CREATIVE
COMPUTER SOFTWARE
FOR
STRATEGIC THINKING
AND
DECISION MAKING

CREATIVE
COMPUTER SOFTWARE
FOR
STRATEGIC THINKING
AND
DECISION MAKING

A Guide for Senior Management and
MIS Professionals

Robert J. Thierauf

QUORUM BOOKS
WESTPORT, CONNECTICUT • LONDON

HD
53
T45
1993

Library of Congress Cataloging-in-Publication Data

Thierauf, Robert J.
Creative computer software for strategic thinking and decision
making : a guide for senior management and MIS professionals /
Robert J. Thierauf.
p. cm.
Includes bibliographical references and index.
ISBN 0-89930-758-2 (alk. paper)
1. Creative ability in business. 2. Decision-making—Data
processing. 3. Strategic planning—Data processing. I. Title.
HD53.T45 1993
658.4′063—dc20 92-18930

British Library Cataloguing in Publication Data is available.

Library of Congress Catalog Card Number: 92-18930
ISBN: 0-89930-758-2

First published in 1993

Quorum Books, 88 Post Road West, Westport, Connecticut 06881
An imprint of Greenwood Publishing Group, Inc.

Printed in the United States of America

The paper used in this book complies with the
Permanent Paper Standard issued by the National
Information Standards Organization (Z39.48-1984).

10 9 8 7 6 5 4 3 2 1

Copyright Acknowledgments

The author and publisher gratefully acknowledge permission for the use of the following copyrighted material.

Idea Tree, courtesy of Mountain House Publishing, Inc.

The information and graphics about OptionFinder® were provided by Option Technologies, Inc. Mendota Heights, Minnesota.

Idea Generator Plus, courtesy of Experience In Software, Inc., copyright © by Gerard I. Nierenberg.

MindLink, courtesy of MindLink, Inc.

IdeaFisher, courtesy of Fisher Idea Systems, Inc. Copyright 1988-1992, Fisher Idea Systems, Inc. All rights reserved worldwide.

Robert C. Klekamp and Robert J. Thierauf, "On Being Boss" *The Cincinnati Enquirer Magazine*, April 4, 1982.

GrandView, courtesy of Symantec Corporation.

Wilson Learning's Innovator, courtesy of Wilson Learning Corporation.

MacFlow, courtesy of Mainstay.

Brainstorm, courtesy of Mustang Software, Inc.

Criterium, courtesy of Sygenex, Inc.

Do what you (as a manager) do best, but now do it better. But how? By integrating creative computer software with information systems technology to improve your strategic thinking and decision-making skills.

Contents

Figures

Preface

Current thinking about how to improve strategic planning (now upgraded to strategic thinking) and decision making by managers at all levels is to employ the latest in information systems technology. Although this approach has worked well for most companies, chief executives are currently asking their managers to do what they do best but now do it better. But how? *Future thinking* about improving strategic thinking and decision making centers on integrating creativity with the latest in information systems. In other words, the power of the computer can be an important means for assisting managers in doing what they do better when employing a creative thinking approach.

The whole concept of creativity is far from new. For centuries, philosophers and teachers have speculated why some human beings are extraordinarily creative and others have merely mortal abilities. The ancient Greeks, for example, thought that creativity was the result of divine inspiration—a gift from the gods. Some modern thinkers have theorized that it is just a lucky combination of genes, a happy but largely accidental coincidence of events. Others have equated creativity with the ability and tenacity to solve problems—a skill, they insist, that can be learned by almost anyone. This last viewpoint is the one advocated in this book, that is, the use of computers is helpful to enhance creativity.

Typically, creative individuals seem to share some common traits: curiosity, an openness to new experiences, a willingness to take risks, and a tendency to think in images. In addition, there appears to be an urge to go beyond established limits and to break rules. These traits of creative persons can, to a large degree, be incorporated into creative computer software such that so-called non-creative people can start thinking like creative ones. Hence a computerized approach to enhance a manager's creativity is explored in some depth in this book. It should be noted that the interaction of the manager with creative computer software needs to be related to where managers get their ideas. Basically, ideas come from working, from getting up every day and going to work. As Sir Isaac Newton put it when he was asked how he was able to discover the law of universal gravitation: "By thinking on it continuously."

This text is designed for both the practicing manger and the academician interested in improving their creativity skills. Managers at all levels can benefit by understanding the subject matter of this book, that is, how they can perform their jobs better in the future. In a similar manner, the book is suitable in an academic environment—an undergraduate or a graduate-level course covering the fundamentals of creative thinking. The student will be exposed to the latest thinking on creativity and will be given ample real-world applications. In turn, this background will be of great use to the student on a new job or on the present job.

This book's structure follows a logical flow for a comprehensive treatment of creativity. The topical areas that are enhanced by creative computer software and real-world applications are as follows:

Part I: Utilization of Creativity to Improve Managerial Effectiveness. Chapter 1 sets the stage for the entire book by looking at a number of areas that are impacted by creativity, with special emphasis on creative computer software as well as virtual reality. In chapter 2, the characteristics of a creative manager are examined along with a quiz to assess a manager's creativity.

Part II: Creativity Techniques and Managerial Decision Making. Current creativity techniques useful to a typical manager are discussed at length in chapter 3. In turn, chapter 4 examines management decision making from a problem-finding or a forward-looking viewpoint that can utilize creative computer software. The traditional approach to problem solving is contrasted with this newer approach to decision making.

Part III: Relationship of Computers to Creativity. In chapter 5, information systems useful for employing creative computer software are set forth within a computerized operating mode. Chapter 6 focuses on the various types of creative computer software, that is, idea organizers, idea networking, and idea generators. These software packages provide the basis for getting managers involved in a computerized approach to creativity.

Part IV: Applications of Creativity in Functional Areas of a Typical Company. Chapter 7 explores a new way of thinking about strategic planning, thereby resulting in a strategic thinking approach for giving overall direction to a company. In a similar manner, chapters 8, 9, and 10 provide the manager with new directions to marketing, manufacturing, and finance and accounting, respectively. In each of these four chapters, real-world applications of creative computer software are illustrated. Particular emphasis is placed on one software package (IdeaFisher 4.0).

For such a large undertaking, I wish to thank the following individuals for their help in this text. First, Dr. Robert C. Klekamp is to be commended for providing helpful materials for selected parts of the text. Second, the following MBA students at Xavier University have provided real-world case studies using creative computer software: John Cunningham, Amy Dwyer, Darryl Hogue, Samuel Kamin, Barbara Kruetzkamp, Steven Levine, Henry Martin, Jeanette Poon, Joseph Ruter, and Noreen Shehata. Third, I am deeply indebted to Jerry Fritsch for his help in developing a number of creative computer software applications using IdeaFisher 4.0. As always, a special note of thanks goes to Thomas Gannon of Quorum Books for his encouragement throughout the project.

Abbreviations

AA	American Airlines
ABC	Activity-based costing
ANSI	American National Standards Institute
ASA	Account services administrator
AT&T	American Telephone & Telegraph
ATM	Automated teller machine
BBB	Battelle-Bildmappen-Brainwriting
B-O-C	Buick-Oldsmobile-Cadillac
CAD/CAM	Computer-aided design/computer-aided manufacturing
CDMA	Code division multiple access
CD-ROM	Compact disc—read-only memory
CEO	Chief executive officer
CIM	Computer-integrated manufacturing
CRT	Cathode ray terminal
CSF	Critical success factor
CSN	Client Services Network
DDP	Distributed data processing
DOS	Disk operating system
DP	Data processing
DRAM	Dynamic random access memory
DSS	Decision support system

EDI	Electronic data interchange
EIS	Executive information system
E-Mail	Electronic mail
Five W's and the H	Who, where, why, when, what, and how
GDSS	Group decision support system
GE	General Electric
HDTV	High-definition television
H-P	Hewlett-Packard
HR	Human resource
IBM	International Business Machines
I-CIM	Interorganizational computer-integrated manufacturing
IFPS	Interactive Financial Planning System
IIE	Institute of Industrial Engineering
IMKA	Initiative for Managing Knowledge Assets
I/O	Input/output
IP	Information processing
IPS	Idea-processing system
JIT	Just-in-time
KPI	Key performance indicator
LAN	Local area network
LCD	Liquid crystal display
Mac	Macintosh
MBT	Michigan Bell Telephone
MIS	Management information system
MIT	Massachusetts Institute of Technology
MRP II	Manufacturing Resource Planning II
NASA	National Aeronautics and Space Administration
NC	Numerically controlled
NGT	Nominal Group Technique
OA	Office automation
PC	Personal computer
PERT	Program evaluation and review technique
PIC	Professional image computer
PIM	Personal information manager
PIMS	Profit Impact of Marketing Strategies

PMI	Plus, minus, and interesting
PMS	Picturephone Meeting Service
R&D	Research and development
ROI	Return on investment
SAS	Statistical Analysis System
SKU	Stock-keeping unit
SME	Society of Mechanical Engineering
TQM	Total quality management
WYSIWIS	What you see is what I see

PART I

Utilization of
Creativity to Improve
Managerial
Effectiveness

1

An Introduction to Creativity to Assist Managers

ISSUES EXPLORED

- To examine a new paradigm of the world that includes the use of creativity
- To explore the current development of new creative ideas at General Electric
- To focus on the use of creativity to monitor a long-term competitive advantage
- To look at newer information systems and organization structures to better utilize company personnel creativity
- To discuss virtual reality, which represents a new direction to assist in creativity of organization personnel

OUTLINE

Today and into the twenty-first century and beyond, creative agility is essential for managers since many businesses are at a crossroads point. Businesses can either go forward or backward. Global events are reshaping business at a very rapid pace. According to creativity expert Edward de Bono, American chief executives are not creative enough to meet the challenges facing their companies today or in the future. This is a sweeping generalization, to be sure, but after 23 years of promoting and teaching creative-thinking techniques in 45 countries, de Bono is convinced that executives lack creativity. He even goes so far as to state that U.S. executives are more uncomfortable with "concepts" than executives in most other developed countries. Thus he feels that creativity has taken a back seat in the information age. Executives and managers below them need "to rethink the policy of not fixing it until it's broken."[1] In other words, they should think in terms of being willing to try something new. The focus should be away from "what is" to "what can be."

Fundamentally, this first chapter sets the tone for the entire book by stressing the need for creativity from a computerized viewpoint. That is, the emphasis is directed away from the traditional approach to teaching creativity and toward demonstrating how computer software packages can help the typical manager operating on an individual or a group basis to be more creative right on the job. Creativity tends to get blocked in companies today because there is a mind-set that overemphasizes one style, a steady incremental change, over a freewheeling experimental approach assisted by creative computer software. In addition, virtual reality, which is a new direction to assist in creativity, is treated in this opening chapter.

VARIOUS WAYS OF VIEWING CREATIVITY

Inasmuch as there are several ways of viewing creativity, although the common thread seems to be making associations of dissimilar things, each creative mode is almost a discipline entirely unto itself. The first is *theoretical creativity*, associated with profound and abstract concepts—the material found in the superpower intellect. Curiously, the Albert Einsteins and Sir Isaac Newtons start with almost childlike questions, primal thoughts such as "What is the universe?" "What is air and light?" and "Why is fire hot?" From this simple beginning, Einstein envisioned himself riding on a beam of light through time. It is a basic concept, but it is the starting point for brilliant and creative thought. On the other hand, *applied creativity* is that of the scientist and thinker. Marie Curie, Henry Ford, Alexander Graham Bell, and Thomas Edison are excellent examples of this type of creativity. They created by taking sensory experiences and things already in existence and translating them into a technological process. Essentially, applied creativity is the main thrust of this book and should be an integral part of a company's corporate philosophy.

Artists and writers fit into two categories that are closely related: *inspired* and *imaginative*. Although their work may be deliberate, inspiration often comes from the subconscious, an almost dreamlike state from which new things suddenly appear. Scientists have for some time been talking about the left and right halves of the brain. The left side controls logic and reason, while the right side contains the intuitive material. Creativity is at its height when there is a flow between the two halves. The artist, for example, may become totally immersed in his process, feeling almost a part of what he is painting; in his mind, he becomes light, shadow, color, and texture himself. Similarly, the writer of good prose feels a certain meter in the use of words and phrases, literature that not only tells a story and imparts information, but reads easily and flows like a melody.

Other ways of viewing creativity include prescriptive and natural creativity. *Prescriptive creativity* is what intellectuals concerned with social and philosophical matters apply to describe the role of man in relation to the universe and his peers. From Plato to Machiavelli and religious thinkers, these persons come up with new observations—creative observations—of how humans can live. *Natural creativity* deals with the body and has been most often associated with great dancers, singers, and performing musicians. It is more than physical ability, for intellect must also go into the performance. In this same vein, professional basketball stars are a creative as any dancer when they appear to float through the air, executing moves never seen before.

LESSONS TO BE LEARNED FROM THE PAST

A logical starting point for a broad-based view of creativity is to look at the past, especially in terms of what went wrong badly for businesses who lack a proper vision of the future. Xerox Corporation recently celebrated the twenty-fifth anniversary of the first commercial fax machine, which it introduced. The company controlled 7 percent of U.S. fax sales in 1989, while Japanese companies had two-thirds. As another example, Raytheon in 1947 sold its first Radarange, a microwave oven marketed to restaurants. When the company introduced a household version twenty years later, sales boomed. Now four of five

American homes have microwaves, but three out of four microwaves sold here are made in the Far East. Still another familiar example is the American-owned companies that built 80 percent of the automobiles sold in the United States in 1979. Over the following decade or so, U.S. automakers have shut numerous North American car and truck assembly plants, while many new plants have opened under Japanese management. The Big Three's share of domestic sales have fallen to less than 66 percent. The same type of story can be told for a number of other industries.

These examples are among the great U.S. industrial blunders, mistakes so massive that it is hard to imagine what on earth could have caused them. No single factor explains them. A number of suspects have been identified, including government policy, foreign conspiracies, the consumers themselves, Wall Street buccaneers, and even the Harvard Business School. Of course, none of them is innocent. However, the finger of blame keeps pointing back to one place, today's U.S. managers. Lack of purpose and direction by management means more than anything else. In the histories of "lost" industries, some management misconceptions appear time and again. American business has paid dearly for them. Here are some of the worst of these misconceptions that have led to very large mistakes: too-high labor costs, walking away from low-margin businesses, not knowing how to sell the product, and buying rather than building operations. Hence past mistakes by managements dictate a new direction in their thinking about the future of U.S. businesses.[2]

A NEW PARADIGM TO REPLACE THE PAST VIEW OF THE WORLD

Due to the many mistakes made in the past by managers of U.S. businesses, AT&T, Procter & Gamble, and DuPont are offering employees personal growth experiences of their own, hoping to spur creativity, encourage learning, and promote ownership of the company's results. A handful of visionary leaders, such as General Electric's chairperson Jack Welch, are going beyond training seminars to a fundamental reordering of managerial priorities. Meanwhile, a small network of consultants, managers, and academics is working to transform businesses. Believing that the world is undergoing major change, they call for a new paradigm, that is, a new framework for seeing and understanding business that will carry humankind beyond the industrial age. The result is a convergence of managers seeking ways to reverse America's fall from dominance with thinkers drawn to business, perhaps as the most powerful institution in global society.

The new framework might be described as New Age without the glazed eyes. The word "paradigm" comes from the Greek for "pattern," and the new paradigm is just that: a new pattern of behavior that stems from a new way of looking at the world. The old worldview—Newtonian, mechanistic, and analytical—is present in everything from the Constitution, with its clockwork system of checks and balances, to the assembly lines devised by Henry Ford.

The new paradigm takes ideas from quantum physics, cybernetics, chaos theory, cognitive science, and Eastern and Western spiritual traditions to form a worldview in which everything is interconnected, in which reality is not absolute but a by-product of human consciousness. This paradigm is not promising universal enlightenment in the near future. However, it is an attempt to deal with a very difficult period of time in business.

What has emerged so far is a host of management theories and practices befitting an age of global enterprise, instantaneous communication, and ecological limits. Some are familiar: hierarchical organizations being replaced by more flexible networks; workers being empowered to make decisions on their own; organizations developing a capacity for group learning instead of waiting for wisdom from above; and national horizons giving way to global thinking. Others may still seem a little far out: creativity and intuition joining numerical analysis as aids to decision making; nurturing and caring being recognized as motivators in the workplace; even the importance of the profit motive being questioned by those who argue that the real goal of enterprise is the mental and spiritual enrichment of those who take part in it.

Currently, each of these developments individually is just one manifestation of progressive management thinking. Together, they suggest the possibility of a fundamental shift in management thinking. Applied to business, the old paradigm held that numbers are all-important, that professional mangers can oversee any company, and that control can and should be held at the top. In contrast, the new paradigm puts customers and employees at the center of the business universe and replaces the rigid hierarchies of the industrial age with a network structure that emphasizes interconnectedness. To illustrate this new paradigm, Levi Strauss chairperson Robert Hass sketched his idea of the corporation of the future: a global enterprise relying on employees who are able to tap their fullest potential and managers who act not as authority figures but as coaches, facilitators, and role models. Levi Strauss is striving to transform itself along these lines because it needs creative thinking and rapid response to satisfy a fashion-conscious public. The point of the new paradigm is to encourage people to think for themselves.

Another executive who is using the new paradigm is General Electric's chairman Jack Welch. Having streamlined General Electric organizationally with a number of sales, acquisitions, and plant closings, Welch has now turned to this new framework. However, GE's moves bear the twin hallmarks of new paradigm thinking, that is, the systems view (seeing everything as interconnected) and the focus on people. Welch's goal is fast turnaround, and to get it he intends to create what he calls the "boundaryless organization": no hierarchical boundaries vertically, no functional boundaries horizontally.[3] In a subsequent section, more detailed information is given about this new paradigm at General Electric.

CURRENT TECHNIQUES TO UNDERTAKE CREATIVE THINKING

Initially, it would be helpful to examine current techniques for undertaking creative thinking. Among the common techniques is the use of brainstorming for idea generation. This technique was developed by Alex Osborn in the 1960s. Basically, brainstorming attempts to "storm" a problem quickly by allowing the participants to suggest off the top of their heads ideas concerning the problem's solution without allowing criticism. Great emphasis will be placed on this group technique throughout this book. Another creative thinking technique is synectics, which attempts to teach creativity. Its purpose is to improve the quality of creative output. Still another technique is the Nominal Group Technique (NGT), which uses the features of brainstorming and brainwriting. Basically, there is a silent generation of ideas in writing, round-robin recording of ideas, serial discussion for clarification, and then subsequent rounds of writing. In this approach, the inhibiting factors of both brainstorming and brainwriting are reduced while public sharing of ideas to stimulate new ideas is retained. Another group technique includes the five W's and the H: that is, the technique asks "who, where, why, when, what and how?" to ensure that all alternatives are considered. Other techniques for groups include the following: assumption reversals, metaphors, relational algorithms, and symbolic representations. On the other hand, techniques for individuals include the following: component detailing, force fit, stimulus analysis, and systematized directed induction. Many of these techniques will be found throughout this book.

A particularly helpful creativity technique has been devised by Edward de Bono (mentioned earlier), the British author of more than thirty books and a well-known creative luminary. De Bono's "Six Thinking Hats" technique is used by Nippon Telephone and Telegraph as well as many other corporations. For this technique, people in a group discussion actually put on different hats that represent different modes of thinking. It is an effective way to switch thinking without offending anyone. The white hat represents information and data, while the red hat legitimizes feelings, intuition, and hunches without the need for justification. In contrast, the black hat is the logical negative, that is, why something will not work. The yellow hat is the logical positive that talks about benefits, feasibility, and the like. The green hat is the creative hat, which allows someone to ask for creativity. Finally, the blue hat is the process control hat that thinks about and plans the thinking itself. Another useful technique for creative thinking is PMI. In this approach, the plus, minus, and interesting points of a decision are listed in separate columns.

Currently, from an overview standpoint, the process of creativity is considered to have four stages: preparation, incubation, illumination, and verification. This process will be treated in more depth in chapter 3 and subsequent chapters. Although several variations of depicting this process exist in the literature, they are basically the same. It should be noted that there may be a lengthy period between stages. An example of the gap between discovery and use is illustrated by the invention of cellulosic materials by the Swiss chemist George Andeman. Almost fifty years elapsed before any practical use was made of artificial silk, under the name of rayon by Comte Hilaire de Chardonnet. Although there can be long time lags between the four stages in the creative process, this does not have to be true, as will be evident in the newer approach to creativity found in this book, namely, utilization of creative computer software.

CREATIVE THINKING DEFINED

Numerous definitions of creativity are recorded in the literature. Creativity is often defined by use of synonyms. These include productive thinking, divergent thinking, originality, imagination, and lateral thinking. Because there is no generally accepted definition of creativity, it would be helpful to look at some definitions to date. Parnes, Noller, and Biondi defined creativity as "the association of thoughts, facts, ideas, etc. into a new and relevant configuration, one that has meaning beyond the sum of its parts—that provides a synergistic effect."[4] J. E. Arnold defined the creative process as "that mental process in which past experience is combined and recombined, frequently with some distortion, in such a fashion that one comes up with new patterns, new configurations, that better solve some need of mankind."[5] Adding a decision-making viewpoint, Ackoff and Vergara defined creativity in problem solving and planning as "the ability of a subject in a choice situation to modify self-imposed constraints so as to enable him to select courses of action or produce outcomes that he would not otherwise select or produce, and are more efficient or valuable to him than any he would otherwise have chosen."[6]

Although this sampling of definitions reveals diverse elements found in creativity, these definitions do suggest a common thread found in creative thinking, that is, a new way of doing things. From this overview standpoint, the author defines creative thinking as *a process that solves a problem in a new and original way that is useful to those involved in the creative undertaking*. It should be noted that the elements of uniqueness of solution and value of results are incorporated into the definition. Both of these elements are essential in defining creative thinking.

COMMON BARRIERS TO CREATIVE THINKING

Barriers to creative thinking can cause a well-designed creativity session to be a waste of time. A company's most resourceful employees may wind up contributing little or nothing to a company in transition. Common barriers to creative thinking are attitudinal, behavioral, and environmental oversights that often occur during staff meetings, in training or idea-generation sessions, and in less formal meetings where employees meet over time to solve the company's problems.

Alexander Graham Bell studied the interworkings of the inner ear before designing the first telephone. It struck him that the bones of the ear were large compared to the delicate eardrum that moved them. The thought occurred to him that if a membrane so thin could move such relatively heavy bones, "why should not a thicker and stouter piece of membrane move my piece of steel?" Bell, therefore, derived the solution to his complex electromechanical problem from a seemingly unrelated, anatomical frame of reference.

Like Bell, creative individuals possess an uncanny ability to integrate principles and information from a wide variety of sources to solve problems. Unfortunately, these employees are often perceived as being out in left field, disengaged from the topic at hand. Their suggestions are usually discounted immediately because they do not seem to fit the discussion's precise frame of reference. Creative problem solving at its best occurs only when judgment is suspended, at least during the initial stages of the process. New ideas and solutions blossom only when individuals are left unencumbered by practical considerations and habitual lines of corporate thinking.

During the initial phase of any problem-solving process, it is critical that employees be allowed to contribute ideas and suggestions without feedback or criticism of any kind. Judgment, disapproving glances, power intrusions, or practical considerations must be suspended until the idea-generating session has concluded. An unusual suggestion from one individual may serve as the springboard for other, more useful perspectives, and this crucial interplay of ideas can occur only if there is an environment devoid of mental obstacles. Another principal reason for suspending judgment of possible solutions is that obvious answers are not necessarily the best answers. There is also need to be wary of solutions that surface quickly. If accepted too readily, these answers may stifle the output of even more rewarding results.

All too often, an employee who makes an insightful contribution to the problem under study is assigned the task of implementing the idea. The task is assigned for expediency's sake, and the intent is an understandable one, that is, the group leader wants to have one neatly packaged meeting. For effective problem solving, this approach can be disastrous and represents one of the most common barriers to creativity. The group leader or supervisor who immediately assigns responsibility to the idea generator will never get another good idea from the person again. Also, the other participants who were asked to generate ideas will all suddenly develop severe cases of laryngitis or will not be forthcoming with their best ideas.

Typically, group participants need to know in advance the exact nature of the idea-generating meeting, that is, what is hoped to be accomplished. The manager should not send a cryptic memorandum the day before and expect an avalanche of ideas. For example, Albert Einstein was unable to formulate his theory of relativity until he stepped away from his equations and blackboards and went home for a good night's rest. When he awoke the next morning, he vividly remembered an image from a dream in which he was astride a rocket speeding away from earth. The remembrance of the dream, a seemingly irrational occurrence, prompted Einstein to return to his blackboard with the solution to his mathematical puzzle.

A final common barrier to creativity is failing to give credit where credit is due. The first time a manager takes a subordinate's good idea and passes it off as his or her own, company creativity will suffer significantly. Tactics like these tend to be commonplace. The news of this plagiarism spreads quickly via the grapevine. In a few weeks, employees perceive management as a self-serving pack of company wolves. In contrast, a good approach when an employee contributes an idea for the betterment of the company is that he or she write and sign a memorandum explaining the new approach. The individual should be assured that the memo will reach the right person and that a report will be sent back as soon as possible with a response. If the idea is incorporated as a new policy or procedure, the employee should be recognized at a formal awards ceremony or luncheon. Also, the award could be announced in the company newsletter. Rewarding creativity is a wise investment that will pay high company dividends for many years.[7]

CREATIVITY AS PART OF A COMPANY'S CORPORATE PHILOSOPHY

In the past, the conventional suggestion box in many companies served as employee input for improving operations. Fortunately, this uncreative, assembly-line mentality has given way to employee involvement and more participatory decision making via the creative process. Today, progressive managers realize that most employees want to be involved in the process of change, to have input in streamlining procedures and brainstorming suggestions to help the company progress. Most important, these managers are realizing that employees who do the actual work, regardless of their relative status or educational level, are usually the ones with the most interesting and progressive ideas. Frontline employees ask the right questions and offer relevant suggestions because they have hands-on experience and are the ones who are most affected by change. To state it simply, these employees frequently know what will work and what will not.

As an example, a manufacturing company decided to computerize its operations to maximize efficiency. The project was an immense undertaking because the company had subsidiaries in ten states. On the surface, the computer linkage would greatly enhance communications and standardize procedures on a companywide basis. However, the company made one bad mistake. Without asking for any employee input, it hired an outside consultant, who had ample computer knowledge but little knowledge of the company's idiosyncrasies, to install the network. Not one employee who would actually use the system was consulted. Twelve months and many thousands of dollars later, the company was still backtracking to correct the mess. Needless to say, the company had to resort to its employees for answers.

LINK OF CREATIVITY TO KEEPING OPERATING UNITS SMALL

Many times, creativity that ultimately becomes an integral part of a typical company's corporate philosophy has its roots in thinking like a small firm. In many types of companies, especially nonmanufacturing ones, bigger usually means less efficient and more wasteful. Staff and overhead expenses tend to take on a life of their own in large companies. In addition, decision making becomes sluggish and inefficient, and communication becomes haphazard. As a result, large companies often cannot make the fast decisions and timely actions that are needed to remain competitive. Companies are finding that they have a lot to lose, in addition to profits, as they grow larger. But more important, creativity is often linked to keeping operating units small.

In the case of mergers and acquisitions, long-time employees may be dismissed, and new time-consuming reports and procedures may be implemented. As a result, managers begin spending more time completing reports and less time managing their staffs and working closely with their customers as well as coming up with new and creative ideas for the company. Such companies become lost very quickly in a bureaucratic nightmare. When that happens, profits and morale plummet. Nevertheless, it is possible to retain the advantages of smallness as a company grows larger. Examples include Worlington Steel in Ohio and Magnum International, a Canadian automotive parts dealer. Both emphasize smallness by keeping the size of their operating companies to fewer than 100 employees. Whenever a company grows larger than 100 employees, the companies create a new subsidiary with its own identity. Overall, Worlington and Magnum are able to retain the advantages of a small, efficient operation that allows them more time for creativity to improve operations even though the total corporation continues to expand.

Other large companies are finding different ways to stay small. For example, many corporations, such as General Electric, Hewlett-Packard, Lockheed, 3M, Digital Equipment, and IBM, form independent project teams that are sheltered from the bureaucracy of the organization for creative thinking. (General Electric will be used as an example of this approach in the next section of this chapter.) These teams have become a primary source of new products, and the products are helping their companies stay competitive.

Other examples include Campbell Soup, which reorganized its company into fifty independent business units such that each unit has a mission to develop its own new products. Within five years, Campbell Soup has produced 334 new products. Another company, Levi Strauss, has set aside more than $3 million to fund new product ideas. Budgets of up to $500,000 were offered for some of the best ideas presented by employees in simple two-page marketing plans. Still another company, Ore-Ida Foods, created a fellowship programs in which five individuals are given $50,000 each year for two years. This money is invested in product development, cost reduction, or new processes. Overall, programs such as these help nurture the spirit of smallness that has traditionally been the springboard of invention in American companies.[8]

No matter what the project to be undertaken by a typical company is, employee input and creativity should be an integral part of the company's corporate philosophy. Representative workers from all levels of the company should be involved during a transition period, should be included in departmental planning meetings and brainstorming sessions, and, when appropriate, should be part of companywide, long-range strategic thinking. Even though the final decisions will still be made by top-level managers, such input can only save time and money and reveal new and more profitable vistas for the company to explore. Whenever possible, company training managers and personnel managers can help break this major barrier to corporate creativity by promoting the need for employee input to upper management and by implementing strategies to make use of this untapped potential.

DEVELOPMENT OF NEW IDEAS AT A TYPICAL LARGE CORPORATION—GENERAL ELECTRIC

At General Electric today and tomorrow, the accent is on developing new ideas. The emphasis is on getting all employees in the organization involved in creativity. The company believes that if this is done right, the best ideas will rise to the top. To get these ideas to rise to the top, General Electric has hired Harvard Business School professor Len Schlesinger and about two dozen academics and consultants to coach employees through the change. This is a large planned effort to alter people's behavior.

General Electric's chairperson Jack Welch and his lieutenants have selected three management techniques called Work-Out, Best Practices, and Process Mapping. The first jimmies the locks that keep employees out of the decision-making process; the second seeks to smash the "not invented here" syndrome and to spread good ideas quickly from one part of General Electric to another; and the third is the tool on which the others most depend. All foster employee involvement. Combined, they are designed to sustain the rapid growth in productivity that is the key to GE's or any corporation's survival in a competitive environment.

Management Techniques to Stimulate Ideas at General Electric

The first management technique, Work-Out, is a forum where three things can happen. Participants can get a mental workout; they can take unnecessary work out of their jobs; or they can work out problems together. Work-Outs started in March 1989. Like kernels of corn in a hot pan, they began popping one at a time—at GE Plastics' silicones unit in Waterford, New York, at NBC, and in the lighting business—then in a great rush. No one keeps count, but it is estimated that eventually 40,000 employees (better than one in eight) will have taken part in at least one Work-Out in 1991 and shortly thereafter.

Initially, all followed the same format, which can be likened to a New England town meeting. A group of 40 to 100 people, picked by management from all ranks and several functions, goes to a conference center or hotel. The three-day session begins with a talk by the manager in charge, who roughs out an agenda—typically, to eliminate unnecessary meetings, forms, approvals, and other items. Then the manager leaves. Aided by the outside facilitator, the group breaks into five or six teams, and each tackles part of the agenda. For a day and a half, they go at it, listing complaints, debating solutions, and preparing presentations for the final day. However, it is the third day that gives Work-Out its special ability. The manager in charge, ignorant of what has been going on, comes back and takes a place at the front of the room. Often senior executives come to watch. One by one, team spokespersons rise to make their proposals. By the rules of the game, the manager can make only three responses. The manager can agree on the spot, can say no, or can ask for more information, in which case he or she must charter a team to get it by an agreed-upon date.

As an example, Armand Lauzon, the head of plant services at the GE Aircraft Engines factory in Lynn, Massachusetts, had to answer to 108 proposals. The employees had set up the room so that Lauzon had his back to his boss. He had about a minute to say yes or no to each one. Ideas ranged from designing a plant services insignia as a moral booster to building a new tinsmith shop. Lauzon answered yes to all but 8 proposals.

The second management technique, called Best Practices, took GE more than a year to develop. GE found that there is an important difference between Best Practices and the benchmarking many companies use. Benchmarkers usually study nonpareils in particular functions, such as "What can our shipping department learn from other well-run companies?" General Electric was looking less for nuts and bolts than for attitudes and management practices. Basically, GE was looking for the secret of companies' successful operations. The end result was a surprise in that the answers were remarkably similar. Almost every company emphasized managing processes, not functions. That is, they focused less on the performance of individual departments than on how they worked together as products moved from one to another. They also outhustled their competitors in introducing new products and treated their suppliers as partners, and they managed inventory so well that they tied up less working capital per dollar of sales than General Electric.

The implications of the Best Practices study were tremendous for GE. It realized that it was managing and measuring the wrong things. The company was setting goals and keeping score. GE should have focused more on how things got done than what got done. Essentially, Best Practices provided an empirical basis for changing what GE manages. For example, the corporate audit staff altered its methods. Auditors, who were picked for their high potential, used to come from finance backgrounds. Now half are from operations or information systems.

Currently, Best Practices is a course that GE gives to a dozen people a month from of its ten manufacturing businesses. The service businesses that need to pay special attention to issues like managing information technology have their own course, based on research at nonmanufacturing companies like American Express. The class teaches three essential lessons. The first is that other companies have much to teach General Electric. Second is the value of continuously improving processes, even in small ways, rather than taking large jumps. To develop a new product, for example, GE learned to make a multigenerational plan: aiming to introduce a first version that uses only tried-and-true technologies, then gradually introducing new ones as they are perfected. That gets the product to market faster and eliminates costly mishaps when an unproven technology turns out to be full of bugs. GE also learned that rotating executives through new jobs quickly, long a practice at the company, created problems in new product introductions, which go more smoothly when managers have long tenure.

The third lessons is that processes need owners—people whose responsibility and authority reach through the walls between departments. That is how Best Practices folds back into Work-Out and explains why, more and more, the people who take this course are not senior management but Work-Out teams that are wrestling with, say, a supplier-relations issue. For example, ties established in the Best Practices study are still going strong. GE and AMP visit one another several times a year, for example. Recently, General Electric has been studying how AMP purchases, while AMP executives have been boning up on GE's executive development programs. GE businesses have begun to copy the technique on their own, making a best practice of Best Practices. For example, NBC visited the United Nations, Citicorp, and others to learn how they cope with the frustrations of moving supplies and equipment in congested Manhattan.

The third management technique is Process Mapping, whereby managers, employees, suppliers, and customers work on a map together to make sure that what the company thinks happens really does. When a team from GE's Evendale, Ohio, plant mapped the process of making turbine shafts for jet engines, the job took more than a month, and the map went all around a conference room. When a process is mapped, GE has the ability to manage an operation in a coherent way from start to finish. Before, this plant strove for worker efficiency and machine efficiency. Now what drives employees is the efficiency of total asset management. For example, in pursuit of 100 percent machine utilization, all rotating parts used to go to a central steam-cleaning facility between operations. Now the shaftmakers have their own cleaning booths because the process map revealed that the time saved more than paid for the additional equipment. The map also helped the shaft team pinpoint sources of imperfect parts and rearrange equipment to achieve a more continuous flow through the factory. The result was a 50 percent time savings, a $4 million drop in inventory, and a good shot at getting 7 inventory turns a year versus 2.6 before.[9]

DEVELOPMENT OF NEW IDEAS BY COMPARING TO THE BEST

As indicated in the previous discussion, development of new ideas and ways of doing things can come from outside the company. When the GTE Corporation wants to know whether it is doing a good job delivering telephone service, it compares itself to local Bell companies or to overseas telephone companies. When it wants to see if its telephone equipment matches the highest quality standards, it compares its methods and products against Sweden's L. M. Erickson and other highly regarded competitors. In addition, when it realized that its billing system was confusing customers, it went to the American Express Company, one of the country's most experienced billers, for guidance. By going outside its own industry, GTE wound up with a billing system so much better than the industry standard that several competitors have paid GTE to help them replicate it.

Utilization of Benchmarking

Benchmarking, the formal name for identifying and emulating the companies that are best at a given activity, has come a long way since the 1970s when the term was first used. Back then, benchmarking was confined mostly to manufacturing companies like the Ford Motor Company or the Xerox Corporation, both of which reclaimed market share by dissecting competitors' cars and copiers and applying what they learned to their own. By the mid-1980s, benchmarking had reached a second phase. Companies had realized that they could use benchmarking techniques and principles to model their customer-service, accounting, and other nonmanufacturing departments after the competitors who do it best. When data about the internal workings of competitors' operations proved difficult to get, consultants could generally be counted on to provide suitably disguised descriptions of best industry practices.

Currently, benchmarking has moved into a third phase in which companies are looking beyond their own industries. Executives, particularly those in charge of quality, are scouring trade magazines, calling consultants and professional associations for recommendations, and browsing through electronic data bases, all in hopes of ferreting out the expert practitioner in any given function. They are no longer asking who is the best in the industry at doing something, but rather who is the best in the world. In effect, companies that have gone outside their industry to pick up tips often can document terrific savings. For example, Motorola, Inc.,'s finance department began to apply electronic data transfer and other techniques it picked up from the First National Bank of Chicago's check-clearing operations to its own operations for closing and auditing its book each month. The net result is that Motorola takes 8,000 fewer person-hours to close and audit the company's books today versus just a few years ago despite a sales increase of more than 50 percent.

Indeed, executives bent on benchmarking report that as long as there are no proprietary secrets involved, companies are quite proud to show their systems. L. L. Bean, Inc., the catalog distribution company, has played host to a number of companies looking for tips on how to spruce up their distribution or warehousing operations. When Bean decided that it wanted to benchmark its succession planning and management development systems against companies with good human-resources reputations, it visited 3M, IBM, and Disney. A team of Bean managers also went to London, where they studied Marks & Spencer's inventory management systems.

L. L. Bean was happy to share information on distribution and found that companies are happy to share information on the areas where they excel. The information flows particularly freely when companies benchmark against their own customers. When American Express wanted to learn about self-directed work teams, it went to the General Electric Company. It sought guidance from Motorola on training. Because they are customers of American Express and American Express is a customer of theirs, exchange of information is easier. Hence an exchange of information on new ideas and procedures can assist a company in improving its operations.[10]

COMPETITIVE ADVANTAGE FROM USING COMPUTERS IS GENERALLY SHORT-LIVED

One approach that has been applied over the years to rectify some mistakes from the past is to utilize computer information technology. According to a recent poll of top MIS executives in *Computerworld Premier 100* companies, respondents said that the use of information systems for competitive advantage lasts no more than twelve to eighteen months. Overall, nearly three-quarters of MIS executives in the *Premier 100*, the annual survey of top technology users, said that their organizations have implemented information systems during the last year solely to get ahead of the competition. Because companies are leapfrogging each other, computer information technology gives companies the ability to catch up quickly. With higher hopes pinned to computer information technology, it is no surprise that fifty-three of the *Premier 100* executives received increases in their MIS budgets.

Organizations in banking, financial services, manufacturing, and aerospace were the biggest advocates of using computer information technology for competitive gain. More than three-quarters of the companies in each of these groups implemented strategic systems recently. One notable shift among respondents concerned the focus of strategic systems. In the past, external or customer applications were presented to be the best use of computer information technology. Now, many say that the biggest payoff comes from deploying strategic systems inside the organization.

The most strategic use for computer information technology today is to improve internal processes. Gencorp has taken steps toward reengineering various cost centers in the company with an eye toward leveraging computer information technology. At the Paine Webber group, MIS has concentrated on simplifying and consolidating internal information feeds to traders. MCI Communications Corporation reduced double planning and double billing and trimmed staff by two-thirds after integrating a network and data-center operations at an Ohio facility. Finally, the FMC Corporation finished the first phase of an IBM mainframe-based procurement tracking system that will completely automate the company's purchasing. Once the computer technology is in place, advantage springs from maximizing it. In addition, well-deployed computer information technology poses a very significant barrier to entry for new companies in an industry.[11]

Although computer information technology may keep some newer companies from entering the field, what about established companies who all are now employing about the same level of computer information technology? In many cases, the answer is to start a new round of computer information technology that gives a company a temporary lead. However, this approach is generally short-lived again. Because a short-lived competitor approach is replaced by another, a better approach is to take a broader-based view of the company that includes, among other things, the use of creativity by company managers as well as non-managers.

CREATIVITY: AN ALTERNATIVE APPROACH TO MAINTAIN A LONG-TERM COMPETITIVE ADVANTAGE

A more positive alternative to maintaining a competitive advantage in the long run is to employ creativity. As noted previously in this chapter, keen competition and sophisticated consumer demands are forcing companies to take more risks, to modify products and services, and to move in new directions to keep pace. Hence the need for creativity is paramount. Creative thinking is no longer an abstract concept or fad. The process has very real implications in the workplace for the typical company and can, if nurtured properly, have a positive impact on the bottom line. The barriers to corporate creativity can occur subtly within the ranks and invade strategic planning sessions, meetings, and workshops like a virus. However, if widely attended by the safeguards noted previously in this chapter, creativity will thrive and greatly improve the health of any company or organization.

Currently, creativity has become an important tool in the executive suite, corporate America's reaction to global competition and runaway technology. Nearly one company in three now offers creativity training to its employees. The figure was more like one in twenty-five just five years ago.[12] Organizations from General Motors and IBM to Coca-Cola and the U.S. Department of Defense are sending employees to workshops and seminars where they learn, among other things, which quadrant of their brains is dominant: the logical upper left, the organized lower left, the visionary upper right, or the emotional lower right. When people are aware of their own brain characteristics, creativity becomes more predictable and comfortable. For those anxious to exercise their own creative lobes, hundreds of books, tapes, games, and software (even brain workout salons) promise to turn an uptight number-cruncher into a one-person idea factory.

As will be seen in future chapters of this book, the challenge is to think up ideas that are novel and innovative and, at the same time, pragmatic. This type of creativity requires being open to new ideas while avoiding the problem of coming up with the same answers. If company personnel continually come up with the same solutions, it could be that these are the only answers or that people are only looking at the market from one perspective. Companies like Levi Strauss are buying into the notion that rather than being the province of artists and inventors, creativity is a learnable skill that can be enhanced through practice and training, especially with the utilization of creative computer software.

Utilization of Creativity Games

As a starting point to creativity, reference initially can be made to playing with games. Generally, playing with creativity games comes close to sanctioned goofing off; that is, the best ideas emerge when people loosen up and act a little crazy. Typical low-cost creativity games include the following. Circles of Creativity (from New Product Development) is a brainstorming tool that helps ideas, objects, or images fit together in interesting, non-obvious ways. Arrows on the chalkboard device rotate, pointing to dozens of phrases arranged in six concentric circles. The "try to" arrow, for instance, can be turned to suggestions like "moisten it," "jiggle it," or "freeze it," yielding responses from other arrows like "failure," "gears," and "cold." When the director of research and development for Hershey Foods in Hershey, Pennsylvania, was putting together a business analysis, he gave Circles a whirl and landed on "bag it." After mulling that for a moment, he pictured himself putting whole pieces of the company into a bag. That gave rise to the notion of breaking the company's Canadian hard-candy market, which had been simply defined as either "sugar" or "sugar-free," into smaller categories such as breath mints, mini-mints, and individually wrapped candies. By looking more closely at specific areas, the company was able to pinpoint growth potential in mint candies that it had never noticed. Hershey now keeps a Circles in every conference room for moments when executives feel "blocked."

Another creativity game is the Creative Whack Pack (from consultant Roger von Oech). It is nothing more than a deck of sixty-four cards with bold labels, like "Be Wacky," "Do Something to It," and "Break the Rules," all aimed at making people move off the well-worn and predictable corporate path. "Reverse Your Viewpoint" rang a bell with the chairperson of Metaphor Computer Systems (Mountain View, California) as he flipped through the Whack Pack during a meeting with his managers about quality problems. What would they do if they were competitors who had infiltrated executive ranks to hamstring the company? It turned out that the managers were guilty of some of the very sins they listed. For instance, by letting the product engineers dot every *i* on a new design proposal before getting feedback from manufacturing or marketing specialists, they had complicated the route from idea to marketplace and wasted time and money.[13]

Utilization of Creative Computer Software

Since the main thrust of this book is a computerized approach to creative thinking, there is need to go beyond the manual creative games presented above. Games often work best when people meet as a group. However, that is not always necessary with creative computer software, although the focus of this book will be on using a group approach for creative thinking. In addition, it is comfortable to know that a person's electronic brainstorming partners will not laugh at the most idiotic suggestions. An overview of three typical current creative computer software programs is given here.

IdeaFisher 4.0 (from Fisher Idea Systems, Inc.) is a kind of brainstorming thesaurus with two data bases that work together. The "QBank" is a collection of nearly 6,000 questions that nudge the user to define the job at hand. The user might be quizzed, for example, about the engineering of a proposed product, its timeliness, and the history of similar products. The "IdeaBank" contains more than 700,000 cross-referenced words and phrases organized into 28 "major categories" and 387 "topical categories." Typing "blue" triggers a spurt of associations that offer fodder for everything from advertising slogans to new product names, for example, midnight blue, blue whale, and so on. As an example, a marketer is trying to name a new laundry detergent and wants to convey the message that the product is efficient and environmentally sound. The individual would enter such terms as "environment," "clean," and "detergent," and the IdeaBank would give back suggestions that included Breathe, Back to Nature, and Purify. Another example would be a financial planning company wishing to devise an advertising metaphor for safe money. The result was to think of a person's money as wearing a seat belt.

Another creative computer software package is the Idea Generator Plus (from Experience in Software). It makes the user examine the problem from unexpected angles by having the person respond to such questions as "What similar situations have you been in?" "What is the opposite of what you want to achieve?" "Can you think of metaphors that apply?" "What does the pessimist in you think?" "Who are the people affected by your decision and what solutions might they offer?" As an example, a creativity consulting company (Mattimore Communications) used this package while devising an adult board game in which the players pretend to be inventors. By figuring out what advice his mother-in-law would give, Bryan Mattimore imaged that she would urge him to "keep it simple." He created a game good enough that it is now under development at the Game Gang, the New York toy company that sells Pictionary and Balderdash.

Still another package is MindLink (from MindLink, Inc.), which gets at a creative quandary in a seemingly roundabout way, sending the user on improvisational tangents called "idea triggers." The user might be instructed to pick up the nearest magazine at hand and extract two ideas from each of five articles. Or the user may have to jot down ten objects in view around the room. Perhaps the user will have to work these observations into a short story. Other triggers urge the user to conjure up images by pairing words such as "time" and "confetti" or "fun" and "cowlike." After each exercise, the user is asked to figure out how these thoughts might be brought together to help him or her deal with the creative dilemma.[14]

NEWER INFORMATION SYSTEMS TO BETTER UTILIZE COMPANY PERSONNEL CREATIVITY

To utilize creative computer software (as set forth in the previous section and throughout this book) in a more effective manner, it is helpful that companies employ the newer directions in information systems. More specifically, the focus in on group decision support systems (GDSSs). These systems provide computer-based facilities for the exploration of structured, semistructured, and unstructured problems in a group setting. Their goal is to improve the productivity of decision-making meetings, either by speeding up the decision-making process or by improving the quality of the resulting decisions. There are a number of GDSS aids for decision structuring, such a alternative ranking and voting tools, and for idea generation or issue analysis. Other new information systems that lend themselves to creativity will be given in chapter 5 as well as in the last part of this chapter.

Accent on Electronic Meeting Rooms

Typically, GDSSs are implemented as electronic meeting rooms that contain several networked workstations, large computer-controlled public displays, and audio/video equipment. Some of these facilities require a specially trained operator; others assume operational competence among the group members. A well-known example is the PlexCenter Planning and Decision Support Laboratory at the University of Arizona. The facility provides a large U-shaped conference table with eight personal workstations; a workstation in each of four breakout rooms; a videodisc; and a large-screen projection system that can display screens of individual workstations or a compilation of screens. The conference table workstations are recessed to enhance the participants' line of sight and to encourage interaction. They communicate over a local area network and run software tools for electronic brainstorming, stakeholder identification and analysis, and issue analysis.

Recent work at the University of Arizona has concentrated on the support of larger groups. The current large-group facility has twenty-four workstations designed to support up to forty-eight people. The support of large groups presents unique challenges and opportunities.[15]

A lower-cost version of an electronic meeting room is one that, for example, utilizes OptionFinder (an idea generator). William Law, president of Law and Associates Inc., often works with small to medium-sized businesses on strategic plans, that is, to help them sort through priorities as a prelude to the entire planning process. A sales force might be queried as to the success of a certain product in the field, using criteria developed beforehand, such as reliability, delivery time, technical support, and training. The OptionFinder software package pairs the questions to rank their importance, asking participants whether they value reliability or delivery time more, for example. Participants press numbers on the keypads to record their opinions, and the computer analyzes the results, weighting and ranking the criteria. It also shows how the votes were clustered: on which issues most participants agree, for example. These issues can be put aside so the discussion can center on issues where there is disagreement. If there is diversity, it should be discussed, since one person may know something that the others do not. In addition, the system can divide the participants into subgroups, showing how middle managers voted in comparison with senior managers. It should be noted that the keypad system allows for anonymity.[16] Further discussion of OptionFinder and other idea generators will be found in chapter 6.

NEWER ORGANIZATION STRUCTURES TO BETTER UTILIZE COMPANY PERSONNEL CREATIVITY

To better utilize employee creativity, companies are also changing their organization structures accordingly. Organization charts are being changed in favor of ever-changing structures that center on teams, projects, and alliances. In tomorrow's company teams, managers, shop-floor workers, technical experts, suppliers, and customers will join together to do a job and then disband, with everyone going off to the next assignment. This new model is called by many the *adaptive organization*. It will be useful to serve customers better and make the company more competitive. Instead of looking to the manager for direction and various types of helpful suggestions, tomorrow's employee will be trained to look closely at the work process and to devise ways to improve upon it, even if this means temporarily leaving his or her regular job to join an ad hoc team attacking a problem. In essence, companies will allow the task to determine the organization.

Currently, the adaptive organization exists more as an ideal than as a reality. However, aspects of it can be seen taking shape not only at Becton Dickinson, but also at companies such as Apple Computer, Cypress Semiconductor, Levi Strauss, Xerox, and AES (formerly Applied Energy Services). For example, an informal Xerox team made up of people from accounting, sales, distribution, and administration saved the company $200 million in inventory costs. Cypress (a San Jose, California, maker of specialty computer chips) has developed a computer system that keeps track of all its 1,500 employees as they crisscross between different functions, teams, and projects. Apple is developing a computer network called Spider that tells a manager instantly whether an employee is available to join his or her project, what the employee's skills are, and where the employee is located in the company.[17]

Relationship to the Informal Organization

In today's organization, there is something quite similar already going on. In every company of more than a few people, there exists an informal organization that operates alongside the formal one. It consists of the alliances between people and the power relationships that actually get work done. It may be as simple as some workers banding together to go outside channels to do a job despite the obstacles set in their way by the formal organization. This, in itself, is not new. What is new is that companies are finally realizing the need to recognize the informal organization, free it up, and provide it the resources it needs.

Basically, the adaptive organization incorporates the informal organization and draws its power from the same fund of energy. It provides openings for the creativity and initiative too often found only in small, entrepreneurial companies. It does this by aligning what the company wants—innovation and improvement— with what turns people on, namely, a chance to use their creativity and expand their skills. Traditional hierarchies, on the other hand, usually have the opposite effect.

Adaptive organizations have one thing in common: fluidity. They work much the same way that large construction firms, such as Bechtel, Fluor, and Brown & Root, do, gathering handpicked groups of employees and outside contractors with the right skills for each new dam, refinery, or airport. For example, Becton Dickinson found itself worrying about the competition despite a history of fast growth. To regain its edge, the maker of high-tech diagnostic systems such as blood analyzers started exploring ways to let its informal organization come into its own. While the company still maintains traditional functions like marketing, sales, and manufacturing, it now encourages its people to take the initiative and form teams to innovate in creative ways and go after business in new ways. The focus is on creating a hierarchy of ideas.

Instead of directing strategy from the top, the chief executive officer lays out a very broad vision—to develop proprietary ideas and beat the competition to market with them—and then lets the fifteen divisions develop their own business strategies. Part of the point is to send a message to employees that there is no rigid master plan. In essence, the company reorganized itself by the way it works. It organized cross-function teams that include not only its own people, but also vendors, suppliers, and people from other divisions. The company set the strategy, and the team carries it out.[18]

VIRTUAL REALITY: A NEW DIRECTION TO ASSIST IN CREATIVITY

Another way of improving one's creativity today is to think in terms of *virtual reality*. A person's first encounter with virtual reality is very much like a dream, but electronic in nature. For example, using virtual reality hardware and software, an individual found himself flying above a kitchen that he somehow knew was his, though it resembled no room he had ever floated above. A big blue hand hung in front of his face and arthritically mimicked every movement of his own right hand. He turned his head and saw that the room stood roofless and alone on a vast, unmarred plane. Hungry, he floated down to the kitchen floor and opened up the white refrigerator. Since there was no peanut butter, cold chicken, or beer, his head began to itch and his eyes ached. This was becoming a nightmare. But even nightmares are usually more comfortable than this. Such is the feeling from virtual reality, the sensual computer illusion forecast by William Gibson and other science-fiction authors. In Gibson's books, this electronic hallucination is called *cyberspace*.

In real reality, this scenario takes place at VPL Research, Inc. (Redwood, California). The user wears a black Lycra data glove, looking like the world's oldest Nintendo player. Three sophisticated, interactive computer programs, written in Forth, C, and Pascal, put the person inside a world of computer graphics. This allows him or her to treat system-generated objects almost as if they were real things. The user interacts with the environment using special clothing and fiber-optic sensors that interpret body positions as computer commands. In theory, the user can create a world limited only by his or her imagination and programming capabilities.

Generally, an ankle-to-wrist jumpsuit is used for a complete virtual reality experience. Complete with fiber-optic piping that looks like something June Lockhart wore to bed in *Lost in Space*, the garment is designed to translate an average-size person's body movements into computer commands for a more realistic approach to virtual reality. The more the super-sensitive fiberglass is flexed, the less light is transmitted. The computer senses the lost light, then translates it into a movement command. However, a data glove can be used in place of the jumpsuit.

In addition, the user must strap on VPL's patented goggles, called Eyephones, a combination of twin-color LCD monitors, cushy earphones, and lead weights. The granulated lead, which hangs in a bag at the back of the phones, acts as a counterweight to the monitors. Resembling a black cyclist's helmet with front and rear bumpers and weighing as much as two very heavy wet towels, the Eyephone is an interface to be reckoned with. Putting it on is cumbersome: one person pulls apart the headphones while the other steadies and lowers the bulky Eyephone onto the wearer's head. Wearing it is akin to putting on a welder's mask and a hard hat. The person feels secure but a little claustrophobic.

Once a person adjusts, the resolution is good, similar to what one would see if a Sony Watchman were taped to his or her forehead, but nowhere near as good as the of the average IBM Video Graphics Array monitor. A person can clearly see dots on the screen. The overall effect is a washed-out, shadowy world with a lot of hard angles and no smooth curves.[19]

Essentially, virtual reality is created by a display and control technology that surround a person with an artificial environment mimicking real life. The person interacts with objects and settings as he or she would in the real world—no passive viewing of computer graphics, the way it is done on most of today's screens. While some advanced design programs let a person manipulate objects on a screen, virtual reality allows a person to be a full participant in a three-dimensional setting that envelops him or her completely.

Practical Uses of Virtual Reality

Virtual reality has a number of commercial applications. For example, inside a Boeing computer laboratory in Seattle, Washington, an engineer dons a bulky headset equipped with blacked-out goggles and pulls on a Lycra glove bristling with wires. Then he points his forefinger at an airplane that looks almost real as it seems to sit on a runway in front of him. In response to his gesture, the scene shifts and he finds himself in front of the airplane. He lifts his finger to walk around it and stops to open a maintenance hatch, revealing a life-support system and a pressure gauge. His next command puts him inside the cockpit. He touches a button on the instrument panel to start the engine, then pulls back the throttle. The plane, a hypothetical tilting-rotor aircraft that Boeing calls VS-X, rumbles down the runway and takes off while he sits back and admires the green and brown landscape below through a porthole. After the plane lands, he walks back to the cargo bay and reconfigures the seats inside the plane. Actually, only the engineer is real. The airplane is made entirely of equations residing in computer memory, yet he says that flying it feels "pretty convincing."

Due to the potential of virtual reality, the company has organized a corporationwide steering committee to explore potential applications. Also, another company, Caterpillar, is testing virtual reality models of its earthmovers to improve their performance and driver visibility. Virtual reality shows promise as a tool for industrial development, design, and testing that goes far beyond now-familiar computer-aided design and manufacturing (CAD/CAM) programs. Also, it could revolutionize entertainment, ease complex surgery, and increase the effectiveness of education by having schoolchildren become parts of equations or travel through a virtual universe of subatomic particles. In essence, virtual reality will probably change the way people use computers since the applications are countless.[20]

Virtual reality programs, along with stereo goggles and inexpensive data gloves, may well bring rudimentary virtual reality to PCs in the next few years. By pointing at the screen, the user will be able to flip through a spreadsheet as if it were a stack of papers. Or the user will be able to take an almost lifelike walk through a model of a new office building. Inside, the user can move the furniture around, lengthen or shorten the walls, turn lights on and off, repaint the rooms, and redo the design to one's taste. Says the noted computer designer C. Gordon Bell: "By the end of this decade, virtual reality will be commonplace. You'll be sitting in front of your terminal and once you put on your 3-D glasses and a data glove, you'll be able to ride on an electron or in a car."[21]

Lower Hardware Costs Expected

VPL Research, Inc., the principal supplier of virtual reality headsets and data gloves, sells the headset for about $10,000 to $50,000 each and the gloves for a Tiffany-like price of $8,800. Since the VPL system uses two powerful Silicon Graphics computers, one for each eye, the total system cost can easily be $250,000. To reach the mass market, a race is on to cut the costs of these key items drastically. Mattel markets a $50 version of the data glove. Run by a separate $99 Nintendo game cartridge, Mattel's Power Glove allows its user to play virtual handball on a virtual court against a virtual opponent. Mattel has sold a million of the gloves since it introduced them in 1989.

Currently, VPL is working on a $200 data glove for PC users. It would allow the user to manipulate items on the PC screen. To this must be added a pair of stereo glasses ($1,300) and a virtual reality chip board (another $1,000 to $2,000) for a PC. Cheaper still may be TV eyeglasses under development at Sony and other Japanese companies. Although intended as TV receivers, they could be used to project virtual reality scenes. As a person uses a laptop PC to write a report, he or she could put on the TV glasses and see the text suspended in the air in front of himself or herself. Some virtual reality experts envision a portable window into the virtual world four or five years from now, an attachment that would fit over a PC or laptop screen and serve the same purpose as more cumbersome headsets or stereo glasses. Silicon Graphics (Mountain View, California) makes the powerful graphics workstations that run most virtual reality applications.[22]

Current Virtual Reality Software

In addition to the software mentioned above, other software has been and is being developed for virtual reality. One such package is Virtus WalkThrough, the product of Virtus Corporation (Cary, North Carolina). Basically, it is a modeling and visualization package that takes the concept of virtual reality from esoteric experiment to practical tool. Virtual reality makes it possible to explore worlds and interiors that exist only in the minds of their creators and, with Virtus WalkThrough, in the bits and bytes of Macintosh (Mac) software.

Virtus WalkThrough lets architects and interior designers create conceptual designs of buildings and interiors and then move through and around them on-screen. For the pre-CAD, visualization phase of spatial design, it is a viable tool. WalkThrough is the only program currently available that provides a completely interactive spatial presentation. Several modeling programs for the Macintosh let the user animate fly-throughs, but restrict the user to a fixed path through the design. WalkThrough lets the user move about freely, viewing the design from many different perspectives, in real time. Also, it does not limit the user to wire frames. The program renders scenes so the user can move through a suite of rooms in seconds. It does all this with files no bigger than word-processing documents. By comparison, eight-bit PIC animation files of a two-bedroom house can easily grow to 150 megabytes. A similar WalkThrough file, on the other hand, is 15 K, or one ten-thousandth the size of the animation file.

The program uses two types of viewing windows for navigating through models: a two-dimensional Design View, which is also used to create designs, and a three-dimensional Walk View, which creates the rendered perspectives as one moves through the model. Although Walk View rendering is not photo-realistic, it does have advanced features such as translucent surfaces for glass or water, twenty-four-bit color, and, as mentioned previously, impressive speed. The user can maneuver through a model by using a mouse or a trackball. If a mouse is used, the user holds down the mouse button and moves the cursor up to move forward, down to go back, and right and left to rotate. The farther the cursor is from the center cross hairs, the faster it is. The user can also move up and down or just look around in all directions without changing position. The focal-length tool adds a wide-angle or telephoto lens to the view.

Creating and editing models in Virtus WalkThrough is almost as quick and easy as moving around in them. Top View, the default two-dimensional Design View, is where the user does most of the drawing. The user can also open windows for the Front, Back, Left, Right, and Bottom Views. An object drawn in Design View immediately appears in Walk View as a rendered three-dimensional object. Virtus WalkThrough, which costs less than $1,000, lets the user experience on a Macintosh what not even the most expensive graphics workstation can reproduce. Virtus WalkThrough provides ease of model navigation and creation, speed, and minute file size (so it can run on any two-megabyte Mac, including a Plus). It is not a drafting took by any measure, but it is an important conceptualization tool. For those who need to look at a design from all angles, Virtus WalkThrough is indeed a breakthrough project.[23]

Virtual Reality's Improvement of the User's Capabilities

A very important feature of virtual reality is that people comprehend images much faster than they can grasp columns of numbers or lines of text. The human brain is unbelievably fast. However, a person's mental "text computer" is limited by the fact that a person can read only about 100 characters a second. Since about half the brain is dedicated to visual processing, virtual reality is the most natural way of all for people to understand and manipulate computerized data, and to do so in three dimensions.

In the Boeing example mentioned earlier, researchers are looking into ways to use what they call "augmented" or "see-through" reality. Workers would wear clear goggles with three-dimensional images reflected onto the lenses. The goggle would superimpose a virtual image of the desired result on a real object, so that workers would know what to do with the object without consulting manuals or blueprints. For example, an assembler inside a fuselage would see the real openings for hydraulic ducts or communications cables with a virtual image of the installed ducts or cables superimposed on them. The goggles could also reflect schematic and wiring diagrams, locations of drill holes, and other information. The end result is better quality in less time.

Some virtual reality experts predict that virtual reality will eventually have an impact as great as the invention of writing. If they are wrong, it will not be for any want of ambition or confidence among pioneers in the field. The major drawbacks are the complexity of the software programs and the speed of light, that is the limitations of the physical world.

VIRTUAL REALITY'S TIE-IN WITH CREATIVITY

Although present virtual reality software does not include the built-in capability to enhance an individual's creativity skills per se, it does allow the user to go beyond traditional boundaries of design and to view designs in new and unusual ways. From this perspective, present virtual reality software would qualify as a creative computer technique to assist a typical designer. As an example of this point, Eastman Kodak quickly gained new insights after it used a supercomputer to process in three dimensions the intricate interactions of such variables as heat, temperature, and pressure in the injection process the company uses to make plastic items from film spools to camera cases. Actually to see six or seven variables is an unusual experience since polymers do an unexpected dance to untangle themselves. Hence Kodak engineers started to see things that could not be seen through equations.

By making these polymer pirouettes visible, Kodak engineers can design lighter, thinner parts that require less material and meet environmental standards. Larry Smarr, who has almost single-handedly pushed the United States into a dominant position in the use of supercomputers for visualization, says that he wants researchers "to become 'infonauts'—to swim among those polymer molecules, to enter the interior of galactic black holes."[24]

On a similar level, virtual reality can be viewed from another perspective, that is, in terms of "virtual work groups." The idea is simple, if at first unsettling: true work groups do not necessarily sit together, at adjacent desks. They are often spread across the building, across the country, and sometimes across the world. Many true work groups are so "virtual" that some members of the groups are on the move much of the time, visiting corporate branches, making customer calls, attending executive retreats, and going on vacation.

Today, there is software available that work groups can use to act as if they are in the same room. One such software package is Notes from the Lotus Development Corporation (this software will be discussed in chapter 6). Notes becomes very valuable in a company that embraces this idea of virtual work groups: people who might, in fact, be quite distant from one another, not all of whom can be found in the same chair every morning—in other words, people bound into a group that is defined not by geography, but by the task at hand. The lives of these groups might be very long (the Southeastern Sales Team) or very short (the group planning the big-customer golf weekend next month). Yet in every case, their information needs are such that they must stay in touch. They need to be able to access several constantly updated pools of information. They need to be able to send one-to-one, one-to-many, and sometimes many-to-one messages. Subsets of the group need to prepare documents and exchange, review, and revise them; other subsets might need to turn these documents into presentation-level work. Also, group members need to track the progress of their projects, track performance against plans, and track actual costs versus budgeted costs. Notes allows company personnel to do their jobs better by binding together into constantly shifting work groups, thereby allowing them to bring into play the creative processes of "virtual members."[25]

SUMMARY

A number of topical areas were discussed in this opening chapter that relate directly to creative thinking. Initially, a new paradigm to replace the past view of the world set the stage for a new way of looking at the world today and well into the twenty-first century. General Electric was shown as a good illustration of how company personnel using creativity can better interconnect internally and externally. Next, important concepts underlying creativity were examined and formed a basis for defining it. Additionally, common barriers to creative thinking were examined.

In the second half, the focus was on the use of creative computer software to assist typical managers and their personnel in gaining a competitive advantage as well as maintaining it. Not only were sample creative computer software packages set forth, but also newer information systems and organization structures were identified as a way of better utilizing company personnel creativity frequently, even daily, as deemed appropriate. In addition, the emerging field of virtual reality was discussed as it relates to creativity. In the next chapter, the essential characteristics of a creative manager are treated along with an opportunity for the reader to determine his or her level of creativity.

NOTES

1. Edward de Bono, "Why CEOs Are Not Creative," *Chief Executive*, July/August 1991, p. 37.

2. Thomas A. Stewart, "Lessons from U.S. Business Blunders," *Fortune*, April 23, 1990, pp. 128–141.

3. Frank Rose, "A New Age for Business?" *Fortune*, October 8, 1990, pp. 156–164.

4. S. J. Parnes, R. B. Noller, and A. M. Biondi, eds., *Guide to Creative Action* (New York: Scribner's 1977), p. 14.

5. C. S. Whiting, *Creative Thinking* (New York: Reinhold, 1958), p. 2.

6. R. L. Ackoff and E. Vergara, "Creativity in Problem Solving and Planning: A Review," *European Journal of Operational Research*, May 1981, p. 9.

7. Richard Lombardo, "Breaking the Barriers to Corporate Creativity," *Training and Development Journal*, August 1988, pp. 63–65.

8. Ken Blanchard, "Successful Companies Think Small," *Today's Office*, May 1991, p. 26.

9. Thomas A. Stewart, "GE Keeps Those Ideas Coming," *Fortune*, August 12, 1991, pp. 41–49.

10. Claudia H. Deutsch, "Emulating the Best of the Best," *New York Times*, December 30, 1990, Business Section, p. 23.

11. Michael L. Sullivan-Trainor and Joseph Maglitta, "Competitive Advantage Fleeting," *Computerworld*, October 8, 1990, pp. 1, 4.

12. Amy Saltzman and Edward C. Braig, "Plugging In to 'Creativity,'" *U.S. News & World Report*, October 29, 1990, p. 95.

13. Ibid., pp. 96–97.

14. Ibid., p. 97.

15. J. F. Nunamaker, Jr., Alan R. Dennis, Joseph S. Valacich, Douglas R. Vogel, and Joey F. George, "Electronic Meeting Systems to Support Group Work," *Communications of the ACM*, July 1991, pp. 40–61.

16. Gigi Verna, "PCs Powerful Tools for More Productive Meetings, The Record Report: Maximizing Productivity," *Greater Cincinnati Business Record, A Supplement*, April 29–May 5, 1991, pp. 1B–2B.

17. Brian Dumaine, "The Bureaucracy Busters," *Fortune*, June 17, 1991, pp. 36–37.

18. Ibid., pp. 37, 42.

19. Jim Nash, "Our Man in Cyberspace Checks Out Virtual Reality," *Computerworld*, October 15, 1990, p. 109.

20. Gene Bylinksy, "The Marvels of 'Virtual Reality,'" *Fortune*, June 3, 1991, pp. 138–139.

21. Ibid., p. 139.

22. Ibid., pp. 139, 142.

23. John Rizzo, "Virtus WalkThrough," *MacUser*, July 1991, pp. 73–76.

24. Bylinsky, "Marvels of 'Virtual Reality,'" p. 150.

25. Jim Seymour, "Tools Help Virtual Work Groups Keep in Touch," *PC Week*, April 29, 1991, p. 65.

2

A Look at Managerial Creativity

ISSUES EXPLORED

- To examine how an understanding of a company's intellectual capital gives it a competitive advantage
- To examine in some depth the characteristics of a creative manager
- To explore reasons why a typical manager is not creative
- To assess a manager's creativity quiz
- To reflect on those factors that are found in a creative manager

OUTLINE

A logical starting point for creativity is to look at those characteristics that are found in a typical creative manager. Such characteristics are examined in this chapter. For the most part, these characteristics will be quite different from those found in an uncreative manager. Generally, an uncreative person thinks of himself or herself as a machine programmed to accept certain inputs and produce results according to an assembly-line schedule. In contrast, a creative person thinks in terms of analogies and metaphors, that is, how the problem is being solved like something previously encountered. Likewise, a creative person tries to put himself or herself in someone else's shoes: How would my chief competitor think about this? Also, a creative person utilizes dreams, whether daydreams, those thoughts that come between waking and sleeping, or strange notions that come while asleep. Because dreams help to pull ideas from the mental muck, they are very helpful to a creative person.

In addition to examining the characteristics of a creative manager, this chapter presents a short quiz at its end to test one's creativity. The reader will be able to compare his or her result with prior research conducted by the author. However, before examining the characteristics of a creative manager, the initial focus of this chapter is on intellectual capital (i.e., assets) of a company and how it can be used by a company to gain a competitive advantage. In other words, the accent is on harnessing employees' brainpower to be used as a company's advantage in today's competitive environment. Needless to say, employees' brainpower is related to the degree of creativity that is practiced by company personnel.

COMPETITIVE ADVANTAGE OF A COMPANY'S INTELLECTUAL CAPITAL

Employees' brainpower has always been an important asset of a typical company. However, it has never been as important as it is today. Every company depends increasingly on knowledge: management skills, technologies, patents, processes, information about customers and suppliers, and everyday experiences. Added together, this knowledge leads to a company's intellectual capital. Even Pope John Paul II recognized it in a recent encyclical, writing of a new, important form of ownership: ''The possession of know-how, technology, and skill.'' Hugh MacDonald, futurologist for ICL (the large British computer manufacturer), calls it knowledge that exists in an organization that can be used to create differential advantage. In other words, it is the total of everything everybody in a company knows that gives a company a competitive advantage in the marketplace.[1]

Although collective knowledge is hard to identify and harder still to deploy effectively, it can make a big difference. As Dr. P. Roy Vagelos, chief executive officer of Merck & Company, stated: ''A low-value product can be made by anyone anywhere. When you have knowledge no one else has access to—that's dynamite.'' Merck, voted five years in a row America's most admired company in *Fortune*'s annual survey, has invented more new medicines than any other U.S. pharmaceutical company.[2]

Examples of Intellectual Capital

Typically, intellectual capital is a very viable asset and a highly valued one that is associated with the leading edge of science. To understand the importance of intellectual capital, reference can be made to the Polaroid Corporation, Pioneer Hi-Bred International, and American Express. Helios, a new medial imaging system from the Polaroid Corporation, will reach the market after just three years in development, twice as fast as predicted. The basic reason is the interdisciplinary teamwork in the laboratories. The company's researchers are not any smarter, but by working together, they get the value of each other's intelligence almost instantaneously.

As a second example, at Pioneer Hi-Bred International, scientists breed special strains of corn for disease resistance, high yield, or specific attributes like oil content. A decade ago, such work ate up hundreds of acres of farmland and consumed untold numbers of person-hours. These days, scientists can do the work by manipulating the plant's DNA directly, using a petri dish. Apart from the cost savings, the company expects to reduce by two years the seven- to ten-year time it takes to develop a new hybrid. Moreover, Pioneer now can focus on individual customers, breeding strains rich in cornstarch for industrial users or in specific oils for food processors.

The third example is IDS Financial Services, the financial planning subsidiary of American Express Company. It codified the expertise of its best account managers in a software program called Insight. Now even the worst of its 6,500 planners is better than the average planner used to be. One result is that in four years, the percentage of clients who leave has decreased by more than one-half. Basically, these three companies have learned to exploit their intellectual capital. In Pioneer Hi-Bred's case, brainpower is replacing land, the elemental form of wealth. IDS has turned the talent of a few employees into an asset available to all its planners. Polaroid is managing its knowledge to shorten development time significantly.[3]

Management of Intellectual Capital

In most companies, the management of intellectual capital currently is regarded as uncharted territory. Managers know about its assets that take tangible form, like patents and copyrights. They have an inkling of the value of others, such as the computer software that runs their information systems. They know that training and the experience gained on the learning curve belong somehow in their asset base. On the other hand, talent is intellectual capital too. The value of a lab, for instance, includes its scientists' ability to make new discoveries in the future. How managers put a price tag on these discoveries or on intangibles like design, service, and customizing that distinguish winners from losers is a different story. In the area of cost, competition increasingly centers on how well intellectual assets are used and not the number of them. These intellectual assets sometimes behave in ways that defy ordinary rules. Managing know-how is not like managing cash or buildings, yet intellectual investments need to be treated every bit as painstakingly, if not more so. Fundamentally, managing knowledge as an asset creates a new way of thinking about a company. It alters how managers think about strategic plans, technology, human resources, decision making, and the like.

Getting More from Intellectual Capital

Essentially, there are three steps in getting more from a company's intellectual capital. The first step is to find the intellectual capital. As an example, how much could a company get if it sold the research and development department that does not bear fruit? The company can determine what its payroll is, but what is the true replacement cost of research and development personnel—the value of skills that would have to be replenished if they left tomorrow? For the most part, no one even knows what these skills are. Jeffrey Staley, a management consultant (Scientific Generics) helps companies map their technology assets, that is, he locates them, defines them, and lays out routes for getting them to other parts of the company. One division of AMP, for example, knows how to drill minuscule holes in ultrathin plastic and metal rings to make connectors for fiber-optic cables. Its driller are the best in the world, and the precision of their work allows AMP to make some connectors for half its competitors' cost. Yet it was not until the company, working with Staley, mapped its technology assets that AMP learned how to make connectors for copper wiring systems. Surprises like that are typical in intellectual assets.

In the second step, the company matches its intellectual needs with its strategic plans. Polaroid is loaded with scientists who know all there is to know about the chemistry of film. But the age of digital photography is dawning, and Polaroid needs electronics experts. To get them, the company revamped its human-resources management. It made a sophisticated model of its hiring requirements. The forecast combines historical employee-turnover trends with data about the current work force, such a probable retirement date, to estimate how many people with what skills will leave in the next decade. That information is then merged with the company's long-range strategic plan to show whether departing employees should be replaced by newcomers with similar or different training, for example, a chemist by a chemist or by a software engineer.

Additionally, Polaroid wants the present work force to equip itself for those jobs. It has them linked to Harvard University, MIT, and Northeastern University. Polaroid has hooked up a satellite relay from the National Technological University—a consortium of thirty-nine institutions—to offer advanced degrees in disciplines like materials science. As an added incentive, Polaroid pegs raises and promotions to acquiring new skills. A worker who masters a skill that his or her department needs gets a raise, whether or not a promotion comes with it. The old system had no way of compensating employees who invested intellectually in the future of the company. Now there is a connection between human-resources planning and strategic business planning.

In most companies, intellectual capital enters the strategic planning process too late, if at all. Even if scientists and engineers come to strategy meetings, they sit in the back of the room. If their managers ask what they think about this idea, they say that it is OK. Rarely is there a systematic attempt to find out what technologies the company will need to carry out the plan, or to analyze the strategic implications of technology gaps, such as whether to make or buy a critical component.

In the third step, there is need to capture, capitalize, and leverage a company's floating brainpower. One approach is to automate it. For example, at Xerox, when a repairman finds a part that has failed, he logs the fact into an information base that will guide engineers to problem areas when they design a new copier. Carnegie Group has formed a joint venture with US West, Digital Equipment, Ford Motor, and Texas Instruments called the Initiative for Managing Knowledge Assets (IMKA). IMKA's aim is to make intellectual assets available through software that links data bases, artificial intelligence, and traditional rules of thumb. IMKA software just installed at Ford keeps track of the equipment and processes used to make electronic components at every manufacturing plant around the world, down to such details as how solder flows across a circuitboard. Why would that matter? When employees in a plant in another country tried to speed up production by rotating the boards made there ninety degrees, the failure rate jumped. Flowing at a new angle, the solder shorted out the circuits. IMKA software could have told them that would happen before they wasted their time and money trying.

Another way to capture intellectual capital is to employ ordinary storytelling. Referring again to Xerox, a study by the company's Palo Alto Research Center revealed that repairmen learn most about fixing copiers not from company manuals, but from swapping stories among themselves. Companies should make opportunities for storytelling at informal get-togethers and loosely organized off-site meetings, and through videotapes and bragging sessions.

Harnessing a company's intellectual capital is not easy, since it forces management to think hard about company operations and maybe even change them significantly. Typically, getting results from investing in knowledge requires a corporate culture that allows it to flow freely, which means breaking down hierarchies and changing corporate policies that stifle new ideas. Overall, a rethinking of a company's entire operations may be necessary to reap the benefits of its intellectual capital.[4]

Vast Superiority of the Human Brain to Today's Fastest Supercomputer

Much has been publicized about the capabilities of today's fastest supercomputers, but very little about the human brain. Recently, the National Commission on Superconductivity recommended developing a superconducting computer operating at petaflops speed, or about one million times faster than today's fastest supercomputers. Peta*flops* is a spectacular feat of *floating-point operations per second*. It is one quadrillion, a million billion, 10^{15}, or 1,000,000,000,000,000 calculations in the time it takes to flick a fly off one's nose. Also, it is the amount of work the fastest Cray supercomputer can do running nonstop for about two weeks or an Apple Macintosh with a robust service contract could turn out in 8,000 years. The prefix *peta* is just beginning to creep into computer terminology, extending up the family of power prefixes that includes kilo, mega, giga, tera, peta, and exa.

Because enthusiasts like to talk about the high, high end of computing, generally the low, low end gets neglected. As an example, reference can be made to the slide rule. It is good for maybe .2 flops if one is really good at it, and that is with poor accuracy. The slide rule was invented in the seventeenth century and disappeared for all practical purposes in the mid-1970s, abruptly shoved aside by the electronic calculator. Seymour Cray, the patriarch of supercomputing, once said that he had a "social problem" as a graduate student at the University of Minnesota because he had a circular slide rule while nearly everyone else had the straight-stick kind. But Seymour was not daunted. In his first job, he used a slide rule to help design what was to become the Univac 1101 mainframe.

Over forty years later, Cray uses a Macintosh personal computer to help him design the next generation of supercomputers, machines whose gallium arsenide logic chips will give them a theoretical top speed of 16 billion flops (gigaflops), or six times faster than today's fastest Cray computer. By one estimate, Cray Computer will spend more than $300 million to bring the Cray-3 to market, and that machine is likely to survive competitive onslaughts for a few short years, at best.

Actually, the slide rule does not perform floating-point operations. It just finds a few significant digits, leaving the placement of the decimal point to "wetware"—what the scientists call the user's brain. No one really knows how fast that is, but one estimate says that the brain computes at 10 trillion operations per second. At 10 teraops, the brain is faster than today's best supercomputer by a factor of 10,000 and uses neither superconductivity nor gallium arsenide.

Today's computer developers have a significant way to go to beat the human brain—the primary source of intellectual capital in a company.[5]

CHARACTERISTICS OF A CREATIVE MANAGER

Once the value of intellectual capital is recognized, there is need to place it in its proper context for a typical company. This takes the form of using a manager's creativity to enhance a company's intellectual assets. Hence it would be helpful to understand what makes people creative, that is, to take a look at specific characteristics that underlie creativity. Essentially, these characteristics are related to improving a company's intellectual capital. The creative manager has distinct characteristics that set him or her apart from less creative colleagues. However, there is no perfect example because no one person could have all the attributes of creativity to a uniformly high degree. Thus there are many gradations of attributes and skill levels among creative persons, but all such people have some measure of these characteristics in common.

As a starter, the creative manager tends to have more energy, is more inquisitive, and is more responsive to emotions and feelings than the less creative manager. The person has something researchers call "flexible repressions," which means that the creative person can bring a lot of material buried in the subconscious to conscious awareness. As will be seen in later chapters, a creative person's real well of ideas is found in the subconscious. In turn, the person has a distinct lack of inhibitions to explore these ideas in new surroundings.

Capability to Generate a Wide Range of Ideas

Creative managers can generate a wide range of ideas rapidly. Being flexible in their thinking, they can choose and investigate a wide variety of approaches to problems, discard one frame of reference for another, change approaches, and adapt quickly to new developments. On the other hand, a less creative manager suffers from "hardening of the categories"; that is, a lack of flexibility often results from overfamiliarity with objects or ideas. The really creative manager allows his or her thoughts to mill about without categorizing.

Seemingly, there is often a light side to the creative manager's involvement in work. The individual may seem to be lost in an irresponsible play of ideas, relationships, and concepts that he or she shapes into all kinds of ostensibly incongruous combinations. However, this apparently purposeless exercise strengthens and, at the same time, loosens the "muscles" of imagination. It enables the person to come up with more inventive solutions to problems.

Typically, creative managers have found that playful sketching and shaping of ideas helps them come upon really valuable ones. Furthermore, this toying serves to get them in a proper mood to start ideas flowing. These quasi-serious exercises relax the everpresent critical and conservative orientation of the conscious. By putting this watchful censor to sleep, they can set the stage for the emergence of novel ideas and solutions.

Constant Sensitivity to Problems

The creative manager not only finds fresh ideas to solve problems, but also detects problems. The ability to see "need" areas or to be aware of the odd or promising allows the manager to note gaps in the company's products, processes, and applications. Also, such managers can see the significance or possibility in situations that a less sensitive manager might overlook. The sensitive creative managers are acutely aware of people's needs and of the unrealized potential of their staffs. Always interested in improving upon existing products or situations, these creative managers are like the Socratic philosopher with a "thorn in his flesh"—perpetually disturbed by something. For the creative manager, there is hardly a situation free of problems. This somewhat happy state of dissatisfaction keeps the individual's ever-present problem orientation alive.

Examination of Cause-and-Effect Relationships

Creativity is contingent upon how much the manager's innate curiosity and youthful sense of wonder have remained intact. Unfortunately, these attributes are educated out of most people by the pressures of conformity and conservatism. Very few adults retain them, but the creative manager holds on to an intense curiosity about everything. An interested, expectant, and responsive attitude toward life keeps the creative mind well stocked with all kinds of information that can be drawn on when engaged in creative activity. Creative managers are not content just to see how something works, but they delve into the whys, that is, the cause-and-effect relationships of what they see and perceive. Their curiosity is not centered just on their own fields; their spectrum of interest embraces disparate areas and generates spontaneous enthusiasm toward almost any difficulty to solve problems.

Capability to Concentrate on Fundamental Aspects of a Problem

Creative managers differ from the less creative ones in the quality they show in their selection of elements when confronting a problem. They are able to choose more fundamental aspects of the problem and cast the superfluous aside. In creative problem solving, it is not necessarily the manager who is highly fluent with the problem who shows the highest degree of creativity. In contrast, the manager who can grasp the heart of the matter quickly shows the highest degree of creativity. Hence it is quality that counts, not necessarily the quantity of ideas.

Many times, creative solutions to problems are often simple and even obvious. Yet solutions often escape those trying to solve problems. In the following number problem, for example, the solution may not lie in the mathematical manipulation of the symbols. With that caution in mind, it is necessary to find the general rule that governs this series: 18, 11, 15, 14, 19, 16, 13, 12, 20. The solution is to translate the digits into words and arrange them alphabetically: eighteen, eleven, fifteen, fourteen, and so forth. In essence, there is need to concentrate on the fundamental aspects of the problem.

Proper Utilization of Creative Memory

Because the subconscious is a storehouse of facts, observations, impressions, and other memory items, the creative manager's mind is always stocked fully with these memories. However, this does not in itself indicate creativity. As a matter of fact, it can act as a deterrent to creativity. What makes memory creative is the dynamic mobility of the components. That is, its boundaries are permeable. All kinds of related and unrelated data and ideas can always be cross-indexed and interrelated. Typically, the creative mind is continuously rearranging, pruning, discarding, relating, and refining these data and ideas. In such a permeably structured memory, there is the ever-present possibility for new configurations and combinations.

Creativity also requires exact, recallable observations and discriminating use of the senses. For example, the manager is asked to draw the face of his or her watch without first looking at it. This test illustrates the effect of overfamiliarity. Because a person looks at his or her watch so often, the individual ceases "seeing" it. That is what happens when behaviors become automatic and when the manager takes objects too much for granted.

Allowance of Time for the Incubation Period

When thinking becomes clogged and no significant insights occur, the creative manager stops working on that particular problem and turns to something entirely different. The individual admits the limits of his or her conscious power in forcing the problem to solution. At some point, called *incubation*, the creative manager treats the problem as if it had a life of its own. In its time and in its relation to his or her subliminal or autonomous thought processes, a solution will come to the person. The creative manager also likes to contemplate, reflect, meditate, or just "chew the mental cud." During the incubation period, the creative manager often gets some of his or her best ideas and solutions to problems.

Some managers tackle problems with a dogged effort. Although commendable, keeping busy without time for relaxation or change of activity frequently serves as a barrier to creative solutions. The manager who knows when persistence with a difficult problem begins to result in diminishing returns, and who then drops it for a while, frequently finds that when he or she returns to it, a fresh approach comes with greater ease. There is a fallacious notion that the creative manager relies on effortless insight and spontaneity. In reality, true creativity requires a great deal of time for the subconscious to mull a problem over before a new idea or solution to it comes to mind.

Need to Assert One's Self-Confidence

Daring to transcend traditional methods of thinking and to stick to convictions in the face of possible discouragement or censure is very necessary in creative work. Rare indeed is the established creative manager, and even rarer is the novice, who can maintain complete detachment from criticism. Hence the creative manager needs to assert self-confidence that can be developed only through experience and exercise. It has been said that nothing breeds success like success, and this is probably true, but the corollary that failure breeds failure need not also be true. Though fear of making a mistake can be a devastating emotional block to creativity, a manager should realize that progress is made through failure as well as through success. Just look at some of the successful inventions of the nineteenth and twentieth centuries.

Since most manager's careers are governed by the degree of success, the specter of failure looms large. In the risk-taking enterprise of creativity and innovation, however, failures do not occur. Failure should be regarded as a situation from which new or improved ideas may arise. Almost every area of corporate development has had its history of failures that ultimately led to success. Perhaps the greatest failure is not to attempt any new ideas.

Need to Tolerate Ambiguity and Complexity

An important reason for the lack of creative ideas among many managers is their strong preference for predictability and order. Many immediately reject ideas that either do not fit into an established pattern or are too elusive for immediate comprehension and categorization. In contrast, creative managers can tolerate a high degree of ambiguity. They are somewhat suspicious of traditional explanations and have developed a healthy respect for groping around and for the unknown during the creative process. Creative managers can perceive a variety of possibilities and are able to consider and balance different, even conflicting and contradictory, frames of reference and concepts simultaneously.

Capability of Originality in Thought

Originality in thought is another trait of creative managers. They can think of unusual solutions and can see relationships between phenomena outside traditional boundaries. Such persons are likely to perceive the unexpected, the novel, and the fresh in everything they encounter. Their openness to unusual ideas sometimes extends to the point of being far out. Such managers are usually quite ready to entertain unheard-of ideas and frequently play around with them seriously before discarding them. New perspectives, new concepts, and venturesome ideas offer an endless source of mental exercise.

High Motivation to Succeed

Today, some managers blunt their effectiveness by excessive motivation or the desire to succeed too quickly. The overmotivated manager may narrow his or her field of observation, looking for and using only clues that provide a fast solution to a problem. This person frequently passes up leads to better solutions by picking the first workable solution rather than considering viable alternatives. Overmotivation can also result in excessively ambitious goals. Some managers want to tackle only very big and complex problems. Failure to solve their subparts first successfully can undermine their confidence to tackle problems well within their capabilities.

A lack of persistence or a feeing of flagging interest is often a signal to get away from a problem and relax for a while. Many creative managers turn to another problem because they find that they function best when involved in several undertakings simultaneously, each at a different stage and each affording the chance to relax when necessary. During the creative process, however, creative managers maintain an uninterrupted rapport with the proposals that emerge from their subconscious as they form them into something that make sense in the business world.

Utilization of a Computer's Power to Enhance Creativity

Essentially, the previous characteristics have focused on those items that are an integral part of a creative manager's personality. As will be seen in this book, it is also necessary that the manager utilize the computer's power to enhance his or her creativity. More specifically, this refers to utilizing creative computer software, that is, idea generators. For a manager operating alone, an idea processor can be instrumental in opening his or her creative channels and generating new solutions. If the manager has a decision to be made and has a number of different options on his or her mind, he or she can bring up an idea generator program and explore those ideas that are most important to solving the problem. Typically, this software will assist the manager in determining what the solution should be. In like manner, idea generators are quite useful in assisting a group of managers in a brainstorming or similar mode. The utilization of creative computer software by a manager operating alone or in a group will be highlighted throughout this book, with special emphasis on application of idea generators in part IV.

The rationale for managers using idea generators is that it is often more difficult for them to visualize all possible options than it is to select the most attractive choice from that list. Psychological research shows that people tend to anchor their thoughts early in the problem-solving process, using their first ideas as a starting point from which other ideas arise. Thus solutions are often variations on a central theme rather than genuinely different options. With the added pressure of problem solving under real-world time constraints, coming up with new ideas can often be a frustrating process. Although idea generators are unable to suggest new ideas on their own, they can aid the manager in systematically exploring a broader scope of possibilities. Needless to say, this is a very important benefit in these fast-changing times.

A CHECKLIST OF TRAITS FOUND IN A CREATIVE MANAGER

As can be seen from the foregoing discussion, a creative manager has certain traits that are far different from those found in other organization personnel. To assist the reader in getting a handle on them, a checklist of these important traits is found in figure 2.1. Basically, this checklist of behavioral and personality traits offers important insights into the makeup of a creative manager. Also, it can be used by the reader to see where improvements can be made in on-the-job and off-the-job behavior. A thorough understanding of this checklist indicates that a creative manager is restless, that is, he or she is irritated by the status quo and refuses to be restricted by habit and the environment. The creative manager is looking for ways to improve not only his or her own performance, but also that of the people around him or her. There is a relentless search to reach important short- to long-range goals. It should be noted that the typical creative manager does not possess each and every one of these traits found in figure 2.1, since people do vary in terms of behavioral and personality traits. However, the person has a sufficient number of these traits to qualify him or her as being creative.

Figure 2.1
A Checklist of Important Traits Found in a Creative Manager

- Has the ability to examine his or her own ideas objectively.
- Has a constant sensitivity to problems and their solutions.
- Has great initiative.
- Has the ability to examine cause-and-effect relationships.
- Is capable of concentrating on the fundamentals of a problem.
- Has the capability to generate a wide range of ideas.
- Can open up to new experiences and abandon traditional defenses.
- Is not afraid to ask questions that allow for better understanding of the problem.
- Likes ventures involving calculated risks.
- Believes, even after repeated failures, that the problem can be solved.
- Has the confidence to explore new problems and find out new approaches to problem solving.
- Is willing to stand alone if integrity demands it.
- Does not blame others or make excuses for errors or failures.
- Has neither fear nor resentment toward authority at all levels of the organization.
- Knows how to use creative memory.
- Is willing to allow sufficient time for the incubation period.

Figure 2.1 (continued)

- Is capable of asserting his or her self-confidence.
- Has the capability to tolerate ambiguity and complexity.
- Is capable of originality of thought.
- Has great motivation to succeed.
- Is willing to give up immediate gain or comfort to reach long-range goals.
- Is determined to finish work even under conditions of frustration.
- Has a great amount of energy that can be channeled into productive effort.
- Perseveres despite obstacles and opposition.
- Is open and direct with company personnel and respects their rights.
- Wants to examine things from a new viewpoint.
- Knows how to inspire and encourage employees.
- Is governed by inner stimuli and has a rising level of aspiration.
- Believes that fantasy and daydreaming can be an important part of the creative process.
- Has an inherent desire and respect for perfection.
- Moves toward solutions using intuition.
- Knows that getting stuck on a problem is frequently caused by asking the wrong questions.
- Is alert to new perspectives and knows that much depends on the angle from which a problem is seen.
- Is willing to listen to suggestions but makes the final judgment.
- Tries to think in terms of analogies and metaphors.
- Makes use of dreams to separate good ideas from far-out ideas.
- Makes use of a computer's power to enhance creativity.

REASONS WHY MANAGERS ARE NOT CREATIVE

Once a list of important traits found in creative managers has been developed, there is a need to examine why managers in the United States do not possess them while managers in Japan generally do. According to Edward de Bono, the Japanese are more game to risk direct-market tests. For example, they test approximately 1,000 soft drinks a year. He also claims that *negativity* is far higher in the United States than in Japan. Basically, negativity is being enhanced by the current movement in U.S. colleges and universities to teach "critical thinking." By definition, critical thinking is analytical. It focuses on "what is," and presumably such an emphasis in U.S. schools of higher learning is designed to turn out future managers with more of the same analytical skills. Certainly, the recent flap in academe over "political correctness" has produced an orgy of analysis, much of it negative and backward-looking.

In contrast, de Bono feels that U.S. schools of higher learning should be teaching constructive, creative thinking skills, focusing on "what can be." He believes that what is needed is a whole change of attitude toward creativity in this country. Even competition, so dear to most chief executive officers, comes in for a knocking from de Bono, since competition too is mostly hung up on "what is" and the way things are in the present marketplace. He is telling managers that it is not enough to move information around, no matter how many personal computers are strung together. De Bono's essential message is that a company's success will be fueled by new ideas and concepts and by chief executive officers eager to embrace them.

Overall, de Bono calls for a change in attitude toward creativity if U.S. business firms are going to reap the benefits from available global markets, available capital, personnel effectiveness, and business competence. Success in global markets is going to need a baseline of competence on which to build. This is related to the development of new ideas and concepts that emanate from serious creative thinking. As noted above, the concept of negativity, which can be interpreted as conservatism and complacency, is the biggest enemy of creativity. To think that the company is doing well or is creative enough is eventually fatal in the long run.[6]

A QUIZ TO ASSESS THE MANAGER'S CREATIVITY

An approach to determine where managers are in terms of their creativity is to use a quiz. The author and a colleague (Dr. Robert C. Klekamp) developed such a quiz several years ago that is set forth below.[7] Many of the statements found in the quiz are based upon the prior discussion on the characteristics of a creative manager.

Creativity Quiz

In this quiz, there are twenty statements to test one's level of creativity. The reader should circle whatever he or she feels is the appropriate answer based upon his or her mode of operation.

1. When under stress, you trust what has worked in the past rather than experiment with new ideas.
    a. Very seldom.
    b. Once in a while.
    c. Occasionally.
    d. Fairly often.
    e. Often.
2. Many of your successful strategies resulted from playing around on paper with the components of a problem.
    a. Very seldom.
    b. Once in a while.
    c. Occasionally.
    d. Fairly often.
    e. Often.

3. You have brainstorming sessions with others.
    a. Almost never.
    b. Once in a while.
    c. More often than not.
    d. Fairly often.
    e. Frequently.
4. You leave a present problem that stumps you in order to face an earlier problem that remains unsolved.
    a. Never.
    b. Seldom.
    c. Occasionally.
    d. Often.
    e. Always.
5. When faced with an important issue, believing that you have made the right decision is more important to you than winning over the opinions of peers and bosses.
    a. Strongly disagree.
    b. Mildly disagree.
    c. Indifferent.
    d. Agree.
    e. Absolutely agree.
6. You use scraps of time, such as in waiting rooms and at lunch, to work on simple problems.
    a. Never.
    b. Seldom.
    c. Occasionally.
    d. Often.
    e. Always.
7. You list ideas as they occur to you for possible future thought.
    a. Very seldom.
    b. Once in a while.
    c. Occasionally.
    d. Fairly often.
    e. Often.
8. To assure rational decision making, you disregard your sense of intuition.
    a. Almost never.
    b. More often than not.
    c. Unaware of intuition.
    d. Often.
    e. Always.
9. You turn to publications within your field to help you identify new solutions.
    a. Usually not.
    b. Occasionally.
    c. More often than not.
    d. Often.
    e. Entirely.
10. You use others as sounding boards to separate the important from the unimportant.
    a. Not at all.
    b. Comparatively little.

    c. Occasionally.

    d. More often than not.

    e. Fairly often.

11. You count on successful ideas rather than unsuccessful ones to lead you to more promising ideas.

    a. Once in a while.

    b. Doesn't matter.

    c. Often.

    d. Very often.

    e. Always.

12. You devote as much effort to defining the problem as to determining its solution.

    a. Never.

    b. Seldom.

    c. Occasionally.

    d. Often.

    e. Always.

13. You schedule your projects according to what comes to you.

    a. Never.

    b. Seldom.

    c. Occasionally.

    d. Often.

    e. Always.

14. You permit all subordinates to use their own judgment in solving problems.

    a. Seldom.

    b. Sometimes.

    c. More often than not.

    d. Often.

    e. Always.

15. Concerned about motivation, you praise good performance rather than admonish poor performance.

    a. Seldom.

    b. Occasionally.

    c. You comment on neither.

    d. Often.

    e. Always.

16. You prefer quarterly performance appraisals rather than annual ones.

    a. Strongly disagree.

    b. Mildly disagree.

    c. Indifferent.

    d. Agree.

    e. Strongly agree.

17. The best-dressed and best-mannered subordinates generally have the most success in completing projects.

    a. Once in a while.

    b. More often than not.

    c. Often.

    d. A great deal.

    e. Consistently.

18. You have found that the presence of external consultants diminishes your managerial aura.
    a. Strongly disagree.
    b. Mildly disagree.
    c. Indifferent.
    d. Agree.
    e. Strongly agree.
19. Your job gives you a real sense of achievement.
    a. Never.
    b. Seldom.
    c. Occasionally.
    d. Fairly often.
    e. Often.
20. If you had a good friend looking for a managerial position, you would recommend the company for which you work.
    a. Never.
    b. Seldom.
    c. Occasionally.
    d. Fairly often.
    e. Often.

Upon completion of this quiz, proceed to the Appendix of this chapter and score your answers. Next, sum the results for the twenty statements. To determine what your level of creativity is for the twenty statements, reference can be made to the grading scale below:

Category 1, 87–100: Creative manager of the future

Category 2, 73–86: Manager with definite creative potential

Category 3, 59–72: Status quo manager likely to be in same position three years from now.

Category 4, 45–58: Lucky to make it through next year as a successful manager

Category 5, 31–44: Consider a non-managerial position or learn a trade

Research Results of Creativity Quiz

This quiz was administered to five graduate-level classes at Xavier University before the appearance of the article in which it was published. The results are as follows:

Category	Number of Graduate Students	Percentage
1	0	0
2	14	15.5
3	67	74.5
4	9	10.0
5	0	0
	90	100%

The research results indicate that there is room for improvement. Essentially, an important part of this book is to improve one's creative skills by utilizing the latest creative computer software. Not only will this software assist in improving strategic thinking and decision making at the top-management levels, but it will also assist those in lower- and middle-level management. In addition, operating personnel who perform managerial activities as part of their jobs can benefit from using creative computer software.

REFLECTIONS ON A CREATIVE MANAGER

From an overall standpoint, creative managers do not know the meaning of an eight-hour business workday. Their preoccupation with problems is typically incessant. Creativity, in whatever field, is generated by hard thinking and prolonged conscious reflection over problems. Frequently, an intense conscious struggle with problems is useless. But these efforts, futile as they seem to be, are not necessarily wasted because they activate the subconscious processes of cerebration and incubation. Without preparatory work, the subconscious can be unproductive.

Essentially, creation is a product of conscious hard thinking, prolonged reflection, and subconscious incubation. There is a continuous assimilation of data and observations, a continuing pondering on the causes of regularly met difficulties, and a sorting out of hunches and ideas that are a part of consciousness. Creative managers develop a retrospective awareness of when they have solved problems creatively. They take note of the methods that have succeeded and failed. They try to learn "why" by retracing as far as possible the routes followed and those avoided.

Creative managers schedule their creative thinking periods for times when they have their most favorable mental set for producing ideas. They are aware of their personal rhythms of output. By keeping a record of the most creative periods during a day, they can establish a pattern and plan ahead, reserving peak periods for concentration, contemplation, and uninhibited thinking, and using the less productive times for reading or routine tasks. But even without a time sheet of productive periods, the creative manager develops a sensitivity to moods that promise good returns and knows when these periods are approaching.

SUMMARY

A thorough understanding of the chapter's subject matter indicates that the creative manager is quite different from an uncreative person. Typically, the creative manager acts just like the person who is not very well planned or scheduled, sensual, poetic, and so on. However, using the creative process, the creative manager transforms far-out ideas into the realities that power the company into the future. Because an important thesis of this book is that creativity can be improved, future chapters will help the typical manager move in this direction, especially with the help of creative computer software.

NOTES

1. Thomas A Stewart, "Brainpower," *Fortune*, June 3, 1991, p. 44.

2. Ibid., p. 44.

3. Ibid., pp. 44–45.

4. Ibid., pp. 45–50.

5. Gary Anthes, "You Still Can't Beat the Brain," *Computerworld*, September 17, 1990, pp. 29, 39.

6. Edward de Bono, "Why CEOs Are Not Creative," *Chief Executive*, July/August 1991, p. 37.

7. Robert C. Klekamp and Robert J. Thierauf, "On Being Boss," *Cincinnati Enquirer Magazine*, April 4, 1982, pp. 31–33.

APPENDIX: ANSWERS TO CREATIVITY QUIZ

1. a. Very seldom: 5 points.
    b. Once in a while: 4 points.
    c. Occasionally: 3 points.
    d. Fairly often: 2 points.
    e. Often: 1 point.
    No matter what the stress, your old ideas are likely to perpetuate the past and permit the situation to recur.

2. a. Very seldom: 1 point.
    b. Once in a while: 2 points.
    c. Occasionally: 3 points.
    d. Fairly often: 4 points.
    e. Often: 5 points.
    Moving ideas around on paper often is a successful method of triggering creativity.

3. a. Almost never: 1 point.
    b. Once in a while: 2 points.
    c. More often than not: 3 points.
    d. Fairly often: 4 points.
    e. Frequently: 5 points.
    Brainstorming is another successful creative trigger.

4. a. Never: 1 point.
    b. Seldom: 2 points.
    c. Occasionally: 3 points.
    d. Often: 4 points.
    e. Always: 5 points.
    Theoretically, our most creative moments come after periods of ego regression such as sleep or alternate stimuli.

5. a. Strongly disagree: 5 points.
    b. Mildly disagree: 4 points.
    c. Indifferent: 3 points.
    d. Agree: 2 points.
    e. Absolutely agree: 1 point.

Creative ideas are worth precious little to a manager's success unless the ideas can be implemented.

6. a. Never: 5 points.
    b. Seldom: 4 points.
    c. Occasionally: 3 points.
    d. Often: 2 points.
    e. Always: 1 point.

These times have high creative potential, so use them for complex kinds of problems.

7. a. Very seldom: 1 point.
    b. Once in a while: 2 points.
    c. Occasionally: 3 points.
    d. Fairly often: 4 points.
    e. Often: 5 points.

List and also rank your ideas according to their practicality and economic feasibility.

8. a. Almost never: 5 points.
    b. More often than not: 4 points.
    c. Unaware of intuition: 3 points.
    d. Often: 2 points.
    e. Always: 1 point.

Rational thinking deals with what is, but a creative manager deals with what might be.

9. a. Usually not: 5 points.
    b. Occasionally: 4 points.
    c. More often than not: 3 points.
    d. Often: 2 points.
    e. Entirely: 1 point.

If you limit yourself to your own field, your managerial style will be dictated by your own competitors.

10. a. Not at all: 1 point.
     b. Comparatively little: 2 points.
     c. Occasionally: 3 points.
     d. More often than not: 4 points.
     e. Fairly often: 5 points.

It is important to you to find out what is important to the rest of your organization.

11. a. Once in a while: 5 points.
     b. Doesn't matter: 4 points.
     c. Often: 3 points.
     d. Very often: 2 points.
     e. Always: 1 point.

Unsuccessful ideas can become successful if they are saved until the right situation and the right time.

12. a. Never: 1 point.
     b. Seldom: 2 points.
     c. Occasionally: 3 points.
     d. Often: 4 points.
     e. Always: 5 points.

You are better off having the wrong answer to the right problem than the right answer to the wrong problem.

13. a. Never: 5 points.
    b. Seldom: 4 points.
    c. Occasionally: 3 points.
    d. Often: 2 points.
    e. Always: 1 point.
    Plan and assign priorities to your projects and your job.
14. a. Seldom: 5 points.
    b. Sometimes: 4 points.
    c. More often than not: 3 points.
    d. Often: 2 points.
    e. Always: 1 point.
    Allowing creative freedom among your subordinates is admirable, provided you are sure that your staff does the right jobs in the right ways.
15. a. Seldom: 5 points.
    b. Occasionally: 4 points.
    c. You comment on neither: 3 points.
    d. Often: 2 points.
    e. Always: 1 point.
    People have a right to know exactly where they stand.
16. a. Strongly disagree: 1 point.
    b. Mildly disagree: 2 points.
    c. Indifferent: 3 points.
    d. Agree: 4 points.
    e. Strongly agree: 5 points.
    Annual feedback is too infrequent to modify behavior over the long term.
17. a. Once in a while: 5 points.
    b. More often than not: 4 points.
    c. Often: 3 points.
    d. A great deal: 2 points.
    e. Consistently: 1 point.
    Your job is to manage productivity, not fashion and etiquette.
18. a. Strongly disagree: 5 points.
    b. Mildly disagree: 4 points.
    c. Indifferent: 3 points.
    d. Agree: 2 points.
    e. Strongly agree: 1 point.
    To build a career on managerial ego is to build on sand.
19. a. Never: 1 point.
    b. Seldom: 2 points.
    c. Occasionally: 3 points.
    d. Fairly often: 4 points.
    e. Often: 5 points.
    If not, there is a good probability that, over time, you will not perform it well.
20. a. Never: 1 point.
    b. Seldom: 2 points.
    c. Occasionally: 3 points.
    d. Fairly often: 4 points.
    e. Often: 5 points.
    If you would not recommend your firm to a friend, better ask yourself why you are there.

Bibliography: Part I

Ackoff, R. L., and E. Vergara. "Creativity in Problem Solving and Planning: A Review." *European Journal of Operational Research*, May 1981.

Alexander, M. "Visualizing Cleared-off Desktop." *Computerworld*, May 6, 1991.

———. "Virtual Reality Still Unrealistic." *Computerworld*, June 24, 1991.

Anthes, G. "You Still Can't Beat the Brain." *Computerworld*, September 17, 1990.

Applegate, L. M., J. I. Cash, Jr., and D. Q. Mills, "Information Technology and Tomorrow's Manager." *Harvard Business Review*, November–December 1988.

Barker, J. "The State of the Art for Decision Making." *Successful Meetings*, November 1989.

Barlow, J. P. "Private Life in Cyberspace." *Communications of the ACM*, August 1991.

Biondi, A. M., ed. *The Creative Process*, Buffalo, N.Y.: D.O.K., 1972.

———. *Have an Affair with Your Mind*, Buffalo, N.Y.: D.O.K., 1974.

Blanchard, K. "Successful Companies Think Small." *Today's Office*, May 1991.

Boyell, J. J., and H. B. Conn. *Workplace 2000: The Revolution Reshaping American Business*. New York: Dutton, The Penguin Group, 1991.

Brown, J. S. "Research That Reinvents the Corporation." *Harvard Business Review*, January–February 1991.

Bylinsky, G. "Where Japan Will Strike Next." *Fortune*, September 25, 1989.

———. "The Marvels of 'Virtual Reality.'" *Fortune*, June 3, 1991.

Carlyle, R. E. "Toward 2017." *Datamation*, September 15, 1987.

Cash, J. I., Jr., and B. R. Konsynski. "IS Redraws Competitive Boundaries." *Harvard Business Review*, March–April 1985.

Clark, C. H. *Idea Management: How to Motivate Creativity and Innovation*. AMA Management Briefing. New York: AMACOM, 1980.

Couger, J. D. "Creativity in IS." *Computerworld*, October 29, 1990.

Crawford, R. P. *Direct Creativity*. Wells, Vt.: Fraser, 1964.

Curran, J. J. "Companies That Rob the Future." *Fortune*, July 4, 1988.

Davis, G. A. *Psychology of Problem Solving*. New York: Academic Press, 1974.

De Bono, E. *Think Tank: Instruction Booklet*. Toronto, Canada: Think Tank Corporation, 1973.

——— . *I Am Right, You Are Wrong: From Rock Logic to Water Logic*. New York: Penguin, 1991.

——— ."Why CEOs Are Not Creative." *Chief Executive*, July/August 1991.

De Groot, M. "3D Graphics: Virtual Reality." *Unix Review*, August 1990.

Deutsch, C. "Emulating the Best of the Best." *New York Times*, December 30, 1990, Business section.

Dumaine, B. "What the Leaders of Tomorrow See." *Fortune*, July 3, 1989.

——— . "The Bureaucracy Busters." *Fortune*, June 17, 1991.

——— . "Closing the Innovation Gap." *Fortune*, December 2, 1991.

Duval Fromson, B. "Where the Next Fortunes Will Be Made." *Fortune*, December 5, 1988.

Dyson, E. "Virtual Reality: Spreadsheets for Industry." *Forbes*, September 17, 1990.

Einstein, A. *Ideas and Opinions*. New York: Bonanza Books, 1954.

Ellis, C. A., S. J. Gibbs, and G. L. Rein. "Groupware, Some Issues and Experiences." *Communications of the ACM*, January 1991.

Evans, J. R. "Creative Thinking and Innovation Education in the Decision Sciences." *Decision Sciences*, Vol. 17, 1986.

——— . *Creative Thinking in the Decision and Management Sciences*. Cincinnati: South-Western Publishing Company, 1991.

Ferguson, C. H. "Computers and the Coming of the U.S. Keiretsu." *Harvard Business Review*, July–August 1990.

Finley, M. "The New Meaning of Meetings." *Communication World*, March 1991.

Fritz, M. "The World of Virtual Reality." *Training*, February 1991.

Fritz, R. "Rate Yourself as a Manager." *Association Management*, American Society of Association Executives, August 1980.

Ganor, G. H. *Achieving the Competitive Edge through Integrated Technology Management*. New York: McGraw-Hill, 1991.

George, J. F., G. K. Easton, J. F. Nunamaker, Jr., and G. B. Northcroft. "A Study of Collaborative Group Work with and without Computer-based Support." *Information Systems Research*, December 1990.

Gibson, W. "Cyberspace '90." *Computerworld*, October 15, 1990.

Glitman, R. "Bringing the Cyber Office to Corporate America." *PC Week*, January 14, 1991.

Goodman, S. E. "The Globalization of Computing: Perspectives on a Changing World." *Communications of the ACM*, January 1991.

Helsel, S. K., and J. P. Roth. *Virtual Reality: Theory, Practice, and Promise*. New York: Meckler Corporation, 1990.

Henry, J., ed. *Creative Management*. Newbury Park, Calif.: Sage Publications, 1991.

Hill, C. W. L., M. A. Hill, and R. E. Hoskisson. "Declining U.S. Competitiveness: Reflections on a Crisis." *Academy of Management Executive*, February 1988.

Huey, J. "Nothing Is Impossible." *Fortune*, September 23, 1991.

Hurst, D. K. "Creating Competitive Advantage: Welding Imagination to Experience." *Academy of Management Executive*, February 1989.

Istvan, R. L. "Competing in the Fourth Dimension—Time." *Chief Information Officer Journal*, Summer 1988.

Jacobson, L. "Virtual Reality: A Status Report." *AI Expert*, August 1991.

Japan Human Relations Association, ed. *The Idea Book: Improvement through TEI*. Cambridge, Mass.: Productivity Press, 1990.

Johnson, V. "Support Systems." *Successful Meetings*, August 1990.

Keen, P. G. W. *Shaping the Future: Business Design through Information Technology*. Boston: Harvard Business School Press, 1991.

Klekamp, R. C., and R. J. Thierauf. "On Being Boss." *Cincinnati Enquirer Magazine*, April 4, 1982.

Konsynski, B. R., and F. W. McFarlan. "Information Partnerships—Shared Data, Shared Scale." *Harvard Business Review*, September–October, 1990.

Lobick, K. "The Seven Keys to Business Leadership." *Fortune*, October 24, 1988.

Lombardo, R. "Breaking the Barriers to Corporate Creativity." *Training and Development Journal*, August 1988.

McFarlan, F. W. "Information Technology Changes the Way You Compete." *Harvard Business Review*, May–June 1984.

Miller, W. *The Creative Edge*. Reading, Mass.: Addison-Wesley, 1987.

Moad, J. "The Second Wave." *Datamation*, February 1, 1989.

Murphy, R. T. "Japan and the World, Power without Purpose: The Crises of Japan's Global Financial Dominance." *Harvard Business Review*, March–April 1989.

Nadler, G., and S. Hibino. *Breakthrough Thinking*. New York: Prima Publishing & Communications, 1991.

Nash, J. "Our Man in Cyberspace Checks Out Virtual Reality." *Computerworld*, October 15, 1990.

Newquist, H. P., III. "A Computer-generated Suspension of Disbelief." *AI Expert*, August 1991.

Nonaka, I. "The Knowledge-creating Company." *Harvard Business Review*, November–December 1991.

Nunamaker, J. F., Jr., A. R. Dennis, J. S. Valacich, D. R. Vogel, and J. F. George. "Electronic Meeting Systems to Support Group Work." *Communications of the ACM*, July 1991.

Osborn, A. F. *Applied Imagination*. New York: Scribner's, 1963.

Paré, T. P. "Who May Thrive Now." *Fortune*, April 22, 1991.

Parnes, S. J., R. B. Noller, and A. M. Biondi, eds. *Guide to Creative Action*. New York: Scribner's, 1977.

Piturro, M. C. "Groupware—Computer Support for Teams." *Data Training*, August 1989.

Portante T. "Cyberspace: Reality Is No Longer Enough." *Patricia Seybold's Office Computing Report*, October 1990.

Porter, M. E., and V. E. Millar. "How Information Gives You Competitive Advantage." *Harvard Business Review*, July–August, 1985.

Rapoport, C. "Why Japan Keeps on Winning." *Fortune*, July 15, 1991.

Reich, R. B. "Who Is Us?" *Harvard Business Review*, January–February 1990.

Rheingold, H. *Virtual Reality*. New York: Summit Books, 1990.

Rice, F. "Champions of Communication." *Fortune*, June 3, 1991.

Richman, L. S. "How American Can Triumph." *Fortune*, December 18, 1989.

Rizzo, J. "Virtus WalkThrough." *MacUser*, July 1991.

Robey, D., and W. Taggart. "Measuring Managers' Minds: The Assessment of Style in Human Information Processing." *Academy of Management Review*, Vol. 6, no. 3, 1981.

Rose, F. "A New Age for Business?" *Fortune*, October 8, 1990.

Saffo, P. "Virtual Reality Is Almost Real." *Personal Computing*, June 29, 1990.

Saltzman, A., and E. C. Braig. "Plugging In to 'Creativity.'" *U.S. News & World Report*, October 29, 1990.

Sellers, P. "Does the CEO Really Matter?" *Fortune*, April 22, 1991.

Seymour, J. "Tools Help Virtual Work Groups Keep in Touch." *PC Week*, April 29, 1991.

Shapiro, E. C. *How Corporate Truths Become Competitive Traps.* New York: John Wiley & Sons, 1991.

Slater, D. "Deep Thought Boggles the Human Mind." *Computerworld*, October 1990.

Sprout, A. L. "America's Most Admired Corporations." *Fortune*, February 11, 1991.

——— . "Who May Thrive Now." *Fortune*, April 22, 1991.

Stein, M. I. *Stimulating Creativity.* Vol. 2, *Group Procedures.* New York: Academic Press, 1975.

Stewart, T. A. "Lessons from U.S. Business Blunders." *Fortune*, April 23, 1990

——— . "Brainpower." *Fortune*, June 3, 1991.

——— . "GE Keeps Those Ideas Coming." *Fortune*, August 12, 1991.

Sullivan-Trainor, M. L., and J. Maglitta. "Competitive Advantage Fleeting." *Computerworld*, October 8, 1990.

Thierauf, R. J. *Decision Support Systems for Effective Planning and Control: A Case Study Approach.* Englewood Cliffs, N.J.: Prentice-Hall, 1982.

——— . *Effective Management Information Systems: Accent on Current Practices.* 2d ed. Columbus, Ohio: Charles E. Merrill Publishing Company, 1987.

——— . *User-oriented Decision Support Systems: Accent on Problem Finding.* Englewood Cliffs, N.J.: Prentice-Hall, 1988.

——— . *Group Decision Support Systems for Effective Decision Making: A Guide for MIS Practitioners and End Users.* Westport, Conn.: Quorum Books, 1989.

——— . *Executive Information Systems: A Guide for Senior Management and MIS Professionals.* Westport, Conn.: Quorum Books, 1991.

Thornbeck, J. "The Turnaround Value of Values." *Harvard Business Review*, January–February 1991.

Thurow, L. "Let's Learn from the Japanese." *Fortune*, November 18, 1991.

Upson, C. "3D Graphics: Tools for Creating Visions." *Unix Review*, August 1990.

Verna, G. "PCs Powerful Tools for More Productive Meetings. The Record Report: Maximizing Productivity," *Greater Cincinnati Business Record, A Supplement*, April 29–May 5, 1991.

Whiting, C. S. *Creative Thinking.* New York: Reinhold, 1958.

Williams, D. "New Technologies for Coordinating Work." *Datamation*, May 15, 1990.

Wiseman, C. *Strategy and Computers: Information Systems as Competitive Weapons.* Homewood,, Ill.: Dow Jones–Irwin, 1985.

Young, L. F. *Decision Support and Idea Processing Systems.* Dubuque, Iowa: William C. Brown Publishers, 1989.

PART II

Creativity Techniques and Managerial Decision Making

3

Creativity Techniques Useful to Managers

ISSUES EXPLORED

- To examine the need to promote managerial creativity on the job
- To stress the importance of going beyond traditional boundaries and making unusual mental connections in the creative process
- To set forth well-known individual and group creativity techniques
- To set forth cautions when using these individual and group creativity techniques
- To show the tie-in of these individual and group creativity techniques with typical creative computer software packages

OUTLINE

Improving Managerial Creativity on the Job
   Promoting Managerial Creativity
Basic Concepts Underlying Creativity Techniques
   Integrative Thinking Goes beyond Traditional Boundaries
   Generation of New Ideas Stresses Unusual Mental Connections
Individual and Group Creativity Techniques
The Creative Process
Brainstorming
Synectics
Battelle-Bildmappen-Brainwriting (BBB) Method
Accurate Problem Definition
Problem Definition Table
Checklists
   Attribute Listing
   Osborn's Checklist

As expected, creativity techniques produce contradictory opinions. Indeed, creativity is probably one of the most complex and confusing phenomena within a person. It is so diverse in its applications and in the methods by which those applications are derived that any attempt to forge a consensus of what is or is not truly creative can only lead to philosophical gridlock. Although great creative minds are surely precious and rare, it is clear that the potential for creativity lies within us all.

Notions about creativity are generally two-faced: some call it a product, others call it a process. Is creativity divine inspiration or strictly human? Can it be developed in a person, or is it inherited? Can the scientist be as creative as the artist, and are their works due to spontaneous imagination or the result of gritty labor? Can creativity be controlled, or does it rise from the unconscious? Last, is creativity pure reason or a brush with insanity? Some of these notions about creativity will be explored in this chapter. As mentioned previously, the thesis of this book is that creativity can be improved upon by using appropriate creative computer software. Because chapter 6 will focus on this software, the central thrust of this chapter is on creativity techniques that are widely used by business currently. However, a brief introduction to typical creative computer software will be given at the end of the chapter.

IMPROVING MANAGERIAL CREATIVITY ON THE JOB

Today, in small and large businesses across America, managers seem to be looking for new ideas. Of late, however, discouraging words have been heard suggesting that traditional methods of conducting the search will not suffice any longer. Chief executive officers proclaim the need for new ways of fostering entrepreneurship within companies. Others from the area of psychology complain that the manager permits the left half of his or her brain (logical, linear, and analytic) to so dominate the right (the big-picture-seeing hemisphere, full of affect) that the manager has not a chance of generating a fresh insight or idea for the problem under study.

Even if the capacity of the left brain to grasp the full gravity of the problem is questionable, it is good to know that corporate America is finally taking heed of such alarms. For instance, a head corporate planner of a large conglomerate surveyed several major companies to determine what, if anything, they were doing to spark greater creativity among their strategic planners. He found that a majority of the companies had undertaken some sort of formal training in creativity within the last two years. Providers of such training for planners and others—consultants and educators—are doing a brisk business these days, considerably more than previously.

A pressing question, then, is whether corporate America is getting anything for its money. Not that all purveyors of creativity training are charlatans. Customers for these services that include the *Fortune 1000* often report that in sessions with the trainers, their people have come up with promising ideas for new products or interesting new uses for old ones. The real issue is whether a company can, with or without outside help, institutionalize a higher level of creativity among its employees. Can a manager, in effect, build in a creative approach to corporate problems?

Framing the issue this way is itself an indication of how far businesspersons have come in thinking about turning on those mental light bulbs. Harrison Gough, director of the Institute of Personality Assessment and Research at the University of California, posits three popular conceptions of creativity.[1] According to the first view, the creative person leans toward the weird. This corresponds to the corporate notion that "if we need creative people, we can always hire them." Then they can be isolated to do their job. In the second view, the act of creation is held up apart from the person or persons responsible. Attention focuses on the process by which new ideas are generated. For example, a task force is formed to figure out precisely how to come up the new model. From this view, the process can be repeated the next time around. In the third and final view, creativity is latent within everyone. It just needs to be brought out. This is the conception to which most creativity-training types subscribe. Companies buying their services adopt it either consciously or unconsciously.

Which of the three views is correct, that is, most productive? The answer is simply that it is not known at this time. As students of this subject admit, neither psychology nor physiology has yet been able to provide a definitive explanation of how creativity works. The lack of such an explanation is a burden particularly for those who embrace the third view. For their viewpoint to be taken seriously, they have to explain why, if everyone has the potential to be creative, so few people seem to deliver on that potential.

Promoting Managerial Creativity

As companies increasingly realize, the real obstacle to building managerial creativity is not getting managers to come up with fresh ways to look at problems. It is, rather, what happens to these insights when managers go back to the office. Even if the ideas suddenly come in abundance, what do they avail if the company, because of the bureaucratic way it operates, does nothing with them, that is, the company does not draw them out, does not act on them, or does not reward the manager responsible? Serious students of corporate performance, most notably Thomas J. Peters and Robert Waterman, Jr., authors of *In Search of Excellence*, have found that certain companies excel at fostering new ideas and bringing them to market—Minnesota Mining & Manufacturing, for instance, or Hewlett-Packard. At each of these companies, a strong corporate culture (a set of shared values) nurtures and protects creativity.

Two questions confront any company wishing to emulate their example. First, does the company want or need new ideas enough that it is willing to put up with all the agony that building a new corporate culture entails? This centers on endless meetings proclaiming the new values, the constant attempt to alter behavior, and the need to get rid of old-timers who cannot keep up with this change. Second, is it even possible to change a company's culture? To their credit, creativity-training firms acknowledge that acceptance of the ideas they help engender is often a problem, even at the companies that hire them. Their response to the difficulty varies widely. Synectics, for example, with a number of professionals worldwide (probably the largest consulting and training firm devoted exclusively to creativity) takes the view that issues of implementation have to be built into the idea-generation process. This Cambridge, Massachusetts, firm got its start over three decades ago stressing brainstorming—just let those ideas flow, reserve any judgment of them until later. However, it now counsels clients to devote more time to developing ways to make ideas acceptable to the company than was spent coming up with the ideas in the first place. Only when an idea has been debugged thoroughly will it be presented to the management layer that passes on new projects.

In essence, implementation of the new culture is all part of generating a situation that management psychologist Harry Levinson describes as "controlled craziness,"[2] controlled because at least some percentage of what the manager comes up with has to have a chance of succeeding within the company. Typically, most companies do not want a too-radical approach. Moreover, the managers who generate the ideas have to continue to abide by most of the company's norms.

BASIC CONCEPTS UNDERLYING CREATIVITY TECHNIQUES

Too often, time for creative thinking is unduly restricted because there is the ever-pressing demand for immediate results. This is typically the fault of top managers who do not recognize the importance of this creative phase in decision making at the levels below them. A good logical mind is required in creative thinking since it is necessary to reduce a complex situation to its essential elements. Effective managers must think analytically and be highly imaginative in their approaches to decision making. Not only must they be able to visualize the possibilities of alternatives, but also they must be capable of communicating these ideas in an understandable manner. They must take the initiative when required and respond to valid objections to their work. In essence, they must operate effectively in two worlds: the *conceptual* one of problem solving and finding and the *real* one of effective decisions.

For effective creative thinking, managers at the top, middle, and lower levels should work with selected personnel from their departments who can then act as a sounding board for new ideas and alternatives. Departmental representatives, who have the answers to the proverbial questions of who, what, where, when, how, and why, should be imaginative enough to recommend improvements to all proposals. Likewise, they should be objective in their thinking and should accept worthwhile changes. Facts that may be needed subsequently can be gathered under their direction. Managers and their departmental representatives can complement each other. This combination can produce better decisions than just having the managers work alone.

In the development and evaluation of alternative courses of action, creative approaches are necessary. Very often, novel alternative solutions must be tried in order to solve problems. However, trying an unknown approach often frightens managers. Their mental sets of alternatives are limited to the point that viable solutions are screened out or rejected as impossible or inappropriate. Managers should always ask themselves why various possible alternatives are out of the question. To illustrate, consider the nine-dot problem (shown below). It requires that the nine dots be connected by drawing only four straight lines without lifting the pencil from the paper. This problem is a good illustration of how constrained thinking can prevent problems from being solved.

```
    •     •     •


    •     •     •


    •     •     •
```

Many people fail to solve this puzzle because their minds eliminate the possibility of drawing outside the area encompassed by the four corner dots. This is not a restriction, yet many people simply assume that it is. The answer to the problem requires drawing beyond the perimeters:

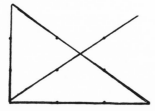

Integrative Thinking Goes beyond Traditional Boundaries

Essentially, the solution of this problem requires going beyond the traditional boundaries that a person imposes upon the problem. Some creativity experts call this *integrative thinking* and some call it *holistic thinking*. No matter what name is used, the focus is to view problems and opportunities integratively such that managers see them as wholes related to large wholes, rather than dividing information and experience into discrete bits assigned to distinct, separate categories that never touch one another. Blurring the boundaries and challenging the categories permits new possibilities to emerge, like twisting a kaleidoscope to see the endless patterns that can be created from the same set of fragments. Harvard psychologist Ellen Langer coined the term "mindfulness" for the ability to make aware choices, to pay attention to the essence and potential of things rather than to be blinded and inhibited by the categories applied to them. Research has associated integrative thinking with higher levels of organizational innovation, personal creativity, and even longer life.

Applying integrative thinking to the nine-dot problem results in a number of equally good or better solutions. A straightforward solution is as follows:

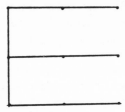

Another solution is expanding the dots so that they become spots that are connected using no straight lines.

Still another solution is to enlarge the line that was originally drawn.

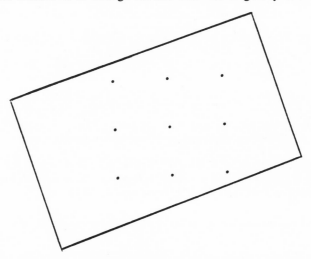

Other solutions also exist. One would be to cut out a plane with the nine dots on it, then fold it again and again so that each fold goes through the center dot; the last fold will form a single line that connects all dots. Yet another solution is to connect the nine dots with a single line by rolling the piece of paper into a cylinder and drawing a springlike line around it until all the dots are connected.[3]

Going one step further, take the nine-dot problem and now try using just three lines to connect the dots. On the surface, it may appear to be impossible. However, if the reader challenges another constraint in the problem, namely, the size of the dots, the problem can be solved as follows:

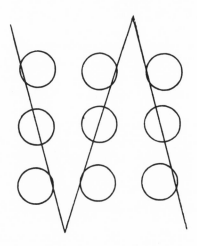

From the preceding discussion about the nine-dot problem, it can be seen that there is need for the manager to rethink categories and transcend boundaries for every aspect of business practice today. As a starter, many companies need a new approach to their business, defined across rather than within industries and markets. For example, a hospital has to think beyond the physical limits of hospital buildings to create new relationships among health-care providers dispersed across many places. Another example is a computer giant that is being challenged on one side by low-cost competition for its products and on the other side by consulting firms taking the high-end systems integration business. Bound by a rigid conception of its industry and organized to fit that conception, the company seems unable to reinvent itself. In contrast, a large bank is prospering by thinking beyond its industry boundaries. By redefining its branch banks as ''stores,'' it can sell many additional products through its branches. If Sears can be in financial services, Banc One can also be in retailing.

Product integrity, an important cause of Japanese success in the auto industry, is the result of thinking across boundaries. In the automobile industry, each functional group contributing to an automobile project thinks across boundaries as it listens to and integrates into its own work the results of the others' efforts. A strong product champion patrols the boundaries, protects the integrity of the whole, and prevents the effort from fragmenting.

Generation of New Ideas Stresses Unusual Mental Connections

The generation of new ideas is itself boundary-challenging. However, innovations grow out of unexpected and even irreverent mental connections. To develop them requires collaborations and adjustments by many parts of a company. Entrepreneurial opportunities do not respect territories; they rarely present themselves to companies in the boxes established by the organization chart. But the more rigid the walls between functions or between divisions, the less likely that managers will venture out of their boxes to try something new.

An integral part of generating new ideas stressing unusual mental connections is to recognize patterns and to see the similarities in different ideas or events. In turn, new ways can be used to see the strange as familiar and the familiar as strange, and from there to start making connections between the two. Of course, the individual must take risks and not be fearful of being wrong. Hence chance can be used to the individual's benefit, taking advantage of the unexpected as Charles Goodyear did with the vulcanization of rubber. Of course, it helps to construct networks, exchanging ideas and questions with other people. One can feed on another's creativity, and it certainly helps to be able to stand on the shoulders of others.

From this vantage point, the individual might be able to see something that does not yet exist. What is important is always what does not exist, and finding it requires incubation, that is, going back and forth between logic and the unconscious. It may be necessary for the individual to use logic in order to understand all the practical elements of the problem before trying to think of a creative solution. It might be helpful to get away to a different place, somewhere outside the individual's normal environment, so that the right half of the brain can start making connections. One should not stop with one idea, but keep ideas going; only when one has several ideas should he or she go back and apply logic to what will work best. Many times, the person will know intuitively what will work best for a client, like a certain design. In the end, it is necessary to create logical reasons for an idea, but first, there must be the inspired product.

INDIVIDUAL AND GROUP CREATIVITY TECHNIQUES

In this part of the chapter, the accent is on identifying current creativity techniques that are useful for an individual or a group. It will be evident from the exposition on each creativity technique what the appropriate basis for its usage is. From an overview standpoint, these techniques can be thought of as consisting of the following steps: defining the problem, collecting new data, breaking down and analyzing, developing useful ideas, easing off to encourage new insight, fitting the odds and ends together, and picking out the best ideas. Formally these steps can be identified as orientation, preparation, analysis, ideation, incubation, synthesis, and evaluation, respectively. These steps include integrative thinking that goes beyond traditional boundaries. In addition, new and unusual contributions are sought. These are combined and rearranged to provide different ways of achieving the same function. These topics were enumerated at some length above.

One final comment should be made regarding the use of these creativity techniques. Sometimes, creative solutions may never be found because not all available information is used. Often the solutions to problems are not obvious even though the problems are well defined. Henry David Thoreau noted that although many objects fall within reach of *visual* view, they are not seen because they do not come within range of one's *intellectual* view. Sometimes, answers lie right before one's eyes, but the individual never finds them because he or she is unable to put the scattered pieces together. Frequently, this is because not all of the relevant, available information is used. Hence managers would be wise to spend time sorting information about problems into categories labeled "usable" and "unusable" and then make certain that all usable information is drawn upon. It is particularly important to do this when it appears that an answer is not forthcoming.

Creativity techniques that are covered below include the following:

- The creative process
- Brainstorming
- Synectics
- Battelle-Bildmappen-Brainwriting (BBB) method
- Accurate problem definition
- Problem definition table
- Checklists
- Redefinition
- Reversal
- Other creativity techniques

Reference will be made to some of these creativity techniques in future chapters from a computerized point of view.

THE CREATIVE PROCESS

Many models have been formulated that relate to the creative process for problem solving by a decision maker working alone. An early descriptive model of the creative process useful to an individual thinker was formulated by Graham Wallas in 1926. This process appeared in his book, *The Art of Thought*.[4] He specified four phases of the creative process: (1) preparation, (2) incubation, (3) illumination, and (4) verification.

In the first phase, preparation consists of gathering facts, knowledge, and information that may be applicable to some problem under study. This phase can include standard and nonstandard approaches and methods that can bring the decision maker to the point where new alternatives can be devised. Typically, the second and third phases of this creative process involve, respectively, an initial pause (incubation) in which some unconscious sifting, sorting, and/or relating of information gathered during the first phase takes place, followed by a sudden awareness or recognition of a new relationship that has importance to the decision maker (illumination). Essentially, incubation is related to the search for and identification of ideas and/or problem-solution alternatives at a subconscious level, which means that this stage can be seen as the actual creative process itself. The illumination stage is the conscious awareness of new ideas and/or solutions to the problem under study by the decision maker. Finally, in the fourth stage, the insight gained from the illumination stage is tested and seen to be viable and acceptable, is determined to be unacceptable, or is reworked until it becomes acceptable. In essence, the decision maker relates the initial notion to other concepts and places it into some logical context. The decision maker imposes closure; that is, he or she accepts or rejects the validity of the idea and/or solution for the problem under study. These four stages of the creative process as postulated by Wallas are set forth in figure 3.1.

Figure 3.1
The Wallas Model of the Creative Process

Stage 1 - Preparation:

Gathering facts, knowledge,

and information relevant to

the problem

Stage 2 - Incubation:

Search and identify possible

ideas and/or solution alter-

natives to the problem at

the subconscious level

Stage 3 - Illumination:

Conscious awareness of new

ideas and/or solutions to

the problem

Stage 4 - Verification:

Testing for viable and acceptable

idea and/or solution to

the problem

Overall, the Wallas model provides a useful framework for describing what happens during the creative process for generating new ideas or solving problems. Also, this framework may be helpful not only to a decision maker working alone, but also to a group of decision makers working together. As noted previously, this model, like other models to be presented in this and subsequent chapters, does not prescribe how the creative thinking process actually works.

BRAINSTORMING

Probably the best-known creativity technique is brainstorming, which was developed by Alex F. Osborn (cofounder of BBD&O) to help solve advertising problems. It is used to improve problem analysis by providing more possible solutions and unusual approaches to the problem under study. A typical brainstorming group consists of six to twelve individuals who assemble to search for solutions to a problem. Most brainstorming experts recommend that the group members have a variety of backgrounds in order to facilitate the analysis of the problem from different points of view. Also, sessions lasting for about an hour are most effective.

Osborn suggests four rules necessary for the utilization of brainstorming: (1) Judgment is withheld; ideas may be criticized and evaluated later. (2) Wild ideas are encouraged; ideas are easier to modify than to originate. (3) Numerous ideas are desired; more ideas increase the possibility of obtaining an excellent idea. (4) The participants are encouraged to utilize the ideas of others to develop additional ideas. Other recommended procedures include the following: The sessions should be recorded, because some ideas may be missed during a meeting; the problem must be manageable, even if it requires breaking large problems into smaller parts; and samples should be available if products are being discussed.

Based upon the foregoing rules, the following guidelines should be observed to provide the proper environment for a brainstorming session:

- Do not attempt to generate new ideas and to judge them at the same time.
- Do try to generate a large quantity of possible solutions.
- Seek a wide variety of solutions by using different approaches to the problem.
- Listen carefully to the input of the others as an opportunity to "hitchhike" onto an idea or ideas as a combination or improvement.
- During a session, no idea, even the most seemingly impractical, should be discarded.
- "Ridiculous" is an unheard-of word in brainstorming. It is both impolite and disastrous to the creative process.
- Before concluding the brainstorming exercise, some time should be allowed for *subconscious* thought about the problem while *consciously* discussing other possible solutions. This incubation can be extended to any appropriate time period, recycling and reorbiting as necessary.
- Recycling and backtracking are useful to a degree, but there should be an attempt to "lean" forward since this is where the solutions are to be found.

After the brainstorming session, the ground rules change radically; that is, the freewheeling, noncritical session ends. Now it is time to apply judgment to the flights of fancy. After brainstorming, the group must set up the criteria for evaluation. Then all the ideas are evaluated based upon the criteria, and the best two or three possible solutions are chosen. An efficient way to begin the evaluation process is to scan the written list and group all ideas that are the same or, at least, very similar. Also, each group is considered as one idea.

Now that constructive criticism is being applied, there may be need to modify any idea in order to make it more closely meet the desired criteria. In this way, a seemingly wild notion can be transformed into a workable solution. No problem-solving process is complete until the most promising solutions are placed into action, so, after the group works through the entire list of ideas, two or three solutions are selected that meet all or most of the desired criteria. The group may spend as much time on explaining and implementing the solutions as it did on their development. The final step is to evaluate regularly and revise the various solutions until one actually alleviates the problem.

After Alex Osborn devised brainstorming, one of his associates observed that when a group really gets going in a brainstorming session, a spark from one mind will light up a lot of important ideas in the others, just like a string of firecrackers. The manager and his or her group who seek a reputation for problem solving may find brainstorming to be a surefire way of reaching that goal. Taking a fresh look by an uninhibited and unrestricted free association by group members can help solve problems by creating proposed solutions that are different from the existing ones.

SYNECTICS

Not as well known as brainstorming, synectics is based on the assumption that creativity can be described and taught. Its purpose is to improve the quality of creative output from those assigned to a synectics team. The people selected to participate in a synectics group determine the group's success. For this reason, team members are chosen only after very thorough testing and screening in order to ensure selection of the best combination possible to solve the problems of a specific company. The selection process results in a tailor-made synectics team composed of individuals best equipped, intellectually and psychologically, to deal with problems unique to their company. After selection, members are assigned to the synectics team and begin studying the creative process and learning the ways of synectics. A synectics team solves problems for the entire company, similar to operations research (management science) or systems analyst groups, and must be fully integrated into the company. For more detailed information on synectics, reference can be made to a book by W. Gordon.[5]

Essentially, the synectic process involves two steps: (1) making the strange familiar and (2) making the familiar strange. The first step requires that the problem be understood and that the ramifications be considered. The mind tends to emphasize one's own experiences and to force strange ideas into an acceptable pattern. Thus it is necessary to reorient these strange ideas into familiar ones. The second step, making the familiar strange, involves distorting, inverting, and transposing the problem in an attempt to view it from an unfamiliar perspective.

To assist in viewing the problem from different angles (making the familiar strange), synectics uses the following mechanisms:

- *Personal analogy*: Members of the group try to identify, metaphorically, with elements of the problem. For example, when a synectics group attempted to develop a new constant-speed mechanism, each member of the group metaphorically entered the box and, using his or her body, tried to effect the speed consistency required. This eventually resulted in an efficient and economical model.

- *Direct analogy*: Parallel facts are compared. Alexander Graham Bell used direct analogy by studying the human ear when he invented the telephone. Biology is an excellent source for direct analogies.

- *Symbolic analogy*: Objective and impersonal images are used to describe the problem. In one case, symbolic analogy was used in developing a jack to move heavy objects, such as houses or freight. The synectics group was making little progress until a member made a symbolic analogy with the Indian rope trick. This analogy proved to be the key and resulted in an innovative jacking mechanism.

- *Fantasy analogy*: Fantasies are used to solve the problem. For example, a vaporproof closure for a space suit was developed using a fantasy analogy of little insects closing the opening. This analogy led to the development of a complex spring mechanism for closure.

BATTELLE-BILDMAPPEN-BRAINWRITING (BBB) METHOD

This method was developed by the Battelle Institute research unit on innovation and creativity located in Frankfurt, Germany. It combines elements of both brainstorming and synectics, thereby resulting in a brainwriting approach. The BBB method starts with brainstorming, is followed by idea stimulation from a picture portfolio (the bildmappen), and then ends with a second round of idea generation using the basic brainwriting method. As described by Warfield, Geschka, and Hamilton, six steps are involved in using this method:[6]

1. A problem is read to a group of five to eight persons.
2. The group verbally brainstorms to develop known or trivial solutions to the problem under study.
3. Each group member is given a folder containing eight to ten pictures that are unrelated to the problem.
4. Each person writes down any new ideas or modifications of old ideas suggested by the pictures.
5. The solutions of each group member are read to the entire group.
6. The group discusses the ideas with the goal of developing additional variations.

An essential benefit of using the BBB method is that the writing of ideas stimulated by the pictures can help to overcome the personal inhibitions often found during face-to-face idea-generation sessions. Furthermore, the use of pictures provides an additional source of idea stimulation not normally present in a brainstorming group. Thus, when the BBB method is used, ideas are generated by individual free association, by stimulation from the ideas of others, and by stimulation from pictures. However, this method does not control the possibility that some individuals might feel inhibited about suggesting ideas after the picture-generated solutions are read. An optional procedure might be to extend the process by allowing for additional individual ideation and evaluation of ideas following the group discussion (i.e., after step 6).

ACCURATE PROBLEM DEFINITION

In practice, most problem-solving failures occur because efforts are directed at solving the wrong problem or only parts of the problem. For one thing, an inability to identify accurately what is going on can lead to inaccurate problem identification. As an illustration, a company discovers that its sales have declined for the past three months. The vice president of marketing accepts the notion that sales volume is directly proportional to the number of calls made by company salespersons. He has heard from a number of sources that some of his salespersons have been overburdened with paperwork and have been spending more time on office matters and less time in the field. He might erroneously conclude that the problem of declining sales is caused by too much paperwork by all of his company's salespersons.

In identifying the causes of a problem, creative thinking is extremely helpful. Is it true that all salespersons are overburdened with paperwork? Has the number of sales calls really dropped off? Are sales falling off because of paperwork or for other reasons? Even if increased paperwork is causing the sales decline, is it causing the decline for all salespersons? Are all salespersons experiencing lower sales levels, or just those who are spending more time with paperwork? Specific questions can be asked to identify the real cause of declining sales.

Incorrect inferences can also lead to inaccurate problem identification. Inferences are conclusions based on observations and the facts at hand; if accurate, they are usually used as the basis for some kind of appropriate action. For example, smoke is seen pouring from a building. One might infer that there is a fire inside, and one might also, knowing that volatile or explosive substances are nearby, call the fire department and avoid going near the area until it is safe. Unfortunately, many decision makers cannot distinguish between their inferences and what they actually observe. There is no problem with this as long as their inferences are correct, but when they are not, there can be trouble. If people were aware of what they infer, they might be more cautious about taking actions based on their inferences. Decision makers, then, are advised to think through the probable consequences of their actions if their inferences are incorrect.

To assist in defining the real problem, a *cause-and-effect diagram* is recommended. Because problems cause other problems, a whole complex of symptoms and problems emerges in need of a solution. A problem-diagramming procedure can help to isolate root causes. First, list all the problems, symptoms, and related problems. Number each one. Next, write the numbers at random on a piece of paper and draw a circle around each one. Then draw arrows to show what causes what. For example, if problem 1 causes problem 2, draw an arrow from circle 1 to circle 2. Consider each circled number, asking, "Which of the other problems causes or helps cause this one?" After all the arrows have been drawn, the root problems become clear. They are represented by the circles with arrows leading only away from them. In figure 3.2, the problem identified by circle 3 is the *root* or *real problem*.

In some cases, this procedure will reveal several unrelated problem complexes. As an example, a company is experiencing declining profits. Is the cause declining sales, lower prices, inadequate inventory turnover, lack of product line for changing times, inadequate warehousing of finished goods, lack of trained sales personnel, or something else? A wide range of symptoms and problems can be identified. By using a cause-and-effect diagram, the root or real problem can be identified.

PROBLEM DEFINITION TABLE

Typically, many different problems have no predetermined solution. Because managers have difficulty in defining problems for which they have no immediate answer, it is exceedingly useful to perform a thorough job of defining problems and developing solutions later. It is sometimes just as important to state what the problem is *not* as it is to state what it *is* in order to identify and define it. Charles Kepner and Benjamin Tregoe have devised a helpful table for this

Figure 3.2
A Cause-and-Effect Diagram That Centers on Diagramming Symptoms and Problems In Order to Determine the Root or Real Problem (Circle 3)

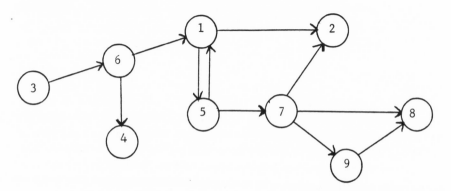

purpose.[7] By filling in the blank spaces in their table, the problem becomes more clearly defined and, as a result, closer to being solved. To complete this table, the problem solver will ask the following questions about the problem and the overall situation:

- What is happening? What is not happening?
- When is it happening? When is it not happening?
- To whom is it happening? To whom is it not happening?
- Where is it happening? Where is it not happening?
- To what extent is it happening? To what extent is it not happening?

With answers to these questions, the manager or managers are better prepared to define the problem more precisely before proceeding to solve it.

CHECKLISTS

Because problems can be broken down into subproblems, which, in turn, can be solved by taking a series of identifiable steps, a checklist can be a particularly useful format in which to present these steps and make sure that all aspects have been examined. Checklists may represent a consensus while assuring the user that most relevant factors have been considered and all necessary actions have been taken. Overall, checklists represent a logical-analytical framework—an attempt to ensure that everything relevant to the problem will be taken into consideration before a decision is reached. A number of specific types of checklists have been developed to facilitate creative thinking about problems:

- *Word simulation* uses lists of words to scan ideas and suggestions that spark creativity in the minds of the people trying to solve the problem.
- *Attribute listing* identifies all the attributes or characteristics of a problem and examines each in turn.
- *Area thinking* uses three or four major areas of consideration in a problem as starting points, then works toward detail in each area.
- *Osborn's checklist* lists words, such as *magnify, substitute*, and *rearrange*, that can be used in sequence to consider alternatives to each subsection of a problem.

Attribute Listing

In attribute listing, the first step is the enumeration of all the attributes of the object, subassembly, or component under study. When this list is as complete as possible (the more complete the list, the easier the task will be), the second step is to change or modify the characteristics of the system or process. Thus the following questions can be asked and answered:
Can we

Modify: meaning? color? odor? taste? form? shape? motion?

Magnify: size? frequency? strength? quantity?

Minify: size? weight? speed? amount?

Rearrange: atoms? enzymes? sequence? pace? tempo?

Reverse: opposite? backward? upside down? inside out? left to right? right to left?

Combine: blend? mix? homogenize?

Osborn's Checklist

Another checklist described above is Osborn's checklist, which lists words that can be used to consider alternatives to a subject area, such as those found below for value analysis of product design:
Can we

Change: dimensions? specifications? container?

Reduce: weight? number of parts? size? visual requirements?

Eliminate: frills? burrs? sharp edges? loose pieces?

Substitute: metal for plastic or wood?

Standardize: gauges? tolerances? locating pads?

Relocate: locating pads? brackets? mating edges?

Simplify: visual requirements? assembly? inspection?

Combine: assembly parts? gauges? loose pieces? packaging?

Increase: grasping surfaces? interchangeability of parts?

Improve: appearance? color? specifications? quality?

Rearrange: packaging, mating surfaces, loose pieces?

Caution is necessary in using such a checklist, because the checklist implies limits and restrictions and, when completed, gives little scope to pioneer new lines of thought. Also, a checklist considered adequate today might be inappropriate tomorrow. Improving the checklists currently in use should be a continuous process. Although properly devised or well-though-out checklists can be real time-savers, managers must always be aware of the obvious omissions in them.

REDEFINITION

Many times, the solution to a problem depends on the way it is stated. If it is defined narrowly, the answer will also be narrow or limited, but if the problem is defined broadly, a whole range of possibilities is opened up. For example, take a family with one car and four drivers. As long as they ask, "How can we make the car available to everybody who needs it?" they are in trouble. What they could ask is "How can we meet our needs without using the car?" The father could join a car pool and the mother could do the grocery shopping just once a week. If the problem is redefined in a larger context, it may be easier to solve.

REVERSAL

To understand this problem-solving technique, reference can be made to an ambulance. Going along a narrow country road, it comes up behind a flock of sheep. To get the ambulance past the sheep would be slow and might harm the sheep. The secret to solving the problem is to reverse the problem and get the sheep past the ambulance. This entails stopping the vehicle, turning the flock around, and leading the flock back past the stationary ambulance. Another example is a used-car salesperson who loathed his job because it sometimes involved unloading questionable cars on unsuspecting buyers. He longed to quit, but the only thing he knew was cars. So he reversed: He set up a used-car locating and inspection service. For a modest fee, he helps prospective buyers find used cars and lists the car's present and potential problems, along with repair estimates. His business is a success, and he is much happier than he was as a salesperson. The advantage of reversal as a problem-solving technique is that it frees the individual from old ways of looking at a problem.

OTHER CREATIVITY TECHNIQUES

There are a number of other problem-solving techniques. Typical ones include the following:

- A *check sheet* is used to log problems within a certain sphere of influence within a certain time frame.
- A *Pareto chart* graphically demonstrates check-sheet data to identify the most serious problem, that is, those 20 percent of the problems that cause 80 percent of the major mistakes.
- *Histograms* or *bar charts* are graphed showing the frequency and magnitude of specific problems.
- *Scatter diagrams* or *"measle charts"* identify major defect locations by having dots on the pictures of products, thus identifying dense dot clusters.
- *Graph* and *control charts* monitor a production process and are compared with a production sample.

CAUTIONS WHEN USING INDIVIDUAL AND GROUP CREATIVITY TECHNIQUES

Although creativity techniques have a very decided upside to their usage, there is a downside, that is, cautions. One of these comes from middle managers who feel that there is a need to impress the boss upstairs and consequently want to deal only in facts. Hence they tend to present solutions that can be proven with logic and reason. However, creativity is intangible and involves some risk. On the plus side, top managers tend to be delighted when they are shown how creative ideas can be put to use. Still, there is a great need for top managers to be more accommodating of creative managers below them since there are many problems that only creativity can solve.

As just noted, creativity inherently means taking risks. The manager can be afraid of being ridiculed because many of his or her ideas for a new product or service will sound great to the individual, but might well be stupid. Still, within the business world, it is difficult getting managers to take risks on creative ideas. When a lot of money is at stake, playing the safe route is a detriment to good creativity.

EMPLOYMENT OF CREATIVE COMPUTER SOFTWARE FOR STRATEGIC THINKING AND DECISION MAKING

In many companies today, managers emerge from marathon meetings where the goals, seemingly so reachable at the start, disappeared in a morass of argument and trivia. To assist in alleviating this problem, software developers have developed creative computer software packages to bring order and clarity to such meetings via the personal computer. Group brainstorming software programs, individual decision-making software, and combinations of them have been marketed for the past several years, and many of the larger corporations use them, such as AT&T, General Electric Aircraft Engines, and Procter & Gamble. Typically, the technology has not trickled down to many small and medium-sized companies, but this has not been for lack of products. Current software ranges from systems running into the tens of thousands of dollars to simpler programs that retail for a few hundred dollars and address some of the main problems that cause meetings to become long and drawn out in companies of all sizes. Hence there is need to employ creative computer software to assist managers at all levels to assist in strategic thinking and decision making.

Tie-In of Creativity Techniques with Computers

In the previous discussion on individual and group creativity techniques, the focus was on their usage without employing the computer. As just noted, a wide range of creative computer software is currently available that utilizes many of these creativity techniques. Although exposition of current computer software is found in chapter 6, several examples of software programs that include creativity techniques are found below.

A typical example of this software is Decision Pad, by Apian Software, Inc. (Menlo Park, California). This software takes the ideas, or choices to be made, and helps to quantify them, eventually producing a "winner" based on the group's assessments. Users consider it a leading-edge creativity and productivity tool since it allows them to bring it into a meeting with PCs and an overhead projection screen. A list of the decisions to be made and the criteria for each can be worked out beforehand. For example, a group deciding what kind of laptop computer to buy can come up with several product choices and a list of attributes, both subjective and objective: price, portability, keyboard design, user-friendliness, feel and others. The program offers a "hint list" for criteria and the option to add explanatory notes along the way. The computer weights each criterion as the participants discuss its relative importance and displays it in a spreadsheet format or as a bar graph. The group may feel that keyboard design is more important than price. The software assigns a weight and a score to each criterion. At the bottom of the screen, it keeps track of the total scores and ranking for each product. The software also generates a printout of the discussion as it was recorded on the computer so participants can review how they arrived at the decision. Essentially, it is a tool for trade-off discussions, purchasing decisions, hiring and evaluating personnel—for whenever the participants are choosing between similar things. The computerized process provides anonymity. With each participant using a PC, comments are stripped of their personal and political connotations.

Another example of creative computer software is OptionFinder from Option Technologies, Inc. (Minneapolis, Minnesota). The program, used in many cases with a Toshiba T1600 personal computer, works like this. Prior to the start of a meeting, the facilitator sets the agenda and enters up to fifty-two key questions to be addressed during the meeting into the OptionFinder software program. Then OptionFinder response pads (ten-button keypads) are placed throughout the room. When critical questions are addressed during the meeting, all meeting attendees can respond by making a selection on their response pads, rather than having just the most vocal people answer. Additionally, OptionFinder software processes answers and, via video projection, displays the group opinion back to the group in the form of a single-axis bar chart or a two-axis X-Y grid. Because of this ability to display immediately the results, total involvement is achieved as the participants review, react to, and explain their responses. The participants are providing both breadth and depth to the group's communications, facilitating buy-in by the meeting participants, and preparing them for the follow-through activities that will be critical to implementation.

OptionFinder is used to focus, improve, and speed decision making on a wide range of management/planning topics, such as company direction and strategy, product quality, and production/operation issues. The OptionFinder/Toshiba combination is currently being used in large companies as well as midsize companies in the banking, manufacturing, insurance, health-care, and marketing/advertising fields. Small consulting firms are also finding the system indispensable.

An illustration of OptionFinder is using the system in meeting customer needs. Customer complaints in two-product areas of a large information systems company were increasing. Key management in the two product areas met in a planning session to identify what they needed to do collectively to improve their ability to meet customer needs. The session began with a review of customer complaints and identification of where they were occurring. Then, using creative brainstorming techniques, the managers identified the key areas that needed to be managed more effectively to meet their customers' needs, including response, reliability, training, and post-sale technical support.

Basically, OptionFinder was used to assist the managers in evaluating the relative importance of each customer need and then to measure the level of satisfaction with the organization's current operations. The post-results analysis permitted the managers to clarify what their roles and responsibilities were in meeting customer needs and to evaluate how well each of their departments was doing, both individually and collectively. Once they saw the results of their votes, discussion that followed focused their attention on working more closely together to be more responsive to their customers. All group responses can be stored on disk or printed in various formats, including bar charts and two-dimensional grids. This is useful for strategy sessions, board meetings, and other planning meetings that require follow-up activities.

A last example of creative computer software that ties in with the preceding creativity techniques is IdeaFisher 4.0. Because IdeaFisher has the ability to facilitate free association and is exceptionally easy to use, it will be featured in part IV of this text with examples in the areas of strategic thinking, marketing, manufacturing, finance, and accounting. This idea generator attacks the problem of automating idea generation by linking its checklist of questions in the QBank question data base, which helps users analyze their problems, with the IdeaBank idea data base, which helps users think about their problems from different perspectives. IdeaBank's ability to trigger a listing of new ideas by helping the user recall information or make new associations sets IdeaFisher apart from other current software packages. It should be noted that not all of the ideas generated with IdeaFisher will be useful. Nevertheless, IdeaFisher is very easy to use and makes it relatively easy to change perspective on a problem by jumping to different topics so that creative thinking becomes less of a chore for managers.

SUMMARY

Initially, the chapter looked at improving managerial creativity, which is linked directly with promoting it on the job. This was followed by basic concepts underlying creative techniques that stressed going beyond the traditional boundaries of problem solving and generating new ideas by looking at new and unusual approaches to the problem under study. The mainstay of the chapter was examining individual- and group-oriented creativity techniques useful to company personnel. This background served as a framework for introducing creative computer software not only in this chapter, but also in future chapters.

NOTES

1. Walter Kiechel III, "Getting Creative," *Fortune*, July 25, 1983, pp. 109–110.

2. Ibid., p. 114.

3. "Crossing Boundaries: The Nine-Dot Dilemma," *Harvard Business Review*, March–April 1991, pp. 208–210.

4. Graham Wallas, *The Art of Thought* (New York: Harcourt, Brace and Company, 1926).

5. W. Gordon, *Synectics: The Development of Creative Capacity* (New York: Harper & Row, 1961).

6. J. N. Warfield, H. Geschka, and R. Hamilton, *Methods of Idea Management* (Columbus, Ohio: Academy for Contemporary Problems, 1975).

7. Charles H. Kepner and Benjamin B. Tregoe, *The Rational Manager* (New York: McGraw-Hill, 1965), p. 72.

4

Creativity and Managerial Decision Making

ISSUES EXPLORED

- To examine the need for synergism in managerial decision making
- To examine the general types of problems that can be solved in a typical company
- To explore the traditional approach to the problem-solving process
- To explore the newer approach to decision making: the problem-finding process
- To show that creativity is an important part of the problem-finding process

OUTLINE

Today as well as in the twenty-first century, decision makers increasingly face and will continue to face an uncharted business environment that has differing and sometimes contradictory degrees of complexity. As a consequence, new demands are continually being made for their attention. It is no longer enough that a manager be good at a specialized skill. Increasing demands of the job force the cultivation of a wider perspective. Simply put, managers must be able to spot quickly the economic, political, and social trends that will affect their companies. In turn, managers must be able to chart a strategic course of action that is *proactive* as opposed to being *reactive*. Essentially, this is the direction taken in this chapter, where the focus is on relating creativity to improving managerial decision making so that the manager takes the appropriate action based upon the present and upcoming business environment.

COMPLEXITY OF MANAGERIAL DECISION MAKING

Managerial decision making has become a truly complex process because the quality of a business decision is now measured by many factors. Managers find themselves with responsibility for not just the bottom-line profitability, but also the political, social, and ethical effects of their decisions. New social pressures force the manager to consider the wide ramifications of his or her choices when evaluating outcomes and alternatives. The dilemma constantly facing top management is how to produce quality decisions that will withstand the pressures of a new business climate.

No matter how complex the situation, the key is information; that is, the critical requirement for quality decisions is timely, appropriate information for the specific situation. Basically, the manager must have information about two specific aspects of the environment: (1) the desired outcome and (2) alternative paths to reach the outcome. Furthermore, the manager must have a clear understanding of the obstacles and costs associated with each available alternative before the feasibility of reaching specific goals can be determined.

The Need for Synergism in Managerial Decision Making

As the information base grows to encompass a wider perspective, the manager can experience information overload. Above a certain point, increased information is no longer a positive help to the typical manager. In fact, too much information can be associated with a drop in the manager's effective response. To overcome this problem of the manager, the more desirable property of information is *synergism*. To state it another way, if the information is organized and presented in just the right way for a particular problem, the individual pieces reinforce each other and the decision-making process of the manager improves greatly.

In a typical synergistic computerized environment, managers and their staffs use computer information in conjunction with their judgmental abilities to change strategic, tactical, and operating plans more rapidly in order to have more cost-effective resources. They combine information and judgment for planning and decision making rather than limiting them to the areas of control for which information, by itself, has been most widely used in the past. Similarly, they use information and judgment to evaluate performance and the organization's responsiveness to its growing and varied constituencies in order to complement the profitability measurements. Finally, they use both for tracking product and service performance on a longer-term basis. Essentially, a synergistic approach is a unifying bond that allows the company's managers to use effectively the resources at their disposal.

Advances in computerized information-processing technology have created the potential for the synergism to take place. Managers are capitalizing on the special attributes of their organizational information systems to improve their decision making. Although the computerized information system means various things in different companies, there is a current consensus that the system can operate such that company personnel (managers, staffs, and operating personnel) can meet their operating needs. Additionally, the computerized information system can be capable of including creativity where this is deemed necessary. Due to the various directions that an information system can take, this important area is covered in some depth in the next chapter along with reference to enhancing the manager's creativity. At this time, it is sufficient to say that the appropriate computerized information system can assist the typical manager and supporting staff in handling present and future complex business environments.

TYPES OF PROBLEMS TO BE SOLVED

Before discussing the essentials of the decision-making process and areas related to it, it would be helpful first to look at the types of problems that are associated with decision making. The environment in which a problem exists determines its type regardless of whether the approach to decision making is to be on an individual or a group basis. Problems to be solved can be categorized in terms of their essential nature as (1) well-structured, (2) semistructured, or (3) unstructured.

Well-structured Problems

A problem is said to be *well-structured* if all of its elements can be identified and quantified in order to determine an answer. Typically, the time frame is of short duration, say, up to one year. For example, in a production allocation problem, the time available this month and next month on the first and second shifts as well as the costs to produce the products in the manufacturing departments can be identified. Also, the level of production is known based upon the forecasted sales for these months. Thus the problem is well defined and can be solved within the parameters set forth using a quantitative approach to decision making.

Since the problem is fully structured, a computer approach is generally desirable because an appropriate mathematical or statistical model can be employed to reach a good solution. The model may be a simple, straightforward rule or procedure or a very complex, computerized mathematical model. The approach is not as important a criterion as the ability to identify all the important parameters surrounding the decision.

Semistructured Problems

A problem is said to be *semistructured* if it contains both well-structured and unstructured elements. The time frame can range from the short run to the long run. For example, an investment problem is considered to be semistructured. From one viewpoint, a systematic search through data on portfolios and securities is required; this can be effected through retrieval, reports, and display via a CRT terminal using mathematical and statistical analytic models. At the same time, the criteria for making investments for a specific portfolio need to be left to the manager's judgment. Thus output from the computer is combined with the portfolio manager's judgment to select appropriate securities to solve the investment problem.

Because the semistructured problem makes use of both computer decision making and human judgment, the user-machine interface is just as important as the quantitative model used. Failure to use this combined manager and computerized model approach will generally result in reaching less favorable decisions.

Unstructured Problems

If the significant parameters of the problem cannot be identified precisely, it is said to be unstructured, since human intuition and judgment are generally needed to reach a decision. Typically, the rationale for the inability to identify specific parameters in the problem is that the time frame is too long, say, beyond five years. As an example, consider the problem of determining a company's personnel needs ten years hence. Because there are a large number of unknowns relating to sales and production, the net result is that the appropriate level of personnel to support these areas is also unknown. In effect, the parameters of the problem are too loosely defined to solve it with a high degree of accuracy.

If the problem is unstructured from the perspective of the executive, computerized mathematical or statistical models are generally inappropriate. To reach a decision, there is a need for meaningful experience, know-how, intuition, judgment, and past experience. This may mean taking a qualitative approach to decision making. However, *rules of thumb* (i.e., heuristic methods) may be appropriate to resolve unstructured problems. This may require resorting to hypotheses, evaluations, educated guesses, and the like. Essentially, it is problem solving under uncertainty. The attendant circumstances must be surveyed to determine whether or not heuristic methods are appropriate for solving unstructured problems.

Typical examples of well-structured, semistructured, and unstructured problems found at various managerial levels are given in figure 4.1. Numerous other examples of these three problem types appear later in the text, in part IV. Also, they are related to creativity and managerial decision making.

THE DECISION-MAKING PROCESS

Initially, it is helpful to discuss a framework for the decision-making process from a broad perspective. This includes two processes. The first approach, known as the *problem-solving process*, is the traditional approach to solving problems and consists basically of problem identification, solution, and implementation. Rather than solve only the problems that managers are confronting today, there is need to go further and determine problems and opportunities in the future that have not been anticipated and explored. The second approach is called the *problem-*

Figure 4.1
The Relationship of Top-, Middle-, and Lower-Level Managers to Types of Problems (Well-structured, Semistructured, and Unstructured)

Managerial Level	
	Well-Structured Problems:
Top-level manager	Manufacturing facilities problems
Middle-level manager	Budget problems
Lower-level manager	Production problems
	Semistructured Problems:
Top-level manager	Merger problems
Middle-level manager	Sales forecasting problems
Lower-level manager	Purchasing problems
	Unstructured Problems:
Top-level manager	Future anticipated new product problems
Middle-level manager	Motivational problems
Lower-level manager	Group behavior problems

finding process. As Albert Einstein put it: "The formulation of a problem is often more essential than its solution, which may be merely a matter of mathematical or experimental skill. To raise new questions, new possibilities, to regard old questions from a new angle, requires creative imagination and marks real advance in science."[1] The quality of the problem posed is crucial not only to science, but also in all business situations requiring thought. From this dual perspective, computerized information systems support managers in decision making to resolve current problems and future ones of great concern. Later in the chapter, the essentials of the problem-solving and problem-finding processes are discussed.

A definition of decision-making activity, whether it be for one manager operating alone or for managers working on a group basis, is associated with making a choice among alternatives. As P. C. Fishburn stated: "Solving the decision model consists of finding a strategy for action, the expected relative value of which is at least as great as the expected value of any other strategy in a specified set. The perspective criterion of a strategy will be a maximization of the decision maker's total expected relative value."[2] From this definition, it is clear that the decision-making process centers on moving one or more decision makers from a current position to the position in which the individual or group wants to be. The essential ingredients in this generalized definition are that one or more decision makers have several alternatives and that a choice involves a comparison among these alternatives and the evaluation of their outcomes. From the context of the manager's view, the *decision-making process* can be defined as a series of steps that start with an analysis of the information and ultimately culminate in a resolution—a selection from the several available alternatives and verification of this selected alternative (now and at some time in the future) to solve the problem under study.

CATEGORIES OF MANAGERIAL DECISION MAKING

Decision making can be thought of at one extreme as an individual manager making a determination and at the other extreme as a group of people coming to an agreement. Some decisions may be so elementary or the manager so capable that the individual will be able to access the raw data and determine the best solution. However, as the complexity increases, the manager may need help from other experts to process the data in order to arrive at the necessary information for the appropriate solution.

After a thorough analysis of the decision-making process, three primary categories of decision making can be identified. Typically, in the first category, a manager makes a decision without any counsel or actively searches out information from others without sharing the nature of the problem. Both approaches employ what could be termed an *authoritative* decision-making mode. In like manner, the second category has two approaches. With one approach, the manager shares the nature of the problem with others and asks their advice separately.

In the other approach, the manager searches out knowledgeable people and brings them together to discuss the problem but maintains the right to make the final decision. Using either approach is classified as the *consultative* mode. Finally, the manager who is a member of a team of knowledgeable people who reach a decision through mutual consensus is using a *consensual* decision-making mode.

Given the typical modes of decision making and the various forms that information can take, the current business environment does have an important impact on decision making. As the amount of relevant information grows, the relationships become more complex. Also, the changes are coming so fast that the older methods are frequently becoming ineffective. When using authoritative approaches to decision making, the manager seeks out the help of experts to condense the data. However, as the amount of data that is supporting a solution increases, it becomes progressively more difficult to perceive what is going on, let alone interpret and utilize the information.

When the manager employs the consultative approach, people are used to process data so that the decision can be based on all the relevant data without the manager having to personally review it. This approach can minimize the occurrence of information overload and thus can rise above the limits of an individual to grasp the complex implications of available actions. In very complex situations, a broad perspective could be critical. Such a perspective is provided by the consensus-seeking approach. Ideally, the consensual approach allows each person to supply a unique insight toward the final decision, unhindered by peer approval or data overload. The key to the ultimate potential for this kind of synthesis is the unrestrained flow of different perspectives on the problem and the solutions.

The Need for Participatory Decision Making

From this analysis, it is clear that no one decision-making approach is optimal for all managerial situations. What is evident, however, is that as the environment becomes more complex (i.e., there is more information and greater change), the manager will have to call upon more resources if effective decision making is to exist. Thus the real question facing a manager is not which decision-making mode should be used, but rather when it is appropriate to use each one. Studies have shown a relationship between characteristics of decisions and the nature of the decision-making process. Decisions were found to be more participatory when decision quality and user acceptance were important. Participation was also preferable when the problem was complex or unstructured. Studies have shown that decisions were found to be less participatory when the manager had all the necessary information, the problem was routine or structured, or time was limited and immediate action was required.

To further emphasize the need for participatory decision making, reference can be made to figure 4.2, where *data* (the unstructured facts and figures) represent the lowest level of inputs for the manager. This is followed by *information* (the

Figure 4.2
A Summary of Decision Approaches That Are Most Suited to Participatory Decision Making

Level of Summarization	Definition	Problem Importance	Decision Approach	Nature of Problem	Number of Persons Affected
Truth	Conformance to fact and reality	Critical	Consensus	Structured to un- structured	Multitudes
Wisdom	Ability to judge soundly	Critical	Consensus	Unstructured	Multitudes
Knowledge	Obtained from experts based upon actual experience	Major	Advisory Group	Semi- structured	Numerous
Information	Structured data useful for analysis	Major to minor	Advisors	Structured and semi- structured	Several
Data	Unstructured facts and figures	Minor to trivial	Individual	Structured	Few

next level up), which is structured data that is useful for the manager in analyzing and resolving critical problems. At the next higher level, there is *knowledge*, which is obtained from experts based upon actual experience. This book, for example, is knowledge about how the typical manager can enhance his or her creativity by using creative computer software. At the second-highest level, *wisdom* is the ability to judge soundly, while *truth*, the highest level, is conformance to fact or reality.

Basically, an analysis of this figure emphasizes that, generally, decisions with the most significant ramifications for the operations of a company tend to have characteristics that are most suited to a participatory decision-making process. The decisions that are best made by an individual do not appear, in general, to have as wide-ranging or overall an organization impact. Hence the implication of figure 4.2 is that group decision making is the way to go for quality decision making for many business situations.

The Need for a Group Synergistic Approach

The complex managerial decision-making environment of today is reflected in the pervasiveness of consensual decision making. In the conduct of organizations from a small company to a *Fortune 1000* firm, group decisions have come to play an increasingly important operational role. Since survey after survey shows that managers spend a lot of time in meetings, top-level managers, for example, can spend over half of their work in meetings. If anything, the need to make more decisions in groups will escalate in the future.

When organizations deal with high levels of complexity (as most private- and public-sector organizations do), group computerized information-processing systems can provide a mechanism to create the necessary information synergism. That is, the MIS department is in a good position to generate a holistic view that is supplied by a group of consensus-seeking decision makers who are supported by experts. Essentially, the goal is the combining of individual perspectives to form a broad perspective, with each of the members refining data from his or her particular resources and supplying his or her expertise to the decision team. The specifics of information-processing systems that are oriented toward an individual and a group basis are given in the next chapter. But more important, emphasis will be placed on those systems that allow managers to employ software that enhances a manager's creativity for solving problems and identifying new ideas for possible implementation as well as new opportunities for products and services.

PRIOR APPROACHES TO DECISION MAKING

Before discussing the processes to solve and/or find problems that are the focus of decision making, it would be helpful at this time to take a look at their development over the centuries. One of the oldest models for resolving problems is the *dialectic model* that was formulated by the early Greek philosophers. It was employed to discern truth when solving all types of problems. The dialectic model thrived because of its simplicity; that is, it was easily understood and easily employed. It was followed centuries later by the scientific method.

The Dialectic Model

The dialectic model is considered to be very crude in terms of today's advances in problem solving. It consisted of three basic steps. First, the *thesis* was a basic premise, statement, or belief. The purpose of the dialectic model was to either confirm the veracity of the thesis or disprove it and act accordingly based upon the outcome. A thesis would be formulated and then subjected to the antithesis. The *antithesis* was typically the converse of the thesis. It always supported an entirely contradictory approach, purely for the sake of argument. Formal presentations of a thesis and an antithesis were a popular mental sport in Greek times when orators enjoyed a high status as artists. The first two steps often constituted formal debate for a group, but the method could be employed by an individual. In the third step, a *synthesis* or a new understanding was reached by subjecting a thesis to its antithesis. In actuality, it was a yielding of both sides to a middle ground that embraced more truth and less absolutism. Sometimes the synthesis would actually confirm wholeheartedly the original thesis, but this in part implied a weak antithesis.

By the advent of the Italian Renaissance, the dialectic model was waning and would soon yield to the forerunner of the modern scientific method. The dialectic model may have solved many business problems centuries ago, such as "Should we sail in search of Phoenician treasure?" but it has little practical application today. It is noteworthy in that it can be held up as the first formal exercise that was used for problem analysis.

The Scientific Method

Another important problem-solving model that is currently enjoying wide usage is the *scientific method*. Essentially, this method is employed as the chief means for both scientific and nonscientific research. It is commonly used in research, surveying, sampling, and testing. Because it is a proven and rigorous model, it is useful for testing a hypothesis in controlled settings, with a baseline (control case) for comparison of the outcome.

The scientific method consists of five basic steps: (1) identifying the problem to be analyzed, (2) collecting facts that are pertinent to the problem, (3) selecting one or more tentative solutions, (4) evaluating all solutions to see which one fits all of the facts, and (5) selecting the optimal solution. This method, as utilized by Charles Darwin, had these underlying tenets: a natural explanation exists for all phenomena; a solution may be supported by evidence alone (not a hypothesis) and, wherever possible, will substitute actual observations for logic. As will be seen in the discussion to follow, current decision support problem-solving approaches are actually variations of the traditional scientific method to solve clearly defined well-structured problems.

TRADITIONAL APPROACHES TO DECISION MAKING: THE PROBLEM-SOLVING PROCESS

In a survey of the current literature in many disciplines, a large number of approaches to solving problems would be found. Rather than try to explore and compare most of them, two approaches that are germane to the problem-solving process will be examined. The first is the *quantitative-centered approach*, which is oriented more toward solving well-structured problems facing managers and which is a variation of the scientific method. The accent is on using mathematical models that optimize performance (maximize profits, minimize costs, or some other criterion) for one or more functional areas of an organization. In contrast, the second is the *decision-centered approach*, which is oriented toward solving semistructured and unstructured problems. The accent is on finding a limited number of acceptable solutions to the problem under study versus many solutions. In turn, the solution is selected from this small number.

Quantitative-centered Approach

The quantitative-centered approach to the problem-solving process is an extension of the scientific method mentioned in the previous section. The scientific method was originally formulated by Francis Bacon in the sixteenth century and elaborated by John Stuart Mill in the nineteenth century.[3] Its traditional steps have been altered to accommodate the ever-changing business environment by the establishment of proper controls over the final solution. As shown in figure 4.3, the approach consists of the following six steps.

1. *Observation*. In the first step, there is a thorough observation of the phenomena surrounding the problem—the facts, opinions, symptoms, and so on. Observation may be a casual glance or a concentrated, detailed, and lengthy study, depending on the requirements of the problem. Observation is used to identify problems. The capable manager is always alert and sensitive to the presence of problems. The individual must be certain that the basic or real problem has been identified, not just the symptoms of it.

2. *Definition of the Real Problem*. The real problem that is impeding the accomplishment of one or more desired objectives is defined in the second step. To do so, the manager should gain a deeper understanding by discussing the matter with knowledgeable people. Because defining the real problem can be a difficult task, the manager must investigate as broadly as possible the factors surrounding the problem. A thorough analysis of all the factors in collaboration with the appropriate parties should lead to a definition of the real problem.

3. *Development of Alternative Solutions*. In the third step, alternative courses of action or tentative solutions to the real problem are developed. The alternative courses of action can take the form of quantitative models that can be developed to accommodate the real-world problem. They are generally computer oriented for a final solution. As each model is developed, deficiencies may become apparent if the model's behavior is inconsistent with that of the modeled problem. Certain models that looked promising at the outset may have to be discarded. Instead of half a dozen models, the choice might be narrowed to one, two, or three candidates.

4. *Selection of Optimum Solution*. The fourth step centers on the evaluation of the alternative quantitative models or tentative solutions that remain in order to select the optimum one. If one fits, a solution may be obtained by using one of the *standard* quantitative models. If the mathematical relationships of the model are too complex for the standard techniques, a *custom-made* quantitative model is required. Thus the selection of the appropriate model using experimentation is dependent on the problem's nature and complexity. Where deemed appropriate, *sensitivity analysis* can be employed to select the optimum solution. Sensitivity analysis is a way of observing output changes while varying inputs to determine their relative impact on the optimum solution.

5. *Verification of Optimum Solution*. Verification involves most or all of the target population (as defined in statistics) for the fifth step. Implementation is

Figure 4.3
A Comparison of Steps in the *Problem-Solving Process*: The Quantitative-centered Approach and the Decision-centered Approach

Basic Phases	Quantitative-Centered Approach	Decision-Centered Approach
Identification	Step 1 Observation - review the phenomena surrounding the problem	Step 1 Intelligence - search the environment for conditions that call for a decision
	Step 2 Definition of the Real Problem - state the root or real problem underlying the major difficulties	
Solution	Step 3 Development of Alternative Solutions - alternatives are based on factors affecting the problem	Step 2 Design - invent, develop, and analyze possible courses of action
	Step 4 Selection of Optimum Solution - best alternative is selected, based on a thorough analysis of feasible alternatives using experimentation. If deemed necessary, sensitivity analysis is used.	Step 3 Choice - evaluate courses of action and select the best one. If deemed necessary, sensitivity analysis is used.
Implementation	Step 5 Verification of Optimum Solution - implementation of the optimum solution in areas that are representative of the entire company	Step 4 Implementation - place the chosen solution into operation
	Step 6 Establishment of Proper Controls - controls are used to detect how changes affect the existing solution	Step 5 Control - monitor the outcome and make the necessary adjustments

NOTE: There is *feedback* from the last step of both approaches of the first step.

necessary because reaction of competitors, consumer buying habits, and comparable factors observed in the limited sample during the development of alternative courses of action (and the selection of the optimum solution) may not hold true for the target population. To verify the optimum model or solution, it must be translated into a set of operating procedures capable of being understood and applied by the personnel who will be responsible for their use. Major or minor changes must specified and implemented.

6. *Establishment of Proper Controls.* Once action has been recommended and implemented and the results have been interpreted, the sixth and final step establishes controls over the solution. A solution remains an optimum one as long as the factors retain their original relationships. The solution goes out of control when the factors and/or the relationships change significantly. The importance of the change depends on the cost of changing the present solution versus the deviation under the changed conditions from the true optimum solution.

For effective control over the model (solution), it is necessary to establish a monitoring system, preferably as a part of an MIS. This will permit *feedback* to the various managers who are responsible and accountable. Continuous monitoring through feedback provides a means for modifying the solution as external and internal conditions and demands change over time. The foregoing steps are seldom, if ever, conducted in a particular order, since there is usually a constant interplay among the steps. However, they provide a conceptual framework for the quantitative-centered approach to problem solving.

Typical Applications of the Quantitative-centered Approach

The readers should have no difficulty in applying the quantitative-centered approach to well-structured problems since this approach is widely used. As one example, it is necessary to allocate production facilities to the company's products on a least-cost basis. This problem is solvable by utilizing a standard mathematical model called *linear programming* from the discipline of management science, which allocates production resources on a lowest-cost basis first before moving on to a higher-cost basis. Another example is the problem of allocating a number of vehicles by size to shipments for a transportation company. This problem is solvable by the *transportation model* from management science, which solves for the proper allocation of transportation vehicles to minimize total transportation costs. Essentially, these illustrations are for relatively well structured problems. Because many of the problems solved for a typical company are not always well structured, managers must also be familiar with the decision-centered approach to problem solving.

Decision-centered Approach

In the quantitative-centered approach to the problem-solving process, managers try to choose the best or optimal alternative, one that balances the costs, benefits, and uncertainties best and is therefore most likely to achieve the most satisfactory results. Optimizing a decision means making the best one available to the organization at a given time. In practice, however, managers may lack important information affecting the decision, may be under pressure to act quickly and with apparent decisiveness, or may have overlooked alternatives in the early stages of the problem-solving process. These limitations restrict decision making and thereby result in satisficing. The word *satisficing* means finding and selecting a satisfactory alternative (as opposed to the best one) that achieves a minimally acceptable solution.[4] There is one word of caution: managers should not select the first satisfactory alternative developed but should take the opportunity and time to develop other good, feasible alternatives.

Included in satisficing is the concept of *bounded rationality*. That is, the fact that managers often make decisions without knowing all the alternatives available to them and their possible consequences means that there is a limit to how logical or rational their decisions can be. In everyday organizational life, managers make the most logical decisions they can, limited by their inadequate information and by their ability to utilize this information, thereby resulting in bounded rationality.[5] Rather than make the best or ideal decision, managers more realistically settle for a decision that will "satisfice" rather than one that will "optimize."

This satisficing approach does not mean that managers should give up trying to make the best possible decisions. It simply means that they recognize that at some point it is too expensive, time-consuming, or difficult to acquire additional information or attempt to analyze it. For example, it is more practical for a finance manager to try to decide what must be done to earn an "acceptable" level of profits than to try to "maximize" potential profits.

In light of the realities of the business world, Herbert Simon's three steps of problem solving are set forth below,[6] along with a fourth step he added later. One last step has been appended by the author for a more complete decision-centered approach to the problem-solving process.

1. *Intelligence.* The first step is concerned with searching the environment for conditions that call for a decision, that is, problem recognition. It is basically a data-gathering phase in which the manager seeks information to define the problem more clearly and provide some input to the solution process. The manager assesses the extent of the problem and obtains data to be used in the design phase.

2. *Design.* The second step centers on inventing, developing, and analyzing possible courses of action. It involves manipulation of the data obtained to develop various alternative solutions to the problem. The manager's perception of the problem is used as the data are assembled and manipulated to provide input in the development of alternatives.

3. *Choice.* In the third step, the task is one of evaluating alternatives. This phase of the problem-solving process also requires selection of the best from among the alternatives developed in the design phase. The choice is generally made under a satisficing perspective versus one of optimization. Also, *sensitivity analysis* can be employed to select the best alternative.

4. *Implementation.* The fourth step puts the chosen solution into effect. The best alternative selected in the third step is placed into operation for better or for worse. If a good alternative has been selected, the results should be favorable.

If a poor alternative has been implemented, the results will generally be poor. This step parallels step 5 of the quantitative-centered approach.

5. *Control.* The fifth step is the monitoring of the outcome and making necessary adjustments. This last step links to the first step, intelligence, by recognizing that a new problem has arisen and needs to be solved. This step is like step 6 of the quantitative-centered approach.

These steps are summarized in figure 4.3 and related to the quantitative-centered approach. As with that approach, the decision-centered approach provides for *feedback*.

Typical Applications of the Decision-centered Approach

The analysis of bad debts in the accounts receivable department is a good illustration of the decision-centered approach. Essentially, it consists of structured elements, that is, the experience of the firm in the past on bad debts, and unstructured elements, that is, what impact the expanding or contracting economy will have on the company's customers' ability to pay. Based upon the integration of both structured and unstructured elements utilizing the decision-centered approach, the amount of the reserve for bad debts can be determined. Another illustration is the determination of what investments should be offered to clients by an investment counselor. Because each client has different investment objectives and information about investments is semistructured in nature, it is advisable for the investment counselor to use a decision-centered approach to assist in the selection of appropriate investment opportunities for his or her clients.

NEWER APPROACHES TO DECISION MAKING: THE PROBLEM-FINDING PROCESS

In the prior approaches to the problem-solving process, the accent has been on some type of analytical technique, which has been the main thrust of information systems. However, there is a need to go a step further by incorporating creativity in the form of "logical-analytical thinking." Logical-analytical thinking goes beyond analyzing present problems of an organization, the approach typical of the problem-solving process. Its accent is on identifying future problems and their impact on the organization today and tomorrow. In addition, logical-analytical thinking is directed toward future problems that are actually future opportunities in disguise. In order to solve future problems and/or opportunities, it is helpful to employ one or more of the creativity techniques set forth in the previous chapter and to tie them in with creative computer software. Generally, a manager who has identified future problems has also identified opportunities. Thus the problem-finding process can be separated into a problem-centered approach and an opportunity-centered approach.

For the *problem-centered approach*, logical-analytical thinking centers on examining the environment with the idea of looking out into the future and exploring problems that have an impact on the organization now or will have an impact at some time in the future. Essentially, the process is one of projecting into the future, determining important problems (i.e., problem finding), and bringing them back to the present to examine their cause-and-effect relationships. Likewise, logical-analytical thinking is needed in the *opportunity-centered approach*. However, the perspective is somewhat different in that the main focus is on identifying opportunities for the organization to persue that generally come from problems uncovered. In effect, managers need to change an organizational liability into an asset, that is, identify problems that can result in important opportunities for the organization. Also, the opportunity-centered approach need not always be related to future problems. It can center on current opportunities that are identified by top management and/or the corporate planning staff. Specific opportunities can be addressed directly by organization members at the higher levels of management.

Creativity Underlies the Problem-finding Process

In both problem-finding approaches, the focus is initially on information useful in getting at a company's future problems and opportunities. But more important, the focus then shifts to exploring ideas that can be useful to solve future problems studied a well as new ideas that can enhance further important opportunities for a company. This new point of view displaces the prior belief that more information will solve a company's problems. There was a time when information was indeed the limiting factor and more information made for better decisions. Generally, this is no longer the case; ideas are the limiting factor today, since detailed analysis does not necessarily yield new ideas. The manager's mind can only see what it is prepared to see. The manager needs to start ideas on his or her own. Hence the current emphasis on problem solving even to the extent that all thinking is called "problem solving" in American psychological usage needs to changed to an emphasis on the manager's creativity in terms of developing new ideas. Such is the approach found in the problem-centered and opportunity-centered approaches presented below.

Problem-centered Approach

The problem-centered approach set forth here is taken from one of the author's previous publications with some modifications to include the generation of new ideas using creative computer software.[7] As shown in figure 4.4, it consists of four steps plus the solution and implementation phases from the quantitative-centered approach or the decision-centered approach.

1. *Generation.* The first step is the most important one in a problem search because it focuses on the probing of potential problems that might have a great impact on the organization. Initially, the analysis is "forward-looking" because this is a search for future problems. Once these problems are identified, the analysis

becomes "backward-looking" since there is a need to evaluate the cause-and-effect relationships of each problem and its possible effects on the organization currently. Accent is placed on each problem, from the short range to the long range. It may also be necessary to look at each problem in different economic climates (good, average, and bad conditions).

To generate important problems, the best approach is to use *brainstorming*. Generally, top managers and their staffs, along with members from the corporate planning staff, meet periodically to brainstorm future organizational problems. In a typical session, all important problems uncovered are recorded; then analysis is performed to explore the important aspects of each problem. These steps are performed in a back-and-forth fashion; that is, the original question concerning the *problem as given* and the subsequent spontaneous ideas are all written down. When participants' minds have cleared, they concentrate on reformulations produced from the collected material, and a choice of one or more is made before the participants continue with questions in sequence concerning the *problem as understood*. (As noted, the initially forward-looking analysis becomes backward-looking.) This can be repeated until all aspects have been considered. Complex problems may require the application of other creativity techniques in order to uncover an unexpected, new angle.

2. *Evaluation.* After the problem-generation phase, the second step centers on examining problems in terms of their being worthy of managerial concern. Because many of these problems are found in the future—the next two to five or possibly ten years—the question can be asked, "Which problem or problems should be considered for solution?" To answer this question, there is a need to evaluate the impact the solution to a problem has on the organization, as in terms of net profit and return on investment. In other cases, consideration might be given to other important areas of an organization, such as sales and customer service. Similarly, it may be necessary to relate the problem or problems back to the organization's critical success factors.

If a computerized mode is used, appropriate creative computer software can be employed to generate new methods and ideas that are related to help in the evaluation of future problems. In this manner, a broader approach can be used to evaluate the problems uncovered in the first step. In this evaluation process, it is possible that more problems may be apparent. If this happens, it may be necessary to add these problems in this evaluation step. As will be seen in chapter 6, there is a wide range of software to assist managers and their staffs in this step.

Generally there is need to perform a *cost-benefit analysis* to determine the impact of the solution on the financial aspects of the organization today and tomorrow. This task can be relegated to managers at the appropriate levels and their staffs to determine which problems are of valid concern for managerial action. The problems generated are then evaluated in terms of benefits versus costs, thereby becoming the basis for validation in the next step.

3. *Validation.* The third step builds on the prior step of problem evaluation. Actual problems are selected as being worthy of managerial concern for today

Figure 4.4

A Comparison of Steps in the *Problem-finding Process*: The Problem-centered Approach and the Opportunity-centered Approach

Basic Phases	Problem-Centered Approach	Opportunity-Centered Approach
Search	Step 1 Generation - probe for potential problems that might exist in the future using a brainstorming approach Step 2 Evaluation - review problems uncovered for managerial concern, backed up by a cost-benefit analysis. Use creative computer software (if appropriate) to generate new ways to evaluate future problems	Step 1 Exploration - examine the environment for opportunities that come from problems uncovered using a brainstorming approach. Use creative computer software (if appropriate) to explore new ideas to exploit these opportunities
Identification	Step 3 Validation - select actual problems for managerial concern	Step 2 Selection - determine that one or more opportunities should be explored by management, as related to the company's critical success factors
	Step 4 Establish Boundaries - define each potential problem within its boundaries so as to cover the whole area that the problem encompasses	Step 3 Examine Boundaries - survey the environment for each opportunity and determine the proper boundaries
Solution	Steps 5 and 6 Solution - use steps 3 and 4 of quantitative-centered approach or steps 2 and 3 of decision-centered approach	Steps 4 and 5 Solution - use steps 3 and 4 of quantitative-centered approach or steps 2 and 3 of decision-centered approach
Implementation	Steps 7 and 8 Implementation - use steps 5 and 6 of quantitative-centered approach or steps 4 and 5 of decision-centered approach	Steps 6 and 7 Implementation - use steps 5 and 6 of quantitative-centered approach or steps 4 and 5 of decision-centered approach

NOTE: There is *feedback* from the last step of both approaches to the first step.

and tomorrow. The validation for solving these problems is generally backed up by a cost-benefit analysis. If such an analysis is not available or too difficult or costly to develop, it may be necessary to use alternative means, such as the consensus of the majority of the problem-finding group, to substantiate this selection as an important problem to be solved. For example, to determine what problems should be validated and solved, the problem-finding group meets again and reviews the recommendations of the managers and their staffs. For the most part, the staffs have prioritized the important problems to be solved. It is up to the problem-finding group to pass judgment on them. As noted, some of the problems cannot be resolved in terms of a cost-benefit analysis. Input from managers and their staffs is generally necessary to finalize the prioritized list for implementation.

4. *Establish Boundaries.* After the problems have been validated in step 3, it is necessary to describe (define) each problem within its boundaries in the fourth step. This ensures that areas that the problem might touch or come into contact with will be included in the problem-finding process. The net result is that there is need for some fine tuning such that the appropriate boundaries of the problem will be considered in its solution. Typically, to establish realistic boundaries, the problem-finding group must have a good knowledge of the future (good, average, or poor economic conditions), a clear description of performance that a solution must fulfill, and a clear idea of what to expect from solving the problem. These areas must be as clear and as accurate as possible, because if the problem is badly defined, the solution is generally of no value to management.

5 and 6. *Solution.* Solution to the problem-centered approach can take one of two directions. One is the use of step 3 (development of alternative solutions) and step 4 (selection of optimum solution) of the quantitative-centered approach. The other is the use of step 2 (design) and step 3 (choice) of the decision-centered approach. The appropriate approach is dictated by the type of future problems being solved. In either case, the solution centers on solving future problems before they actually occur. The accent is on practicing management by perception, rather than the management by exception that is traditional in the problem-solving process.

7 and 8. *Implementation.* In these final steps for the problem-centered approach, the implementation steps for the problem-solving process are usable. Fundamentally, these steps for the quantitative-centered approach and the decision-centered approach are the same. In addition to implementation, it is necessary to establish control over the solution in order to detect how changing times are affecting it.

The foregoing eight steps are normally conducted in the order in which they were presented because of the uncertainty of the future. However, there may be circumstances that warrant changing this sequence. As in the problem-solving process, there is need of *feedback* in the problem-centered approach.

Typical Application of the Problem-centered Approach

As an illustration of the problem-centered approach, a chemical products company is currently offering a line of chemical products that are sold to retail and industrial laundry and drycleaning plants. Recently, the president and the vice-presidents (who assist the corporate planning staff) became concerned about the direction the government is taking in terms of regulation and control of the drycleaning industry because of hazardous wastes. This waste problem will force a decline of drycleaning chemical sales in favor of laundry products. Since drycleaning sales are 75 percent of the company's total sales, there was concern by the company's management. Upon brainstorming of the overall problem by the corporate planning staff, a number of problems were generated (first step). One of these was the effect of shifting the manufacturing plants over to production of more laundry chemicals. An equally important problem was the need to change sales and marketing strategies toward the laundry market. Needless to say, other problems were identified. In turn, ideas related to overcoming these problems were evaluated using a creative computer software package. A cost-benefit analysis and compliance with organizational objectives and government regulations served as a final evaluation basis (second step).

At this point, the corporate planning staff met with top management to validate the overall problem and the related problems (third step). After examination of their impact on customers, production, and other concerns, a list of priorities was set forth for the specialized problem areas. Next, the scope of boundaries of each problem was addressed (fourth step). Changes in production and inventory levels were outlined for the manufacturing facility. The marketing efforts were defined in terms of advertising media and markets to address. Other boundaries, like personnel, budgets, and time frames, were set for each problem.

Possible solutions to each of the problems were identified (fifth and sixth steps). Solutions for the manufacturing department included building a manufacturing facility exclusively for laundry products, contracting the additional work to other manufacturers, or having existing plants updated. After analysis of potential solutions, top management needs to decide which is the optimum solution for each problem after considering all of the factors. If updating the present manufacturing facility is identified as the best alternative, funds must be allocated to facilitate its completion. Next, the optimum solution for each problem must be implemented (seventh and eighth steps). In addition, there is need to place proper controls over the implemented solutions.

Opportunity-centered Approach

The opportunity-centered approach to the problem-finding process is also taken from a prior publication by the author.[8] As illustrated in figure 4.4, three steps plus the solution and implementation phases from the quantitative-centered approach or the decision-centered approach are set forth. This opportunity-centered approach is related to managers and their staffs.

1. *Exploration*. The first step examines the internal and external environment for opportunities that come from problems uncovered. As in the problem-centered approach, brainstorming is generally used by managers and their staffs. The focus

is directed away from the short range to the medium and long ranges where every effort is used to determine what opportunities are presented by the problems discovered in the future. As in the prior approach, the analysis is initially forward-looking in that there is a search for future problems. Once the problems have been identified, they are examined from the standpoint of identifying opportunities for improving the company's operations (from the standpoint of sales, profits, or whatever). From this perspective, the concept of opportunities has a "positive" connotation, while the concept of problems has a "negative" meaning.

If a computerized mode is utilized, appropriate computer software can be gainfully employed to assist managers and their staffs in developing new ideas that exploit appropriate opportunities for a company to pursue. Generally, creative computer software results in the exploration of more new ideas than if step 1 is performed manually. This will be apparent in the various examples given in part IV of this book. The selection of more opportunities helps to assure managers that this exploration step is performed in a most comprehensive manner.

2. *Selection*. When appropriate opportunities have been identified, the second step is to determine what opportunities (one or more) should be explored by managers and their staffs. The selection process should focus on opportunities that relate to a company's *critical success factors*, the areas in which satisfactory results are critical to its success. Typically, these factors include price, sales promotion, customer service, product mix, inventory turnover, cost control, and quality dealers. In turn, the interrelationships of the critical success factors and the company's goals and objectives are discussed for further clarification. But more important, this discussion determines what opportunities should be pursued by the company, thereby identifying them in a clear and meaningful way. Moreover, it takes into consideration all the important facts that bear on important company opportunities. Where deemed necessary, a *cost-benefit analysis* can be used to determine what opportunities are more important than others in terms of how they affect the company's future profits.

3. *Examine Boundaries*. The third step centers on surveying the environment for the opportunities identified before pursuing an opportunity solution. Due to the nature of some opportunities, the boundaries may be quite wide; that is, they may extend beyond the company and may be related to emerging and established organizations and industries. Generally, greater opportunities are found when boundaries are extended. Thus top management and the corporate planning staff need to examine the boundaries surrounding the opportunities from a narrow to a very wide perspective. The net result is that the proper boundaries are used in the solution and implementation of the opportunity.

4 and 5. *Solution*. As in the problem-centered approach, the solution to the opportunity-centered approach can take one of two directions, the quantitative-centered approach or the decision-centered approach. Current problem-solving approaches require that the decision maker pick the best solution from the set of feasible ones. An opportunity solution, then, requires that the decision maker pick the best opportunity from the set of feasible opportunities under study. As

with the problem-centered approach, the main thrust is on practicing management by perception.

6 and 7. *Implementation*. For these last steps of the opportunity-centered approach, the implementation steps for the problem-solving process are used. The opportunity must be monitored and implemented, making the necessary adjustments to changing times.

As shown in figure 4.4, the seven steps of the opportunity-centered approach are related to those for the problem-centered approach. Also, this approach provides for *feedback*.

Typical Application of the Opportunity-centered Approach

To illustrate an opportunity-centered approach for the chemical products company (as set forth previously), managers and their staffs need to examine the environmental issues in more depth. That is, they need to identify future opportunities that may exist. If they feel that biodegradable products hold an edge in the future market place, then they need to examine such implications. This could include not only a more thorough exploration of the retail and industrial laundry market, but also the home products market (first step). Utilizing the same creative computer software packing set forth previously, important ideas to exploit market opportunities were introduced by group members. The resulting opportunities for the company in the home market centered on private labeling for an established firm, buying a firm for its distribution and marketing efforts in the home market, or breaking into the home market itself.

By looking at the trade-offs of each alternative, one was selected for further review. Using a cost-benefit analysis, private labeling was determined to be the best alternative because of the company's contact (second step). The boundaries of the private labeling issue were examined (third step): that is, what companies would be interested in such a product line, what is the target home market, and what are the cost and pricing needs of offering such a product? These boundaries would lead to the best solution (fourth and fifth steps) and implementation of the best alternative (sixth and seventh steps). Additionally, controls need to be implemented to make sure that the solution is best for the times.

Comparison of the Problem-solving and Problem-finding Processes

The major elements of the problem-solving and problem-finding processes are set forth in figure 4.5. The accent of the problem solving is on management by exception for solving all types of problems in the short range and some in the medium range. This represents a *micro* or a *reactive* approach to problems. In contrast, the focus of problem finding is on management by perception for solving semistructured and unstructured problems covering the long range and some in the short and medium ranges. This is representative of a *macro* or a *proactive* approach to problems.

Figure 4.5
A Comparison of the Problem-solving and the Problem-finding Processes

Problem-Solving Process	Problem-Finding Process
Accent on Management by Exception	Accent on Management by Perception
Basic Phases of Problem Solving	Basic Phases of Problem Finding
Identification, Solution, and Implementation	Search, Identification, Solution, and Implementation
Useful to Solve These Types of Problems	Useful to Solve These Types of Problems
Well-Structured Semistructured Unstructured	Semistructured Unstructured
For the following time periods:	For the following time periods:
Short Range Some Medium Range	Some Short and Medium Range Long Range

Since the problem-finding process encourages the integration of the manager's capabilities with those of creative computer software if this is deemed appropriate, the quality of the final decision is enhanced. The human-machine interface allows the manager to retain control throughout the problem-finding process. From this view, creativity is an important part of these decision-making activities, just as intuition, judgment, and experience are helpful in understanding how the environmental factors react to the stimuli that decisions provide. Of equal importance is a systematic approach that forces the manager to evaluate the facts critically before reaching a final decision.

SUMMARY

The initial focus of the chapter was on the complexity of managerial decision making, which was supplemented by discussion of the need for a synergistic interaction between the manager and the computer. Next, the decision-making process, which is at the center of a manager's activities, was discussed, along with the need for participatory or group decision making. Typically, managers have two basic approaches to the decision-making process: the utilization of the problem-solving process or of the problem-finding process. In the problem-solving process, the quantitative-centered approach is useful in solving well-structured problems, and the decision-centered approach is helpful in solving semistructured and some unstructured problems. In the problem-finding process, the problem-centered approach pinpoints future problems that can be solved today to minimize their impact in the future. Related is the opportunity-centered approach, which searches the environment for opportunities that derive from uncovered problems. In the problem-finding process, there is especially need for creativity since the manager is operating in uncharted waters. As will be seen in succeeding chapters of this book, more effective decisions can be made by utilizing creative computer software.

NOTES

1. Albert Einstein, *Ideas and Opinions* (New York: Bonanza Book, 1954), p. 35.

2. P. C. Fishburn, *Decision and Value Theory* (New York: John Wiley & Sons, 1964), p. 11.

3. Robert A. Raitt, "Must We Revolutionize Our Methodology?" *Interfaces*, February 1974, p. 2.

4. James G. March and Herbert A. Simon, *Organizations* (New York: John Wiley & Sons, 1958).

5. Herbert A. Simon, *Models of Man: Social and Rational* (New York: John Wiley & Sons, 1957).

6. Herbert A. Simon, *The New Science of Management Decision* (New York: Harper & Row, 1960), pp. 2–3.

7. Robert J. Thierauf, *A Problem-finding Approach to Effective Corporate Planning* (Westport, Conn.: Quorum Books, 1987), chap. 2, pp. 17–43.

8. Ibid.

Bibliography: Part II

Abrams, W. N. "Mind Management Techniques." *Data Training*, August 1987.

Agor, W. H. *Intuition in Organizations: Leading and Managing Productivity*. Newbury Park, Calif.: Sage Publications, 1989.

Argyris, C. "Teaching Smart People How to Learn." *Harvard Business Review*, May–June 1991.

Barker, J. "The State of the Art for Decision Making." *Successful Meetings*, November 1989.

Behling, O., and N. L. Eckel, "Making Sense out of Intuition." *Academy of Management Executive*, February, 1991.

Courtney, J. F., Jr., D. P. Paradice, and N. H. A. Mohammed. "A Knowledge-based DSS for Managerial Problem Diagnosis." *Decision Sciences*, Vol. 18, no. 3, 1987.

Cox, E., and M. Goetz. "Fuzzy Logic Clarified." *Computerworld*, March 11, 1991.

"Crossing Boundaries: The Nine-Dot Dilemma." *Harvard Business Review*, March–April 1991.

Dery, D., and T. J. Mack. "Information Support Systems for Problem Solving." *Decision Support Systems*, Vol. 1, 1985.

Drucker, P. F. "Principles of Innovation: The Do's and Don'ts." *Modern Office Technology*, February 1986.

Einstein, A. *Ideas and Opinions*, New York: Bonanza Book, 1954.

Evans, J. R. *Creative Thinking in the Decision and Management Sciences*. Cincinnati: South-Western Publishing Company, 1991.

——— . "Creativity in MS/OR: Creative Thinking, A Basis for MS/OR Problem Solving." *Interfaces*, September–October 1991.

Fishburn, P. C. *Decision and Value Theory*. New York: John Wiley & Sons, 1964.

Forgionne, G. A. "OR/MS and Decision Technology in the 1990s." *OR/MS Today*, June 1990.

Freedman, D. H. "Cultivating IS Creativity." *Infosystems*, July 1987.

Gordon, W. *Synectics: The Development of Creative Capacity*. New York: Harper & Row, 1961.

Grosswirth, M. "Creative Consultancy." *Datamation*, April 1979.

Handy, C. *The Age of Unreason*. Boston, Mass.: Harvard Business School Press, 1990.

Hickson, D. J., R. J. Butler, D. Cray, G. R. Mallory, and D. C. Wilson. *Top Decisions: Strategic Decision-Making in Organizations*. San Francisco: Jossey-Bass Publishers, 1986.

Houghton-Allico, D. "Creative Thinking Aids Documentation Focus." *Software News*, March 1984.

Huber, G. P. "A Theory of the Effects of Advanced Information Technologies on Organizational Design, Intelligence, and Decision Making." *Academy of Management Review*, Vol. 15, no. 1, 1990.

Isenberg, D. J. "How Senior Managers Think." *Harvard Business Review*, November–December 1984.

Kepner, C. H., and B. B. Tregoe. *The Rational Manager*. New York: McGraw-Hill, 1965.

Kiechel, W., III. "Getting Creative." *Fortune*, July 25, 1983.

Kostanecki, A. T. "Solving Problems Is an Art." *Inc.*, March 1981.

Kotter, J. P. "What Effective General Managers Really Do." *Harvard Business Review*, November–December 1982.

Lasden, M. "Intuition: The Voice of Success?" *Computer Decisions*, February 26, 1985.

Lindley, D. V. *Making Decisions*. 2d ed. New York: John Wiley & Sons, 1985.

Lindo, D. "How to Sell Good Ideas." *Computerworld*, December 21, 1987.

March, J. G., and H. A. Simon. *Organizations*. New York: John Wiley & Sons, 1958.

Martin, A. P. *Think Proactive: New Insights into Decision Making*. New York: Professional Development Institute, 1984.

Mason, J. "Technical Problems, Creative Solutions." *Computerworld*, October 29, 1990.

McKenney, J. L., and P. G. W. Keen. "How Managers' Minds Work." *Harvard Business Review*, May–June 1974.

Mintzberg, H. "The Manager's Job: Folklore and Fact." *Harvard Business Review*, July–August, 1975 (and March–April, 1990).

Morley, E., and A. Silver. "A Film Director's Approach to Managing Creativity." *Harvard Business Review*, March–April 1977.

Nadler, G., and S. Hibino. *Breakthrough Thinking*. New York: Prima Publishing & Communications, 1991.

Neustadt, R. E., and E. R. May, *Thinking in Time: The Uses of History for Decision-Makers*. New York: Free Press, 1986.

Peters, T. J., and R. Waterman, Jr. *In Search of Excellence: Lessons from America's Best-Run Companies*. New York: Harper & Row, 1982.

Pitt, M., and R. N. Woolley. "Four Views on Problem Structuring." *Interfaces*, February 1980.

Piturro, M. C. "Computer Conferencing: Brainstorming across Time and Space." *Management Review*, August 1989.

Raitt, R. A. "Must We Revolutionize Our Methodology?" *Interfaces*, February 1974.

Roach, J. M. "Simon Says . . . Decision Making Is a 'Satisficing' Experience." *Management Review*, January 1979.

Roth, W. F., Jr. *Problem Solving for Managers*. New York: Prager Publishers, 1985.

Saunders, C., and J. W. Jones. "Temporal Sequences in Information Acquisition for Decision Making: A Focus on Source and Medium." *Academy of Management Review*, Vol. 15, no. 1, 1990.

Schoennauer, A. W. W. *Problem Finding and Problem Solving*. Chicago: Nelson-Hall, 1981.

Simon, H. A. *Models of Man: Social and Rational*. New York: John Wiley & Sons, 1957.

———. The New Science of Management Decision. New York: Harper & Row, 1960.

Simon, H. A., et al. "Decision Making and Problem Solving." *Interfaces*, September–October 1987.

Sirkin, H., and G. Stalk, Jr. "Fix the Process, Not the Problem." *Harvard Business Review*, July–August 1990.

Summers, I., and D. E. White. "Creativity Techniques: Toward Improvement of the Decision Process." *Academy of Management Review*, Vol. 1, no. 2, 1976.

Sussman, L., and R. Herden. "Dialectical Problem Solving." *Business Horizons*, January–February 1982.

Telem, M. "Information Requirements Specification I: Brainstorming Collective Decision-making Approach." *Information Processing and Management*, Vol. 24, Issue 5, 1988.

———. "Information Requirements Specification II: Brainstorming Collective Decision-making Technique." *Information Processing and Management*, Vol. 24, Issue 5, 1988.

Thierauf, R. J. *A Problem-finding Approach to Effective Corporate Planning*. Westport, Conn.: Quorum Books, 1987.

VanGundy, A. B. *Techniques of Structured Problem Solving*. New York: Van Nostrand Reinhold Company, 1981.

Veloso, O. A. S. "On the Concepts of Problem and Problem-solving Method." *Decision Support Systems*, Vol. 3, Issue 3, 1987.

Wakin, E. "Brainstorming: It's Raining Ideas." *Today's Office*, January 1985.

———. "Turning a Problem into a Solution." *Today's Office*, March 1989.

Wallas, G. *The Art of Thought*. New York: Harcourt, Brace and Company, 1926.

Warfield, J. N., H. Geschka, and R. Hamilton. *Methods of Idea Management*, Columbus, Ohio: Academy for Contemporary Problems, 1975.

Whyte, G. "Decision Failures: Why They Occur and How to Prevent Them" *Academy of Management Executive*, August 1991.

Young, L. F. "Knowledge-based Systems for Idea Processing." *Data Base*, Winter/Spring 1991.

PART III

Relationship of Computers to Creativity

5

Creativity as Practiced
in an MIS Environment

ISSUES EXPLORED

- To explore current management information systems that focus on efficient processing with some reference to creativity
- To focus on group decision support systems that are helpful to managers and their staffs for practicing creativity on the job
- To explore current electronic decision rooms that facilitate the creative process
- To focus on idea-processing systems that make use of computer generators to develop new ideas
- To show the tie-in of management information systems to creative computer software

OUTLINE

Current Management Information Systems That Focus on Efficient Information Processing
Real-Time MIS
  On-Line Real-Time Concept
Distributed MIS
  Application of the 80-20 Rule
Current Successful Management Information Systems That Perform Efficient Information Processing
  Shell Oil Company
  Strawbridge & Clothier
  Air Products & Chemicals, Inc.
Newer Management Information Systems Useful to Practice Creativity
Electronic Data Interchange Systems
  EDI Outside the Company
  EDI Inside the Company

Now that creativity techniques have been set forth within a traditional decision-making environment, the next step is to place them within the context of a computerized operating mode. Because the recurring theme of this book has been to improve decision making by employing a creative computerized mode, this chapter will focus on newer systems that can be useful in accomplishing such a desired goal. Initially, however, the focus will be on current management information systems that have provided practical solutions for management to improve customer relations, expand in new markets, and the like. Some typical efficient information-processing systems that are currently in place will be supplemented by other systems that lend themselves to the application of creativity on the job for the typical manager. This background will be helpful for a tie-in not only with the subject matter of the next chapter on creativity software, but also with the remaining chapters of the book, where creative solutions to problems are presented in certain types of computer operating environments.

CURRENT MANAGEMENT INFORMATION SYSTEMS THAT FOCUS ON EFFICIENT INFORMATION PROCESSING

For the most part, past management information systems have not provided managers with the potential to offer creative solutions to a company's information-processing (IP) problems. For example, *integrated management information systems* provide selected decision-oriented information needed by management to plan, control, and evaluate the activities of the organization. They are designed within a framework that emphasizes profit planning, performance planning, and control at all levels. An integrated MIS centers on the integration of required business information systems, both financial and nonfinancial, within the organization.

In the past, the primary interest of information systems was developing financial statements. When an integrated MIS is installed, its *primary purpose* is the production of reports that will assist management. In contrast, its *secondary purpose* is the preparation of periodic financial reports representing a by-product of the information processed to assist in planning controlling operations.

Although integrated management information systems rectified the problem of prior accounting-oriented systems by providing feedback in the form of reports through their various systems and subsystems, they are still deficient in one important respect. Data must be accumulated for a period of time before processing is feasible. Whether sequential or random-access files are used, there is still the problem of time lag. For this reason, all prior systems, including integrated MISs, are called *backward-looking systems*. The methods, procedures, and equipment look to past history before reports are produced for feedback. What is needed is a *forward-looking system*—one that looks to the present and the future. Such an approach is found in subsequent management information systems, in particular, real-time MISs and distributed MISs as discussed below.

REAL-TIME MIS

Although integrated MISs are operating in a few organizations of various sizes, they have been replaced by the implementation of *real-time management information systems*, sometimes referred to as *on-line real-time systems*. Like prior systems, they are essentially transactional processing systems that also provide essential information for management. Typical applications in such an environment include accounts receivable, airline reservation systems, bank deposit and withdrawal accounting, hotel accounting and reservation systems, law enforcement intelligence systems, patient hospital records, savings and loan deposit accounting, and stock market information.

On-Line Real-Time Concept

Such systems focus on the on-line real-time concept. All data is *on-line*, that is, all data are sent directly into a computer system as soon as they come into being. The whole operation is in *real time*, which means that data are processed and fed back to the appropriate source in sufficient time to change or control the operating environment. Basically, then, any system that processes and stores data or reports them as they are happening is considered to be an on-line real-time system. Company personnel will receive a response from the system in time to satisfy their own real-time environmental requirements. The response time may range from a fraction of a second to minutes, hours, or days, depending on the attendant circumstances.

The integrated data accumulated from the many detailed on-line transactions are commonly referred to as the data-base elements or the organization's data base. In addition to having all data collected in one place, the same inventory data base, for example, may be used by a number of departments, such as manufacturing, production planning and control, inventory control, purchasing, and accounting. In another example, a data-base element is an employee skill number that can assist in preparing weekly payroll, referencing personnel records, filling new job openings, preparing contract negotiations, and the like. A data base, then, contains elements or data bits in a common storage medium that form the foundation for operational information although the data base may be physically dispersed. Because designing a structured data base for accommodating the various levels of management is a formidable task, a real-time MIS satisfies the needs of lower and middle management for organizing, directing, and controlling activities around the established plans, being in conformance with the organization's objectives.

Typically, in a real-time MIS environment, a number of on-line input/output (I/O) devices are located throughout the company's operations. Teletypewriters, CRT display devices, and personal computers are capable of sending as well as receiving information. They may be many miles away from each other but are linked through a data communications network from the local computer and/or regional computer to the central computing facility. Essentially, the operating mode can be viewed as a centralized basis versus a decentralized basis. Even though lower and middle managers can obtain updated information about the company's basic business operations through some kind of input/output device on a centralized basis, the same cannot be said for top management with a real-time management information system. Although the system does respond to the managerial needs of the first two levels and does provide immediate feedback on present operations, it falls short of the information desired by top-level executives.[1] As will be seen shortly, this is not the case with decision support systems.

DISTRIBUTED MIS

Distributed MIS, commonly referred to as *distributed data processing* (DDP), is one of the major thrusts in current management information systems. These systems represent a decentralized approach to placing low-cost computing power, starting at the various points of data entry, and linking these points, where deemed necessary, with a centralized computer via a distributed communications network. Like the previous systems, their essential focus is on transactional processing of business activities at the lower level of operations while also supplying appropriate managerial information. In effect, distributed data processing is an approach to placing computing power where it is needed in an organization for efficient and economical data-processing operations. Similarly, it is a feasible alternative to centralized data procession due to the declining costs of programmable terminals, microcomputers, minicomputers, and small business computers. Because the focus of current distributed data-processing systems is placing computer power at the lower levels in an organization, their output generally centers on assisting lower and middle management.

Application of the 80-20 Rule

In the prior computerized MIS, most computing capabilities were dependent on one or more large central processing units that were programmed to perform various data-processing functions. The use of centralized systems created input bottlenecks. Similarly, they created situations where the feedback of business data necessary to run an organization occurred only after substantial delays. Because of these problems, distributed data processing arose out of the need to get computing power where it is needed—at all levels of an organization. Another way of viewing the need for distributed processing is applying the *80-20 rule*: putting computer processing power where 80 percent of the work is done or where results are needed. In general, distributed data processing makes economic sense if 80 percent of the data generated at a down-line site is used primarily for that site. Otherwise, other MIS approaches may be more suitable.

An integral part of a distributed processing system is the use of data communications equipment from the remote processors to the central computer facility. The system allows a number of small computers (microcomputers, minicomputers, and small business computers) to be combined to form an operational data-processing (DP) center at more than one location. A network of these centers sharing computerized files provides a powerful data-processing capability at local and regional levels. The system provides on-line data entry to the local and regional data bases for concurrent processing of multiple independent jobs. An operational DP center performs the required MIS operations of the remote site while it maintains concurrent high-speed communication with the central computer and other DP centers in the network. It permits the development of network applications that can be solved by the existing MIS staff where the accent is on simplicity of operations. The system provides for generating reports within the network that give operational management personnel control over their operations as well as for generating summary information for higher levels of management. Various network configurations can be developed by connecting network elements through communications lines. The attendant circumstances must be surveyed for the proper DDP network. In addition, to overcome objections to a large, centralized data base, MIS strategists came up with the idea of *distributed data bases* whereby the user's files are placed at or near the point where transactions occur. This way, the user's data are always available; the concern about data communications failures is no longer necessary.[2]

CURRENT SUCCESSFUL MANAGEMENT INFORMATION SYSTEMS THAT PERFORM EFFICIENT INFORMATION PROCESSING

To place real-time MIS and distributed MIS into their proper perspective, typical applications of these systems are given below. These centralized and decentralized systems demonstrate that creativity was used by their developers. That is, these transactional processing systems process everyday business transactions so efficiently that their companies are able to get an upper hand on the competition. In turn, their summarized output has proven to be helpful to their managements.

Basically, these successful management information systems have taken non-traditional approaches to everyday information processing such that they represent significant breakthroughs. Their companies recognize that anything that gives one company an advantage is going to be copied by competitors, erasing the innovator's head start. However, these same competitive pressures that make it tough to sustain an advantage make it imperative to try.

Today, companies ranging from energy providers to retailers to hospitals are viewing management information systems not as a cost but as a revenue generator. Company managers are integrating their management information systems with their essential needs. In the process, those information systems that have communications capabilities are changing the way business does business. For the most part, companies can get a competitive advantage by doing even the basic business things, the nuts and bolts, better.

Developing and implementing such systems is no easy matter, with no magic formula. Many times, the biggest hurdles are not technical. Company managers are the real obstacle. For example, top executives at one company could not figure out where all the technology dollars were going. Hence the problem was high-level executives who were not paying attention to the use and planning of information resources. Even when the executives on the business side are paying attention, most organizations have high organizational barriers that make it difficult for business and technology managers to listen to one another. People in the business functions, like manufacturing and informations systems, have their own view of the company. Dominating the middle of each image is the group's own concerns, whether operations, process controllers, or technologies. Off in the corner or on the side are little boxes representing the others.

Shell Oil Company

As an example of a successful management information system, one firm that has managed to mesh these worlds is Shell Oil Company (Houston, Texas). It fills senior positions in MIS with business managers familiar with technology issues. By moving people across functions, the company ensures that MIS is driven by business needs. Thus MIS is not remote from the business, and the business people cannot put their ideas in a mail drop and expect to have them executed successfully. Currently, the oil giant's general manager of technology and development has also worked at Shell as a marketing manager and general auditor as well as researcher and product business manager.

A direct outcome of this process was Shell's initiation five years ago of point-of-sale equipment for credit authorization. Business management was the driving force for the company to rethink the retailing cost structure, where credit is a major tool. The technology people saw that improvements in telecommunications and

microcomputers made possible a nationwide network that had not been economical-
ly feasible before. With the network, Shell reduced its bad debt and its receivables
and shortened the billing cycle.[3]

Strawbridge & Clothier

Strawbridge & Clothier, the $900-million retail chain (Philadelphia, Penn-
sylvania), was getting low marks from customers for its too-long checkout lines.
The company experimented with Universal Product Code bar coding, scanning,
and price lookups at the cash registers. Strawbridge now has bar-coded all items
in its more than twenty discount stores and 40 percent of them in its thirteen department stores.

Although scanning might not be considered to be sophisticated information processing, it is not merely one leg of the way toward a full quick response system,
the retail and textile industries' version of just-in-time. According to a study by
Andersen Consulting in New York, this technology alone can save stores an
amount equal to 1 percent of their sales a year. Not only does it speed the checkout
lines and keep customers happier, but by tying to other back-office operations,
it improves inventory control and reduces the labor needed to reticket goods for
sales and other promotions.[4]

Air Products & Chemicals, Inc.

Air Products & Chemicals, Inc., also needed to improve its customer service.
But as a supplier to other chemical producers, its problems did not stem from
backed-up checkout lines. As the company's chemicals group has shifted its
strategic emphasis from bulk commodity chemicals to specialty chemicals, the
company has moved into a new market with more complex delivery requirements.
The specialty market is also more time-sensitive. Before, orders as large as a
railroad car could be delivered in one or two weeks. Today, same-day delivery
is routine for bag- and pail-size quantities. But the old batch-order processing
system, built in the mid-1970s, was too slow and unable to keep the customer
representatives knowledgeable about their customers' special wants.

A systems planning effort, led by the MIS department, identified an on-line
order-entry system as the highest priority for the chemicals group. In an industry
in which customers have multiple suppliers, improved service is one of the few
ways for Air Products to get ahead of the pack. Its new Advantage system is
connected to its fifteen plants scattered around the country. It enables sales
representatives to fill an order, run a credit check, see if the product is in stock,
identify transportation, and send the order out to the plant, all within a short phone
conversation with the buyer. The end result is that sales representatives are more
productive, inventory control is tighter, and invoicing is faster.[5]

NEWER MANAGEMENT INFORMATION SYSTEMS
USEFUL TO PRACTICE CREATIVITY

As noted in the preceding discussion, management information systems center on producing periodic reports designed not only to recap past operations with an accent on exception items, but also to pinpoint possible control problems in current and upcoming operations for lower and middle management. Although these factors represent improvements over prior information systems, they can be viewed from a two-dimensional framework; that is, the computer gives a periodic answer that is indicative of what should have been done or what should be done to control operations. However, in this fast-changing world, there is need to bring in a third-dimensional viewpoint, namely, that of the manager, who brings judgment, expertise, and other intellectual assets to bear on the whole problem. From this broad perspective, the manager is able to get a *macro* view of the problem. Whereas MIS focuses on structured problem solving, decision support systems (DSSs) extend the range of problem structure to include semistructured and unstructured problems. DSSs allow managers and their staffs to use the query capabilities of the computer to obtain requested information and be at the center of the decision-making process as changes occur. This is in contrast to relying on periodic control reports, as found in MISs.

In the discussion to follow, the focus is initially on electronic data interchange (EDI) systems outside a company with its trading partners and within the company. Next, decision support systems are viewed from both an individual and a group perspective. In addition, executive information systems (EISs) are covered and related to DSSs. Needless to say, these areas are related to the utilization of computers to enhance a manager's creativity.

ELECTRONIC DATA INTERCHANGE SYSTEMS

Electronic data interchange represents the exchange of documents and transactions by a computer in one company with the computer(s) of one or more companies. Prior to EDI, the data flow focused on paper documents. The paper documents, for example, were mailed by the buyer to the seller, and the seller moved the paper documents to the proper departments for appropriate processing. In turn, the buyer undertook the necessary processing as well as the receipt of the goods. In contrast, the application of EDI involves the conversion of a written document into a machine-readable form so that a computer in one company can communicate directly with the computer of the other company. Generally, the bulk of these documents relate to events that would generate input transactions for accounting systems to be processed into information.

A very important means for storing data used in an EDI environment is a company's *data base*. To facilitate the use of data, they should be integrated with the data base so that data used by different departments are available from one record on the data base versus several records. In this manner, not only is the programming effort facilitated, but also the exchange of information with outside companies is much easier. A *data dictionary* describes the precise meaning of data in the data base and related specifications that are used in structuring a transaction. It is helpful in understanding special codes and provides additional information about data elements when necessary.

EDI Outside the Company

Normally, a set of EDI transactions is packaged in an electronic envelope and transmitted throughout a communications network. *Transmission protocols* describe the rules by which an envelope is structured and handled by various communication devices. For example, several electronic transactions such as invoices may be sent together in a package with appropriate standard separators indicating parts of invoices or identifying the beginning and ending of the message. Because the envelopes containing these messages are handled by the various devices in the communication network, it is necessary that standard rules be established for transmission and separators.

EDI transmissions go from application to application between buyers and sellers without human intervention. An EDI system is involved in electronically exchanging purchase orders, invoices, payments, shipping notices, and like transactions. In the process, staffing needs are cut by reducing paper handling, reducing errors by eliminating the need to rekey data, and improving transaction turnaround time. The net result of utilizing an EDI system is a computerized exchange of business documents in a specific format between companies. Fundamentally, an EDI system can be defined as a computer-to-computer exchange of routine paper documents, such as purchase orders, material releases, or receipt advices, by one company with other companies. This computerized information is transmitted in a standard format between a company and other companies. In an EDI system, electronically transmitted data replace paper documents throughout a company's transaction cycle.[6]

EDI Inside the Company

From another perspective, electronic processing can be viewed only from within the company, where image-processing systems use electronic imaging to replace paper-intensive information systems. From an overall standpoint, there is an advantage to automating existing business processes with image-processing systems. The present method of paper processing is replaced by capturing all data initially in an electronic form. In turn, all subsequent processing refers to the same electronic images. Also, there is need to go a step further and to find applications for image processing that transform the business.

Organizations that have faced up to the issue of their survival can be very innovative in changing their business culture. As an example, Xerox revolutionized its own methods by designing and manufacturing copiers when extreme competitive pressures came from Canon. Companywide integration and systems coordination is another key to improving customer service and guaranteeing success. Procter & Gamble pulled together under the umbrella of "product delivery" three formerly separate functions that covered suppliers, manufacturers, and finished-goods delivery.

In light of the preceding comments, image-processing systems can be defined as those systems that focus on replacing paper processing with an electronic processing mode. An image-processing system allows images to be digitized and then processed with computers. In an optical-based system, paper images are fed into a scanner, digitized, and stored under a heading of the user's choice. Subsequent users can reference these same images, thereby eliminating use of paper files, which typically are time-consuming to reference.[7]

DECISION SUPPORT SYSTEMS

Essentially, an individually oriented decision support system is designed to satisfy the needs of a manager at any level in a distributed data-processing environment. The system is designed to support the problem-finding (future problems related to the present) and problem-solving decisions of the manager. It incorporates features found in management information systems and in quantitative models of management science. Such a system emphasizes direct support for the manager in order to enhance the professional judgments required in making decisions, especially when the problem structures tend to be semistructured and unstructured. The use of interactive systems and CRT displays in a decision support system is an example of this point. Emphasis is placed on helping the manager to make decisions by being at the center of the decision-making process rather than on actually making decisions for the manager. This interplay results in a total effort that is greater than that of the manager or computer operating independently (as in MIS), thereby providing *synergistic decision making*. Also, information is presented in a useful form rather than as a mass of all information that might be useful. From this perspective, an individually oriented decision support system builds on present management information systems as well as complements them.[8]

Accent on Group Perspective

Since there is a move toward *group decision support systems* (GDSSs), there is need to define such an approach. Fundamentally, group decision support systems combine computers, data communications, and decision technologies to support problem finding and problem solving for managers and their staffs, which may also include operating personnel in the newer work environments. Technological advancements, such as electronic boardrooms, local area networks, teleconferencing, and decision support software have spurred an interest in this area. In addition, fundamental changes in the external environment of organizations are encouraging organizations to head in this direction. Typically, organizations currently are experiencing the emergence of a postindustrial environment characterized by greater knowledge, complexity, and turbulence. One important effect of this trend is that decision-related meetings are becoming more frequent and more important. At the same time, the decisions confronting groups are becoming more complex and must be made more quickly and with greater participation than in the past. As part of the transition into this new environment, organizations are exploring advanced information technologies that might be employed in group meetings.[9]

EXECUTIVE INFORMATION SYSTEMS

To a degree, an extension of DSS is executive information systems (EISs). EIS is used mostly for highly structured reporting, sometimes referred to as status access. DSS has become almost synonymous with modeling and unstructured, ad hoc querying. Executive information systems are aimed at senior executives who currently have few, if any, computer-based systems to assist them in their day-to-day responsibilities. EIS brings together relevant data from various internal and external sources, delivering important information quickly and in a useful way. More important, it filters, compresses, and tracks critical data as determined by each executive end user. EIS performs the conceptually simple task of informing senior executives on matters relevant to their organizational responsibilities.

Unlike traditional MIS functions that focus on the storage of large amounts of information, EIS focuses on the retrieval of specific information and on status access. The emphasis is on reducing the time and effort that the executive user must expend to obtain useful information.

How EIS Is Different from DSS

Fundamentally, there are four key factors that distinguish EIS from DSS. The first two factors are related: the EIS front end must be easy to learn and easy to use. A touch-sensitive screen or a mouse (instead of—or, in some cases, combined with—a keyboard) and high-resolution graphics are the preferred methods of executive interface. Ease of use depends not only on the physical medium (mouse, graphics), but also on how the information is organized. The executive should be able to navigate the system quickly to locate the desired information. The ability to delivery timely, summary-level information in an easy-to-use format is the key to a product's success among senior executives.

Third, because the EIS will be used by a high-level executive, the response time must be good. Senior executives typically will not be willing to wait in front of the screen as long as their staff. This response-time requirement will affect both the data-base structure and the design. Finally, in order to be helpful to senior executives, EIS must be quite flexible and reasonably comprehensive. It must be able to present a wide array of information about the company, segmented and/or related along any number of dimensions. This can require significant up-front development costs as well as significant ongoing operating and support costs.[10]

GETTING MANAGERS INVOLVED IN A COMPUTERIZED APPROACH TO CREATIVITY

At this juncture, it would be helpful to show how managers can get involved in a computerized approach to creativity. Fundamentally, the cutting-edge creative technology can solve a number of problems found in many types of group delibera-tions. Typically, group work is becoming increasingly critical for the survival and success of companies. In complex environments that are becoming even more complex, many specialists and generalists are needed to cope with decision com-plexity. New information technology that can aid the group deliberation and decision-making processes is now available. Opportunities abound for creating electronic meeting rooms where computing and communications are merged. Terms such as group decision support systems, electronic meeting systems, and computer-supported cooperative work describe the technology that is available to support group activities.

Electronic Decision Room

Present information technology is usually a network that connects a number of PCs with a file server (high-capacity disk storage shared via a local area net-work) and has the capability of displaying input on large-screen monitors in a room designated for the purpose. The information displayed either can come from an individual using a PC or can represent the aggregation of responses made dur-ing a group session. These sessions may focus on any or a number of the following group tasks or processes: (1) brainstorming by a group, (2) nominal group (group suggestions are discussed and commented on without judgmental assertions), and (3) Delphi (surveys of groups in which feedback based on individual suggestions or conclusions is given to the respondents and consensus is sought).

Group decision support systems, originally located at universities (including the University of Arizona and the University of Minnesota) are found now in industry settings. IBM installed six group decision rooms in the late 1980s. The Internal Revenue Service office in Manhattan agreed to participate in experiments using these rooms in the late 1980s and the early 1990s. The systems' configura-tions vary from eight to thirty-two PCs. The rooms are usually U-shaped to facilitate person-to-person communication when the PCs are not being used. The PCs are generally moderately powered with high-resolution graphics. The large screens in the front of the room also have high resolution. In essence, these rooms have been designed to provide a WYSIWIS (what you see is what I see) environ-ment. The networking if fairly standard, with the file server and the external facilitator's PC having more power and storage than the PCs used by the participants. This technology platform can be replicated at a fairly reasonable price.

Activities and Benefits of Electronic Decision Room

Many managerial activities can take place in and will benefit from use of such a room. For example, a group meeting to plan a complex project could use most of the available group tools effectively. Electronic brainstorming permits each person to submit an idea, pass it to the system, receive someone else's idea, add to it, and pass it on, with comments accumulating at each step in the process. The ideas and comments are passed anonymously via the computer program. After the brainstorming has been completed, the GDSS computerized issue analyzer function permits consolidation of the ideas into focus items, such as critical success factor. Voting may occur next as individuals anonymously rank their preferences. If it is necessary, a number of votes can be taken to establish consensus. Finally, the computer files can be printed for further analysis.

This technology is actually an open forum for raising issues and identifying underlying assumptions while allowing participants to rank their preferences. It also allows for person-to-person conversation, an important complement to individual workstation computing. Interaction of the participants with one another and with the facilitator is always possible; participants therefore have the option of contributing to the interaction either anonymously (via the computer) or directly.

Group decision support systems for committee meetings directly address a number of the problems that contribute to nonproductive meetings. Committees have to deliver tangible output from a diverse set of participants, each of whom may have his or her own agenda. With GDSS, individuals may contribute freely and in a nonjudgmental environment. Documentation of each step in the process is instantly available. Domination cannot occur without revealing that someone is attempting to impose certain beliefs on the others. Creativity is encouraged as individuals contribute and respond freely to the input of others. Overall, creativity is right at home in an electronic decision room.

LATEST MANAGEMENT INFORMATION SYSTEMS USEFUL TO PRACTICE CREATIVITY

The latest types of management information systems that can be related directly or indirectly to helping managers practice creativity on the job are expert systems and neural networks. More important, emphasis is being placed on idea-processing systems (IPSs) that employ idea generators. These types of systems are discussed below, followed by their tie-in with creative computer software.

EXPERT SYSTEMS

An expert system arrives at intelligent solutions to user queries by using the rules contained in the system's knowledge base. A *knowledge base* consists of if-then rules, mathematical formulas, or some other knowledge representation structure to represent the knowledge of experts in a certain domain. The expert system scans its knowledge base to find the appropriate rules, formulas, or some other knowledge structure to apply. Knowledge for such a system is extracted from human experts (i.e., domain experts) on the subject in which the expert system is expected to specialize. The knowledge in the form of rules is then stored in the expert system's knowledge base for use when needed.

Knowledge engineers who have been trained in the techniques of obtaining knowledge from domain experts procure the knowledge necessary to develop rules, formulas, or some other knowledge structure for the problem under study. In effect, knowledge engineers develop the expert system that is designed to parallel decisions made by recognized experts in a field by acquiring knowledge about the particular problem and applying appropriate rules. Once the rules are captured and programmed, a panel of domain experts reviews the program's recommendations in a series of test cases to verify the newly designed expert system.

For typical business applications, most often the knowledge is stored in the form of *if-then* statements known as rules. This collection of rules is interpreted by an *inference engine*. Fundamentally, an inference engine navigates through the knowledge base much like a human would reason through a problem. Each rule can have one or more statements in its *if* and *then* parts. If all the premises of the *if* part hold *true*, the conclusions reached by the expert system in the *then* parts are also *true* and the rule is said to "fire."

Forward Chaining and Backward Chaining

Furthermore, the conclusion of a certain rule may exist as a premise of another rule that may itself "fire" and "ignite" other rules in succession until a final conclusion is reached. This process is known as *forward chaining*. Essentially, then, the expert-system program looks for rules that apply. By executing each rule that applies, the computer creates additional data about the problem at hand. Then it begins to search for another rule that applies to the new set of data. The computer goes through this operation again and again until it reaches a final conclusion. Hence forward chaining is defined as a bottom-up, data-driven strategy. A forward-chaining strategy works well for problems with many solutions or where a goal must be achieved. The Digital Equipment Corporation's XCON expert system, as an example, uses forward chaining to configure VAX computer systems.

In contrast, a *backward chaining* strategy starts at the final goal and works top down through various subgoals. This goal-driven approach works best when the number of outcomes is small and the goal is known. Because of these characteristics, backward looking is commonly used for diagnostic applications. To establish a goal, all of the premises of a rule are checked. If a premise is a rule, it becomes a subgoal. This process is applied recursively until a value is established for the top-level goal. Thus the inference engine traverses the knowledge-base rules backward, from conclusion to the initial premises. One of the best-known examples of an expert system that uses this strategy is MYCIN, a diagnostic tool for infectious diseases, developed at Stanford University. Additionally, there are hybrid expert systems with both forward- and backward-chaining control. The particular needs of the user will dictate which of the three chaining approaches is appropriate for the application being developed.

In summary, expert systems are designed to mimic the problem-solving abilities of experts in a particular domain. Because an expert system works roughly the way human experts do, it combines factual knowledge with rules that experience teaches, that is, heuristics, and then makes inferences about the situation at hand, whether it be diagnosing the financial portfolio of a client or the cost of a new product. In light of these facts, an expert system can be defined as a computer program that embodies the expertise in a specific domain that would otherwise be available only from a human expert. It represents a codification of the knowledge and reasoning used by human experts. Once operational, it can be copied and distributed at little marginal cost to assist users, whether they be experts or inexperienced personnel.[11]

NEURAL NETWORKS

Since an expert system contains expertise in the form of a knowledge base, the system goes through its knowledge base and picks out the most appropriate response. The real problem is that if a person queries the expert system about something outside of its knowledge domain, it cannot respond. This is where neural networks come into play. The key distinction between expert systems and neural networks is that neural networks do not involve specific recordings or transcriptions of someone else's thinking. Neural networks can learn from experience.

Neural networks supposedly imitate the way actual neurons operate in a human's brain. The brain contains 100 billion or so neurons. Axons carry a signal away from the neuron, and dendrites carry the signal toward another neuron; synapses are where nervous impulses pass between neurons. Individual neurons thereby reach out to 10,000 or so other neurons.

Currently, "intelligence" is believed to be created via the rich and complex interconnections between the individual neurons. The premise is that particular groups of neurons, through experience and repeated firings, create a favorable connection, or affinity, with other neurons. Properly stimulated, the neurons fire off simultaneously as a group. In neural networks, for example, such collective cellular intimacy is measured as a weighted value. A collection of neurons that work well in unison have a high weighted value. Less unison means a lower weighted value. A higher weighted value might produce an affirmative answer, while a lower or nonexistent value could produce a negative answer. This is the basic idea behind pattern recognition.

Forward-Propagation Learning and Back-Propagation Learning

To recognize patterns, neural networks use back-propagation learning (or supervised learning), forward-propagation learning (or unsupervised learning), and variations in between. Signature recognition on checks, which serves as a means for preventing bank fraud, is a very good utilization of a back-propagation neural-net system. In back propagation, there is need to look for a specific response to a specific stimulus. In contrast, in forward propagation, a small network is dropped into the system to see what it makes of this insertion. This network, being unsupervised, will start detecting patterns in areas one might never have guessed. When this network increases in size, it could serve, as an example, as a productive financial analyst's advisor. It should be noted that unlike a back-propagation system, the pattern that the forward-propagation network detects has no semantic meaning until the human analyst gives it one.

In the neural-net world, several performance criteria seem to come up repeatedly. One is the number of neurons, and the other is the connections per second that a net can make. Hardware vendors, such as Intel, are starting to show off specialized chips that increase the number of connections per second between these neurons. Intel, in fact, is claiming something like a billion-plus connections per second. Even with this increase in processing speed, however, neural nets still have a long way to go before they truly imitate the human brain.[12]

IDEA-PROCESSING SYSTEMS

Today, idea-processing systems (IPSs) are considered to be related to decision support systems. Some in the field consider them a subset of group DSSs. No matter how idea-processing systems are looked upon, they are essentially systems designed to capture, evaluate, and synthesize individual ideas into a large context that has real meaning for problem solving. From this perspective, idea generators are generally used to assist in the idea-formulation stage. In the next chapter, idea generators will be the focus of discussion.

To better understand this type of system, it would be helpful to examine initially the meaning of ideas. An *idea* can be thought of as a formulated thought or opinion. Ideas spring from knowledge, which is essentially derived from observation of the environment in which one lives as well as from an awareness of one's internal emotions and feelings on these observations. This way of viewing knowledge is in line with the definition given in the previous chapter, namely, that obtained from experts based upon actual experience. Knowledge implies more than observations of past experience and also includes some form of interpretation of past experience. Ideas can be thought of as the conscious expression of these interpretations. It should be noted that ideas are separate notions that a person is conscious of, but that may or may not be relevant to any specific purpose that has been predefined.

Essential Stages of Idea Processing

A person's ideas can be further refined; that is, ideas may not only come into and go out of a person's awareness, but also can be consciously related to one another in ways that can be useful, interesting, or just plain satisfying to the individual. From the standpoint of being useful in a business environment, ideas can be related to solving a specific problem using an idea-processing system. As such, an idea-processing system has the following basic stages. *First,* there is need for a problem statement by a group that is studying the problem. The group describes the problem and a specific goal to be obtained by solving the problem. *Second,* the focus in on observation, that is, taking in external events as well as internal awareness by group members. *Third,* there is the formulation of individual ideas that can be used to solve the problem. This stage is generally referred to as idea generation; that is, there is formulation of conscious expression by group members. In the *fourth* stage, the ideas are presented to the group with the purpose of evaluating them to solve the problem under study. The evaluation stage determines whether one or more ideas are viable solutions to the problem under study. The *fifth* stage, report preparation, centers on producing a report that demonstrates how the problem will be solved using new and creative ideas proposed by group members. In the *sixth* and final stage, the information contained in the report is disseminated to those in the organization that desire the output from idea processing. Dissemination of the report's contents can be communicated not only to the functional areas under study, but also to other functional areas that are integrated functionally with the problem. These basic stages of an idea-processing system for a group are set forth in figure 5.1.

Figure 5.1
The Basic Stages of an Idea-processing System

Inputs Stage 1 Problem Statement - group describes the problem under study

Stage 2 Observation - group takes in internal and external events

surrounding the problem

Pro-   Stage 3 Idea Generation - group formulates ideas to solve the problem

cessing Stage 4 Evaluation - group determines if one or more ideas are viable

solutions to the problem

Outputs Stage 5 Report Preparation - group prepares a report on how one or more

ideas can solve the problem

Stage 6 Dissemination - group sends final results to appropriate

functional areas

These basic stages of an idea-processing system center on *inputs* in the form of problem statement and observation about the problem. In turn, *processing* involves idea generation and evaluation of ideas for solving the problem. The end result is *outputs*, that is, report preparation and dissemination of information about specific ideas to solve the problem. Regarding idea generation, the behavioral sciences have not been able to explain how a person's mental process operates nor how a person's knowledge is organized. However, there is ongoing research by behavioral psychologists as well as by computer scientists who are attempting to imitate such functions by a computer.

As discussed in chapter 3, there are a number of creativity techniques useful to the manager. As will be seen in the next chapter, some of these techniques have been computerized. These creativity techniques, whether they are employed for idea generation in an idea-processing system or not, have some common approaches to their processing mode. Idea generation can make use of the following:

- Metaphorical association of ideas—classifying and arranging ideas in a variety of unusual ways
- Divergent searches for alternative ideas—classifying and arranging combinations of juxtaposed ideas
- Problem redefinition and reversal—classifying and arranging ideas into logical hierarchies so that they can be viewed from another perspective
- Scenario building and analysis of ideas—summarizing, associating, and relating certain key items in a historical sequence to get at new ideas

In addition, other methods can be used in a computerized mode to assist in broadening idea generation. In part IV of this book, applications that make use of idea-generation methods will be demonstrated.

TIE-IN OF MANAGEMENT INFORMATION SYSTEMS TO CREATIVE COMPUTER SOFTWARE

The central focus of an electronic meeting for group DSS (as noted previously in the chapter) is a large-scale viewing screen. With graphic capabilities, the screen is used by managers in attendance to display everything from agenda items to financial charts and graphs, slides and videotapes, and even materials they would normally draw by hand on chalkboards or flip charts. With attention focused on the screen, managers use a computer to display and modify all kinds of company data, including up-to-the-minute sales, inventory, receivables, payables, cash, and other information. This computer power makes the meeting a more vivid and vibrant experience full of information that is easy to visualize and absorb. It also means that managers can make quick estimates or projections. For example, managers struggling to increase sluggish sales can immediately look at sales figures product by product, region by region, month by month, or any other way they would like. Instead of relying on past figures, they can work with the most recent information available anywhere within the company.

Going one step further, this electronic meeting approach within a GDSS operating mode can also be utilized effectively by managers to generate new ideas, products, solutions and the like. Employing MindLink (one of the idea generators to be presented in the next chapter), for example, managers can explore new directions that do not come from such analysis as just described. Rather, managers get involved in a five-stage process for creative-oriented problem solving.

In stage 1, there is *a statement and an understanding of the problem*. MindLink's trigger system helps managers gain new perspectives on tough and fuzzy problems. *Wishing* is stage 2, in which the program invites managers to expand the possible solutions open to them through wishing for various outcomes. The triggers help out again by assisting them to generate fresh and surprising perspectives on the range of possible outcomes. State 3 is *idea generation*. After choosing one of the outcomes the managers created, the program now helps them generate the ideas they need to achieve that outcome. The triggers in this portion of the program help them generate more and more speculative ideas for as long as needed. The permutations of idea-generating triggers number many hundreds, each one capable of helping the brain trigger one or more fresh ideas. Managers only quit when they have such an excellent idea that there is no need to go any further.

Stage 4 is, in essence, *solution development*. Often a great idea still has some flaws in it, like an imperfect diamond. It would be a crime to throw it away. Now, managers turn to the development process designed into this part of the program. Key flaws are itemized and, one by one, overcome with the same thinking power the managers used already in the program. Triggers here are designed to help them get this kind of thinking. Finally, this part of the program leads the managers right through to developing an action plan for solving the problem. In the last stage, the focus is on *solution formats*. The crowning touch in coming up with a victorious answer is embellishing on all the little details and wrapping it all up in a clear and attractive report. The predesigned formats in MindLink prod the managers to remember and include the relevant details for many of the standard kinds of problems and opportunities, from new products and businesses to strategies and papers. Also, book outlines and book reports are included. These stages are comparable to the essential stages set forth in figure 5.1 for an idea-processing system.

In the next chapter, other creative computer software—like MindLink—is presented. Special emphasis is placed on idea generators in terms of their current state of the art. IdeaFisher 4.0 will be the final one explored since it will be featured in future chapters. At this point, it is appropriate to say that newer types of management information systems are now encompassing elements of creativity for strategic thinking and decision making.

SUMMARY

The initial part of the chapter focused on current information systems, that is, real-time MIS and distributed MIS, that have the potential to offer some creative solutions to a company's information-processing problems, and presented an exposition of their basic elements. Next, current successful management information systems that perform basic information-processing activities efficiently were explored for three companies. This background set the stage of the newer and latest MISs found next in this chapter.

In the second half, newer approaches to management information systems that are useful to managers for practicing creativity were presented. More specifically, this part focused on electronic systems within and outside a company, along with reference to individually and group-oriented decision support systems and executive information systems. Next, the latest directions in MIS were treated, namely, expert systems and neural networks, with special emphasis on idea-processing systems. It should be recognized that all of the management information systems discussed in this chapter represent continuing developments in the ever-evolving state of the MIS art. It may well be that many of these systems will be replaced by newer ones that will help the manager to utilize his or her creativity to the fullest.

NOTES

1. Robert J. Thierauf, *Systems Analysis and Design of Real-Time Management Information Systems* (Englewood Cliffs, N.J.: Prentice-Hall, 1975).

2. Robert J. Thierauf, *Distributed Processing Systems* (Englewood Cliffs, N.J.: Prentice-Hall, 1978).

3. Mark Breibart, "Business Imperatives," *Computerworld Focus on Integration*, June 5, 1989, p. 26.

4. Ibid., p. 27.

5. Ibid., pp. 27–28.

6. Robert J. Thierauf, *Electronic Data Interchange in Finance and Accounting* (Westport, Conn.: Quorum Books, 1990).

7. Robert J. Thierauf, *Image Processing Systems for Business: A Guide for MIS Professionals and End Users* (Westport, Conn.: Quorum Books, 1992).

8. Robert J. Thierauf, *Decision Support Systems for Effective Planning and Control: A Case Study Approach* (Englewood Cliffs, N.J.: Prentice-Hall, 1982); and *User-oriented Decision Support Systems: Accent on Problem Finding* (Englewood Cliffs, NJ.: Prentice-Hall, 1988).

9. Robert J. Thierauf, *Group Decision Support Systems for Effective Decision Making: A Guide for MIS Professionals and End Users* (Westport, Conn.: Quorum Books, 1990).

10. Robert J. Thierauf, *Executive Information Systems: A Guide for Senior Management and MIS Professionals* (Westport, Conn.: Quorum Books, 1991).

11. Robert J. Thierauf, *Expert Systems in Finance and Accounting* (Westport, Conn.: Quorum Books, 1990).

12. Franco Vilaliano, "Expert Systems and Neural Networks," *Digital Review*, June 10, 1991, p. 15.

6

Creativity Assisted by Computer Hardware and Software

ISSUES EXPLORED

- To explore hardware devices useful in creative problem solving for a typical manager working alone or in a group
- To survey research that indicates that employee creativity is increased by utilizing creative computer software
- To set forth a good approach for the typical manager to employ before using creative computer software
- To classify creative computer software available currently
- To show why idea generators are generally preferred over idea organizers and idea networking for a group of managers involved in developing new ideas

OUTLINE

Relationship of the Creative Manager to Computer Hardware
Hardware Useful to the Creative Manager
   Personal Computers (Microcomputers)
   Micros in Local Area Networks
   Computer CRT Terminals
   Management Workstations
   Personal Computer Visual Systems
   Management Control Centers
   Video Teleconferencing
Relationship of Computer Hardware to Software to Assist in the Creative Process
Software Useful to Improve Managerial Creativity
   Research to Determine the Effect of Using Software to Improve Creativity
   Results of Research on Using Software to Improve Creativity

When managers are making business decisions, typically it is more difficult for them to visualize all possible options than it is to select the most attractive choice from that list. Psychological research shows that people tend to anchor their thoughts early in the problem-solving process, using their first ideas as a starting point from which other ideas arise. Hence solutions are often variations on a central theme rather than genuinely different options. With the added pressure of problem solving under tight time constraints, coming up with new ideas can often be a frustrating process.

Although computers are unable to suggest new ideas on their own, they are free from a human's subjectivity and can aid the human decision maker in systematically exploring a broader range of possibilities. Although these programs are easy to learn, each demands that managers adapt their work styles to fit the program's interpretation of the idea-generation process. These products can help managers organize random or related thoughts; they cannot create new ideas. It is from this perspective that computer hardware and software are presented in this chapter.

RELATIONSHIP OF THE CREATIVE MANAGER TO COMPUTER HARDWARE

Today, some managers have received some type of computer training to assist them in using a PC or a CRT terminal connected to a computer mainframe. Because many managers are still not familiar or comfortable with using computers, a suggested way to get started is using a personal information manager (PIM). Such PIM software is given in the section "Getting Started on Using the Computer on a Day-to-Day Basis." This starting approach provides a natural tie-in for the manager to employ creative computer software when deemed necessary, that is, daily or periodically.

In contrast, future managers will be "computer literate" since computers will have been incorporated into their training, whether it be on a formal or an informal basis. Hence managers of the next century are already well into their careers and are using computer systems as an integral part of their daily activities. During the next decade, these managers will participate in the development of information systems of unparalleled creativity and flexibility that are needed to compete in the global marketplace. These systems will be built upon high-capacity networks, very powerful workstations, and creative software designed for use on a wide variety of computers.

Driving this demand for this set of technologies are managers facing the hard facts of business: demands for greater productivity, the need to meet global competition, and the desire to exploit the capital investments already made in information technology. Inasmuch as computer technology has reached a new stage in the wake of the personal computer revolution of the past decade, it makes possible the capability to meet the information-processing needs of an organization as well as to respond to the desire of managers to share applications and data easily. What is really interesting is that many managers are driving the demand for these systems because they perceive an opportunity to employ computer creativity techniques that provide a competitive advantage for their organizations.

Personal computers, local and global networks, and creative computer software, which are the tools and the foundation of idea-processing systems, cannot be understood in isolation; they depend on each other to an unprecedented degree. Nor can the task of evaluating the potential organization effects of their adoption be ignored. From new product opportunities to improved physical distribution, managers will find themselves dealing with issues addressed by changes in the use of information technology, especially idea-processing systems.

The way the complex of personal computers, networks, and software interacts with an organization—its objectives, its methods, and the work styles of its managers and employees—promises to be as significant to the next century as the assembly line was to this one. Call it what you will: new-wave creative computing, manager-oriented networked computing, manager workgroup computing, manager cooperative processing, or integrated managerial corporate computing —the name is not as important as the capability of managers utilizing their creativity to outmaneuver their competitors, thereby improving the company's net profits over the short and long terms.

HARDWARE USEFUL TO THE CREATIVE MANAGER

When one is considering hardware useful to the creative manager, it is essential that it be tailored to meet the manager's needs. The manager must always come first, and the needs for one or more managers must be defined before the hardware can be selected. The computer hardware needed consists of four basic components: (1) input data-entry devices, whereby the manager can enter, verify, and update data as desired; (2) the central processing unit (CPU), which controls the other computer system components; (3) data storage files, which hold business information useful for the manager; and (4) output devices, which provide a visual or a permanent record for the manager of the desired information. Thus, depending on a manager's needs, hardware generally consists of an input data-entry device, a central processing unit, one or more data storage units, and a visual output device and/or a printer along with other peripheral devices found in a typical computerized environment. In the material to follow, accent will be placed on hardware that is typically found in a creative computing environment whether the manager is operating alone or as part of a group. Such hardware includes personal computers (microcomputers), micros in local area networks, computer CRT terminals, management workstations, personal computer visual systems, management control centers, and video teleconferencing. It should be noted that this material is supplementary to that found in the previous chapter on electronic decision rooms, which will not be repeated again. Hence electronic decision rooms represent a viable alternative for a number of managers and their staffs working together in a productive creative environment.

Personal Computers (Microcomputers)

Personal computers (microcomputers) have made tremendous inroads not only in the home market, but also in the business sector for processing daily business transactions. In the recent past, the most popular of all PCs was the IBM Personal Computer (which was introduced in 1981), for which a number of programs are still available, such as the Personal Decision Series (PDS). The six programs in this series can be bought individually, depending on the executive's needs. The first, Data Edition, is a flexible data-base manager that organizes information and takes it from a variety of sources. When the Host Attachment Edition is used, valuable information from an inside source, the central computer, can be obtained without having to rekey it. By adding PLAN+, the user can answer "what-if" questions with a financial model or spreadsheet that has the capability to remember how the answers were arrived at. Numbers can be transformed into different shapes, sizes, and colors by using GRAPHS. Documents can be customized by making layout and type style decisions with REPORT+. Finally, WORDS helps the user with an easy-to-learn word-processing system.

In 1987, IBM announced its new line of personal computers, called the IBM Personal System/2. Also announced in this same year was the Macintosh II computer from Apple. Not only did both vendors introduce a wide range of models, but also both included a whole host of micro software for users. In addition to a wide range of software packages that cover every facet of a typical business organization from a vast number of vendors, several creative computer software packages have been developed and marketed. Basically, this is the subject matter found in the second half of this chapter. Hence discussion of this software will be left until that time.

Later developments of personal computers that go beyond the traditional desktop market include laptop PCs, which are lightweight and can be carried by users for field use as well as business trips. Although this PC development assists in enlarging the number of PCs, there are two other innovations (both announced in 1991) that will have a great impact on extending the manager's ability to use PCs. First, pen-based computers—small tabletlike devices with electronic pens—use a paper and pen metaphor with no cursor, providing users with more familiar and more direct input control. Not only are these tablets extremely portable, but many observers think that they will change the way managers use information. Another factor expected to propel the market forward is a relatively short learning curve for pen-based systems. The selling and training cycle for stylus systems is considerably faster than that for conventional keyboard PCs.

The result, according to Forrester Research, Inc., a market research firm (Cambridge, Massachusetts), is that pen-based computing could be the next mass market for the computer industry. Surveys have predicted from 7 million to 54 million potential customers for the technology in the near future. With its attendant revenue potential, the pen-based market is attracting all kinds of established vendors, including IBM, NCR Corporation, Microsoft Corporation, Lotus Development Corporation, Apple Computer, Sony Corporation, and Tandy Corporation, as well as substantial investment capital directed at start-up companies such as Go Corporation, Slate Corporation, Pensoft, Pen Pal, and Momenta.[1]

Second, the 95LX, nicknamed Jaguar, is a leading-edge palmtop computer from Hewlett-Packard. It weighs just eleven ounces and takes up no more space than two checkbooks glued back to back. Yet it has Lotus 1-2-3 built in, has as much memory as many desktop computers, is comparable with a PC/XT in its capability, and has a sixteen-line, forty-character screen, all for a suggested retail price of $699. Other built-in software includes H-P's latest business calculator and the most popular features of pocket organizers: appointment book, phone list, stopwatch, currency converter, and so forth. Some analysts are calling this a breakthrough product that will make palmtops, now regarded mainly as gimmicks, seriously useful in business. As the author sees it, they could also be useful to store ideas as they come to the manager's mind.

Micros in Local Area Networks

From a broadened perspective, PCs can be incorporated into a work group. This means that five to twenty managers can benefit from microcomputer-based shared resources as well a from person-to-person communications. This, of course, is in addition to the fact that PCs serve as an individual productivity tool. Thus this is where local area networks (LANs) come into play. Essentially, linkage of PCs in a LAN means improved communications and decision making among managers in a work group. The LAN permits immediate person-to-person communication among managers who are in frequent contact with each other. As will be seen later in this chapter, many creative software packages require that participants utilize a local area network.

Although the current focus is on PCs physically linked to one another in some type of LAN environment, the future emphasis is on wireless LANs whereby local area networks can be changed at will. But more important, computer vendors envision a future of ultraportable communications devices for office, home, and everywhere in between. Pen-based computer manufacturers are planning for wireless links, and consumer electronic giants, along with a few Silicon Valley start-ups, are prototyping new wireless information appliances. Armed with a suitably equipped device, business travelers could stay in constant contact with their offices while on the road, instantaneously exchanging information such a product order, memos, and phone messages along with new ideas that come from being out in the field.

Other wireless devices will be quite different, resembling neither computer nor telephone. For example, researchers at Xerox's Palo Alto, California, Research Center have been experimenting with "active badges"—identification tags that transmit an infrared signal, thereby allowing a computer to track wearers from office to office. Transportation agencies envision wireless systems built into cars for toll collection and even traffic control. Only one detail stands between vision and wireless reality: the lack of space in the crowded commercial radio spectrum. The pinch is already felt by annoyed cellular telephone owners who are discovering a dial tone to be a scarce resource in crowded urban areas.

Nevertheless, wireless researchers are finding new ways to pack more signals into a given space of the radio spectrum without interference. For example, code division multiple access (CDMA) is a scheme theoretically capable of delivering a twenty-fold capacity increase over that of current cellular telephone systems. From this discussion, it is clear that newer computer devices with LANs allow more information and ideas on products and services from field personnel who normally are not a part of the creative process. The end result should be more in-depth ideas to help managers solving pressing problems facing their organizations.[2]

Computer CRT Terminals

While the personal computer represents the low end of the computer hierarchy, the computer mainframe represents the high end. But managers may need a system that fits between these two—something that bridges the gap between personal and corporate computing. That system is the departmental computer. A departmental computer system can be based on a computer mainframe or a minicomputer, depending on a company's organization structure. Generally, it utilizes CRT terminals as its principal means of inputting and retrieving data from the system.

As with personal computers, there are a number of computer mainframe vendors. However, the most notable ones currently are IBM, DEC, Unisys, NCR, Cray, and Amdahl. For these vendors, ongoing technological advances in computer systems have blurred the distinctions that traditionally separated these different classes of computers. A typical computer mainframe at this middle level is the IBM 9370. The IBM 9370 brings mainframe performance in a supermini package. Its compactness, air cooling, single-phase power, and quiet operation allow users to put computing power where needed. This IBM computer mainframe can connect a number of its CRT terminals to almost any interface, network, or protocol. It is an excellent solution, offering low-priced computing, for work groups of managers and departments.

An important advantage of these departmental systems is that they complement the ways in which managers and their staffs in organizations work. Departments are not closed, rigidly defined entities, but are flexible work groups whose makeup and responsibilities shift. A department is often dependent on work that was initially done by a different department and that must be passed on to yet another department. Because managers often work in teams or departments, it is important that they are not isolated from the mainstream of the company in the data or applications they use. Typically, 9370-based departmental systems allow groups to be part of a companywide information network. In addition to bringing individual users into the corporate computing mainstream via their CRT terminals, 9370-based departmental systems provide a way for departments to communicate easily and quickly with one another. For example, PC users in marketing can funnel requests for data through their departmental 9370 to the inventory department, which uses CRT terminals connected to a different departmental 9370. Marketing can then incorporate the inventory department's data into its own applications. Next, the marketing department can upload the information to the corporate mainframe. Financial planners can access that data via their departmental 9370 to answer important questions. This interaction takes advantage of a departmental 9370's ability to customize applications for each department.

Management Workstations

The interface between the manager and the computer can also take place via some type of management workstation. Made possible by the continuing improvements in processing, storage, and communications, a management workstation is designed to support all or most of the information-handling needs of a typical manager. It integrates data, text, and image handling currently supported by separate devices such as telephones, calculators, typewriters, and copiers. Modular in design, it incorporates the necessary hardware and software features to satisfy varying end-user requirements for information storage and retrieval, idea processing, text preparation, mathematical and statistical calculations, and interfaces to internal and external communication systems.

The hardware necessary to provide these capabilities consists of a variety of separate components: an output display (for soft copy), a mini- or microprocessor (for processing), internal storage (for applications and operating software), a printer or access to a conveniently located shared printer (for hard copy), a three-dimensional graphics output capability (for soft or hard copy), communications capability with a computer and data base (for accessing and storing important data), and the ability to use mathematical and statistical models (for solving simple to complex problems). The hardware components of a typical multifunction management control station, then, are adequate to meet the requirements of a manager for an idea-processing mode.

Personal Computer Visual Systems

An alternative approach to management workstations and personal computers is the personal computer visual system. In this system, in addition to each personal computer working with the same information, there is a PC projector that displays the results, which are also shown on the individuals' screens. In effect, the PC visual system will reproduce results on a screen for easier viewing by the entire group. Thus the group leader has more control over the issues and problems being solved.

A typical PC visual system is shown in figure 6.1. This Visualon Multi-Purpose Work Station (Model UCS500) System is a complete instruction/presentation support system. Not only is there provision for an IBM or Apple microcomputer, but also there is a viewgraph PC projector to present visual output for all to see in some detail. As shown, participants have no hard-copy devices attached to their PCs. Therefore, the Visualon system has provision for printing hard-copy output as the meeting progresses so that important items discussed are documented for future reference. The cost is very low, approximately $1,000 for the PC projector system (without the personal computers). However, other costs must be added for the system's stand and for the printer. Overall, the investment is very modest for an idea-processing mode where the group leader and the participants can interact in a computerized mode.

Management Control Centers

When the support of managerial decision making is viewed from a very broad perspective, there is generally need to go beyond the hardware presented above. In a management control center, large display screens are utilized to show various types of planning and control information in graphic form to a group of managers and their staffs (figure 6.2). Whether this environment to support decision making is called by another name, such as a decision support room or a management war room, is purely academic. Its importance lies in its ability to call up a wide

Figure 6.1
A Typical Personal Computer Visual System

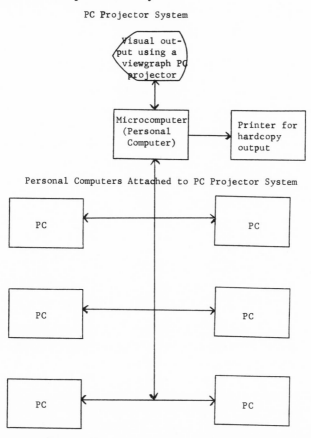

range of management information. Instead of searching manual files and cluttering up the office with paperwork, managers and their staffs can obtain the required information immediately in a conference-room environment. They can, for example, retrieve a host of strategic and operational planning information from the data base and present this information as is or combine it with other information for graphic display. Also, they can obtain sales figures for any time period together with comparable figures for previous periods. Current production schedules, status of back orders, profit analysis by periods and products, equipment utilization, and divisional performance factors are other types of information that are available. In a similar manner, managers can jointly explore ideas and their resulting opportunities that have a great impact on the organization today and tomorrow. From this latter perspective, management control centers are like electronic decision rooms (as set forth in the previous chapter). They were originally built to support various types of management information systems.

Figure 6.2
A Typical Management Control Center Helpful to Managers and Their Staffs for Supporting Decisions and Developing New Ideas

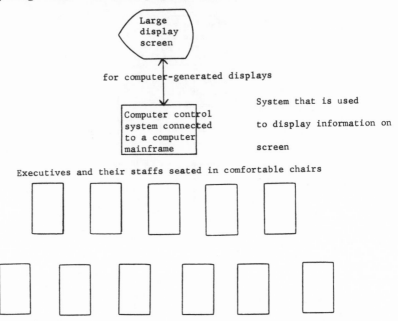

Because data are always current, accurate, and in a form well suited for fast evaluation, graphs, charts, indexes, and the like on the large display screen are employed to simplify and dramatize the information, thereby increasing the managers' understanding of current and upcoming organizational activities. Pages and pages of tabular information can be condensed into one projected picture. Exception reporting can reduce the amount of data for possible viewing. The use of computer-generated displays further reduces the need for paper reporting. The speed and simplification of reporting allow managers considerable time in evaluating their decisions.

Typical management control centers are designed to assist managers at all levels. They can focus on operational and tactical applications, helpful to meet the needs of lower and middle management, respectively, for problem solving and idea generation in the short run. However, they are quite useful to top management and their corporate planning staffs in the long run for idea generation in a problem-finding environment. Likewise, they are helpful to support planning decisions—evaluating new products over their life cycles, allocating available factory capacity in the most efficient manner throughout the organization, and setting long-range plans and objectives for the organization. The use of management control centers, then, allows managers and their staffs to get a handle on present and future operations. Managers from the lowest level to the highest level can put their heads together and generate ideas in the form of important opportunities for the organization. In turn, appropriate plans, strategies, programs, and policies to support these opportunities can be developed for implementation.

Video Teleconferencing

Another hardware approach for effective idea processing is video teleconferencing, which is available for business units that are widely dispersed geographically. Although video teleconferencing is basically hardware, it is designed to be used as a business tool to assist in overseeing dispersed operations. Typically, the meeting room is equipped for audiovisual demonstrations in addition to transmitting and receiving color TV images. Likewise, slides, transparencies, and hard copy can be transmitted. The users can draw on a blackboard or use charts. The meeting can even be recorded on videotape. Users can make a complete presentation on any subject that is appropriate for the situation, even the demonstration of new products and packaging.

In a video teleconferencing environment, there can be an exchange of ideas that involves managers at distant locations. The accent may be on a brainstorming session to seek new ideas on specific issues. From this perspective, the interaction of managers and their support staffs at distant points from one another may signal the need to develop specific ideas covering products and/or services. At the next video teleconferencing meeting, a presentation can be made that focuses on potential answers to the ideas posed in the previous meeting.

Currently, several vendors (and some users) are offering public rooms or sharing their private rooms with others. The public-room concept, pioneered by AT&T, is offered under the name of Picturephone Meeting Service (PMS). (AT&T's original Picturephone service began in the early 1970s). Offered from a number of public rooms, PMS can be rented on an hourly basis. Currently, the service is available in small- to large-sized cities. Besides its public PMS, AT&T also installs private rooms that are compatible with the public ones. For instance, AT&T works cooperatively with such companies as Hilton Hotels, Inc., and the World Trade Center in Boston to provide public videoconferencing rooms, and US Sprint supplies for-hire videoconferencing rooms for companies that are not ready to install their own facilities.

Many large corporations are now making use of private broadcasts by satellite directly into their own facilities or into hotel meeting facilities to deliver corporate communications or training to employees. As they have gained experience with the use of corporate video, companies have installed their own private networks of satellite receiver dishes located at their corporate facilities that enable employees to watch regularly scheduled company programs. Hewlett-Packard, Tandem Computers, IBM, Kodak, Merrill Lynch, J. C. Penney, TRW, and General Motors are examples of major corporations with their own video networks.

RELATIONSHIP OF COMPUTER HARDWARE TO
SOFTWARE TO ASSIST IN THE CREATIVE PROCESS

As can be seen from the preceding discussion there are a number of hardware approaches that can be used by the manager working alone or in groups when involved in the creative process. As indicated previously, this discussion also ties in with that in the previous chapter on electronic decision rooms. The variety of hardware operating modes was presented as a background for the remainder of the chapter. Not all creative software packages are designed for a manager operating alone on a PC. Rather, these software packages cover a wide range of hardware operating environments for one manager or a group of managers and their staffs. It is expected that there will be need for newer hardware environments as more advanced creative software is introduced in the workplace. Hence managers should keep an open mind so that their creative software packages can be upgraded in an appropriate computer hardware environment.

SOFTWARE USEFUL TO IMPROVE MANAGERIAL
CREATIVITY

Creative computer techniques (i.e., tools) have emerged with the promise of enabling decision makers to develop better and more creative solutions to problems they face in an individual or a group DSS operating mode. There are two assumptions underlying this concept. First, individuals can be helped to be more creative, and second, properly designed software can provide this help. Creativity research supports the first assumption and has been the basis of discussion in the prior chapters of this text. An experiment that explores the second assumption is discussed below and explored in more depth in part IV of this text.

When one is faced with a problem, there is a natural tendency to choose the first solution that comes to mind. Furthermore, fear of failure and other mental blocks may inhibit creativity in individuals. Two perspectives in the design of creativity-enhancing decision support systems are (1) a model of the creative process and (2) a component model of creativity. The creative process model consists of the following five stages. It begins with a problem or task presentation, which may be internally stimulated (found by the individual) or externally stimulated (presented to the individual). The next stage is one of preparation, where the individual builds or recalls information relevant to the task at hand. Next, alternatives are produced in the response-generation stage. This is followed by response validation, where various alternatives are evaluated. Finally, the process may terminate with a successful outcome, the process may terminate in failure with no acceptable solution, or the individual may conclude that some (but not sufficient) progress has been made and return to a previous stage in the model.

In the component model of creativity, the individual has (1) domain-relevant skills, (2) creativity-relevant skills, and (3) task motivation. For the first component, the domain-specific knowledge of an individual is directly related to the level of creativity. Creativity-relevant skills, the second component, aid creative thinking and problem solving. These skills include divergent thinking, which refers to the preparation of a variety of alternative solutions, and delayed judgment, which consists of suspending critical evaluation of ideas until a significant amount of "free" thinking has been done. The third component, task motivation, determines the gap between what an individual can and will do.

Generally, a creativity-enhancing DSS is quite different from traditional DSSs. A creativity-enhancing DSS is process oriented, provides an environment that facilitates the use of a number of creativity-enhancing skills, and can be applied to any problem context. Appropriate guidelines for designing creativity-enhancing DSSs are as follows:

- The system should allow users to stop, store work sessions in process, and then resume work later.
- The system should provide feedback as well as positive, meaningful, helpful, and encouraging responses to increase task motivation.
- A full range of qualitative as well an quantitative decision aids should be available to the users.
- The system should be easy to use and conceptually challenging.
- The system should provide an enjoyable computing environment.

In contrast, a traditional DSS is very structure oriented and typically does not encourage the use of individuals' creativity faculties. Accent is on solving problems that utilize the problem-solving process enumerated in chapter 4.

Research to Determine the Effect of Using Software to Improve Creativity

Essentially, the experiment described here addressed the question "Can software influence creativity?" and was directed at two hypotheses. The first hypothesis was that a user of a creativity-enhancing, individually oriented DSS will adopt a multiple-step decision process, whereas a user of no software will adopt a single-step decision process. The second hypothesis was that the user of a creativity-enhancing, individually oriented DSS will generate higher levels of creative responses than the user of no software. The first hypothesis focused on the relationship between the user of a creativity-enhancing, individually oriented DSS and the decision-making process. The second hypothesis addressed the relationship between the use of a creativity-enhancing, individually oriented DSS and the creativity of responses. The software package chosen for the experiment was Consultant. (This software package is discussed later in this chapter.) This package was designed specifically from a creativity-enhancing perspective, includes both quantitative and qualitative thinking aids, and is easy to learn and use. Two of six different process models offered by Consultant were used in the experiment.

The Version 1 process looks backward for causes and depth of understanding, while Version 2 looks ahead for practical solutions. The independent variable in this experiment was the level of software used: Version 1, Version 2, or no software. The two dependent variables were the decision-making process employed and the creativity of responses.

The subjects for the experiment were twelve junior members of the auditing group of one of the largest accounting firms. Most subjects were in their early to mid-twenties, had worked with the accounting firm for an average of two and one-half years, and had a bachelor's degree in accounting. Each subject addressed two tasks, a business application and a public-policy application, yielding twenty-four observations. These tasks were pretested for the following requirements: scenarios were needed that required the making of nontrivial decisions, the tasks had to be complex enough to be addressed by a broad range of possible solutions, they had to be poorly structured with no obvious right or wrong solution, and the tasks had to be addressable in a reasonable time without automated assistance.

Measurement procedures for the decision-making process consisted of transcripts of individual think-aloud protocols recorded during the completion of each task, as well as the saved on-line protocols for those individuals using software. The results were characterized as either single step or multiple step, with the expectation that individuals who used software would be influenced to use multiple steps, while those who did not use software would tend to adopt a single-step process. Experts, assumed to have consistent internal definitions of what constitutes creativity, used their own subjective definitions to assess the creativity of the subjects' responses. The baseline creativity measurement did not show any statistically significant differences. Thus differences in the creativity of responses could not be attributed to individual differences in creative aptitude.

It is worth noting that creativity was never mentioned at any time before, during, or after the experiment. The average time to complete a single task for each subject group was twenty minutes for subjects using Version 1 of Consultant, sixteen minutes for those using Version 2 of Consultant, and four minutes for those subjects not using any type of software. Version 1, which produced the most creative solutions, took the most time. Furthermore, both groups that used software took more time to complete the tasks than the group that did not use software.

Results of Research on Using Software to Improve Creativity

For the first hypothesis, research results showed that the decision process for all subjects using software consisted of multiple steps. For subjects not using software, the decision processes of five subjects were classified as single step and of three as multiple step. Using Fisher's Exact Test, significant differences in the decision processes of subjects using either version of the software and subjects using no software were found. Further research is needed to better understand whether the decision-making process is influenced by the actual capabilities of the decision support system or just by the knowledge that such a model exists. The second hypothesis, which focused on the creativity of responses using a creativity-enhancing, individually oriented DSS, resulted in a statistically significant difference between the three subject groups. The group using Version 1 of Consultant produced more creative responses than either of the other groups, while, surprisingly, the group using Version 2 of the software actually produced less creative responses than the group using no software. These results show that software environments can both enhance and inhibit desired outcomes.

Although the final results can be termed favorable to using software to enhance creativity, there are a number of other factors to take into consideration. First, the results must be interpreted within the framework of how the task was presented to the subjects. Second, the sample was fairly small and homogenous. The experiment should be repeated with a larger number of subjects with different backgrounds. Third, there was no time limit imposed. Forth, the business application task was more familiar to the subjects than the public-policy application. The research results of this experiment indicate that it is difficult to state exactly what a creativity-enhancing DSS for an individual really is. Furthermore, in understanding its effect, the decision support system cannot be looked at in isolation, but must be looked at in the context of the user-DSS interaction. This research provides a basis for more extensive research in understanding the link between creativity and software.[3]

GETTING STARTED ON USING THE COMPUTER ON A DAY-TO-DAY BASIS

Before a typical manager can feel at home using creative computer software on a day-to-day basis, it would be helpful for the individual to get started first on an easy-to-use software package. This can take several directions today. However, because a manager has a schedule that varies from hour to hour and day to day, it would be advisable to employ a personal information manager (PIM) software package. This type of software is essentially a daily scheduler with alarms for appointments, a dialer and phone log, and an address book.

Typical Personal Information Managers

Since managers have strong opinions about overseeing their personal information, some demand accessibility above all else. They want a PIM that allows them to get in and out quickly when they want to enter an appointment or phone number on the fly. Others demand features and power-user extras such as the capability of automatically assigning entered data or performing complex, cross-module searches. Because of different views on handling a manager's personal information, PIM packages vary somewhat from each other. Current PIMs that focus on appointment scheduling, task tracking, and note management include Agenda, Current, Instant Recall, PackRat, SideKick, and Who-What-When.

What all of these PIM software packages have in common is that they are designed to make it easier for managers to keep track of the day-to-day flood of information, whether names and phone numbers, appointments, memos, or project dates. They approach their tasks in a surprising variety of ways. Some programs, such as Instant Recall, emphasize calendar-based appointment and task scheduling. Others, such as Agenda, do not focus quite as heavily on calendaring as on managing and allowing managers to manipulate individual data items. For managers, it is an unusually subjective process to find which program's approach best suits their ways of working. Overall, Agenda and Current are the most customizable. If the manager wants to customize and wants a Windows program, Current is a good choice. However, if the manager is more often dealing with random text than data for field entry, Agenda is a good choice. If scheduling is a priority, Instant Recall and SideKick are the best all-around choices. If the manager wants a Windows scheduler, PackRat is probably the strongest. Also, Who-What-When makes handling multiple schedules easy.

CLASSIFICATION OF CREATIVE COMPUTER SOFTWARE

Once the manager has a day-to-day familiarity with computers using a PIM or otherwise, he or she is now in a position to utilize creative computer software. Because creative computer software is not all the same, it would be helpful at the outset to classify these software packages. Essentially, there are four levels, although the last level is in the developmental stage. At the first level, the computer software is used to organize ideas that have already been developed by managers working on a problem. In turn, the logical hierarchy of ideas is useful to managers for mirroring back their thoughts, thereby facilitating their further development. As such, this software can be labeled *idea organizers*.

At the second level, the focus is on the development of ideas at remote locations. Because personnel are limited by their remoteness from one another, they must utilize some form of networking to tie participants together. Many times, the exchange of ideas is not performed on a real-time or now basis. Rather, the exchange takes place over an extended period of time, say, several weeks. In such cases, participants can supply specific ideas or modify and extend any idea presented. Since this level is similar to checklists, this level of support provides orientation on a problem, calls attention to relevant problem aspects, and provides a format to change ideas presented to date to solve the problem. Typically, many managers and staff members are involved at this second level. An appropriate name for this type of creative computer software is *idea networking*. It should be noted that newer software at this level allows participants to develop ideas interactively in real time versus over a period of time.

The third level provides a framework for developing ideas. Such a framework supports an active exchange of ideas among participants at one location. The software is the centerpiece of the exchange of ideas; that is, the software suggests certain inputs from the participants, captures their responses using a notepad to store suggested ideas to solve the problem, and then provides output based upon the problem studied. From this perspective, the computer software assists in helping participants generate ideas. The participants remain the initiators of the problem to be studied as well as the final judges of what ideas can be retained and developed in more detail. An appropriate name for this level is *idea generators*, which are designed to assist the managers and their staffs to do things better. Essentially, the computer software generates and displays ideas for consideration by the participants for associating, comparing, and synthesizing elements of the problem. In turn, these elements are critical in developing creative ideas to solve the problem.

At the fourth level, which is currently under development, the computer software allows the participants to get inside the ideas presented and test them within a three-dimensional framework for solving the problem under study. By using virtual reality (see chapter 1), a manager, for example, could test out his or her ideas in a virtual world before recommending them as a solution. Hence not only does the computer software generate and display ideas for the individual's consideration (as at the third level), but also it takes the individual through test runs to determine the real feasibility of those ideas. A label that would be appropriate is *virtual idea generators*. It is expected that in the twenty-first century, virtual idea generators will be commonplace for developing new product opportunities as well as solving future problems in a problem-finding environment.

Since computer software is readily available currently for the first three levels only, they are treated below. However, as just indicated, reference can be made to the end of the first chapter for virtual reality and current software available.

IDEA ORGANIZERS

A number of software packages have emerged that focus on improving the organization of ideas and related matters for managers and their staff members who are tired of manually creating and modifying flowcharts. These flowchart packages enable users to generate quickly a large number of decision charts, organization charts, and related business diagrams, including the capability of making fast modifications when new information becomes available. Some of these software packages are discussed below. It should be noted that this class of software can be useful in conjunction with brainstorming for developing ideas and true idea generators.

Idea Tree

Although Idea Tree 2.0 from Mountain House Publishing Inc. is helpful for organizing plans, this software product helps users visually develop ideas the way they think. Basically, users enter ideas into "idea boxes." These boxes are appended to a "root" idea that forms an upside-down hierarchical "idea tree." Each idea is put into an idea box that is connected to other idea boxes to form the components of the tree's branches. Idea boxes can contain as many as sixty characters, of which forty-five characters are displayed on-screen. With a text editor, notes can be appended to each idea box.

An example of Idea Tree 2.0 is shown in figure 6.3. In the first screen, an overview of the steps involved in a new product launch is given. The second screen centers on ideas for market and product research. In the third and fourth screens, a listing of ideas has been developed centering on identifying the target market audience. It should be noted that the final two screens relate back to the first screen, that is, "identify target market audience." This succession of screens, then, contains helpful ideas about a new product launch. Another example of Idea Tree 2.0 is given in a future chapter.

As can be seen from this example, Idea Tree 2.0 is actually an idea outliner or organizer. Even though Idea Tree's interface has command keys, moving idea boxes around to reorganize ideas can be cumbersome at times because people think of ideas much faster than they can create, edit, and organize the little boxes. Typically, a large number of ideas can be placed at any level of an idea tree. Also, any idea or branch of an idea can be copied, deleted, saved as a new tree, or moved to another position in the current tree. To view an idea tree, users can scroll Idea Tree's display right, left, up, and down. However, it can be difficult to work with ideas or their attached notes if, as is the case with large trees, they are not visible on the computer's display. At the end of an outlining session on ideas, idea trees can be viewed or printed out in an outline format that is especially helpful for displaying and printing large idea trees.

Criterium

An important task for managers is choosing among several good alternatives. Additionally, their hardest task is defending their choices, especially to their superiors. Criterium from Sygenex, Inc., makes both tasks easier. It helps weight criteria according to preferences, assigns numerical scores to even the most subjective evaluations, and compares those scores to determine the best choice. It also lets managers play "what if" with the results, which is the most constructive way to respond to critics. To convince others that their alternatives are not flawed, managers can determine preferences that must be changed for their choices to prevail.

Criterium uses the decision-hierarchy metaphor to help users weigh the factors involved in making a decision, letting them build a hierarchy of criteria based on one-to-one comparisons. Factors can be weighted with numerical values, verbal descriptions, or by using a graphical sliding-scale indicator. Users in marketing, human resources, and product development have noted that reports produced by the program are critical to showing clients or management how decision recommendations were reached. With this in mind, Sygenex has enhanced the reports the program produces with Version 1.1.

Figure 6.3
An Example of Developing Ideas for a New Product Launch Using Idea Tree 2.0

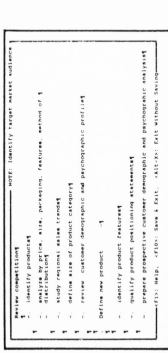
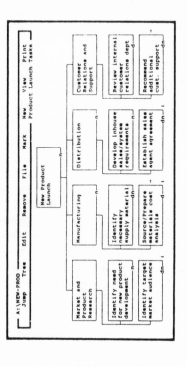

Source: Courtesy of Mountain House Publishing Inc.

Reports can now detail how specific criteria influence the overall recommendation. For example, the new reporting features are important because they allow users to show a customer how specific factors, such as cost of materials, influence the decision to bid on a project or not.

Because each type of comparison in Criterium involves a different way of thinking, users can evaluate criteria in several ways. For example, suppose that a marketing manager is planning a print-advertising campaign and wants to choose the magazine that reaches the largest number of potential customers for the lowest possible cost. He or she must consider each magazine's advertising costs, circulation, editorial content, and reputation. Comparing magazines by cost and circulation is relatively easy, but comparing them by editorial content and reputation is more difficult. Criterium helps a decision maker visualize such comparisons with a bar graph. To indicate subjectively how much better magazine X's reputation is than magazine Y's, for example, just lengthen the bar for magazine X until one obtains the appropriate relationship between the two magazines. Criterium assigns a score to each magazine based on the length of its bar. The user can also make comparisons on scales 1 to 10 or poor to excellent.

Criterium lets the marketing manager build a hierarchy of preferences based on one-to-one comparisons. One can indicate that magazine X's cover is liked more than magazine Y's and that magazine Y's cover is liked more than magazine Z's. If the marketing manager then indicates that magazine Z's cover is preferred over magazine X's, Criterium will warn him or her of the flaw in his or her logic. Because Criterium has the ability to create rules based on combinations of criteria, it can be used to qualify alternatives. For example, the marketing manager may prefer to advertise in a magazine with a circulation of more than 50,000 but will accept a magazine with a smaller circulation if at least 75 percent of the magazine's readership is age thirty or younger. Criterium lets the marketing manager specify these requirements in English. The program flags any alternative that fails to qualify. Screening alternatives this way simplifies the final choice. An example of using Criterium is shown in figure 6.4. Later in the text, another example will be given.

GrandView

GrandView software, which replaces ThinkTank, is an outlining program designed for managers who need an effective planning and organizational tool. Its outlining features are designed to help managers capture and organize their ideas into action-oriented plans. Its Calendar and Category features allow them to delegate, assign, and track tasks, schedules, and priorities. Its writing tools enable managers to create business documents complete with font-enhanced text, customized headers and footers, and a detailed table of contents. With dynamic links to Harvard Graphics and Lotus Freelance Plus, outlines can be transformed into persuasive presentations.

With GrandView, managers can develop a business plan, coordinate an event, or plan a project. It allows managers to enter their ideas in any order. Then, using

Figure 6.4
An Example of Using Criterium to Reach a Target Audience

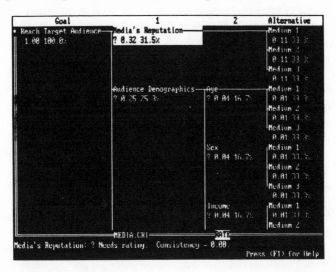

Source: Courtesy of Sygenex, Inc.

the program's intuitive outlining features, they can organize their ideas. Grand-View numbers and aligns the information into a flexible outline format. It will even automatically renumber and realign subheads and headings as items are moved around.

Because of GrandView's spreadsheet-like columns, it is easy to delegate and assign the tasks and responsibilities associated with plans and projects. With up to twenty-two categories per outline, managers can quickly cross-reference their outlines for effective tracking. The Column Layouts feature allows them to group and save column arrangements. One layout can have columns for date and priority, while another has columns for person and department. Layouts can be changed for instant update on the status of plans and projects. Also, there is a built-in calendar that lets managers stay up-to-date with appointments, commitments, and priorities. A date can be chosen from the calendar, and the items due that day are seen. Columns can be added for person, priority, and status that track the tasks delegated to others. In addition, a master calendar can be created for use on a network; that is, team members and department staff can enter their due dates, commitments, and assignments.

MacFlow

MacFlow can be used to create a wide variety of more general business diagrams, including decision trees and project-schedule charts. Early versions of MacFlow used only specialized flowchart symbols that had meaning to programmers but not to average users. However, the latest version of MacFlow (Version 3.5) lets managers create custom symbols, making it a good choice for creating graphic representations of business plans and strategies as well as flowcharts. For example, managers can create a MacFlow diagram by selecting a symbol from the Symbol palette and directing it to the document work space. After the symbol is labeled, the manager can bring in another symbol and connect the two with an arrow. What distinguishes MacFlow from all-purpose drawing programs is its ability to remember which objects arrows are attached to—they remain attached even when their position in the diagram is changed.

MacFlow charts can represent complex interrelationships among objects because the charts are hierarchical. Such charts can expand and contract to show various levels of detail, so the program is well suited to the creation of hypertextlike documents. Top-level chart objects work like buttons in HyperCard. Double-clicking on them reveals the underlying detail. The user can also link external programs to symbols and run them by clicking on the symbols.

MacFlow's background text and graphics are also similar to HyperCard's. The user can paste icons into a chart and create two freestanding text fields per chart—an excellent way to incorporate logos, names of document authors, or sensitivity labels such as "confidential." In addition to color support, MacFlow provides a tool for creating curved lines, shadow differentiation for objects that include underlying notes, and varied line widths and arrowhead selections. Reduced and enlarged views as well as alignment tools make document preparation easy.

With MacFlow, a manager can brainstorm a marketing strategy or document a planning process. In addition, MacFlow can be used to draw a decision tree of ideas or define a marketing program's logic. Overall, it is helpful to managers for optimizing the effectiveness of their charts that pertain to communicating plans and ideas.

Flowchart Software Packages

Two early entrants in the flowchart software market were Clear Software Inc. (Brookline, Massachusetts), maker of DOS-based allCLEAR, and Roy Kore Inc. (San Francisco), purveyor of ABC Flowcharter, a Microsoft Windows product. Both products allow users to construct flowcharts that outline ideas, policies, and procedures much more easily than with pen and paper. Because managers deal with logistical information, they are good candidates for these software products. Also, both have a similar appeal to a wide range of business users, including financial auditors, consultants, and systems analysts. One user is the large accounting firm Arthur Andersen & Company, where the software is on their recommended buy list.

The fact that flowcharting software is attractive to a growing number of users has not been lost on suppliers of more generalized presentation packages. Nor has it stopped users of Lotus Development Corporation's Freelance, Micrografx Inc.'s Charisma, Microsoft Corporation's PowerPoint, or Software Publishing

Corporation's Harvard Graphics from attempting to draw flowcharts with their existing software. Typically, however, these packages are more difficult to employ than those designed specifically for making flowcharts. Software Publishing Corporation recently integrated Draw Partner, a flowcharting module, into its top-selling Harvard Graphics package. Version 2.3 of Harvard Graphics now contains a library of 500 flowchart symbols. Draw Partner is an advanced drawing program, and users can certainly draw flowcharts with it.

Another flowchart software package is TopDown, Version 3.0. It lets its users create idea charts, organization charts, procedure diagrams, and training materials quickly and easily. The package allows users to draw and update their diagrams and connect symbols with just two mouse clicks. Also, connecting lines are automatically rerouted whenever the drawing is revised. Ten different line paths provide users with the maximum versatility possible. TopDown has 110 different charting tools, including 12 ANSI symbols and a Custom Symbol creation capability. Text importing, Notecards, color, and On-Line Help are available on Top-Down 3.0

A summary of typical current outliners and flowcharting software products for organizing ideas that are available from vendors is found in figure 6.5.

IDEA NETWORKING

Going beyond software packages that are basically idea organizers, there are idea software products that focus on networking participants. Called "groupware" or "collaborative computing," this software has the goal of making it possible for widely dispersed people to participate jointly on a common problem. One of the first such programs was Notes, introduced in 1989 by the Lotus Development Corporation. It can be used to help people schedule meetings, track progress of different projects, and exchange views and information on particular topics. In the discussion to follow, a number of software packages that are useful for idea networking are examined.

Brainstorm

Brainstorm 2.0 helps users develop new ideas with coworkers on a network by facilitating the exchange of ideas about different discussion topics. The product's central group-discussion concept helps justify implementing Brainstorm as a DOS-based E-mail system. Although brainstorming is generally more productive if problem-solving groups meet face-to-face, Brainstorm may be an efficient way to communicate for LAN-based users who cannot meet to discuss a topic.

A Brainstorm meeting begins with a user sending an invitation over E-mail for others to join a discussion on a certain topic. Once the topic has been set up, the networked users are automatically routed to that topic. Reference can be made to figure 6.6, which illustrates a discussion of the current telephone system.

Figure 6.5
Typical Current Idea Organizers and Flowchart Software Products

Product	Vendor	Description
ABC Flowcharter	Roy Kore Inc.	ABC Flowcharter is a Microsoft Windows product that allows users to outline ideas, policies, and procedures and change them more easily than pen and pencil.
allCLEAR	Clear Software Inc.	AllCLEAR allows users to construct flowcharts that outline ideas, policies, and procedures much more easily than pen and pencil.
Criterium (Version 1.1)	Sygenex, Inc.	Criterium is a software program that lets the user combine hard data and gut instinct, facts, and opinions. It helps the user make informed decisions - decisions that are well organized, clearly documented, and completely supportable. Criterium allows the user to detail each step in the decision-making process. It helps organize and analyze the parts of a decision, then calculates the best choice based on the information supplied. Last, Criterium provides the user with comprehensive background data reports and concise executive summaries so that the user can present his or her decisions with complete confidence.
GrandView (Version 2.0)	Symantec Corporation	GrandView is an outliner to keep a to-do list. If the user wants to track projects, GrandView has much to offer. Also, it is a traditional PIM. If a user's needs are outlining, it is not necessary to resort to another program for scheduling since GrandView has added calendar features that satisfy the scheduling needs of many users.

Figure 6.5 (Continued)

Product	Vendor	Description
Idea Tree (Version 2.0)	Mountain House Publishing Inc.	Idea Tree captures a user's thoughts as they come to mind. It displays a user's thinking in a two-dimensional tree structure. At the touch of a key, Idea Tree turns it all into an outline showing flow from idea to idea. The user can browse across trees, set bookmarks, turn arbitrary idea groups into a new tree, and move it to any point in any tree in memory. Research notes, reminders, and data to individual ideas can be added with the Note Processor. Idea Tree can print complete documents automatically from the individual idea documents, with optional outline, table of contents, and notes as references.
MacFlow (Version 3.5)	Mainstay	MacFlow, once a single-task tool, goes beyond programmer productivity into the realm of business communication with version 3.5. Unlike previous versions, which limited the user to programming symbols, version 3.5 lets the user create and edit a host of multipurpose symbols for various types of charts, using graphics imported from other programs. Additional tools, such as Bezier curves and varied line widths and arrowhead selections, help the user optimize the effectiveness of his or her charts for communicating plans and ideas.
TopDown (Version 3.0)	Kaetron Software Corporation	TopDown 3.0 allows the user to create idea charts, organization charts, procedure diagrams, and training materials.

Figure 6.6

A Typical Discussion Topic Using Brainstorm 2.0 for the Quote and Reply Screen

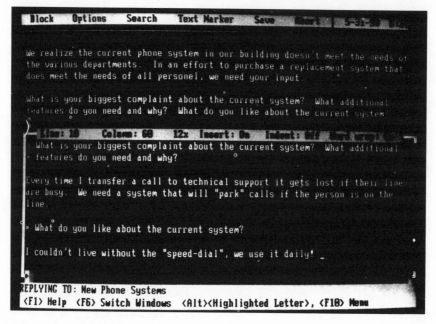

Source: Courtesy of Mustang Software, Inc.

Brainstorm's Topic feature supports three types of communication: public (everyone is automatically included), private (a topic administrator assigns certain users to the topic), and request (users are asked if they want to join the discussion). Once users have been registered by the topic manager, they are updated as new E-mail messages are posted. Typical topic areas for discussion are "What new product or products should be developed and marketed?" and "What are the products to be called?"

Brainstorm is easy to install and configure. Its E-mail service works well, but its E-mail system security may be a concern in some organizations since there is only one level of password protection. The package is compatible with Novell NetWare 2.0a or above, Banyan VINES 2.X or above, or any network that supports DOS 3.X file and record locking or the DOS Share command.

Notes

The Lotus Development Corporation has developed a groupware program called Notes. The program is designed to let users of personal computers on a network plan meetings, share comments on such areas as new product ideas, track projects, and examine libraries of documents. It can work with an operating system for

IBM's personal computers called Presentation Manager. Currently, several hundred employees in several different buildings at Lotus's Cambridge, Massachusetts, headquarters are using Notes. One use lets Lotus track discussion of potential products or corporate acquisitions by various executives and its corporate-strategy group.

When a company approaches a Lotus executive with a proposal, details are recorded on an electronic form that can be called up from a central data base by authorized employees. Subsequently, as other executives review the proposal and make recommendations, they update the form, leaving an electronic "paper trail." The net result of using Notes is that group productivity is boosted by letting people avoid or shorten meetings. Many times, items are resolved before the meetings. In addition, Lotus uses icons to symbolize various categories, making it easier for Notes users to find information. In the system being used at Lotus, a drawing of an insect symbolizes the category "software problem reports"— bugs, in industry parlance.[4]

Instant Update

On Technology Inc. (Cambridge, Massachusetts), headed by Lotus's founder, Mitch Kapor, markets another collaborative system called Instant Update. Designed for preparing documents, the program allows each user to obtain the largest version of a work in progress, such as ideas for a new product or service, and discloses who made which changes when. It is a way to free people so they can work at the time and place that are most convenient for them. In neither Notes nor Instant Update, however, do the different participants interact directly. Users contribute to a document individually and at different times. Essentially, this approach accommodates people with different schedules and allows flexible input from different sources. However, the participants lose some of the spark that comes from bouncing thoughts off one another. Thus other software packages that follow may be preferable to this one and preceding ones.

VisionQuest

To help businesses sidestep time-consuming and ineffective meetings, Collaborative Technologies Corporation's VisionQuest transforms PC LANs into electronic meeting places. VisionQuest streamlines the meeting process by helping participants define objectives, generate ideas, and exchange opinions. The software reduces the time that middle-level, white-color workers spend in meetings—a figure some observers estimate to be as much as 30 percent to 80 percent of each workday.

VisionQuest has made meetings much more productive by reducing meeting times and increasing the clarification of ideas generated. VisionQuest, which can be run on most standard PC networks, uses Novell Inc.'s Btrieve data base as a repository for storing and organizing meeting commentary. To keep participants focused, VisionQuest presents users with a predetermined meeting agenda and action-item list, prompting participants for their responses. After soliciting feedback, the software compiles responses and distributes them among meeting participants for evaluation. VisionQuest meetings can take place between users on both local and remote networks. Either way, ideas evolving from a Vision-Quest session are usually more thought-out than ideas generated verbally. Testing has shown that every meeting has a surprising amount of clarity to it as a result of writing down the ideas.[5]

Aspects

Basically, Aspects is a collaborative system for the Apple Macintosh that is useful for brainstorming. In an attempt to mimic the process of solving problems by placing people together in a room, Group Technologies, Inc. has developed the first computer program that lets organization personnel in far-flung locations work simultaneously on a single problem. The program is designed to fill gaps left by electronic mail and video conferencing in what amounts to a conference call over a computer since it allows participants to work together simultaneously on the same document. Each person can change or add material—a word, a paragraph, a notation, or a graph—while seeing what the others are doing. As a result of the program's operating mode, synergy gets going when people work together. A typical example is illustrated in figure 6.7, where the PC to the left initiates the meeting.

Figure 6.7
Example of Collaborative Work on Documents by Participants in Different Locations Using the Aspects Program

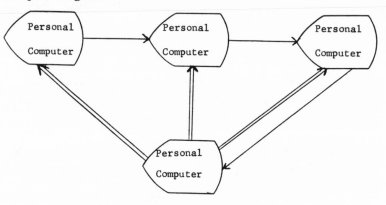

_____ Updating changes instantaneously

_____ Distributing documents

Aspects allows organizational personnel using Apple Macintosh computers to collaborate in either free-form "meetings," in which everybody can contribute at once, or more structured encounters in which participants take turns. For example, a team of managers and lawyers split between Houston and New York might want to work together on a legal brief. Typically, the participants would talk over an ordinary telephone conference call while watching the legal brief evolve on computer screens. Using Aspects, in what amounts to an enhanced conference call, a lawyer in Houston might write comments in the margins, asking colleagues to bolster a particular argument with better precedents. A second lawyer could then circulate the decision from a similar case, and the group could decide which lines from that decision to insert into the new filing. Most changes appear on each screen in less than a second. Hence managers working with lawyers in this situation may well be able to resolve this legal brief faster than if a typical telephone conference call were undertaken.

A summary of typical current idea-networking software packages from vendors is shown in figure 6.8.

IDEA GENERATORS

As noted previously, each of the first two levels of creative computer software has its own particular strengths that make it amenable to certain situations. The same is true at this third level; that is, an idea generator is better for certain creative situations than idea organizers an idea networking. For example, Michael Kelly, president of Techtel Corporation (a market research firm in Emeryville, California) operates in this manner. If he has a decision to make and has a number of different options on his mind, he brings up a creative software program and lets it pull out of him the things that are most important. Eventually, it just dawns on him what the solution is. Currently, Kelly is using Experience in Software Inc.'s Idea Generator Plus 3.1.

In his experience with this software package, one situation stands out. He found that he was spending too much time on receivables and needed a solution to this problem. In small businesses, there are too many ups and downs. A business tends to spend time concentrating on either sales, operations, or collections. By using Idea Generator Plus, he realized that more time had to be spent on each of these other factors. The solution in this case was to have someone else handle receivables, allowing him more time to do selling. This had a noticeable effect on his sales. Hence Kelly found that the ability to allow him to define, clarify, and focus on problems and then come up with alternative solutions is the most valuable feature of Idea Generator Plus. Even in the blur of everyday activity, this enables the user to devise a helpful new solution.

As another example, Lex Young, vice president and director of communications services at DDB Needham Worldwide Advertising Inc. (an advertising firm in Chicago), said that a critical feature of idea generators is their ability to help the user break out of cyclical thinking patterns and generate alternative solutions.

Figure 6.8
Typical Current Idea-networking Software Products

Product	Vendor	Description
Aspects	Group Technologies Inc.	Aspects is a software product that is designed to fill gaps left by E-mail and video conferencing. It is actually a conference call using a computerized mode that allows its participants to work together simultaneously on the same document or idea. Each participant can change or add material while seeing what the others are doing.
Brainstorm (Version 2.0)	Mustang Software, Inc.	Although Brainstorm includes a complete E-mail system, it is specifically structured to provide individual topic conversations to discuss areas of user interest. These individual conversations are known as "topics" in Brainstorm paralance, and can range from gathering feedback for the purchase of a better phone system to improving everyday scheduling of a company's operations.
Instant Update	On Technology Inc.	Instant Update is a collaborative system that allows users to obtain the latest version of a work in progress, such as an idea on a new product, and discloses who made which changes when. It is a way to free people so they can work at the time and place when it is most convenient for them.
Notes	Lotus Development Corporation	Notes is a program designed to let users of personal computers on a network plan meetings, share comments on new product ideas, link projects, and examine libraries of documents. It can work with an operating system for IBM's personal computers called Preseutation Manager.
VisionQuest	Collaborative Technologies Corporation	VisionQuest streamlines the meeting process by helping participants on both local and remote networks define objectives, generate ideas, and exchange opinions. Basically, it makes meetings more productive by reducing meeting times and increasing the clarification of ideas.

Young uses IdeaFisher 4.0, from Fisher Idea Systems, Inc., to help DDB Needham attract clients. Essentially, IdeaFisher gives him the capability of looking at many versions of the end product and picking out which is best. Young uses IdeaFisher to help develop advertising strategy statements for his clients, and he finds that it facilitates this process.

A strategy statement is a single-page document having to do with advertising. However, Young had to go through mounds of materials to get down to a simple statement. IdeaFisher is useful to Young because it has a question bank relating to advertising positioning. This enables him to come up with a basic idea of what the product is and then to put that into words. IdeaFisher then gives him a list of key words to be used in the product-positioning and strategy statements. Young is currently using IdeaFisher on the Macintosh.

Previously, he worked on a PC/XT, on which he employed Symantec Corporation's GrandView and ThinkTank (covered in previous sections of this chapter), outline processors with word-processing capabilities. Neither package was robust enough for his advertising demands. Because he wanted something that would do a little more than be an outliner, he then tried Idea Generator Plus, but found it too rigid for his needs. He eventually switched to IdeaFisher when he moved over to the Macintosh. Hence this example and the prior one demonstrate that idea generators serve different needs of their users.[6]

Consultant

Consultant, a software product by ODS, Inc. (Des Plaines, Illinois), uses the Macintosh interface and icon logos. Consultant's goal is to help knowledge workers use their whole brains to think and work more productively. Consultant offers the user three types of functions: (1) procedures, (2) aids, and (3) helps. They may be used at any time and in any mix or order. The procedures, the first type of function, consist of a series of steps presented as questions or directions that lead the user to effect a change from some present condition. They include a descriptive problem-solving procedure, a planning procedure, and a procedure to help the user sell his or her plan. The aids, the second type, consist of idea-generation aids and decision-making aids. Helps, the third type, are useful in assisting the user to complete the task at hand.

In reference to the second type, idea-generation aids include Brainstorm (which solicits a large number of user idea responses to a previously supplied stimulus question), Questioner (the user supplies as many potential answers as possible), Combines (which generates a list of all combinations of items), and Scenario (which leads the user through defining the elements of a scenario). On the other hand, decision-making aids encompass Prioritizer (which supports prioritizing or preference ranking of items by means of soliciting a series of paired comparisons), Grader (which facilitates assignment of 0–10 scale values to items), Rater (which creates a score for items consisting of the product of user-supplied values on two equally weighted 0–10 scales), Evaluator (which evaluates one or more alternatives on a variety of factors), Relator (which facilitates assigning and considering task procedures and interdependencies, such as in PERT), and Categorizer (which facilitates the identification of categories and the assignment of items to them).

Basically, Consultant goes beyond the standard DSS microcomputer software consisting of spreadsheets, data-base query, and graphics. It adds procedures and aids not found in DSS software. Being the first idea generator (introduced in 1985), it is being supplemented by newer ones that are more group oriented. Thus many of the succeeding idea generators presented in this section focus on a collaborative approach versus an individual working alone.

The Innovator

The Innovator, which is marketed by the Wilson Learning Corporation, is a computer-assisted group decision support process designed specifically for the organization that is facing change. The organization recognizes that its success in dealing with and adapting to change will depend, to a large extent, on its ability to support effective group action. The Innovator is capable of assisting an organization in improving the quality of its group decision making and the effectiveness of the actions that result from these decisions. These outcomes derive from the fact that The Innovator process is designed specifically for a number of situations. These include the following:

- Stimulating and focusing the creative energies of the group on the task
- Integrating and synthesizing qualitative as well as quantitative data generated by the group
- Overcoming the limitations on creativity and participation often resulting from the dominating influence of powerful or high-ranking group members
- Permitting immediate analysis and consideration of data generated by the group
- Focusing group energies on an outcome rather than a problem frame of reference toward the situation
- Facilitating the identification of the high-priority opportunities in the situation that promise the greatest payoff for action taken
- Identifying the specific areas of disagreement within the group and providing an efficient process for resolving the sources of that disagreement
- Producing an effective yet flexible plan of action that has the active commitment of the group

Because The Innovator process has been designed to be versatile yet directly applicable to the specific needs of changing organizations, its product line is organized to address particular business applications. The group-meeting portion of each application module is designed so that it can be accomplished in the equivalent of a one-day session or less.

Each participant uses a wireless audience-response keypad to register his or her opinion on a particular question or issue. Functions include issue pair-comparing, issue rating, and performance/value prioritizing. The results of the opinions are immediately displayed for the group to view, and they show information such as group agreement and disagreement and demographic information by function. The Innovator is suitable for both small and large groups. Although most sessions involve 15 to 25 participants, it is not uncommon to use The Innovator with over 100 participants.

Applications for using The Innovator are limited only by the imagination and have ranged from quality assessment to the development of a mission statement. A sample of some typical applications and uses includes the following:

- Developing and mapping out strategic priorities for organizations
- Assessing and prioritizing the needs of corporate divisions, departments, and teams
- Conducting surveys with a tool that immediately and accurately collects information
- Job futuring, used to facilitate group review of job data to identify performance and prioritize current and future job functions
- Conflict resolutions, used by teams and groups to resolve conflicts by identifying and prioritizing key issues anonymously

The Innovator is used by organizations, associations, and universities. It can be applied to all levels of individuals, including frontline employees, senior managers, committees, and teams.

The initial "family" of applications of The Innovator is directed at supporting effective group problem solving around the variety of increasingly complex human-resource issues facing business today. The Innovator human-resource family members include The Problem Solver, The Work Culture Analyst, The Team Builder, The Human Resource Developer, The Diagnostician, The Strategic Planner, The Performance Communicator, and The Personnel Planner. For example, The Problem Solver is designed to assist problem-solving groups at all levels of the organization in their effort to (1) clarify understanding of a problem and redefine it in terms of a positive outcome, (2) develop high-quality, creative alternatives to the situation, (3) discover and resolve sources of substantive differences among group members, (4) identify key opportunities for taking action, and (5) develop a plan of action that has the active commitment of the group. In addition to the human-resource application area, additional Innovator applications focus on marketing and sales and on issues specifically affecting line management.

OptionFinder®

OptionFinder, a software program designed by Option Technologies, Inc. (Mendota Heights, Minnesota), is useful to enhance the effectiveness of the group process. OptionFinder is a general-purpose opinion-collection and analysis software that connects up to 250 participants with an IBM-compatible computer via individual 10-button keypads. The computer is also connected to several types of large-screen or overhead display units for immediate presentation of voting results as graphs and charts. OptionFinder can increase the likelihood of achieving desired outcomes since it is a way for every individual to have input. Typically, in almost any group, there are people who dominate the discussion. OptionFinder allows everyone to have input to questions asked of the group. Experience has shown that people who dominate before input is requested speak up less after seeing the results, while the quiet ones tend to speak up more. This may be due to the participants being more willing to discuss the issues afterwards because they have had to take a stand.

OptionFinder software allows a meeting leader to ask participants to vote anonymously via the keyboard provided for each participant on as many as fifty-two items or issues that previously have been generated by the group for evaluation. For example, senior management has developed nine critical success factors (CSFs) for the organization. To evaluate organizational performance with OptionFinder, the senior staff is first asked to rank the relative importance of the nine CSFs by using an evaluation process that assures dispersion from high to low importance. Then the staff is asked to rate the performance by using a 7-point scale, where 1 = no performance, 4 = just OK for now, and 7 = fantastic.

In the two-dimensional graph shown in figure 6.9, the importance ranking is plotted on the vertical axis and the performance rating is plotted on the horizontal axis. A CSF that appears in the upper right quadrant would be very important relative to the others and the organizational performance would be high. A CSF that appears in the lower right quadrant would be relatively unimportant, but the performance would be high. The upper left quadrant represents an area of high importance to organizational success, but low performance.

Figure 6.9
The Power of OptionFinder: Leveraging Organization Opportunity

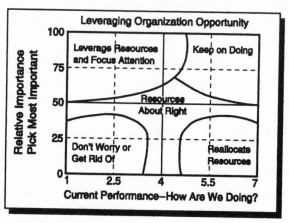

Source: Courtesy of Option Technologies, Inc.

By analyzing the location of individual CSFs within the meaning of each of the quadrants, the staff can determine quickly where it will obtain the greatest leverage for achieving desired organizational outcomes. In figure 6.9, suggested actions are labeled in different areas of the X-Y plot. For example, a CSF in the upper right quadrant is a real strength of the organization, so the staff "keeps on doing" it. However, any CSF that falls into the lower right quadrant would represent an area where the organization could release additional resources by pulling back some of the effort that is being applied to that CSF. These additional resources could then be reallocated to CSFs that appear in the upper left quadrant, which represents the area of greatest opportunity for "leveraging organizational resources and focusing attention."

By engaging the staff in a discussion of results plotted in this X-Y format, the program can quickly clarify their understanding of the CSFs under review and the actions that should be taken to improve them. This, in turn, will help to focus the attention and energies of the staff on the truly high-priority actions that it should be taking.

Idea Generator Plus

Idea Generator Plus, a product of Experience in Software, Inc. (Berkeley, California), is based on a logical three-step approach to problem solving. First, the user enters a problem into the program and works on clarifying it by answering questions generated by the program. Second, new ideas are cultivated when the user answers another series of questions that help put the problem or situation into a new perspective. Third, the user evaluates and prioritizes these ideas based on the original goals. This gives the user the opportunity to prune or discard less useful ideas or solutions and to rate the remaining ideas on the basis of costs, benefits, and the effects on people involved in the process. Although the program's analytical question-and-answer setup is helpful to the user, it is time-consuming. This makes Idea Generator Plus more suitable for analyzing problems that must be solved using highly structured reasoning.

Not all of Idea Generator Plus's questions are applicable to every problem, and many of its questions are difficult to answer. Reference can be made to figure 6.10. For example, the program asks the user to list goals and then reverse them (in order of importance, for example), and then to consider ways to reach the reversed goals. Finally, the program asks the user to try to determine whether the plans to achieve the reversed goals provide any insight into new ways to reach the initial goals. By reversing the priority of these goals, the user may consider different options, one or more of which could satisfy the original goals.

Because Idea Generator Plus's questions require careful consideration, it takes the user several hours to work through the broad range of questions that are relevant to the problem under study. Nevertheless, thinking about the problem from different perspectives helps the user to break away from circular thinking patterns. A useful feature is the Idea Screen, which tracks the user's train of thought.

Figure 6.10
Idea Generation Technique Found In Idea Generator Plus

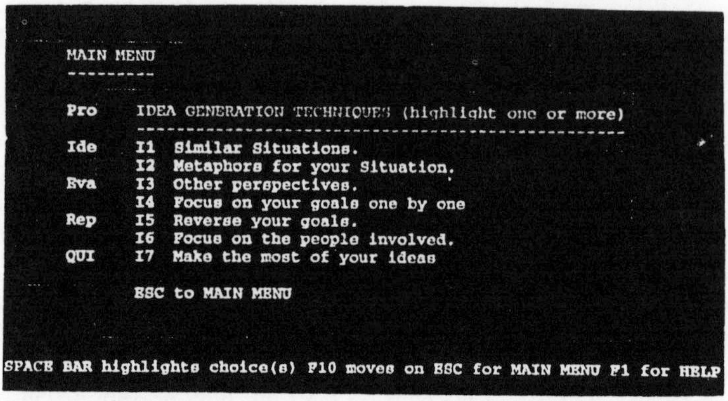

```
  MAIN MENU
  ---------

  Pro    IDEA GENERATION TECHNIQUES (highlight one or more)
         ----------------------------------------------------
  Ide    I1  Similar Situations.
         I2  Metaphors for your Situation.
  Eva    I3  Other perspectives.
         I4  Focus on your goals one by one
  Rep    I5  Reverse your goals.
         I6  Focus on the people involved.
  QUI    I7  Make the most of your ideas

         ESC to MAIN MENU


SPACE BAR highlights choice(s)  F10 moves on ESC for MAIN MENU F1 for HELP
```

Source: Courtesy of Experience in Software, Inc. © copyright by Gerard I. Nierenberg.

The Idea Screen can be accessed via a hot key at any time. It incorporates a text editor to record new ideas, associations, and conclusions. In addition, Idea Generator Plus provides a useful summary report that includes a description of the situation, a list of the people involved, and ratings of the individual's or group's goals, in order of importance. The information in the summary report can be printed out or exported to applications, such as Symantec Corporation's Grand-View and ThinkTank as well as Lotus Development Corporation's Agenda (refer to the section on PIMs).

MindLink

Codeveloped by Synectics, Inc. (the Cambridge, Massachusetts–based consulting firm) that literally invented creativity consulting over thirty years ago, MindLink asks the user to do no less than throw away a good deal of his or her normal associational thinking and consider how seemingly unrelated things—the crossings of an elephant with an oil well, the headline of today's newspaper, a trip to the shopping mall, or the feeling that a poem gives the user—might ultimately provide the solution to the problem under study. Typically, most untrained users will quickly find themselves violating the cardinal rule of brainstorming—namely, to withhold judgment—and grumbling, "What does this have to do with anything?" "Why am I wasting my time here?" The software challenges users to transcend their traditionally linear ways of thinking and make the leap into irrelevant, absurd, or even contradictory thoughts that the developers believe will increase the chances of creating a truly novel, or breakthrough, idea. Sometimes, users need to forget a problem to solve it.

One way to approach MindLink—at least until users become comfortable with its method—is with a spirit of play, almost as a kind of Nintendo for the mind.

That is one reason why the developers have included a program section called the "Gym." The Gym is a creativity warm-up session that encourages a non-goal-oriented, non-judgmental spirit of mental play. The three other sections are "Idea Generation," "Guided Problem Solving," and "General Problem Solving." All sections use "idea triggers" to force divergent thinking.

In all, there are more than forty idea triggers in the program. For example, one idea trigger uses poems to help the user create ideas. Any one of more than thirty poems could appear at a given time. Another trigger invites the user to put himself or herself into someone else's situation, from Mahatma Gandhi to an investment banker or a traffic cop. After each seemingly unrelated-to-the-problem trigger exercise, the user is asked to imagine how the imagery, wishes, thoughts, or ideas generated from each could be used to help solve his or her particular problem. The best ideas are then brought through a disciplined "building" process until, finally, the user ends up with an action plan for the ideas he or she would like to pursue. A typical solution worksheet is found in figure 6.11.

IdeaFisher 4.0

IdeaFisher 4.0's brainstorming and problem-solving capabilities are based on the principles of free association, memory retrieval, and analogical and metaphorical reasoning. The program provides two data bases: (1) IdeaBank, which cross-references words and phrases, and (2) QBank, which is a repository of questions that help the user define the problem. QBank contains nearly 6,000 questions that help the user clarify a problem or objective. The questions are organized into three divisions: (1) Orient-Clarify, for identifying the aims of a task and clarifying goals and problems, (2) Modify, for reshaping ideas and potential solutions, and (3) Evaluate, for assessing goals, assumptions, and ideas.

From the user's answers, QBank generates a list of key concepts that the user can explore in the program's IdeaBank. IdeaBank is organized into 28 major categories such as colors, places, government/law/politics, and shape/position, and 387 topical categories, such as verbs, descriptors, and people/animals. IdeaBank's topical categories contain more than 60,000 words and phrases with more than 700,000 predefined associative links that make IdeaBank much more powerful than a simple thesaurus. IdeaBank can be customized for each user by adding topical categories, words, and phrases.

Both IdeaBank and QBank help the user free-associate and trigger new ideas. The program cannot create new ideas, but its cross-referenced links can remind the user of thoughts, feelings, facts, images, and personal knowledge that can stimulate new ideas. This idea generator also includes an Idea Notepad, which automatically records each association selected during a session and provides a basic text processor to record the user's train of thought.

When using the program for the first time, users will have to spend a little time to figure out which topic makes the most sense to explore. Going to an

Figure 6.11
A Sample Solution Worksheet Using MindLink

Source: Courtesy of MindLink, Inc.

illogical topic, however, can trigger associations that would not occur through more linear associations. For example, a user can free-associate from "foods" to "sticky" and to a non-linear association of "office products," developing a new type of Post-it note that contains gourmet recipes. Needless to say, not all of the ideas that are generated by IdeaFisher will be useful, but the program helps the user explore a broader range of possibilities. A three-screen example is found in figure 6.12.

A summary of typical current idea generator software from vendors is found in figure 6.13.

APPLICATIONS OF CREATIVE COMPUTER SOFTWARE
TO FUNCTIONAL AREAS OF A TYPICAL COMPANY

The idea generators described in the previous section represent some of the better ones developed to date. On the other hand, there are some other less expensive

Figure 6.12
A Three-screen Example of IdeaBank Used to Develop New Ideas in IdeaFisher 4.0

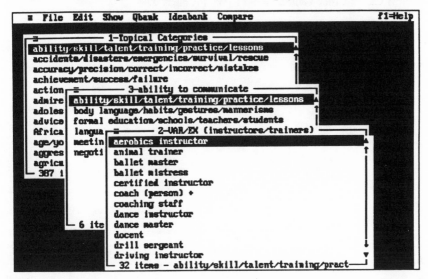

Source: Courtesy of Fisher Idea Systems, Inc. Copyright 1988–1992, Fisher Idea Systems, Inc. All rights reserved Worldwide.

software packages that treat problems these programs address. If the user just wants a good data base of phrases to bounce around, Writer's Dreamtools has a number of them. The Heizer Software catalog lists several random-word data bases designed to help users overcome thinker's block. However, none of these programs is as focused as the ones included in the previous section.

At this point, it would be helpful to show how creative software packages differ from one another. Due to space limitations, only IdeaFisher and MindLink are contrasted here. IdeaFisher is especially helpful when the goal of brainstorming is words (product names, titles, advertising slogans, and so forth). MindLink is better suited for tackling large, multifaceted problems whose end result is likely to be a strategy or plan of action. MindLink imposes a reasonable methodology on brainstorming that can prove helpful. It also provides a place for "brainstorm stuff." But after a few runs, it can prove monotonous. Once users have internalized the process, there is need for something more—a data base like IdeaFisher's or more helpful summary reports. From this perspective, IdeaFisher's data base gives it an edge over MindLink and the other software packages presented in this chapter for generating ideas to solve a wide range of business problems.

Because the focus of this book is oriented toward work that supports brainstorming, there will be examples of IdeaFisher 4.0 in the remaining chapters of this text. Also, there will be selected examples of some of the other software packages presented in this chapter. In this manner, the reader will have a better

Figure 6.13
Typical Current Idea Generator Software Products

Product	Vendor	Description
Consultant (Version 1.6)	ODS, Inc.	Consultant's mission is to help knowledge workers use their whole brains to think and work more productively. Consultant offers the user three types of functions: procedures, aids, and helps. The procedures consist of a series of steps presented as questions or directions that lead the user to effect a change from some present situation. They include a descriptive problem-solving procedure, a planning procedure, and a procedure to help the user sell his or her plan. The aids consist of idea generation and decision-making aids.
Idea Generator Plus (Version 3.1)	Experience in Software Inc.	Idea Generator Plus utilizes a logical three-step approach to problem solving. The first step is to enter the problem and clarify it by answering questions generated by the program. Second, another series of questions helps cultivate the new ideas and puts the problem or situation into perspective. Third, the user evaluates and prioritizes these ideas based on the original goals. Idea Generator Plus offers an Idea Screen which tracks the user's train of thought. This screen can be accessed via a hot key at any time and incorporates a text editor to record new ideas, associations, and conclusions. It provides a useful summary report that can be exported to other applications.

170

Figure 6.13 (Continued)

Product	Vendor	Description
IdeaFisher (Version 4.0)	Fisher Idea Systems, Inc.	IdeaFisher is a massive data base of words, phrases, cliches, and titles. About 60,000 idea words and phrases are cross-referenced in several ways. They are categorized under 28 "major categories" and 387 more specific "topical categories" (a hierarchical organization like that of a real, nondictionary-style thesaurus). Each word is also linked in surprising and idiosyncratic ways to dozens of other words for a total of more than 700,000 cross references. The user can add words, categories, and cross-reference associations.
MindLink	MindLink, Inc.	Based on more than 30 years research in the field of creativity by the Synectics Corporation, MindLink guides the user through a step-by-step problem-solving sequence enriched by industry-proven idea generation techniques. The program helps the user create new ideas to apply to the problem or opportunity under study. Because the ideas are one's own, the solutions the user generates will fit the situation and one's capabilities. MindLink automatically organizes the user's thoughts in a logical pattern and keeps the user moving toward actionable solutions.

Figure 6.13 (Continued)

Product	Vendor	Description
OptionFinder (Version 3.2)	Option Technologies, Inc.	OptionFinder is a hardware/software system that uses keypads in place of PCs. This system is based on the premise that the largest untapped resource is the people that are never asked about their ideas. OptionFinder uses a PC or laptop computer, an overhead projection system for the meeting facilitator, and keypads for the participants, each with 10 buttons. Depending on the number of keypads for the participatns, a meeting can be conducted with a small group of managers or gather opinions from a group of up to 120 people.
The Innovator	Wilson Learning Corporation	The Innovator is a group facilitation tool that combines the best understanding of the complex human dimensions of group facilitations with the capacity to increase the efficiency and creativity of group deliberation and problem solving. Its family of applications includes human resources, marketing and sales, and issues specifically affecting line management.

understanding of how these creative computer software packages can be used under various circumstances for functional areas of a typical company.

SUMMARY

In the first part of this chapter, the focus was on computer hardware that is needed to support computer software. Although there are a number of hardware platforms that are useful to support idea processors of various types, it should be recognized that the software to assist a manager in a creative problem-solving environment may require a certain size of memory. Hence a fundamental consideration before acquiring new computer hardware is its ability to handle present and proposed creative computer software.

In the second half of the chapter, idea processors at four different levels were presented: idea organizers, idea networking, idea generators, and virtual idea generators. Since only the first three levels are commercially available, major creative software packages in these levels were examined. Some of these software packages will be illustrated in the final part of this book. However, because of its innovative approach to free association, its unique idea data-base concept, and its ease of operation, IdeaFisher 4.0 will be demonstrated in each of the remaining chapters.

NOTES

1. Patricia Keefe, "Pen-based PC Poised for Breakthrough," *Computerworld*, June 3, 1991, p. 111.

2. Paul Soffo, "A Wireless Computing Revolution Is Just around the Corner," *InfoWorld*, June 10, 1991, p. 73.

3. Joyce J. Elam and Melissa Mead, "Can Software Influence Creativity?" *Information Systems Research*, March 1990, pp. 1–23.

4. William M. Bulkeley, "New Software Helps PC Users Work as Groups," *Wall Street Journal*, February 24, 1988, p. 25.

5. Steve Higgins, "VisionQuest Reduces Time Spent in Meetings," *PC Week*, April 22, 1991, p. 40.

6. Sally Winship, "Packages Stimulate Creative Process, Buyers Say," *PC Week*, March 18, 1991, pp. 109, 116.

Bibliography: Part III

Altieri, R. P. "A Memo to the EIS User." *Information Center*, February 1990.
Angehrn, A. A., and H.-J. Lüthi. "Intelligent Decision Support Systems: A Visual Interactive Approach." *Interfaces*, November–December 1990.
Bacon, D. C. "Brainstorming with Your Computer." *Nation's Business*, December 1989.
Ball, M. "EDI Takes Root." *Computerworld Focus*, September 7, 1988.
Bar, J. "A Systematic Technique for New Product Idea Generators: The External Brain." *R & D Management*, January 1989.
Barker, J. "The State of the Art for Decision Making." *Successful Meetings*, November 1989.
Barney, D. "Fishing for the Right, Ummm, Idea." *Computerworld*, May 15, 1989.
Barron, J. J. "Solving the Nearly Unsolvable." *Byte*, June 1989.
Belitsos, B. "EDI Becomes a Necessity." *Computer Decisions*, October 1988.
Benbasat, I., and B. R. Nault. "An Evaluation of Empirical Research in Managerial Support Systems." *Decision Support Systems*, Volume 6, Issue 3, 1990.
Betts, M. "EDI Shreds Federal Paperwork." *Computerworld*, September 5, 1988.
———. "Lawyers Fret over Risks of EDI Growth." *Computerworld*, January 16, 1989.
Beulens, A. J. M., and J. VanNune. "The Use of Expert System Technology in DSS." *Decision Support Systems*, Vol. 4, 1988.
Bittlestone, R. "Future Developments in EIS." *Information Center*, July 1989.
Bochenski, B. "Workgroup Goals Push Groupware Boundaries." *Software Magazine*, November 1990.
Bonner, P. "Pilot Executive Systems: Lightship 2.0" *PC Week*, March 4, 1991.
Bowerman, R. G., and D. E. Glover. *Putting Expert Systems into Practice*. New York: Van Nostrand Reinhold, 1989.
Brandel, M. "Executive Information Systems." *Computerworld*, July 22, 1991.
Breibart, M. "Business Imperatives." *Computerworld Focus on Integration*, June 5, 1989.
Briggs, G. "Quaker Oats Builds Decision-Support System to Gain Marketing Edge." *MIS Week*, June 18, 1990.

Bruns, W. J., Jr., and F. W. McFarlan. "Information Technology Puts Power in Control Systems." *Harvard Business Review*, September–October 1987.

Bulkeley, M. "New Software Helps PC Users Work as Groups." *Wall Street Journal*, February 24, 1988.

Burden, K. "Software Helps with Creating Magic Ideas." *Computerworld*, November 14, 1988.

Campbell, T. L. "Technology Update: Group Decision Support Systems." *Journal of Accountancy*, July 1990.

Carlson, P. A. "Cognitive Tools and Computer-aided Writing." *AI Expert*, October 1990.

Coale, K. "Digging through Workgroups." *InfoWorld*, June 17, 1991.

Connolly, T., L. M. Jessup, and J. S. Valacich. "Effects of Anonymity and Evaluative Tone on Idea Generation in Computer-mediated Groups." *Management Science*, June 1990.

Cooper, J. K. "On the Road to Distributed Processing." *Mainframe Journal*, July 1990.

Corr, R. M. "Successful EIS Implementation Requires Commitment from Top Management." *InfoWorld*, February 8, 1988.

Couger, J. D. "Creativity in IS." *Computerworld*, October 29, 1990.

Dalton, G., and K. Way. "Reach Out and Touch Some Vendor with an EDI System." *Chief Information Officer Journal*, Fall 1988.

Daly, C. "Pen-based Computing Breaking Through." *Computerworld*, July 29, 1991.

Davenport, T. H., M. Hammer, and T. J. Metsisto. "How Executives Can Shape Their Company's Information Systems." *Harvard Business Review*, March–April 1989.

Davis, L. "Retailers Go Shopping for EDI." *Datamation*, March 1, 1989.

——— . "On-Line Applications Grow Up." *Datamation*, January 1, 1990.

Davis, M. W. *Applied Decision Support*. Englewood Cliffs, N.J.: Prentice-Hall, 1988.

Dayton, D. "Idea Generators Spark New Solutions." *PC Week*, March 18, 1991.

DeGarmo, S. "Creative Attack! No Joke—Here's How to Get the Jump on the Competition." *Success*, June 1990.

DeSanctis, G., and R. B. Gallupe. "A Foundation for the Study of Group Decision Support Systems." *Management Science*, May 1987.

Dunkle, J. V. "Working Well in a Work-Group Environment." *Computerworld*, June 4, 1990.

Dvorak, P. "Development Software Helps Get a Grip on Concepts." *Machine Design*, September 6, 1990.

Dyson, E. "Why Groupware Is Gaining Ground." *Datamation*, March 1, 1990.

Elam, J. J., and M. Mead. "Can Software Influence Creativity?" *Information Systems Research*, March 1990.

Ellis, C. A., S. J. Gibbs, and G. L. Rein. "Groupware, Some Issues and Experiences." *Communications of the ACM*, January 1991.

Eom, H. B. "The Emergence of Global Decision Support Systems." *OR/MS Today*, October 1990.

Eom, H. B. and S. M. Lee. "A Survey of Decision Support System Applications (1971–April, 1988)." *Interfaces*, May–June 1990.

Er, M. C. "Decision Support Systems: A Summary, Problems, and Future Trends." *Decision Support Systems*, Vol. 4, Issue 4, 1988.

Evans, D., and A. Morantz. "Computer Linkages: The Next Revolution." *Canadian Business*, October 1990.

Farham, A. "The PC You Put in Your Pocket." *Fortune*, May 20, 1991.

Ferranti, M. "Lotus Targets Pen-based PCs, Multimedia." *PC Week*, June 17, 1991.

Finley, M. "The New Meaning of Meetings." *Communication World*, March 1991.

Fisher, M. J. "Digging Out with Image Technology." *Datamation*, April 15, 1989.

Foley, J. "Sharing Resources to Improve Productivity." *Communications Week*, June 24, 1991.

Forgionne, G. A. "OR/MS and Decision Technology in the 1990s." *OR/MS Today*, June 1990.

Foster, E. "Enterprise Computing." *InfoWorld*, October 15, 1990.

Fox, J. "Groupware Tomorrow—Software Today." *PC Today*, November 1990.

Francis, B., J. McMullen, and J. Moad. "PC Portables: Join the Executive Ranks." *Datamation*, March 1, 1991.

Freedman, D. H. "Cultivating IS Creativity." *Infosystems*, July 1987.

Friend, D. "Benefits of An Executive Information System." *Information Management Review*, Winter 1989.

———. "EIS and the Collapse of the Information Pyramid." *Information Center*, March 1990.

Gallagher, J. P. *Knowledge Systems for Business: Integrating Expert Systems and MIS.* Englewood Cliffs, N.J.: Prentice-Hall, 1988.

George, J. F., G. K. Easton, J. F. Nunamaker, Jr., and G. B. Northcroft. "A Study of Collaborative Group Work with and without Computer-based Support." *Information Systems Research*, December 1990.

Gillin, P. "Group(ware) Therapy: Tips for Success." *Computerworld*, November 5, 1990.

Glitman, R. "Pen-based PCs Herald Era of Handwritten Input, NCR Readies Stylus System." *PC Week*, October 8, 1990.

Gold, E. M. "Moving into the Fast Lane." *Networking Management*, June 1991.

———. "The International Picture Clears Up." *Networking Management*, August 1991.

Gupta, J. N., and T. M. Harris. "Decision Support Systems for Small Business." *Journal of Systems Management*, February 1988.

Hackman, J. R., ed. *Groups That Work (and Those That Don't): Creating Conditions for Effective Teamwork.* San Francisco: Jossey-Bass, 1989.

Haight, T. "The Dawn of a Distributed Decade." *Network Computing*, October 1990.

Halliday, C. "Presentation Graphics Ease Chart Creation." *PC Week*, June 24, 1991.

Hammer, M. "Reengineering Work: Don't Automate, Obliterate." *Harvard Business Review*, July–August, 1990.

Harmon, R., R. Maus, and W. Morrissey. *Expert Systems: Tools and Applications.* New York: John Wiley & Sons, 1988.

Harrison, B. T. "Workgroup Integration Strategies." *DEC Professional*, October 1990.

Heymann, H. G., and R. Bloom. *Decision Support Systems in Finance and Accounting.* Westport, Conn.: Quorum Books, 1988.

Higgins, S. "VisionQuest Reduces Time Spent in Meetings." *PC Week*, April 22, 1991.

Holsapple, C. W., and A. B. Whinston. *Business Expert Systems.* Homewood, Ill.: Dow Jones–Irwin, 1987.

———. eds. *Decision Support Systems: Theory and Applications.* New York: Springer-Verlag, 1987.

Hwang, M. I. H., and B. J. P. Wu. "The Effectiveness of Computer Graphics for Decision Support: A Meta-Analytical Integration of Research Findings." *Data Base*, Fall 1990.

Jessup, L. M., and D. A. Tonsik. "Decision Making in an Automated Environment: The Effects of Anonymity and Proximity with a Group Decision Support System." *Decision Sciences*, Vol. 22, 1991.

Johansen, R. *Groupware: Computer Support for Business Teams*. New York: Free Press, 1988.

Jones, K. "Executive Support Systems Come of Age." *Modern Office Technology*, October 1989.

Joslow, S. "Case Study: Building an EIS." *Information Center Quarterly*, Winter 1991.

Joyce, E. J. "A System for the 21st Century." *Datamation*, May 15, 1989.

Kador, J. "Developing a Decision Support System Strategy." *System Builder*, August/September 1989.

——— . "Decision Support for Middle Managers." *EDGE*, November/December 1989.

Kapoor, A. "Electronic Imaging and Information Processing." *The Office*, December 1988.

Keefe, P. "Pen-based PC Poised for Breakthrough." *Computerworld*, June 3, 1991.

Kendall, R. "The Idea Generator." *PC Magazine*, December 13, 1988.

Keyes, J. "Getting Caught in a Neural Network." *AI Expert*, July 1991.

Kolodzeij, S. "EIS Is a Prestigious Strategic Weapon!" *Software Magazine*, July 1989.

Korzeniowski, P. "International Software Trends: EDI, Overseas Signals Making More Sense." *Software Magazine*, March 1989.

Korzeniowski, P., and J. Desmond. "And Now the Software Delivers the Software." *Software Magazine*, May 1991.

Leigh, W. E., and M. E. Doherty. *Decision Support and Expert Systems*. Cincinnati, Ohio: South-Western Publishing Company, 1986.

Leonard-Barton, D., and J. J. Sviokla. "Putting Expert Systems to Work." *Harvard Business Review*, March–April 1988.

Lewis, L. F., and K. S. Keleman. "Experience with GDSS Development: Lab and Field Studies." *Journal of Information Science*, May 1990.

Lindquist, C. "Quest for Machines That Think." *Computerworld*, November 18, 1991.

Lovett, P. D. "Meetings That Work: Plans Bosses Can Approve." *Harvard Business Review*, November–December 1988.

Loy, S. L. "The Interaction Effects between General Thinking Skills and an Interactive Graphics-based DSS to Support Problem Structuring." *Decision Sciences*, Vol. 22, 1991.

Mace, S. "Firms Find New Uses for Conferencing Software." *InfoWorld*, May 23, 1988.

Main, J. "At Last, Software CEOs Can Use." *Fortune*, March 13, 1989.

——— . "How to Go Global—and Why?" *Fortune*, August 28, 1989.

Marshall, M., and D. Coursey. "The Super PC." *InfoWorld*, May 6, 1991.

Marshall, P. "Organized and Ready for Action, Six Personal Information Managers That Focus on Task and Time Management." *InfoWorld*, February 19, 1990.

——— . "Personal Information Managers: Names and Notes at Your Fingertips." *InfoWold*, June 3, 1991.

Martin, J. "DSS Applications Should Shed New Light on a Problem." *PC Week*, May 1, 1989.

——— . "DSS Tools Help Build, Analyze Models to Make Decisions." *PC Week*, May 8, 1989.

Mason, J. "EDI Is Starting to Take Off." *Computerworld*, February 6, 1989.

Mattimore, B. W. "Mind Blasters: Software to Shatter Brain Block." *Success*, June 1990.

McCarthy, P. "The Idea Bank." *Omni*, September 1989.

McCartney, L. "Brainstorming Problems with the Computer." *Dun's Business Month*, January 1987.

McClatchy, W. "EIS Powers Executive." *Information Week*, October 9, 1989.

McCormick, J. "Agenda Is at Top of PIM Heap and Provides a Lot of Power." *Government Computer News*, July 9, 1990.

Melymuka, K. "High-Impact EIS." *CIO*, February 1989.

Methvin, D. "Wireless LANs Offer Networking Options." *PC Week Special Report: Networking*, June 24, 1991.

Milbrandt, B. "Making EDI Pay Off." *Corporate Cashflow*, December 1988.

Miller, R. "Executive Information Systems Help You Conduct Your Business." *Today's Office*, April 1989.

Moad, J. "The Software Revolution." *Datamation*, February 15, 1990.

Moskowitz, R. "Electronic Meetings Raise Effectiveness." *Office Systems*, August 1991.

Murphy, J. A. "Software Improves Work-Group Productivity." *Today's Office*, November 1990.

Myers, K. "The Write Stuff." *Information Week*, April 30, 1990.

Nash, K. S. "PC-based Support Tool Helps Decision Makers." *Computerworld*, July 22, 1991.

Nelson, F. "Notes 2.0 Flexibility Share Information." *InfoWorld*, August 12, 1991.

Nunamaker, J. F. Jr., A. R. Dennis, J. S. Valacich, D. R. Vogel, and J. F. George. "Electronic Meeting Systems to Support Group Work." *Communications of the ACM*, July 1991.

Ohmae, K. "Managing in a Borderless World." *Harvard Business Review*, May–June 1989.

O'Leary, M. "EIS Brings Bottom-Line Decision Makers to the PC." *PC Week*, April 14, 1987.

Patterson, W. P., and J. Teresko. "Managing in the '90s: New Tools." *Industry Week*, April 18, 1988.

Peak, M. H. "When You're Fishing for Ideas." *Management Review*, January 1991.

Pinella, P. "An EIS for the Desktop." *Datamation*, May 1, 1991.

Piturro, M. C. "Computer Conferencing: Brainstorming across Time and Space." *Management Review*, August 1989.

——— . "Groupware—Computer Support for Teams." *Data Training*, August 1989.

Powell, D. "Videoconferencing: A Wise Strategy." *Networking Management*, December 1989.

Proctor, T. "Experiments with Two Computer-assisted Creative Problem Solving Aids." *Omega*, March 1989.

Rappaport, A. S., and S. Halivi. "The Computerless Computer Company." *Harvard Business Review*, July–August 1991.

Rifkin, G. "Packing Some Sense into Computers." *Computerworld*, October 15, 1990.

Rockart, J. F., and D. W. De Long. *Executive Support Systems: The Emergence of Top Management Computer Use*. Homewood, Ill.: Dow Jones–Irwin, 1988.

——— . "Moments of Executive Enlightenment." *Information Strategy: The Executive's Journal*, Fall 1988.

Rouse, N. C. "Brainstorming Software Unlocks Creativity." *Machine Design*, October 12, 1989.

Runge, L. "Prototype That EIS!" *Information Center*, February 1989.

Rupley, S. "Meeting Makers: Four Workgroups Schedulers That Coordinate People and Resources." *InfoWorld*, November 20, 1989.

Sanders, B. D. "Making Work Groups Work." *Computerworld*, March 5, 1990.

Schatz, W. "EDI: Putting the Muscle in Commerce and Industry." *Datamation*, March 15, 1988.

Scheler, R. L. "Lotus Notes Conquers Groupware Frontier." *PC Week*, June 3, 1991.

Schlack, M. "IS Puts Notes to the Test." *Datamation*, August 1, 1991.

Schlender, B. R. "Hot New PCs That Read Your Writing." *Fortune*, February 11, 1991.

Skillings, J., and R. Glitman. "Pen-based PCs Herald Era of Handwritten Input, Applications Evolving Slowly." *PC Week*, October 8, 1990.

Soffo, P. "A Wireless Computing Revolution Is Just around the Corner." *InfoWorld*, June 10, 1991.

Solter, J. H., and G. M. Rothermel. "Small Business Decision Support Systems." *National Public Accountant*, May 1989.

Southcott, J., and B. Hooey. "EIS: Big League Decision Support." *EDGE*, November/December 1989.

Sprague, R. H. "A Framework for the Development of Decision Support Systems." *MIS Quarterly*, June 1980.

Sprague, R. H., Jr., and H. J. Watson. *Decision Support Systems: Putting Theory into Practice*. 2d ed. Englewood Cliffs, N.J.: Prentice-Hall, 1989.

Swasey, L. "Executives Eye EIS Software." *MIS Week*, November 6, 1989.

Tanniru, M. R., and H. K. Jain. "Knowledge-based GDSS to Support Reciprocally Interdependent Decisions." *Decision Support Systems*, Vol. 5, Issue 3, 1989.

Tansey, F. M. "Idea Generator: This Program Can Turn Your IBM PC into Brainstorming Tool." *InfoWorld*, September 29, 1986.

Thierauf, R. J. *Systems Analysis and Design of Real-Time Management Information Systems*. Englewood Cliffs, N.J.: Prentice-Hall, 1975.

——. "Distributed Processing Systems." Englewood Cliffs, N.J.: Prentice-Hall, 1978.

——. *Decision Support Systems for Effective Planning and Control: A Case Study Approach*. Englewood Cliffs, N.J.: Prentice-Hall, 1982.

——. *Effective Management Information Systems: Accent on Current Practices*. 2d ed. Columbus, Ohio: Charles E. Merrill Publishing Company, 1987.

——. *A Problem-finding Approach to Effective Corporate Planning*. Westport, Conn.: Quorum Books, 1987.

——. *User-oriented Decision Support Systems: Accent on Problem Finding*. Englewood Cliffs, N.J.: Prentice-Hall, 1988.

——. *Group Decision Support Systems for Effective Decision Making: A Guide for MIS Practitioners and End Users*. Westport, Conn.: Quorum Books, 1989.

——. *Electronic Data Interchange in Finance and Accounting*. Westport, Conn.: Quorum Books, 1990.

——. *Expert Systems in Finance and Accounting*. Westport, Conn.: Quorum Books, 1990.

——. *Executive Information Systems: A Guide for Senior Management and MIS Professionals*. Westport, Conn.: Quorum Books, 1991.

——. *Image Processing Systems for Business: A Guide for MIS Professionals and End Users*. Westport, Conn.: Quorum Books, 1992.

Thornburg, D. D. "Creativity and Computers." *California Management Review*, Fall 1988.

Tsay, B. "Electronic Data Interchange—Current Developments and Prospects." *Journal of Systems Management*, September 1988.

Turban, E. *Decision Support and Expert Systems*. 2d ed. New York: Macmillan Publishing Company, 1990.

VanGundy, A B. "Idea Collection Methods: Blending Old and New Technology." *Journal of Data Collection*, Spring 1987.

Verity, J. W. "Rethinking the Computer." *Business Week*, November 26, 1990.

Vilaliano, F. "Expert Systems and Neural Networks." *Digital Review*, June 10, 1991.

Wallace, S., and M. Semilof. "What Can Groupware Do?" *Communications Week*, June 24, 1991.

Waterman, D. A. *A Guide to Expert Systems*. Reading, Mass.: Addison-Wesley Publishing Company, 1986.

Weixel, S. "How to Tempt Resistant Execs to Use Computers." *Computerworld*, March 25, 1991.

Williams, J. I., and L. Dome. "Turbocharging Senior Management with Executive Information Systems." *Chief Information Officer Journal*, Fall 1988.

Winship, S. "Packages Stimulate Creative Process, Buyers Say." *PC Week*, March 18, 1991.

Wohl, A. D. "Executive Information Systems Give You the Big Picture." *Today's Office*, April 1990.

Worchel, S., W. Wood, and J. A. Simpson. *Group Process and Productivity*. Newbury Park, Calif.: Sage Publications, 1991.

Yeo, J. "MCI Counts on Intuitive Systems to Help Make Decisions." *Computing Canada*, January 17, 1991.

Young, L. F. "The Metaphor Machine: A Database Method for Creativity Support." *Decision Support Systems*, Vol. 3, Issue 4, 1987.

———. *Decision Support and Idea Processing Systems*. Dubuque, Iowa: William C. Brown Publishers, 1989.

———. "Knowledge-based Systems for Idea Processing Support." *Data Base*, Fall 1990.

Zaleznik, A. "Executives and Organizations: Real Work." *Harvard Business Review*, January–February 1989.

Ziber, J. "IdeaFisher and MindLink." *MacUser*, May 1990.

PART IV

Applications of
Creativity in
Functional Areas of
a Typical Company

7

Creativity in Corporate
Strategic Thinking

ISSUES EXPLORED

- To examine the need to change from corporate strategic planning to corporate strategic thinking
- To explore the relationship of corporate strategic thinking to creative visioning
- To explore the relationship between creative visioning and a company's mission and goals
- To examine the essentials of critical success factors (CSFs) and their measurement using key performance indicators (KPIs)
- To explore real-world applications that show the linkage of corporate strategic thinking to creative computer software

OUTLINE

As companies move toward the twenty-first century, a number of important factors are clamoring for attention by company managers. The economy does not have the vitality it did in the past. Foreign competitors are becoming tougher. Workers, many aging and underskilled, are becoming more demanding. But more important, customers are demanding the highest quality, the latest technology, and the speediest delivery, all at the lowest cost. In essence, these are times of immense uncertainty for managers trying to improve the profitability of their companies.

Due to the extreme uncertainty of these times, companies must take a new and expanded view of their operations and how they plan for these operations. As will be seen in this chapter, there is need for managers to take a different perspective by incorporating creativity in how they will anticipate the future. An unpredictable future demands new creative approaches that center squarely on specific markets and, at the same time, are flexible enough to move with unexpected changes in the economy and its impact on the marketplace. Not only will an expanded approach to traditional corporate strategic planning be explored, but also applications that tie into creativity will be examined in this chapter. This broadened perspective provides the essential framework for applying creativity to the other areas of a typical company, namely, marketing, manufacturing, finance, and accounting, the subject matter for the remainder of this book (part IV).

CHANGE FROM TRADITIONAL CORPORATE STRATEGIC PLANNING TO CORPORATE STRATEGIC THINKING

In light of the preceding comments on future uncertainty, how do companies plot strategies when the shape of the future keeps changing? Typically, the old methods will not do since strategic planning at too many companies has become bureaucratic, too quantitative, and somewhat irrelevant. In executives suites across the United States, countless five-year plans, updated annually and documented in binders, are gathering dust. Their specific projections about prices, costs, and market share are long forgotten. For example, asks John Walter, chief executive officer (CEO) of R. R. Donnelley & Sons (America's largest printer): "Do I have the books in my closet with all the numbers in them? Yes. Do I look at them? No."[1]

Such comments do not mean that Walter and other CEOs have abandoned a strategic planning approach. Rather, they have begun to forge a company's planning that thinks and acts strategically not just once a year but every day. The term "strategic planning," starting in the 1960s, no longer describes what they do. The phrase gaining in recognition is "strategic thinking." Executives use it to describe what a company does in becoming smart, targeted, and capable of prospering in an era of constant change. William Lawrence, executive vice president for planning, technology, and government affairs at TRW, speaks for many when he says, "The key words for the Nineties are 'focus' and 'flexibility.'"[2]

Key Elements of Corporate Strategic Thinking: Focus and Flexibility

Fundamentally, *focus* means figuring out and building upon what the company does best. It means identifying the evolving needs of a company's customers, then developing the key skills (often called the core competencies) critical to serving them. It means setting a clear and realistic mission and then working to ensure that everyone, from the chairman of the board to the middle-level manager to the hourly employee, understands it. Such self-assessment led TRW (Cleveland, Ohio), once a loosely knit agglomeration of eighty businesses, to eliminate half its units and establish early leadership in the burgeoning market for automotive air bags. It led Chicago-based Donnelley to become a high-tech global communications company that adds value not just by putting ink on paper, but also by transmitting, customizing, and packaging information.

On the other hand, *flexibility* means sketching rough scenarios of the future—what General Electric chairman Jack Welch calls bands of possibilities—then being ready to capitalize on opportunities as they arise. GE was once the corporate citadel of quantitative forecasting. The 350-member planning staff churned out voluminous reports, meticulously detailed and exquisitely packaged. Now GE has but a score of full-time planners. Called business development specialists, they are there only to advise line managers, who have the prime responsibility for formulating strategy. The heads of GE's thirteen businesses each year develop five one-page "charts," memos that alert them to possible opportunities and obstacles in their industries over the next two years. When Hungary opened its doors to foreign ownership in state-run companies, GE needed just sixty days to cut a deal for 50 percent of Tungsram, the country's leading lighting company. Tungsram had been on GE's charts for years.[3]

An Example of Loss of Focus: Northern Trust Corporation

Northern Trust Corporation, an asset-management and bank holding company (Chicago, Illinois), is an example of a company that had lost its focus. Long expert at ministering to the private banking needs of affluent clients, Northern aggressively expanded into such areas as energy and real-estate lending in the late 1970s and early 1980s. However, the bank was outmaneuvered by larger and more seasoned competitors. A number of bad loans to Third World countries forced it to take a $179-million write-off in 1987 and post the only loss in its history. What the bank finally realized was that it was a small, marginal bank in these areas.

In the spring of 1990, the thirteen members of Northern's policy committee, accompanied by a senior vice president of Boston Consulting Group, undertook an in-depth study of its operations. During three days of soul-searching, the managers assessed the company's strengths and weaknesses and hammered out a ten-page vision for the next decade. Northern decided to refocus on its core skills: asset management, private banking, and targeted commercial lending mainly for local midsize companies. Capitalizing on its expertise in serving wealthy customers, Northern has been expanding into Florida, Texas, Arizona, and California and is considering the Northeast. The bank has also exported its operational excellence to London, becoming a leader in cash-management and custodial services for international pension funds. Recognizing that its key asset is people, Northern has beefed up management training programs and, thinking even further ahead, has donated $1 million to a Chicago community group to help improve preschool, elementary, and secondary education. While other banks are having a difficult time, Northern looks to be on course for many years of record earnings.[4]

STARTING POINT FOR CORPORATE STRATEGIC THINKING: CREATIVE VISIONING

In the example just cited, the Northern Trust Corporation developed its vision for the coming decade in a ten-page report. That is, its management executives determined what they saw as the important directions that the corporation should take. Hence a logical starting point for corporate strategic thinking for a typical company is *creative visioning*. Creative visioning encompasses farsightedness by a company's executives that focuses on an eagerness to look ahead, but, at the same time, to be of a practical sort. Effective executive visionaries are not necessarily those who can predict the shape of the twenty-first century. Rather, they are creative individuals who can draw a conceptual road map (using a problem-finding approach if deemed necessary) from where the organization is now to some imagined future, who can say, "This is how we get there." Generally, creative visioning implies a change from the status quo, which helps explain why visionaries are overrepresented in the ranks of entrepreneurs and also why they come in handy to an organization in deep trouble—think of Lee Iacocca saving Chrysler. Creative visioning is not for the complacent. While the executive visionary sees things in a different light, he or she is no mystic. The person's sources of information are down-to-earth—customers and suppliers, for example—and extend beyond his or her gut-level feelings. The most creative visionary executive can take in large amounts of information, and not just from inside himself or herself.

Typically, a broad grounding in a particular industry is almost always a prerequisite to successful direction setting. It is helpful to look at the early career of an executive who comes to be regarded as visionary. Usually, the creative individual finds an assignment or a series of assignments that enables him or her to see the company from many different perspectives; that is, the individual has served as vice president of marketing, then production, then finance, or has had a tour as executive assistant to the president. As examples, Jan Carlzon held all sorts of positions in the travel business before becoming head of SAS, and Louis Gerstner studied the financial services industry as a McKinsey consultant before taking over American Express's credit card and traveler's check businesses.

From another view, there can be situations where the creative executive does not need to be steeped in an industry to conceive a vision of its future. Upstarts like Steve Jobs, such outsiders dwell on the dangers of falling prey to the Standard World View, thereby missing opportunities that arise when that standard world begins to show a few cracks. The skeptics concede, though, that someone who has grown up in the business stands a better chance to realize his or her vision.

Creative executives with vision typically share a couple of other characteristics. They have a high degree of self-confidence. It takes a lot of inner strength to imagine a future at variance with the common expectation and to sustain that imaging in the face of responses ranging from incredulity to derision. The creative visionary may also be a bit of a loner. Ego strength can mean that the individual has less need of other people. But executive vision has a way to excite others somehow. A creative visionary has an appeal to the emotions and aspirations of people that goes beyond the usual carrot-and-stick approach.

Most creative corporate visions come out looking like tarted-up strategies. William Hewlett and David Packard established a company that is dedicated to producing the best instruments for the world's scientists—that surely counts. Ray Kroc build McDonald's and Kemmons Wilson the Holiday Inns chain, both visionary achievements of twentieth-century American capitalism. Vision of the future by itself is not enough for the creative executive to possess. The executive visionary must be able to communicate what he or she has dreamed, and the company must have the required skills needed to execute it. Creative leaders of the organization must act consistently with the vision in everything they do.

The execution of creative visioning can be facilitated by the use of an idea-processing system (refer to chapter 5). Too often in the past, top-management teams have worked up a statement of corporate vision, promulgated it, and then thought that their work was done. What they overlooked, and what dooms this kind of superficial effort, is the need to plan and control this vision over time. An idea-processing system is an excellent vehicle for fulfilling a company's vision.

Principal Reason Why Corporate Visioning Is Not Implemented

The principal reason why farsightedness or creative visioning is not widely used is that managers are preoccupied with, as well as rewarded for, the critical present-day tasks of boosting sales, increasing market share, and enhancing profit margins. In most American companies, the urgency for short-term results has driven out the important long-term vision of a company. The traditional building block of American corporations, the semiautonomous strategic business unit, can actually impede a company's ability to focus on the future. Most companies still use rigid financial formulas for deciding whether they should invest in or dispose of individual units. Such an approach not only focuses on current market conditions, but also makes it easy for competitors to determine what a company will do with a particular business. As an example, why did American companies pull out of the color TV business? Because traditional strategic analysis said that it was a mature industry. However, the remaining players, who now compete in the growing markets for VCRs and video cameras, will likely get into such new products as high-definition TV.

Additionally, the dividing of a company into strategic business units can interfere with its ability to identify its core competencies and key people. Essentially, core skills often have nothing to do with the way the company is organized. At General Electric, Jack Welch is determined to create what he calls a boundaryless organization in which technology, information, managers, and management practices flow freely from one division to another. When inspectors at the aircraft engines division check the integrity of metal parts, for example, they use X-ray technology developed by the medical systems unit.

As another example, focusing on the future needs of customers has prompted R. R. Donnelley to reinvent not just itself but its competition as well. The company visions its principal competitors not as other printing companies, but rather as televisions, radios, telephones, computers—any medium of communication that can lure the company's customers away from print. To keep customers and win new ones, Donnelley has invested heavily in advanced technology and has stepped up expansion overseas. Using satellites, the company can print a securities prospectus simultaneously in the United States, Europe, and Japan. When a computer manufacturer wants a new user manual, Donnelley can use digitial technology to do the job on glossy paper, magnetic disk, compact disc, or all three. What is next? Perhaps customized yellow pages (each would encompass a circular geographic area with the consumer's house at the center) or college textbooks tailor-made for a professor's class. The company estimates that about 50 percent of its revenues by 1995 or 2000 will come from new business operations that did not exist ten years ago.[5]

Scenario Planning Can Be Helpful in Corporate Visioning

To keep top-level executives from being trapped by unexpected external factors when undertaking creative visioning, there is generally need for scenario planning. Royal Dutch/Shell has been doing scenario planning for nineteen years and is widely regarded as the master of scenario planning. Currently, it has two twenty-year scenarios in place. The first, called "Sustainable World," predicts increased concern about global warming trends and an expanded emphasis on conservation, recycling, and emissions controls. The second scenario, called "Mercantilist World," postulates an increase in protectionism, a slump in world growth, and a deemphasis of environmentalism.

The company's group planning coordinator believes that scenario planning has helped Shell be better prepared than its competitors for external shocks. In the early 1980s, for example, while most forecasters were predicting a steadily increasing price for crude oil, Shell, in one of its scenarios, entertained the possibility that the price would slide to fifteen dollars a barrel. As a hedge against such an eventuality, the company began looking into cost-saving exploration technologies. When the slump hit, Shell was able to sustain a higher level of drilling activity than many of its competitors. Shell realizes that its two scenarios do not encompass everything that might happen in the future, and that neither will be a perfect predictor. However, they do provide a framework for visioning the company's future in a creative way.[6]

An Example of Using Corporate Visioning to Overcome a Crisis

Often, it takes a crisis to jar companies into using thinking that is realistic about the future. At Trinova (formerly Libbey-Owens-Ford, a manufacturer of engineered components and systems), the catalyst was would-be corporate raiders who wanted to break up the company and sell off pieces. Trinova was until recently a loose confederation of three businesses with no clear direction. The CEO did not have a good understanding of what the company was, let alone what he wanted it to be. Figuring these things out took the CEO and his senior managers many years. They decided that Trinova's glass business was too capital-intensive and too dependent on the cyclical automobile industry, so they sold it to Pilkington Brothers, a leading British glassmaker.

To assist in getting a handle on its operations today and tomorrow from a creative visioning perspective, Trinova asked itself what kinds of products and services its customers would likely need fifteen years hence and what kind of core competencies the company would have to develop to serve them. Its Vickers division, for example, was already a global leader in hydraulic components for airplanes. But Vickers' customers were thinking about enhancing or replacing some of their hydraulic components with electric, electromechanical, and electronic parts and systems. The net result was that Vickers resolved to master these new technologies through acquisitions, joint ventures, licensing agreements, and its own research and development. Trinova does not want to lose a customer because it does not have the technology. Trinova does not know exactly what Boeing and McDonnell Douglas will be ordering in the twenty-first century, but it is confident that it has the skills and flexibility to meet their evolving needs.[7]

RELATIONSHIP OF CORPORATE VISIONING TO A COMPANY'S MISSION AND GOALS

As chief executives strive to get their companies to think strategically, they are discovering the importance of their line managers at the various operating levels. Line managers are reemerging as the missing link in the drive to turn creative visions into realities. In many cases, the most important strategic decisions get made in the trenches and not by executives and their corporate planners. Managers below this highest level formulate strategy day in and day out since they respond to competitive pressures by virtue of the products they promote, the price concessions they make, the distribution channels they choose, and similar items.

Too often, the corporation vision and mission statements that issue from top-level executives bear only slight relation to reality. For example, a company's current vision is to be a world-class leader in certain products and/or services and its mission is to keep all of its customers happy with these products and/or services. Such a statement can be valuable, but only if it is used as a constant guide for the actions of managers and workers in terms of specific goals to be achieved. The real test of a mission statement's effectiveness is how well it helps managers obtain their goals on a day-to-day basis.

Defining a Company's Corporate Mission and Goals Realistically

As an example of relating a company's mission and goals realistically, Intel Corporation's stated mission in the early 1980s was to be a major competitor in both memory chips and microprocessors. In turn, specific goals were developed around this mission. However, Intel pulled out of the dynamic random access memory (DRAM) business in 1985 and focused its energies almost exclusively on microprocessors because the company suffered large losses at the hands of Japanese competitors. It is now clear that the company had already decided to retreat from memory chips, perhaps as early as 1983, by its marketing, pricing, and investment choices.

Currently, Intel's mission is to become the premier building-block supplier to the *new* computer industry, and the company has formulated specific goals to accomplish this enlarged mission of its operations. The company intends to keep concentrating on microprocessors, such as its successful 386 and 486 chips, the brains of personal computers, and many successor chips, such as the 586 and

686. Also, Intel has begun, on a small scale, to make personal computers that are sold by customers (including AT&T and Unisys) under their own names. If there should be a shift in the marketplace by its customers to increasingly buy finished or semifinished systems, Intel will be able to respond to the changing marketplace.[8]

CRITICAL SUCCESS FACTORS SUPPORT THE ATTAINMENT OF A COMPANY'S CORPORATE GOALS

For any business, critical success factors are the limited number of areas in which results, if they are satisfactory, will ensure successful competitive performance. They are the few key areas where things must go right if the organization is to flourish. If results in these areas are not adequate, the organization's efforts for the period will be less than desired. As a result, the critical success factors are areas of activity that should receive constant and careful attention from management. The current status of performance in each area should be continually measured, and that information should be made available to higher levels of management.

As shown in figure 7.1, critical success factors support the attainment of a company's corporate goals. Goals represent the endpoints that a company hopes to reach. Critical success factors, on the other hand, are the areas in which good performance is necessary to ensure attainment of these goals. As figure 7.1 shows, the automobile industry has four industry-based CSFs: (1) having the right styling for the times, (2) having a good-quality dealer system, (3) having effective cost control over selling and manufacturing operations, and (4) having the capability to meet current energy standards in terms of average mileage per gallon for all cars produced. Though the automobile manufacturers must pay attention to many other factors, these four areas represent the underpinnings of successful operations.

Sources of Critical Success Factors

From a broad viewpoint, the principal sources of critical success factors have been identified as follows:[9]

- *Structure of a particular industry.* As shown in figure 7.1, each industry by its very nature has a set of CSFs that are determined by the characteristics of the industry itself.
- *Competitive strategy, industry position, and geographic location.* The actions of the major companies in an industry that is dominated by one or two large companies will often produce new problems for the smaller companies in the industry. The competitive strategy for the latter may mean establishing a new market niche, getting out of a product line completely, or redistribution of resources among various product lines.
- *Environmental factors.* As the economy changes, potential factors change, the energy problem becomes more acute, and the like, critical success factors can change for an organization.

Figure 7.1

How Attainment of Organizational Goals Is Supported by Critical Success Factors for the Automobile and Supermarket Industries

Example	Company's Goals	Critical Success Factors
For-profit	Earnings per share	Automobile industry:
concern	Return on investment	Styling
	Market share	Good-quality dealer system
	New product success	Cost control
		Meeting energy standards
		Supermarket industry:
		Product mix
		Inventory
		Sales promotion
		Price

Source: John F. Rockart, "Chief Executives Define Their Own Data Needs," *Harvard Business Review*, March–April 1979, p. 86.

- *Temporal factors.* Internal organization considerations often lead to temporal critical success factors. Inventory, for example, which is rarely a CSF for top management, might become a high-level CSF if there is far too much or too little stock.

Although these four sources for identifying CSFs are determinable, critical success factors are different for an individual industry and even for companies within that industry.

Tie-in of CSFs to Key Performance Indicators (KPIs)

The concept of key performance indicators (KPIs), developed at MIT's Sloan School of Management, is a way of formalizing and measuring critical success factors. As a starting point, it is necessary to show the relationship of corporate visioning (first component) and a company's corporate mission (second component) to a company's goals (figure 7.2). Essentially, a company's corporate goals (third component) are broken down into appropriate goals for its divisions and business units. In turn, each business unit identifies a number of critical activities (CSFs) (fourth component) that must be performed well in order to achieve its goals. These activities are then assigned to the people responsible for their completion. Finally, each business unit establishes a measurement system to quantify success. These measures are the key performance indicators (fifth component).

For example, a company has decided that one of its corporate goals is to improve customer satisfaction. At the corporate level, a periodic survey of customers would be a key performance indicator, since corporate executives are responsible

Figure 7.2

The Relationship of Corporate Visioning to a Corporation's Mission and Its Specific Company Goals, Which Are Related to Critical Success Factors (CSFs) and Key Performance Indicators (KPIs)

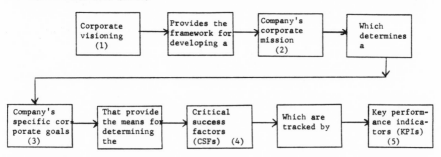

for the overall company effort. Activities that contribute to improvements might be improved product quality, improved customer service and support, improved delivery times, and more customer-suggested product improvement. Each of these activities suggests its own key performance indicators. The most important part of this process is that the KPIs be measures that people responsible for them can actually control and for which they can be held accountable. Because of this combination of responsibility, control, and accountability, these KPIs are certain to be relevant and important to the executives assigned to them.

Measurement of a Company's KPIs against the Best

A way to judge the performance of a company unit in terms of KPIs is to compare it to other units within the company. However, comparisons with outsiders can highlight the best industry practices and promote their adoption. This technique is commonly called "benchmarking." When the Xerox Corporation started using benchmarking, management's aim was to analyze unit production costs in manufacturing operations. Uncomfortably aware of the extremely low prices of Japanese plain-paper copiers, the manufacturing staff at Xerox wanted to determine whether its Japanese counterparts' relative costs were as low as their relative prices. The staff compared the operating capabilities and features of the Japanese machines, including those made by Fuji-Xerox, and tore down their mechanical components for examination.

As somewhat expected, the investigation revealed that production costs in the United States were much higher. Discarding their standard budgeting processes, U.S. manufacturing operations therefore adopted the lower Japanese costs as targets for driving their own business plans. Top management, gratified with the results, directed that all units and cost centers in the corporation use benchmarking.

In contrast, distribution, administration, service, and other support functions of Xerox found it difficult to arrive at a convenient analogue to a product. These nonmanufacturing units began to make internal comparisons, including worker productivity at different regional distribution centers and per pound transportation costs between regions. Next, they looked at competitors' processes. In logistics, that meant comparing the transportation, warehousing, and inventory management of Xerox's distribution function with those of the competition.

The initial step in the process is to identify what will be benchmarked, that is, measured, such as expense-to-revenue ratios, inventory turns, service calls, customer satisfaction—whatever the "product" of the particular function is. Then it is necessary to pinpoint the areas that need improvement. In Xerox's experience, managers tend to concentrate first on comparative costs, but as they become more knowledgeable about benchmarking, they discover that understanding practices, processes, and methods is more important because these define the changes necessary to reach the benchmark costs. Moreover, as managers become more confident about benchmarking, they can readily extend it beyond cost reduction to profit-producing factors, like service levels and customer satisfaction.[10]

Important sources for the purpose of comparison are annual reports and other easily available publications. They can uncover gross indicators of efficient operation. Universally recognized measures like return on assets, revenue per employee, inventory turns, and general and administrative expenses will help identify the well-managed companies. To identify superior performance in specific functions, a company can utilize trade journals, consultants, annual reports and other company publications in which "statements of pride" appear, and presentations at professional and other forums. The same well-run organizations keep turning up. Overall, comparison of a company's key performance indicators against the best can determine whether or not the creative process should be applied to improve operations.

CORPORATE STRATEGIC THINKING AND CREATIVITY

Corporate strategic thinking, as can be seen from the foregoing discussion, is somewhat different from the traditional strategic planning approach. Accent is very heavy on the *focus* of a company's operations today and tomorrow and *flexibility* when focusing on the company's core areas. However, it should be noted while constructing alternative visions of the future that strategic thinking can also carry a price. That is, there is a word of caution. If a company tries to be flexible and ready for everything, it could end up raising its costs and not being good at anything. Managers ultimately have to make hard choices. This is where creativity can be of great assistance to managers.

When it comes to thinking and acting strategically in creative ways, managers have to depend on a number of quantifiable and unquantifiable factors, like experience, instinct, guesswork, and luck. That is, managers will have to link strategic thinking with corporate visioning, which, in turn, is linked to a company's mission and goals. In a similar manner, there must be a linkage to day-to-day operations, which take the form of a company's critical success factors and key performance indicators.

Overall, strategic thinking allows managers to marry together a company's quantitative and qualitative factors in creative ways in order to get a handle on a company's present and future operations. As discussed in the last chapter, this means incorporating creative computer software in a manager's daily mode of operations. Such an approach will be evident in the applications to follow in this chapter and the remaining ones.

APPLICATIONS SHOWING LINKAGE OF CORPORATE STRATEGIC THINKING TO UTILIZING CREATIVE COMPUTER SOFTWARE

In the applications to follow, a number of managers at the various levels of the corporation focus their attention initially on corporate strategic thinking. Typically, these managers utilize creative computer software to support them in their strategic thinking activities. From this perspective, they use creative computer software "to do it better." That is, appropriate software is utilized to assist management in going the final step in reaching higher-quality decisions. Needless to say, improvement in decision making has the capability to meet and, hopefully, beat competition in the short to the long run.

AMERICAN AIRLINES

In the airline industry, American Airlines (AA) has set the standard with its highly profitable Sabre reservation system. Its strategic system has profoundly shaped the structure of this industry in the past and continues to do so. The Sabre system is still reaping benefits today for American Airlines. After many years of use, it is being enhanced to the airline's advantage. Five years ago, American Airlines tripled the size of its application development staff, an increase that is just now beginning to yield solid results. For example, a recent demonstration of new systems at the airline's Fort Worth, Texas, headquarters revealed an impressive range of technology.

New Systems and Applications Recently Implemented

One of the major projects currently under way at American Airlines is the development of a companywide office automation (OA) system. Dubbed "InterAAact," the $150-million effort aims to deliver 18,000 personal workstations based on the Intel Corporation 80386 microprocessor. The integrated package of third-party OA software includes a combination of the Windows and NewWave computing environments from Microsoft Corporation and Hewlett-Packard Company, respectively; the Paradox relational data-base-management system from Borland International Inc.; and the Word word-processing software and Excel spreadsheet from Microsoft. Connectivity is also provided to an internal E-mail system and to American's Sabre airline reservation services.

Another part of American Airlines' new systems is the $25-million airlines operations center. Housed in a building located south of the Dallas/Forth Worth International Airport, the center controls all operations of the 550 air fleet and associated support systems. Among the departments using the building are flight dispatch, weather services, operations analysis, central load control, cargo operations, and crew scheduling. The system operations control facility, opened in 1990, also includes a command and communications center used for teleconferencing and emergency coordination.

To accommodate future growth, the system can manage flight operations of up to a third more aircraft than American now flies. A maintenance, operations, and control expert application in the center is expected to save three hours of time for each operations controller in an eight-hour shift. The software, incorporating seventeen work-years of development and the expertise of the airline's most experienced controllers, was produced on a Macintosh incorporating a Micro Explorer Lisp board from Texas Instruments Inc. (Dallas, Texas) and the ART expert-system software from Inference Corporation (El Segundo, California).

Other applications demonstrated included landside analysis. American Airlines Decision Technologies, a consulting subsidiary, developed the PS/2-based application to forecast the results of physical changes in an airport. A color display shows an animated view of airport concourses and passenger traffic patterns based on proposed changes. American is now using the software to analyze the results of changes in security procedures begun during the recent Persian Gulf war.

Hub slashing, a knowledge-based application, was recently implemented to assist operations staff in choosing the best flights to cancel when such an action is required. The selected flights out of American's seven hub airports are rated by the Macintosh-based software as having the least impact on operations and passengers. American developers constructed the hub slashing application with the use of Clisp, a C-language expert system shell developed by the artificial intelligence section at the National Aeronautics and Space Administration (NASA) and a Macintosh HyperCard stack software development system.

Another interesting application demonstrated was Sabre Vision imaging. As an adjunct to the company's popular airline reservation system, American installed videodisc applications at travel agencies across the country. The system provides agents with pictures and background information on hotels. Travelers can specify up to 100 requirements, including hotel services and location, and are given a list of lodgings that meet the criteria. They can then view images of the hotel exterior and rooms. To develop Sabre Vision, American developers used OptiNet, a networking product for sharing CD-ROM data bases across a Novell NetWare LAN, and OptiWare, a data-base system tuned to allow faster network access to CD-ROM data, both from On-Line Computer Systems Inc. (Germantown, Maryland).

Still other applications centered on load planning and food preparation. The Macintosh-based load-planning expert-system application can assist land planners in checking weight limits, center of gravity, and payload fuel efficiency of the aircraft. The software can recommend runway selection, cargo-hold temperature, and flap settings. The package was built using the expert software shell from Neuron Data Corporation (Palo Alto, California) and the Macintosh HyperCard software. VideoSpecs food preparation, two years in development, will ultimately be deployed in 170 kitchens across the country for American Airlines flights. A computer touch-screen will allow chefs to pull up visual demonstrations of some 1,000 recipes. The multimedia application also includes text ingredient lists. The company expects to yield $200,000 in annual savings through the elimination of paper-based recipes.[11]

Enhancing Creativity at American Airlines by Using Creative Computer Software

As can be seen from these new systems and applications, American Airlines is not sitting still and letting its competition gain an edge. In fact, American may be commanding such an impressive lead in systems now that the current smaller and medium-sized as well as weaker airlines may never be able to compete effectively. However, the more aggressive airlines, such as United Airlines and Delta Airlines, have comparable systems that prod American for further improvement. But how will American move forward against it stiffest competition?

American Airlines, like other airlines, has developed new systems and applications that basically come from past or current internal needs. In some cases, the demand for new systems has come from the development of new ideas. That is, if planning or brainstorming sessions at American have been productive, MIS personnel must have both specific direction and sufficient time to explore various alternatives. In such cases, creativity can be reinforced by a change in environment and dress code. On the downside, meetings that are held with a picture of American's founder on the wall are not the way to go. (This statement can be made about any company.) The only observable creative activity in such a formal environment will be the clever methods used by MIS participants to stifle their yawns. Fresh corporate perspectives of American's MIS personnel come to the fore more readily when meetings are held at a site that lacks the usual reminders of business as usual. An egalitarian seating arrangement also proves to be beneficial. Additionally, MIS participants will be more involved and enthusiastic if they leave their blue pin-striped suits at home and attend in more casual attire.

Generally, this is the environment that is currently used by many companies, including American Airlines, to employ creativity in developing new systems and applications. However, as discussed throughout this book, a preferred approach to enhance creativity is to go beyond this traditional approach and employ idea generators and idea-processing systems. If this approach were implemented on a widespread basis, AA managers would feel more comfortable with the solutions or ideas from "the guy in left field." Such a computer approach would loosen up some of the inhibitions of American's managers, who oftentimes tend to have a one-track mind regarding solutions to the problems they face. By using other means of looking for creativity such as computerized idea generators and idea-processing systems, American's managers can get beyond traditional limitations in strategic thinking and decision making. These comments are designed to show that an industry leader, like American Airlines, can do things better creatively in the future to meet and preferably beat competition.

GENERAL ELECTRIC AIRCRAFT ENGINES DIVISION

General Electric Aircraft Engines Division produces aircraft engines for military and commercial use. It sells military engines to the U.S. government as well as governments of other nations, such as Turkey, Israel, Greece, Egypt, and Japan. For a foreign government, there are many factors to be included in that nation's decision to purchase an aircraft and a particular engine for the aircraft. For example, it is already known that South Korea has chosen to purchase the F-16 aircraft produced by General Dynamics. There are two possible engines that can power the F-16. The F110-GE-129 is made by GE Aircraft Engines Division. Its alternative is the Pratt & Whitney F100-PW-229.

Because GE would like to determine which manufacturer will win the South Korean engine contract before South Korea actually makes its decision, there are a number of factors involved, namely, economic, logistic, and political ones as well as the performance of the engine. As will be seen in the material to follow, there are various ways to analyze these factors using Criterium, a software package discussed in the previous chapter.

Background on the F110-GE-129 Engine

In the 1970s, GE focused on developing new engines for military use. GE initiated development of the 27,000-to-29,000-pounds-thrust-class Derivative Fighter Engine, called the F110. Unfortunately, government spending on defense mechanisms was reduced drastically at the same time. The government did not purchase many of the engines. However, with this engine, the company was poised for success in the 1980s. In 1984, the U.S. government began purchasing GE's F110 engines. The F110 engine is used to power General Dynamic's F-16 and F-16XL fighters and Grumman's F-14 fighter aircraft. It is also now used in F-16s owned by Israel, Turkey, Greece, Bahrain, and Egypt. GE's F110 represents 89 percent of the aircraft engine contract selections made by international competitors since competition for the engine began in 1985. Since the U.S. government is cutting defense-budget spending, it is necessary for GE to get more orders for military engines from foreign nations.

Corporate Vision, Mission, and Goals for GE Aircraft Engines Division

Initially, it is helpful to define General Electric's corporate vision, mission, and goals for its division before trying to determine the outcome of South Korea's engine decision. In this case, this division has a vision of being the world leader in powering air and land transportation vehicles of all types well into the twenty-first century and beyond. Its mission is to provide engines that meet the needs of business and government customers today and into the future. In light of this division's vision and mission, its specific corporate goals are defined as follows:

1. Sell as many engines as possible.
2. Produce a quality product.
3. Service the customer.

To meet these corporate goals, there are several factors considered critical to GE's success, that is, critical success factors that are measured by key performance indicators. First is the financial position of the South Korean government compared to that of the United States, as measured by the value of the U.S. dollar. Likewise, South Korea's perception of the U.S. government is important and is indicated by purchases of other goods from the United States. Engine quality is also critical. Engine performance may be measured by thrust and maximum speed. The engine must be reliable and maintainable, which may be determined by the amount of time between repairs. Customer service, including delivery of engines, can be measured by GE's ability to meet the customer's required delivery schedule. Additionally, spare parts must have zero defects. Maintenance is based on GE's service to South Korea.

The linkage of corporate goals to critical success factors and key performance indicators is found in figure 7.3. In turn, this information is useful in answering specific questions, as will be seen below.

Figure 7.3
Linkage of Corporate Goals to Critical Success Factors and Key Performance Indicators—General Electric Aircraft Engines Division

Corporate Goals	Critical Success Factors	Key Performance Indicators
1. Sell as many engines as possible	Financial position of South Korean government	Value of US dollar
	South Korea's perception of US government	Purchases of other goods from United States
2. Produce a quality product	High performance	Thrust and high speed
	Low maintenance	Time between repairs
3. Service the customer	Delivery	Meet delivery schedule
	Spare parts	Zero defect spare parts

Questions That Can Be Answered Using Criterium

Currently, GE is trying to determine a foreign nation's choice of engine for the F-16 fighter aircraft. The foreign nation may choose either GE's F110-GE-129 or Pratt & Whitney's F100-PW-229. GE would like to predict this nation's decision before the choice is made. As noted previously, such is the case with South Korea. The Criterium software package was used to create a decision hierarchy consisting of the decision to be made, the four contributing factors, and the two alternatives. The model defines the decision as "Buy Engine for F16." The decision is divided into four contributing factors. The first factor is the performance of the engine, which includes speed, thrust, and reliability. Next are the economic factors of price and number of engines previously sold to the nation. Third, logistics such as delivery schedule, availability of spare parts, and engine service are defined. Finally, politics influence the event of the threat of war and by U.S. friendship with the foreign nation. Reference can be made to figure 7.4

Initially, all factors in the model were given an equal percentage of the rating. That is, each of the four main factors was rated as contributing 25 percent to the final decision. Values were then assigned to each attribute either qualitatively or quantitatively. The qualitative data were converted to a numerical value by Criterium, and a total score was computed for each engine type. This first model created served as the base model. If the South Koreans were to make a decision based on the base model, they would buy their engines from GE (GE had a rating of 51.99 percent to Pratt & Whitney's 48.01 percent). Reference can be made to figure 7.5, which ties in with figure 7.4, the Criterium software structure.

After evaluating these results, it was decided that a country preparing to buy engines would not weigh the four main factors equally. Hence two additional models were created. In the first Criterium model or peace model (when South Korea is not at war), potential customers would probably be most interested in the logistical aspects of the engines. In the peace model, Pratt & Whitney scored higher in delivery and spare parts while GE scored higher in service. Because service and delivery cancel each other out, spare parts tips the scale in favor of Pratt & Whitney. Engine performance was weighted as 39.05 percent of the decision. Next important were economic factors at 27.61 percent. Third were logistics factors at 19.53 percent. Finally, political factors had much less influence on the choice of an engine and were given a rating of 13.81 percent. The model was recalculated with the new weight scales. This time, the GE engine became the leader with a core of 51.53 percent compared to Pratt & Whitney's engine, which scored 48.47 percent.

In the second Criterium decision model or the war model (when South Korea is at war), the political factor will have a greater weight in the decision to purchase an engine. Engine performance and logistics will also be important, with economics having less of an effect. The war model weighted political and logistics factors each as 33 percent of the model. It should be kept in mind that GE has the better political track record, but Pratt & Whitney rates higher on logistics,

Figure 7.4
Criterium Software Structure—General Electric Aircraft Engines Division

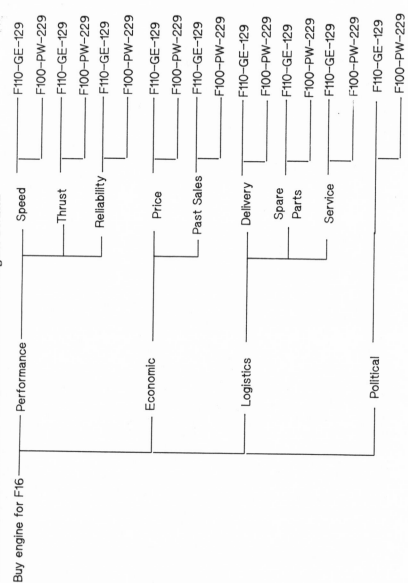

Figure 7.5
Criteria Ratings of Alternatives for F-16—General Electric Aircraft Engines Division

BASE MODEL

Criteria Summary

CRITERIA BLOCK: Buy engine for F16

```
Rank    Score    Block Name
====    =======  =========================================
  1     25.00%   Performance
  1     25.00%   Logistics
  1     25.00%   Economic
  1     25.00%   Political
```

CRITERIA BLOCK: Performance

```
Rank    Score    Block Name
====    =======  =========================================
  1     49.33%   Reliability
  2     31.08%   Thrust
  3     19.58%   Speed
```

CRITERIA BLOCK: Economic

```
Rank    Score    Block Name
====    =======  =========================================
  1     66.67%   Price
  2     33.33%   Past Sales
```

CRITERIA BLOCK: Logistics

```
Rank    Score    Block Name
====    =======  =========================================
  1     33.33%   Spare Parts
  1     33.33%   Delivery
  1     33.33%   Service
```

Figure 7.5 (Continued)

BASE MODEL

Ratings of Alternatives from Buy engine for F16

Alternative	Result
=============	========
F110-GE-129	XXXXXXXXXXXXXXXX 51.99
F100-PW-229	XXXXXXXXXXXXX 48.01

CRITERIA BLOCK: Past Sales

Rank	Score	Block Name
======	=======	============
1	87.50%	F110-GE-129
2	12.50%	F100-PW-229

CRITERIA BLOCK: Delivery

Rank	Score	Block Name
======	=======	============
1	66.67%	F100-PW-229
2	33.33%	F110-GE-129

CRITERIA BLOCK: Spare Parts

Rank	Score	Block Name
======	=======	============
1	83.33%	F100-PW-229
2	16.67%	F110-GE-129

CRITERIA BLOCK: Service

Rank	Score	Block Name
======	=======	============
1	66.67%	F110-GE-129
2	33.33%	F100-PW-229

Figure 7.5 (Continued)

BASE MODEL

CRITERIA BLOCK: Political

```
Rank    Score    Block Name
====    =======  =========================================
  1     66.67%   F110-GE-129
  2     33.33%   F100-PW-229
```

CRITERIA BLOCK: Speed

```
Rank    Score    Block Name
====    =======  =========================================
  1     66.67%   F110-GE-129
  2     33.33%   F100-PW-229
```

CRITERIA BLOCK: Thrust

```
Rank    Score    Block Name
====    =======  =========================================
  1     66.67%   F110-GE-129
  2     33.33%   F100-PW-229
```

CRITERIA BLOCK: Reliability

```
Rank    Score    Block Name
====    =======  =========================================
  1     80.00%   F110-GE-129
  2     20.00%   F100-PW-229
```

CRITERIA BLOCK: Price

```
Rank    Score     Block Name
====    =======   =========================================
  1     100.00%   F100-PW-229
  2       0.00%   F110-GE-129
```

having better spare parts and delivery ratings. Performance had a 20 percent weighting. Economics, least important to a country during war, was allotted only 14 percent of the model. As a net result of the changes for the war model, GE scored higher than Pratt & Whitney by a score of 53.55 percent to 46.45 percent. In comparing the war model with the peace model, GE has a greater chance of winning the contract when South Korea is at war than during a time of peace.

Overall, this first application has demonstrated that corporate strategic thinking can be incorporated into models of GE's future performance. That is, GE's Aircraft Engines Division can start with a base model that represents the basic focus of its operations and can then develop additional models, such as peace and war models, where the accent is on flexibility to meet possible forthcoming conditions. In addition, this application has demonstrated the linkage of GE's corporate vision and mission to GE's Aircraft Engines Division in terms of specific goals, critical success factors, and key performance indicators.

ABC BANK, INC.

ABC Bank, Inc., is a regional bank operating in Indiana, Kentucky, Michigan, and Ohio. Last year's revenues exceeded $800 million. Just three months ago, ABC Bank acquired another bank. In the past, ABC Bank focused on serving mostly rural areas and targeted deposit products such as savings accounts, checking accounts, certificates of deposit, and the like. However, with the recent merger, locations have expanded to include many suburban markets as well. In fact, since the merger doubled the deposit base of the bank (ABC Bank did not buy the loans of the other bank), the new focus of the bank will be to market a more diverse portfolio such as trusts, investment services, business services, Visa, and Mastercard.

In addition, ABC Bank would like to identify other areas of expansion so that it may have continued growth in this competitive market. It has looked into targeting such groups as the elderly, small businesses, and the affluent customer. It has explored expanding its services through packaging products, automated teller machine innovations, automatic transfer of funds, and installation of point-of-sale terminals in grocery stores and gas stations.

Strategic Thinking by Bank Managers in Terms of Computer Systems and Software

Like a few other banks, ABC Bank has identified computer systems and software that will assist it in focusing better on its core business and being flexible enough to change with the times. Hence it has employed strategic thinking about its present and future computer systems and software. Within its everyday operations, some of its computer applications, such as financial planning, may be obvious, while more innovative uses of credit scoring are just beginning to gain in popularity. Focusing first on electronic spreadsheet models, ABC Bank was able to utilize software packages such as Lotus 1-2-3 to simplify the hundreds of recalculations necessary during the course of every business day. In addition, Lotus 1-2-3 allows the bank's managers to change variables easily to determine the effects of different changes on the bottom line.

Perhaps even more useful in supporting the complex needs of its financial institutions is the utilization of a fourth-generation language,. Interactive Financial Planning System (IFPS). Such a financial planning language allows the bank's managers to perform advanced tasks such as linear optimization, risk analysis, cash-flow analysis, and the like. These IFPS programs are used on a regular basis for forecasting, investment analysis, and other ongoing needs.

Aside from these well-known computer banking applications, the bank is moving to automation of other banking operations previously unaddressed by the MIS department. As mentioned earlier, one example of this utilization can be seen in the credit scoring system currently in use. Such an automated system assigns point values to various aspects of credit applications and, in turn, calculates a cumulative score. This score is then compared with guidelines set for "minimum" scores needed to gain loan approval. ABC Bank can then use this information, along with its experience and discretion, in making the final lending decision. This is a good example of the synergy that can be created with a manager-machine interface. That is, neither the manager nor the machine can make the best decision alone, but by combining both, they can make better decisions together.

Two areas that have incorporated newer computer systems, that is, a group DSS operating mode, are marketing and market research. Those in market research are making great use of the increased demographic and customer information available to them. They can analyze their customer base to set pricing for services or perform venture analysis over the life cycle of a bank product to determine the offerings. With increased GDSS usage, the bank's marketing managers are better able to quantify larger amounts of information and sell their programs to upper management. By presenting various "what-if" scenarios, marketers are able to demonstrate what an anticipated 40 percent market share "good-case" scenario versus a 20 percent "worst-case" scenario might mean to overall bank profitability.

CSFs and KPIs to Evaluate Product Introductions

Because market research centers on what new banking products should be brought to the marketplace, the success of the bank depends on the ability of management to anticipate future trends and provide better products than the competition. This is supported by advertising intended to communicate the availability of the product to present and potential customers. In figure 7.6., critical success factors and associated key performance indicators have been identified to evaluate new product introductions. Market research applications clearly represent how computerization can be used in conjunction with management experience to improve the quality of decisions.

Figure 7.6
Critical Success Factors and Key Performance Indicators to Evaluate New Product Introductions—ABC Bank, Inc.

Critical Success Factors	Key Performance Indicators
Develop product for a target market	Volume of inquiries and sales from target group
Advertise to the target market	Response from advertising
Build product strength	Volume of sales
Gain product acceptance	Rate of sales growth
Maintain quality of product	Percentage of services discontinued/ number of repeat customers

The continued growth of ABC Bank depends on its flexibility to meet changing market needs. With the diversity of people's attitudes in different cultures and generations, this need for flexibility is magnified. New products must be introduced to replace those near the end of their product cycles. To bring new products to the market requires much from the bank's managers in terms of an analytical and a behavioral viewpoint. However, the use of an idea generator can do much to help managers develop new banking ideas that were not previously known or to solve banking problems that were considered to be difficult to solve or unsolvable.

Questions That Can Be Answered Using IdeaFisher 4.0

As the first step of looking at market research in a group DSS environment, the bank's managers decided to undertake the development of a new service. The managers will generate new ideas for services from which the best service will be chosen. The IdeaFisher 4.0 software package from Fisher Idea Systems is utilized. As described in the previous chapter, IdeaFisher 4.0 is an idea generator designed to help people think more creatively and effectively. IdeaFisher cannot recommend answers to problems presented by the bank's managers. It is not, in that sense, artificial intelligence. However, it can guide them and prod them to identify the relevant issues. In turn, it will inspire them to develop new ideas and insights into problems. IdeaFisher is a cross-reference system of words, phrases, and questions that is composed of two data bases. One, called QBank, contains nearly 6,000 organized questions too clarify, modify, and evaluate the bank's managers' thoughts. The other, IdeaBank, contains more than 60,000 organized words and phrases with over 700,000 associative links.

IdeaFisher utilizes two notepads, one for QBank to hold answers to questions, and one for IdeaBank that is the focal point in capturing the bank's managers' ideas, thoughts, and comments. The Idea Notepad records the managers' train of thought as they explore IdeaBank's relationships. These basic components of IdeaFisher will be explained in each of the IdeaFisher examples in this chapter and the following ones. It should be noted that each figure for the examples of IdeaFisher is a representation of the actual computer screen.

Initially, IdeaFisher will be used to answer this question: "What if we want to develop a new product or service?" In the first screen, shown in figure 7.7a, the second items was selected from the first QBank menu: "2. Developing a New Product or Service—Modifying a Product or Service." As is shown in the top half of figure 7.7a, this gave four menu items regarding clarification questions. IdeaFisher's QBank was then used to get a strategic grasp of a product or service: market, customer, competition, and so on. QBank prods the bank's managers by asking specific questions in these areas. After answering all relevant QBank questions and recording the answers in the question notepad at the bottom of the screen in figure 7.7a, the managers then used IdeaFisher to filter out the key concepts, as shown in figure 7.7b. These key concepts allow the bank's managers a logical starting point to expand their ideas using IdeaBank. The key concepts shown indicate that the bank could help small businesses that have workaholic owners. The small businesses are understaffed and have a lack of expertise. Owners of small businesses are looking for banks to provide convenient, reliable, and effective banking services.

Next, it is necessary to enter IdeaBank in order to explore the ideas and associations. The bank's managers are exploring the "Business-Industry-Occupations-Money" selection from the list of twenty-eight major categories, as shown in figure 7.8a.

Figure 7.7a
Selection of Second Item from the QBank Menu: "2. Developing a New Product or Service—Modifying a Product or Service"—ABC Bank, Inc.

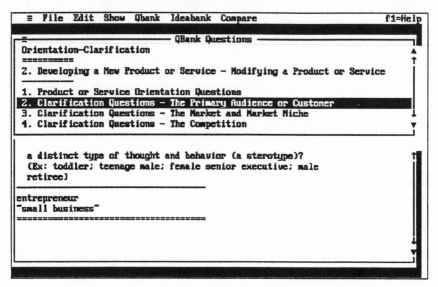

Figure 7.7b
Key Concepts Useful to Bank Managers for Expanding Ideas Using IdeaBank—ABC Bank, Inc.

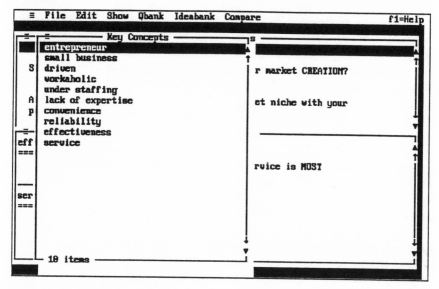

Figure 7.8a
Use of the Major Category from IdeaBank, "Business-Industry-Occupations-Money," by the Managers of ABC Bank, Inc.

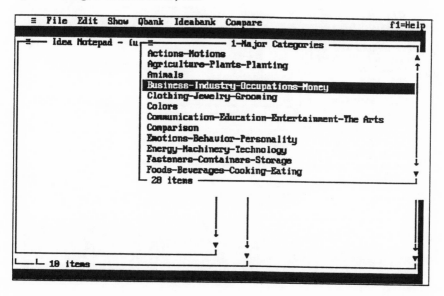

It is obvious that the other major categories are not appropriate for the development of an appropriate banking service. Within this major category are twenty-eight topical categories, of which "Money/Banking/Finance/Economics" was explored, as shown in figure 7.8b. This figure also shows the bank's managers' train of thought as recorded by the Idea Notepad on the left of the screen. As an example in this figure, there was a movement from "Business-Industry-Occupations-Money" to "Money/Banking/Finance/Economics" to "rubber check" and "bad check" down through "accounts receivable." When the Idea Notepad was reviewed, items like checks, accounting department, and accounts receivable were evident in this list. Reminded by Key Concepts that the bank is trying to provide a banking service to small businesses, the managers considered all of this information to create a "lock-box" service. This service would receive accounts receivable at a post office box and deposit the funds into the small businesses' accounts. The deposit information, along with a copy of the checks, would then be sent to the small businesses. The bank can also offer collection services for delinquent accounts. This will help the small businesses with their cash-flow positions and, at the same time, generate an income service for the bank.

It should be emphasized that IdeaFisher did not create the lock-box service per se. It only consolidated the bank's mangers' thoughts. By reviewing the traits of this service in the Question and Idea Notepads, the bank's managers derived a lock box. Another group of bank managers might create something completely different, based on their train of thought and associations made by them. The

Figure 7.8b
**Use of the Topical Category from IdeaBank, "Money/Banking/Finance/Economics,"
to Develop the Idea Notepad, by the Managers of ABC Bank, Inc.**

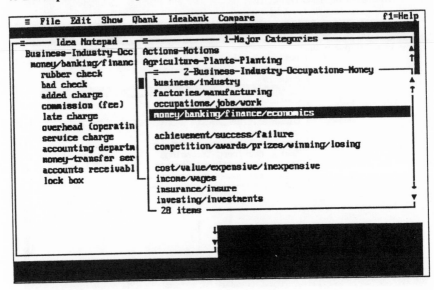

end result of these associations is that the creative talents of the bank's managers have been brought to bear on the problem.

IdeaFisher was then used to create a second option for a strategic decision at ABC Bank, Inc., by the bank's managers. In this case, there was no preconceived reason (such as developing a new service) for the generation of an idea using IdeaFisher. The fact that there was no "goal" allowed greater flexibility in the choice of associations. Because the bank's managers were just looking for ideas, the QBank segment was ignored; that is, they started with IdeaBank. As can be seen from the Idea Notepad on the left of figure 7.9a, the main category of "Business-Industry-Occupations-Money" was selected. Considering that the bank had just merged with another, it was decided to follow the ideas of "new" and "starting over." The topic of "New/Modern/Fresh" was chosen, which displayed a list of things that are new. Since a new service had just been created, the managers chose a "new product" to come up with an idea to complement it. That led them to the list of selections shown on the right of figure 7.9a.

From the list "imagination/creativity" displayed in figure 7.9b, the word "logo" was spotted by the managers. The idea hit them. It was decided to create a new logo for the bank as it moves into anew era. They also noticed the words "Madison Avenue" under the word "logo." This triggered the use of a new advertising campaign to promote the "new" bank, complete with spots to introduce the new logo and service. This is an excellent example of how a strategic decision useful for promoting a "new bank" can be tied back to the CSFs that relate to offering new services to attract more customers.

Figure 7.9a
**Use of the Major Category from IdeaBank, "Business-Industry-Occupations-Money,"
Along with the Topic "New/Modern/Fresh," by the Managers of ABC Bank, Inc.**

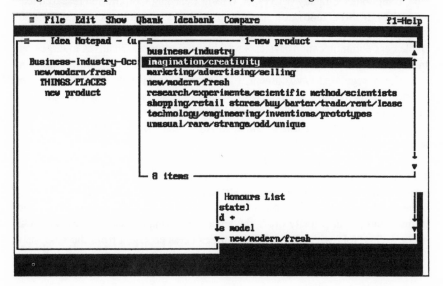

Figure 7.9b
Use of the Topical Category from IdeaBank, "Imagination/Creativity," to Identify "Logo" and "Madison Avenue" by the Managers of ABC Bank Inc.

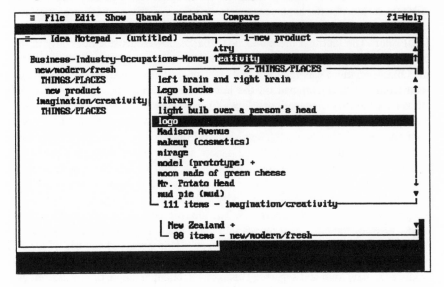

OTHER STRATEGIC THINKING APPLICATIONS THAT MAKE USE OF CREATIVE COMPUTER SOFTWARE

An example of applying creative computer software can be found at the Michigan Bell Telephone Company (MBT). A Wilson Learning Corporation research team recently ran three Innovator sessions at MBT. Company account service administrators (ASAs), their managers, and their customers participated. The ASAs implement communications systems sold by account representatives to large commercial customers. Because they have a great deal of responsibility and work in a highly regulated environment, MBT wanted to provide them with the best possible skills training for their work. The Innovator sessions helped determine (1) changes and trends of the past twelve to eighteen months that have affected ASAs' success, (2) a profile of the ideal ASA, and (3) critical competencies for success of ASAs.

The ASAs, managers, and customers answered questions in these three areas. First, each group defined the main issues and changes that affect the ASAs' work. Second, they addressed the current strengths and weaknesses of the ASAs and identified the characteristics of an ideal ASA two years in the future. Third, they defined and put in priority order the behavorial competencies critical to ASAs' success. The following five critical competencies emerged from the analysis of the Innovator-assisted input groups: influencing skills, communication skills, servicing the customer, creative problem solving, and technical knowledge.

Wilson Learning Corporation's design and development team produced "A Professional Approach to Service," a twelve-day curriculum based on the identified critical competencies. The five-module curriculum includes six generic programs tailored to the ASA environment, three and one-half days of custom-designed material, and three new video segments.

MBT finds the curriculum solid and on target. Ameritech, parent company of MBT, is interested in using it with ASAs in its other Bell Operating Companies. The success of this program is due in no small measure to its foundation: the information gleaned from the "input groups," key stakeholders gathered together and asked for their perspectives. The quality of the information gathered, the clarity of those perspectives, and the ease with which participants could share their views are a credit to The Innovator.[12]

Another application of creative computer software can be found at the *Kansas City Star*, where David Zeeck is facing a series of problems. As executive editor of the *Kansas City Star*, he is, step-by-step, merging his paper's editorial staff with the editorial staff of the *Star*'s former competitor, the *Kansas City Times*. Although the two papers' business operations have already merged, their editorial cultures have remained distinct. For example, to do investigative reporting, the *Star* always had a special-projects team. On the other hand, the *Times* always did it without a special team; its philosophy was that the whole paper should be involved.

To patch together answers to problems like that, Zeeck has turned to MindLink, a HyperCard-based brainstorming tool. MindLink incorporates ideas developed by Synectics (see chapter 6). MindLink leads the user through developing wish lists and free-associating ideas, suggesting images and ideas to help the user's thoughts branch out. For example, on one card, the user might pose a problem; if the user clicks on the Wishing Well button, he or she jumps to another card where he or she can speculate about the problem or ask for triggers—key words, images, or even stories. MindLink may even prompt the user to get up and go for a stroll outside. Meanwhile, MindLink gathers the user's ideas and stores them until he or she is ready for the key task: turning wild ideas back into practical solutions.

What did Zeeck decide about investigative reporting? He believes in a projects desk, but the *Times*' way has benefits too. The resulting answer using MindLink was to do it in a way where the investigative reporters are using other reporters from all over the building. Although MindLink cannot invent an answer, it did assist Zeeck in determining an answer more quickly.[13]

SUMMARY

In this chapter, the change from traditional corporate strategic planning to corporate strategic thinking by company managers was linked to the utilization of creative thinking (as deemed necessary). In effect, today's top-level managers have to be much nimbler than they were in the past. They must be able to spot opportunities and potential problems even before they develop. In turn, the accent has shifted somewhat from strictly the *quality* of the decision to *quality plus*, that is, making an effective decision and implementing it faster. To assist a company's managers in doing things better, idea processors and idea-processing systems that are an integral part of the managers' mode of operation are extremely useful. It was from this perspective that creativity was approached in this chapter. Not only was a broad framework given for linking strategic thinking to creativity, but also several examples were given of using creative computer software in conjunction with other software to solve a company's pressing problems. This specialized approach to study and apply creativity will be found in the remaining chapters of this book on marketing, manufacturing, finance, and accounting.

NOTES

1. Ronald Henkoff, "How to Plan for 1995," *Fortune*, December 31, 1990, p. 70.
2. Ibid.
3. Ibid., pp. 70–72.
4. Ibid., p. 72.
5. Ibid., p. 74.
6. Ibid., p. 79.
7. Ibid., pp. 72–74.
8. Ibid., pp. 74–76.
9. John F. Rockart, "Chief Executives Define Their Own Data Needs," *Harvard Business Review*, March–April 1979, pp. 86–87.
10. Frances Gaither Tucker, Seymour M. Zivan, and Robert C. Camp, "How to Measure Yourself against the Best," *Harvard Business Review*, January–February 1987, pp. 8–9.
11. Steve Polilli, "AA Boasts of New Systems," *Software Magazine*, May 1991, pp. 25–27.
12. Robert Blaine, "The Innovator at Michigan Bell," *Learning Age*, vol. 2, no. 1, 1989, p. 3.
13. David Zeeck, "Breaking Those Mind Chains," *MacWorld*, June 1990, p. 243.

8

Creativity in Marketing

ISSUES EXPLORED

- To rethink the marketing mix today and tomorrow in view of changing times
- To explore the need to examine core competence to create new markets
- To examine why market leaders know what the customers want versus non-market leaders
- To demonstrate the utilization of creative computer software to assist in the development of innovative products and services
- To illustrate applications that show the linkage of rethinking marketing to utilizing creative computer software

OUTLINE

As stressed in chapter 1, it is no longer the case that simply more information will solve today's problems. The limiting factor today is new ideas and fresh concepts. Information, analysis, and problem solving will not yield new ideas because they are all focused on "what is." There is need to refocus on "what can be" such that marketing managers can generate creative and constructive new product and service ideas along with new categories for them. But even that change of mind-set may not be enough. For example, Raytheon, which developed the Patriot missile, also invented the microwave oven years ago, but did nothing with it. Japanese firms turned it into a huge market success.

U.S. corporations spend millions and millions on research and development projects in hopes of inventing creative new products, but if these corporations are run by stodgy chief executives "uncomfortable" with unproven new concepts, creative new products and services will not go anywhere. Besides, new ideas should be a companywide effort. In light of these current problems in U.S. corporations, the whole marketing function should be rethought. The discussion to follow centers on new ways of viewing the marketing function as well as real-world examples of using creative computer software.

LINKAGE OF CORPORATE STRATEGIC THINKING TO RETHINKING THE MARKETING FUNCTION

If companies in the United States are to have global success today and tomorrow, they need to go beyond the "me-too" product attitude. The focus should be on corporate visioning, which is a starting point for corporate strategic thinking. Visioning of the marketing function is envisioning markets for products and services that do not exist today. In other words, a typical U.S. company should generate new products and services such that the company is out there ahead all on its own, as Raytheon could have been with the microwave oven.

In this century as well as into the twenty-first century, marketing battles will be won by companies that can build and dominate fundamentally new markets.

For example, creative new products, such as microrobots, speech-activated appliances, and self-parking cars, not only make the inconceivable conceivable, but also allow a company to influence the direction of the market. In the years to come, more and more companies will close the gap with their rivals on costs, quality, and delivery. But without the capacity to stake out new territories with products and services, many U.S companies will find themselves faced with traditional and shrinking markets for products and services.

RETHINKING THE MARKETING MIX TODAY AND TOMORROW

Before exploring those items that will impact creativity in marketing, it would be advisable to take a look at the marketing mix today and tomorrow. That is, the focus is on rethinking how the typical marketing manager views the marketing mix: product, price, place, and promotion. For a company to be successful in the future, it is necessary that it offer the *right products* at the *right price* in the *right place* along with the *right promotion*. Needless to say, a successful company must change with the times since there are fundamental changes in demographics and consumer preferences ahead for the end of this decade that will force companies to rethink their marketing mix. In addition, there are dramatic changes to take place in the twenty-first century.

Changing Demographics

Demographic projections indicate that the current population will increase 7.1 percent by the year 2000. But unlike previous population rises, this one will come more from increased longevity, not from increasing birth rates. The group aged sixteen to twenty-four will continue to shrink as a percentage of the population. The group aged twenty-five to thirty-four also will continue to decline. This decline may be more significant than the decline in the younger group because those twenty-five to thirty-four years old create new households and therefore purchase home furnishings, appliances, housewares, and similar items. The population in the group aged thirty-five to forty-four has reached its peak and will continue at this level.

The group between forty-five and fifty-four, clearly on the rise since the early 1980s, is projected to increase 31 percent from 1990 to 2000. This age group is at the peak of its earning ability, while its largest expense, its mortgage, mostly is low and close to disappearing. To win loyalty from this group (and capture some of its discretionary income), companies will have to cater to its new needs and preferences. Fueled by the aging of the baby boomers, this group will continue to grow and spend in the 1990s. The group aged fifty-five to sixty-four also will rise from the mid-1990s as the immediately younger group gets older. In addition, the increased longevity due to medical advances will increase the numbers in this age group. Many in this group will go into retirement, which means a necessary slowing of spending. But it also means more time available for shopping. Therefore, companies will succeed by offering these customers merchandise for travel and other leisure activities.

Though the population is aging, marketing executives should not be fooled into thinking that the United States will become a geriatric society. Because the aging baby boomers are active both at home and work, they have been taking good care of their health. Many are better educated than previous generations, live in dual-income families, and have many hobbies and interests.

Not only will the 1990s see more older consumers, but their preferences will change. Also, they will have more money to spend than currently. Because those in the over-fifty age group have already purchased homes and reared families, their expenses tend to plateau. This group controls 50 percent of all discretionary income and earns 42 percent of all U.S. after-tax income. As people age, their consumer preferences change. This group is much more value oriented than younger groups. It is not looking for image products. Research has shown that 83.6 percent of the over-fifty age group say that they are willing to pay more for quality, and 88.8 percent would rather buy a few high-quality items than many items of lower quality. The conspicuous consumption of the yuppie generation will diminish as an older, more sophisticated shopper with a desire for quality and diversity emerges.

Convenience also will emerge as a consumer preference. An increasing number of families are made up of two full-time workers. The buyers in the family have little time and thus need convenient shopping, such as at-home shopping via catalog/direct mail and television shopping. Consumers do not want to spend Saturday on the freeways driving for discounts; they want to spend Saturday on the golf courses and other leisure activities.[1]

Changing Marketing Mix

In the retailing field, marketing executives must be responsive to the changing demographics and preferences (as mentioned above) in order to succeed. Altering *product offerings* is one way retailers can respond. Traditionally, retailers selected their merchandise assortments for breadth and depth. To meet ever-changing consumer preferences, however, retailers need to change their thinking. For example, retailers such as the Limited Stores and The Gap have stuck with their original formulas of offering a small focused assortment in great depth. A stroll through any of the regional malls reveals many similar specialty merchants—stores that sell exclusively sunglasses, nuts, brushes, bathing suits, and so forth. These specialty stores represent the traditional departments in a department store.

From another perspective, there are nationally prominent specialty merchants that dominate their categories. These merchants have successfully developed a following of their own and can make decisions regarding assortment, pricing, and location, independent of competitors. They will continue to wield huge market power, influencing everything from product development to pricing structures.

In the areas of *pricing strategy* and *promotion*, retailers have a method to carve out a niche for themselves. The meteoric rise of discounters in the 1970s and the early 1980s has reached its peak, primarily because of heavy competition in that market. Currently, growth appears greatest among those firms that dominate their categories. The reason is that they are specialists who are able to create their own customers and become market leaders within a chosen segment. The ability of these superspecialists to offer both broader and deeper assortments within a limited category ensures them steady traffic without promotional price-cutting.

In the 1990s, pricing trends will focus on everyday low prices and high/low promotional pricing. Although promotions encourage comparison shopping to obtain the best price, many people with demands on their time refuse to do that and instead will trade potential savings for time. This partially explains the success of Wal-Mart. From a management perspective, everyday low pricing means labor savings because of reduced marking and remarking of price tags, and fewer stock shortages on the promotional items. In addition, rather than ticketing an item with an expected selling price, the retailers sets an artificially high ticket price. Markdowns or promotions then bring the item down to the expected selling price. Retailers that choose this pricing and promotion strategy will have to be good merchants, combining fresh merchandising with crisper visual presentations and perhaps adding store attractions to keep the traffic flowing. The promotions of the department stores will most likely continue since they depend more heavily than others on selling quickly changing fashions.

The changing demographics are best illustrated in the emergence of *new channels of distribution* and the resurgence of some old channels of distribution. The demand for convenience, not just price, has allowed nonstore retailers to flourish. Since the technology is changing so rapidly, it is impossible to guess what the end of the next decade will bring, but here are some of the important trends:

- *Electronic shopping*, including video kiosks (both dedicated and shared), teleshopping (including interactive), and on-line computer shopping. These electronic alternatives address the lack of assortment in small independent stores and the more sophisticated demand of today's consumers. Major players in the retail and computer hardware industry have invested considerably in developing and instituting electronic home shopping technologies. The rise in these technologies coincides with the increase in cable subscription, home computer ownership, use of automated teller machines (ATMs), use of debit cards, and women working outside the home.

- *Mail-order catalog/direct mail.* Catalog and direct-mail retailers have become more competitive because of greater use of technology, smarter buying, less costly and more time-efficient distribution systems, and general economies of scale. In terms of product mix and product development, many catalogers are among the leaders in their specialty markets. Increased computer sophistication in marketing has allowed them to get closer and closer to their target consumers, ensuring them a greater return on investment.

- *Manufacturer's outlets.* Throughout the Northeast and Midwest, manufacturer's outlets are becoming very popular. Many of these are located in outlying rural and ex-urban locations. These centers have been shown time and again to have the power to draw bargain hunters by the busload. Among the nationally known brand names with outlet stores in these centers are Corning Ware, Carter's Childrenwear, Van Heusen, and the like. The number of these outlets may continue to expand as they become one of the stops on retirees' many vacation trips.

- *Hypermarkets.* Truly one-stop shops, hypermarkets offer a huge assortment of products, carrying everything from grocery and fresh foods to soft goods, apparel, hard goods, consumer electronics, and automotive supplies. These new retail formats are intended to eliminate as much of the cost after wholesale as possible. Hypermarket retailers must be willing to accept low margins across a broad range of products to ensure the kind of traffic needed to maintain a large volume. They depend on the lower service and high volume they can get by creating a broadly assorted, no-frills environment for one-stop shopping.

NEED FOR CORE COMPETENCE TO CREATE NEW MARKETS

In order to create new markets for products and services, early and consistent investment in what is called "core competencies" is one important factor. In turn, corporate imagination and expeditionary marketing are the keys that unlock these new markets. A company that underinvests in its core competencies or inadvertently surrenders them through alliances and outsourcing generally robs its own future. But to realize the potential that core competencies create, a company must also have the imagination to envision markets that do not yet exist and the ability to stake them out ahead of the competition. In short, a company must anticipate what the customers want before they are aware of what they want.[2]

A company will strive to create new competitive space only if it possesses an opportunity perspective that goes far beyond the boundaries of its present businesses. This perspective identifies, in broad terms, the marketing territory top management hopes to stake out over the coming years, a terrain that is unlikely to be captured in anything as precise as a five-year marketing plan. The initial enthusiasm that several Japanese companies brought to developing high-definition television (HDTV) grew out of just such a vision. Creative considerations of the many new opportunities that might emerge if HDTV could be made a reality led them beyond the traditional boundaries of the color television business to identify potential markets in cinema production, video photography, video magazines, electronic museums, product demonstrations, and training simulations, among others.

As this example demonstrates, a company's opportunity perspective represents its collective imagination of the ways in which an important new benefit might be harnessed to create new competitive space or reshape existing space. Commitment to an opportunity perspective does not rest on ROI (return on investment) calculations but on an almost visceral sense of the benefits that customers will finally derive should pioneering work prove successful. The more fundamental the envisioned benefits and the more widely shared the enthusiasm for the opportunity, the greater the company's perseverance will be.[3]

Enlarged View of Core Competence to Develop New Opportunities

Although there is need for core competencies to create new markets, there is also need for an enlarged view of these competencies. Conceiving a company as a group of core competencies rather than as a group of products and services is one way to extend the opportunity perspective considerably. Because Motorola sees itself as a leader in wireless communications, it is not just a producer of paging devices and mobile telephones. Rather, the company's charter permits it to explore markets as diverse as wireless local area computer networks and global positioning satellite receivers. Ajinomoto, a giant grocery-products company, is not only in the food business, but also applies the skills it has mastered in fermentation technology to produce an elastic paper for Sony's top-end headphones. The point to be made from these examples is that if company managers are not able to think outside current business boundaries, they will miss important new opportunities that depend on the combination of skills from several divisions.

Another example is Kodak, which recently extended its opportunity perspective by searching for markets that fell between or across its traditional areas of competence in chemicals (film) and electronic imaging (copiers). One of the product opportunities that emerged from this cross-divisional exercise was what insiders are calling the "electronic shoebox." Recognizing that in many homes, family photographs sit in a shoebox, gathering dust in the attic, Kodak's chemical and electronic engineers dreamed of a medium that would let customers store their photographs easily and safely, view them on a standard television, and rearrange them at the touch of a button. The end result is a process available through photo developers that turns chemical images on photographic film into electronic images. These images, in turn, can be viewed and edited on a videodisc player connected to a television. While it is too early to say whether this product will be a great success, it has already shown Kodak how a synthesis of core competence skills residing in different divisions can stretch its opportunity perspective.[4]

DEVELOPMENT OF INNOVATIVE PRODUCTS AND SERVICES

Generally, the development of innovative products and services takes one of the following three forms: (1) adding an important new function to a well-known product (Yamaha's digital recording piano), (2) developing a novel form in which to deliver a well-known functionality (automated teller machines), and (3) delivering a new functionality through an entirely new product concept (fax machines). Standard approaches to market analysis are not likely to lead to innovations like these. They are created when people substitute a matrix of needs and functionalities for the more conventional matrix of customers and products. The end result is a new, reworked view of the market.

To illustrate, consider a line of company personnel waiting to use a copier. Conventional analysis would look at the queue as a customer-product problem. Viewed from that perspective, the solution is an even faster, even larger copier; in other words, an extension of the existing product. However, if the same line is viewed in terms of needs and functionalities, the copier's functionalities include both speed and accessibility. If most of the people in line are making only a few copies of short documents, they may value accessibility over speed. If so, the solution would be an entirely new product, a smaller, slower copier that would minimize the total time each user has to spend getting a copy. Disaggregating a product or service into its functional components is a logical process. Discovering and developing a new product that reconfigures functionalities to satisfy a previously unmet need is a good example of marketing creativity.[5]

Utilization of Creative Computer Software to Assist Marketing

To assist marketing managers in conceiving markets in terms of their needs and functionalities, creative computer software can be very helpful. As noted in chapter 6, idea generators can be a preferred approach to developing new products and services along with market opportunities for marketing managers. Two such creative software packages mentioned in that chapter are IdeaFisher 4.0 and MindLink. Essentially, IdeaFisher uses two tools. The QBank (first tool) guides the user through a series of stock questions (which can be modified or added to by the user) and copies the user's responses to a notepad for further filtering (this process also allows for interactive word searches while the user is answering the questions). The IdeaBank (second tool) lets the user compare two words and phrases and responds with every word or phrase cross-referenced to the two that the user entered. From a different perspective, MindLink leads the user through a series of questions and answers including a non sequitur here and there. After this, the program asks the user to ponder the similarities and differences between the user's topic and some object that the program determines. Included with the program are a number of different objects that the program may ask the user to ponder. This may be considered a wild approach to generating ideas, but that is just the point. The program makes the user shift gears in hope of triggering a solution to the problem. Overall, IdeaFisher 4.0 is better suited to marketing problems requiring the use of words and phrases. In contrast, MindLink is more useful if the solution to the marketing problem is likely to be a plan of action.[6]

In addition to assisting marketing managers in conceiving markets in terms of their needs and functionalities, creative computer software can go a step further by helping marketing managers establish market leadership for their companies. The creation of new ideas for products and services using creative computer software can assist marketing managers in determining what their customers want before the customers themselves know of a particular need. In order to reach this market leadership goal, marketing managers must change their mind-set when viewing current and future products and services for their customers. But more important, marketing managers need to have the capability to utilize creative computer software when this is deemed appropriate. Hence creative computer software should become an integral part of rethinking the marketing function, that is, operating on a proactive or forward-thinking basis.

INFLUENCING THE DIRECTION OF CREATING NEW MARKETS

To influence the direction of creating new markets, it is necessary to go beyond asking the company's customers what they want. A few years ago, how many customers were asking for such items as microwave ovens, cellular telephones, or compact disc players? Of course, it is important to listen to customers, but it is hard to be a market leader if a company does no more than that.

A more recent example is General Motors, which introduced Saturn, a new compact car. The company conducted extensive market research when it began its product development efforts in the late 1980s. Four years later, it introduced the "perfect car" to compete with its Japanese competitors' three-year old models. Although the company was following its customers all right, its customers were following more imaginative competitors. Honda had recently introduced its NSX sports car, a cross between a family sedan and the performance of a Ferrari. Because the NSX was not a car buyer's dream, no car buyer could have dreamt of such a car. Instead, the NSX was a carmaker's dream and represented the fulfillment of the company's long-standing ambition to produce a car that is both exotic and domestic.[7]

Reestablishing and Influencing Direction of Markets

From a different perspective, a company can reestablish itself in its current markets by making essential changes. For example, consider the situation at Cadillac, where a few years ago this division's cars had been "overdownsized." Also, Cadillac had serious quality problems relative to power trains, the life, breath, and heritage of Cadillac. Short-term fixes were instituted. Immediate steps were taken to correct the power-train problems, and the division worked with design staff to effect short-term changes in the cars to give them more presence on the street.

But just lengthening cars shared with other divisions—those short-term changes—was not enough. A study ordered by the B-O-C (Buick-Oldsmobile-Cadillac) group vice president William Hoglund concluded that Cadillac needed more control over its destiny to survive and regain a leadership role in an increasingly competitive luxury segment. He recommended that the Detroit Product Team, the part of B-O-C responsible for the E/K (Eldorado-Seville) and D (Brougham) platforms, be merged into the division. On January 1, 1987, Cadillac was reborn.

Cadillac now has more opportunity to be responsive to what the market needs. It is past the point of responding. Cadillac wants to go beyond being market driven—most companies are market driven. It is working on influencing the direction of the market. Cadillac is working on things beyond the near-term horizon that will have an influence on what people will want to buy, rather than what it has been doing, that is, responding to what the market wants to see. Seville and Eldorado are the first cars developed under Cadillac's new way of business. The next step is the thirty-two-value Northstar V-8 for the Allante and other Cadillac models. The Northstar engine reestablishes significant leadership attributes for power trains at Cadillac. The next important move is consolidating core products—Seville, Eldorado, and C-body De Ville—at the Hamtramck plant.

Going beyond these developments, Cadillac sees a need for a new Cadillac, that is, an entry-level Cadillac. It is a car that is not inexpensive, but is of a different character than the current entry-level Cadillac, which is a Sedan De Ville. The LSS and Aurora concept cars were designed to determine the route Cadillac should take. The idea is to create what will be acceptable to the market and will be a different type of entry-level Cadillac, but maintain Cadillac's overall character. The final design is expected to have a much different flavor than what current Cadillacs have. The Cadillac Division sees itself as being America's luxury-car leader, selling 250,000 to 300,000 cars per year. This means that it has to have a good price value. It cannot be selling only cars priced $45,000 and higher. Cadillac finds that it must broaden its appeal. Its owner body is more traditional in total. Hence it needs to attract young, affluent people at a higher rate. Therefore, the new focus will be on influencing the direction of the market rather than on following the market.[8]

MARKET LEADERS KNOW WHAT CUSTOMERS WANT

There are basically three kinds of companies: (1) those that simply ask customers what they want and end up as perpetual followers; (2) those that succeed for a time in pushing customers in directions they may not want to go; and (3) those that lead customers where they want to go before customers know it themselves. Currently, NEC dreams of (and pursues) a telephone that can interpret between callers speaking in different languages. Motorola envisions a world where telephone numbers are attached to people rather than places and where a personal communicator allows millions of out-of-touch business travelers to be reached anytime and anywhere. Market research and segmentation analysts are unlikely to reveal such opportunities because deep insight into the customers' needs, lifestyles, and aspirations is required.

Need to Go beyond the Traditional Approach to Market Research

There are many ways such insights may be garnered, all of which go beyond traditional methods of market research. For example, Toshiba has a Lifestyle Research Institute, and Sony explores human science as vigorously as it pursues the leading edge of audiovisual technology. Yamaha gains insights into unarticulated needs and potentially new functionalities through a "listening post" it established some years ago in London. Stocked with leading-edge electronic hardware, the facility offers some of Europe's most talented musicians a chance to experiment with the future of music making. The feedback helps Yamaha continually extend competitive boundaries it has staked out in the music business. Yamaha's approach illustrates a basic point. To gain the most profound insights into its customers, the company must observe up close the coming needs of its most demanding customers.

Companies that succeed in educating customers to what is possible develop both marketers with technological imagination and technologists with marketing imagination. In many companies, marketers seem to be winning the long-running debate over whether new product development should be technology driven or market led. Technologists are accused of being out of touch with the marketplace, that is, more interested in technical wizardry than in understanding customers. Much of this criticism is valid. Though technologists often claim that the market was not ready, the truth typically lies in the fact that the technical community either did not understand the customers' underlying needs or missed the appropriate price/performance target. Yet many companies are striving to be more market oriented while their world-class competitors are increasingly using advanced technology to create new businesses that few marketers could have imagined.

It should be noted that neither technology nor marketing can be the sole departure point for creative new competitive territories. Multidisciplinary product teams and communications between sales and development are useful but not sufficient. While many companies have procedures that allow the sales organization to relay customer requirements to technical personnel, few have procedures that work in the reverse, that is, to inform those closest to the customers about new emerging technological possibilities.

As an example, in one Japanese company, senior technical officers spend as many as thirty days a year outside Japan talking to customers. The aim is not to solve technical problems nor to close a sale, but to listen to and observe customers and absorb their thinking. In another example, a Japanese chief engineer of a major new business development program lived for a time with an American family thought to be representative of the customers his company hoped to win. In each case, the goal was not to improve the flow of information between marketers and engineers nor to manage the balance of power between the two groups, but rather to blur organizational and career boundaries by ensuring that both communities had a large base of shared experiences. The net result was a good mixture of market and technical imagination.[9]

TAKING A CLOSER LOOK AT COMPETITION

Finally, as part of the rethinking process of the marketing function, it is quite helpful to take a closer look at competition. Typically, the task of creating new markets for products and services dominates senior marketing managers' agendas because competition is so intense. New competitive products and services do not stay new for long. Building one new product and service after another faster than competitors is the only way to stay ahead. The results of this obsession are quite visible. Yamaha's strong position in electronic pianos, synthesizers, and other digitally based musical equipment or Sharp's strengths in pocket LCD televisions and ultrathin displays are examples of where competitors should be studied to determine where they are strong and where they are weak. In this way, marketing managers of competing firms have an opportunity to meet and possibly beat their major competition. As will be seen in the sections to follow, two approaches will be treated.

An integral part of taking a closer look at competitors is also related to the time it takes a company to develop and launch a new product or service, accumulate insights from the marketplace, and then relaunch an improved product or service. All things being equal, a company with a one-year iteration cycle will be able to close in on a potential market faster than one with a three-year cycle. Each product iteration unfreezes one or more aspects of the product design and thus provides an opportunity for a company to apply what has been learned from the marketplace and improve the product for the next round. Consumers may consider a company an also-ran if its product development cycle is longer than the product life cycle established by a competitor. For example, Toshiba's pace of product introduction allowed it to explore almost every possible market niche and to outrun rivals, including Grid, Zenith, and Compaq. Moreover, if one particular model failed, its withdrawal would hardly cause a ripple in customer confidence.

Utilization of Profit Impact of Marketing Strategies

Profit Impact of Marketing Strategies (PIMS) is a computerized approach for planning market strategy that is run by the Strategic Planning Institute. It is a data pool of information on the marketing experiences of its members.[10] Several hundred corporations submit data annually on a total of about 3,000 of their business units, each of which is a distinct product-market unit. Each member provides PIMS with the most intimate details on matters such as its market share, investment intensity, product quality, and total marketing and R&D expenditures. Through computer simulation, the company can then test its own market strategies against the real experiences of hundreds of comparable companies, including competitors. What it receives are answers to questions such as these: What is the normal profit rate for a business or a product line given its combination of circumstances, and why? If the business continues on its current track, what will its future operating results be? What will happen to short- and long-term performance if certain strategic moves are made? What changes will create the best profits or cash returns?

Typically, what a member company wants from PIMS is to find out what it will cost to make a particular strategic move and how much better off the business will be afterward. For example, consider return on investment, which PIMS considers one of the best measures of how a business is doing. The PIMS models can forecast how much ROI for a business line will change because of a strategic move involving more marketing R&D, capital equipment buildup, or whatever—both what the ROI will be immediately following the move and what it will be several years in the future.

Principles That Have Emerged from PIMS Computer Models. Some new as well as traditional principles have emerged from PIMS computer models of the real-life experiences of its corporate members. Among them are the following:

- There is a set of operating rules that govern all businesses. Some thirty-seven factors—including market share, capital intensity, and vertical integration—jointly explain 80 percent of the success or failure of any business; only 20 percent of a business's return on investment can be attributed to factors that are unique or special, such as the quality of working relations.

- Anything more than a minimal R&D program does not make sense for a company with a weak market position. Copying competitors' products rather than inventing them is probably its best bet. This can be a very profitable strategy.

- High marketing expenditures for low-quality products can have a devastating effect on profits.

- High product quality can offset a weak market position.

- Weak companies should not become vertically integrated, whereas strong ones should.

- High costs in more than one area, such as capital investment, R&D, or marketing, can ruin any business.

When companies are extrapolating form the PIMS data base, it is recommended that they not automatically compare themselves with competitors in the same industry or business category to find out how well they are doing. According to PIMS, industry breakdowns are not all-important. A better yardstick may be the performance of companies in other industries whose total situation is comparable. A tire company, for example, may have even more in common with, and more to learn from the market strategies of, a small-appliance manufacturer than from those of another tire company.

Three Tailor-Made PIMS Reports. For a PIMS member, three tailor-made reports are developed for every business or product line analyzed. First, there is the ''Par Report,'' which specifies the return on investment that is normal or ''par'' for the business line given the characteristics of its market, competition, position, technology, and cost structure. It states whether the business is the kind that normally earns, say, 3 percent or 30 percent, judging by the experiences of businesses with similar characteristics. It also identifies the major strengths and weaknesses of the business that account for the high or low par. Second, the "Strategy Sensitivity Report" tests several possible strategic moves the business can make. It indicates the normal short- and long-term consequences of each move and specifies what the profit or loss is likely to be. Third, and most important, is what PIMS calls the "Optimum Strategy Report." This report picks the combination of changes that promises to give the business the best results in terms of return on investment for the next five years, discounted cash flow over ten years, short-term earnings, and other measures, judging by the experiences of businesses in similar circumstances. The reports are very helpful to top-level executives and their corporate planning staff for giving direction to strategic planning.

PIMS/PC. The PIMS/PC program differs from electronic spreadsheets, such as Lotus 1-2-3 and Javelin, in that it goes beyond simply calculating, storing, and displaying a strategic plan. It attempts to test the plan's viability by comparing it with the actual experience of similar businesses. Until recently, executives of member firms who wanted to use the PIMS program had to get on-line to the mainframe in Cambridge, Massachusetts, to do so. However, PIMS/PC is a personal computer version that now makes telecommunications unnecessary.

To illustrate the tie-in of a typical business with PIMS, Glen Raven Mills' (a Burlington, North Carolina, textile manufacturer) fourteen businesses are in the PIMS data base. They report annually to the mainframe. The vice president and director of planning monitors each unit quarterly and compares its results to PIMS par. He also uses PIMS to test strategic decisions. However, he has found that it is not good for predicting whether the company ought to buy a medium-sized piece of machinery. It is a good indicator of what the consequences would be of investing so many millions of dollars in quality improvements. If the company could improve its relative quality by so much percent, what are the consequences of that? Do those consequences justify this new technology? Thus PIMS is good for important strategic questions.

A few years ago, the vice president and director of planning and his associates sought PIMS's advise about whether or not to acquire a competitor. The model said that the result of the acquisition would be increased relative quality and increased market share, which would raise par. The results from the model said that if the company made this acquisition, its par would drop and would begin to come back over the years. Because the company was willing to face this result, it followed what the model said.[11]

Gathering Information on Competition

Less than a decade ago, the practice of competitive intelligence, that is, amassing and analyzing data about competitors, was considered a legal, but not very savory, version of industrial espionage. However, intensifying global competition now makes that data critical, while the proliferation of electronic data bases and of corporate computer networks makes it easier to assimilate. The upshot is that competitive intelligence activities are springing up all over. Companies that used to ask consultants to do one-shot competitive assessments are now setting up the process themselves.

This is particularly true of companies that face foreign competition. Congress has been holding hearings on whether the Washington intelligence community should help American business learn more about foreign competition. There are ample examples of competitive intelligence coups, both domestic and overseas. In 1987, Motorola's intelligence staff noticed a pattern in the types of capital equipment that Japanese electronics companies were buying. It warned Motorola's top executives that the Japanese were planning a major move into Europe. When more than half a dozen Japanese companies did start selling consumer electronics in Europe in 1989, Motorola was prepared, and it has held on to much of its market share.

One of the Coors Brewing Company's competitors was sued by another company. Coors's competitive analysis people used superficially disjointed information from the court testimony to build a mathematical model that enabled Coors to calculate how many barrels of beer the competitor processed and shipped each quarter. The competitive assessment people at McDonnell Douglas keep tabs on the strengths, weaknesses, and philosophies of competitors' high-level executives. That way, if a key executive at a competing company dies, McDonnell Douglas can anticipate the changes the persons's successor might make.

For the most part, companies use different systems for gathering data. Some, like Corning and Ameritech, bring organization members into the intelligence network. Others, including Motorola and McDonnell Douglas, have separate intelligence departments. Coors and others run the function in tandem with market research. The people handling the functions are equally hard to categorize. The 1,700 members of the Society of Competitive Intelligence Professionals hold degrees in fields as disparate as library science and engineering. Some do competitive intelligence full-time; others do it in conjunction with other jobs. However, all have the same goal, which is to provide early warning of external events that could have an impact on the business. Overall, what they do is to make sure that management is not caught off guard concerning events that have impact on their companies.[12]

THE DOWNSIDE OF RETHINKING THE MARKETING FUNCTION

Even though the foregoing items regarding rethinking the marketing function are implemented within a creative environment, a company can still experience failure with a new product or service. Failure is as often the result of unrealistic expectations as it is of managerial incompetence. For example, in the 1980s, General Electric faced an important opportunity to become a leader in the market for the factory of the future. Integrating CAD/CAM, computer-integrated manufacturing, robots, and automated material handling was an important challenge, and one GE was willing to confront. But unrealistic expectations about how fast the market would develop, combined with an all-or-nothing approach to market entry, set GE up for a major failure and a sizeable financial write-off. GE was able, however, to regroup with more modest, short-term objectives and to find partners with whom to share much of the risk. But GE's confidence in the business opportunity never fully recovered from this self-inflicted wound. The point is not that GE's ambitions were too grand, but rather that what constitutes failure depends on management's initial assumptions. If the opportunity is oversold and the risks undermanaged, failure and premature abandonment of the opportunity are preordained.

Typically, commitment to a new opportunity is measured in terms of investment dollars rather than consistency of effort. Too often, staying power is interpreted to mean large financial commitments rather than sheer persistence in learning from the market. Thus companies need to learn to manage tomorrow's opportunities as competently as they manage today's businesses. If company managers spend more time overseeing the present rather than the horizon, they will find themselves stumbling. If company managers have no shared view of future opportunities, there will be no sense of the opportunity costs of failing to escape the gravitational pull of today's businesses. If customers are given merely what they have asked for when competitors are giving them what they have not yet dreamed of, leadership will be an ever-receding goal. If commitment is measured in terms of investment rather than persistence, risks will be undermanaged and expectations overinflated. If there is no risk- and time-adjusted view of managerial performance, new opportunities will wither from lack of managerial attention. If failure is seen only as dollars lost and not as dollars foregone, new business opportunities will be prematurely abandoned.[13]

APPLICATIONS SHOWING LINKAGE OF RETHINKING MARKETING TO UTILIZING CREATIVE COMPUTER SOFTWARE

In order to compete in today's rapidly changing business environment, marketing managers need the help of group decision support systems in order to gain a competitive advantage. Those systems that incorporate the latest computer software packages enable a company to react to the internal and external factors that affect the industry, and to react to these changes in a positive way. Furthermore, such group decision support systems allow companies to take a proactive, problem-finding approach to situations. Such an approach allows marketing managers not only to predict what will happen in the future with a degree of certainty, but also to prepare for unforeseen events.

In this section of the chapter, several creative software packages will be applied to typical situations. More specifically, Brainstorm 2.0, Idea Generator Plus, and IdeaFisher 4.0 will be illustrated. By using these packages, marketing managers have the flexibility to be more creative in their problem-solving and problem-finding approaches. This allows great flexibility in creating different scenarios to answer typical "what-if" questions. The end result is that the quality of managerial decision making is improved dramatically and the reduced decision-making time enables marketing managers to concentrate more on other important aspects of their jobs.

COMPUTER NETWORK WORLD

Computer Network World is a closely held franchise that operates as a regional reseller of personal and business computer products. It is a full-service company that provides its customers with hardware and software services, training, and ongoing support. Computer Network World serves its clients in Ohio and Kentucky from its seven stores. Currently, its market consists of 80 percent business buyers and 20 percent personal/home buyers. Annual current sales are approximately $3 million and are projected to grow at a rate of 15 percent per year. The sales support department utilizes several promotional activities to increase demand for its products. These include seasonal sales (Presidents' Day, back-to-school, and so on), special incentive programs (system upgrades, free software, and so on), and direct selling. In addition, the company offers a Client Services Network (CSN) as part of its deluxe maintenance agreement package for high-volume business clients. This network provides an electronic discussion arena. The CSN allows the client to dial in directly to the customer support department via an electronic-mail link.

Each client is assigned a unique user ID and password so that his or her access to the CSN can be monitored by the company. Clients can create or join topics. This allows them to post service calls to customer support or inquire of other CSN members.

Goals of the Client Services Network

The goals of the Client Services Network are to provide an electronic environment where (1) existing clients can share information with each other so that previous solutions provided for one client can be shared with other clients who might have the same problem; (2) client service calls can be automatically posted to the service department without going through the receptionist; (3) customer support can post suggestions for system maintenance; and (4) sales support can generate new business by offering incentives to this exclusive group of clients (CSN–Special Discounts). Essentially, the company is offering a new type of service before it is requested by its customers. From this perspective, the company's customers perceive it as being forward-looking and ahead of its competitors.

The CSN is basically a qualitative enhancement to the level of service provided by the company. The intangible benefits to Computer Network World from the clients' perspective are the shift in attitude from perceiving it as a hardware vendor to perceiving it as a full-service partner in servicing the clients' needs. The company can post sales suggestions specifically designed for the CSN to induce existing customers to buy add-on products. For example, what if the company gave CSN members a 10 percent discount on supplies purchased through the end of the month (toner cartridges, tapes, disks, and paper)? These suggestions can be derived from problems identified on the CSN or as a special offer to the exclusive group of clients who belong to the CSN.

Questions That Can Be Answered Using Brainstorm 2.0

The software selected by Computer Network World to provide CSN service is Brainstorm 2.0 by Mustang Software. Brainstorm is an idea-networking technique because it provides an electronic discussion arena in which group dialogue and decision processes can take place. Brainstorm utilizes a DOS-based E-mail environment that supports the capability to permit users to join discussions. This joining process means that an idea or "what-if" question can be posted on the system and suggestions can be requested from the CSN user community. The input from the various users represents ideas or opinions that can lead to a better decision on the issue at hand.

Computer Network World utilizes Brainstorm as the controlling software for its Client Services Network. This tool provides a two-way connection to permit customers to suggest methods that the company can use to support its customers better. This provides a competitive advantage since support after the sale is often more important than the specific hardware or software purchased. As an idea generator per se, Brainstorm is not very helpful. However, in an environment where many diverse users access Brainstorm to request and share ideas, a "virtual meeting of minds" can be undertaken.

Because there are no quantitative capabilities provided by Brainstorm, mathematical modeling of any suggestions would have to be performed by some other software package. The results of such an analysis can be shared with the group by joining the discussion and entering the results. For users, Brainstorm is easy to use since it provides pull-down menus and straightforward commands. It has the capability to invoke other PC-DOS applications so the user can configure his or her PC to boot up into Brainstorm. Brainstorm then becomes a front end to the other applications the user might need. If, for example, the user starts up Lotus 1-2-3, he or she automatically returns to Brainstorm when Lotus 1-2-3 is terminated.

The cost of providing the CSN to the customer includes the cost of one communications server and two workstations to monitor the system. Network cabling and software must be installed to support the system. The central server is accessible from the customer support department to monitor the incoming suggestions and service requests from clients. Computer Network World's telephone system must be upgraded to add additional lines to permit simultaneous multiple access. The addition of ten lines is projected to support the system. The initial setup cost of CSN was about $25,000. Brainstorm software provides the CSN environment. This enhanced E-mail software forms the basis of the CSN design.

There are several benefits to clients when they participate in the CSN. High-volume clients, to whom this product is provided, now have direct access to log service calls in order to have technicians dispatched. Clients can post software operational questions for the software support group. Clients can join discussions to share information/opinions about software or hardware with other clients. Clients receive notification of exclusive sales promotions that foster vendor loyalty.

Overall, the benefits to Computer Network World are qualitative versus quantitative. The CSN is a value-added benefit in providing quality service to clients. In this regard, it differentiates the company from its competition. The goodwill generated by this service should lead to increased market share. The availability of this extra level of customer support may be an inducement to new customers and, therefore, lead to a higher closing percentage among new customers. Computer Network World will have a captive audience from which to extract add-on business at potentially higher margins. The CSN automates the service and support calls, increasing the productivity of these important areas, and provides a feedback mechanism through which the company can stay in tune with its most valuable client needs.

XYZ MEDICAL SOFTWARE CORPORATION

XYZ Medical Software Corporation is a medium-sized software development company headquartered in Cincinnati, Ohio, with branch offices in Columbus, Ohio, Indianapolis, Indiana, and Louisville, Kentucky. Founded in 1981, the corporation currently has over fifty employees in four cities. About 75 percent of these employees are technical support people or consultants. Each branch office consists of seven technical support people (systems engineers) and three sales/marketing representatives. Within each office, one of the marketing representatives also acts as the district manager and is responsible for overseeing the activities of the entire territory. The Columbus branch office covers all accounts in northern Ohio, the Louisville office is responsible for the state of Kentucky, and the Indianapolis branch oversees all of Indiana. Each branch office reports to the corporate office in Cincinnati, which is also responsible for the Greater Cincinnati area and West Virginia. The remaining employees located at the Cincinnati office consist of administrators, sales/marketing representatives, technical support people, programmers/consultants, and the executives/owners.

The primary business of the XYZ Medical Software Corporation is the development of software for the medical industry, specifically, software packages for physicians' practice management. While developing and marketing the software, the company works in conjunction with major computer manufacturers to develop software to meet the specifications of the vendors' product line. This provides an additional channel for the corporation to market its products as well as an additional source of revenue. Relationships with various computer manufacturers are strategic to its success. These relationships are encouraged, enhanced, and utilized while working with associates and customers. Furthermore, the corporation is consistently up-to-date on the latest information systems technology and methodology.

Three Strategic Business Units

The three strategic business units of XYZ Medical Software Corporation are education, information systems consulting/programming, and physicians' practice management system consulting. Education consists of training provided for customers and associates as well as for hardware vendors with which the specific software is compatible. Training and education are on an ongoing basis and are vital to maintaining a competitive edge in this industry. Information systems consulting/programming is a large part of the business and involves a one-to-one working relationship between the corporation's consultants/programmers and an individual customer with a specific need. Together, they work on providing the optimal solution to satisfy the customer's system requirements. The final strategic business unit is physicians' practice management system consulting. In this division, the corporation provides consulting services to users or potential users of a specific physicians' practice management software package.

Consulting is the primary source of revenue for the corporation. This encompasses programming/consulting services rendered by the technical support staff and consultants. Additionally, commissions are received from manufacturers (hardware or software sold), which serve to fuel the consulting business. In addition to its core businesses, the corporation provides a variety of supplemental services. System conversion/migrations are offered for customers who wish to upgrade their current system or who wish to convert to a different system. The corporation provides the necessary program conversion to meet the customer's specific system requirements. Custom programming and modifications are also offered. Programmers work on creating custom programs geared to the customer's business, as well as revising existing programs to meet the changing needs of the organization. Disaster recovery plans are also available. Such plans are designed to enable a customer to get his or her system up and running as quickly as possible in the event that a natural disaster or some other type of failure should occur. Additionally, the XYZ Medical Software Corporation installs networks as requested by the customer and also aids him or her in the selection of specific hardware and software. Finally, the ability to integrate different systems is another service offered.

As can be seen, the corporation offers a wide range of services for the medical profession. In recent years, the corporation has experienced slight decreases in sales. Although part of the reason can be explained by the economy, other factors have affected sales as well. In order to remain competitive, the corporation has to look continually for new areas of growth, which may entail market expansion, broadening the product line, expanding the sales effort, and a host of other alternatives. Complete up-to-date information on all internal and external factors affecting the environment in which the company operates is vital to its continued success and growth. With this information, top-level managers are asking themselves some basic questions concerning the current and future marketing operations of the corporation.

Questions That Can Be Answered Using Idea Generator Plus

Because of the competitive nature of the computer software industry, the corporation realizes the importance of an effective sales support system. More specifically, decision support tools, such as the Idea Generator Plus, to support the sales function are being employed. Examples of the types of questions and situations that can be addressed with this idea generator will be demonstrated in this section. The primary advantage of an effective sales support system comes from the information that is generated. This information is used to evaluate internal and external factors that impact the corporation's operations and leads to a higher quality of decision making.

By way of review, the Idea Generator Plus was presented in chapter 6; it helps users in their decision-making processes to be more creative and to generate new alternatives. Using artificial intelligence techniques, the program is based on a logical three-step approach to creative problem solving. The first step is a statement of the problem. The program generates a series of questions to clarify the problem and its related objectives. The user is prompted to list goals, put them in order of importance, and list people who will be involved in achieving them. In the second step, new ideas are generated when the user answers another series of questions that help put the problem or situation into a new perspective. This step provides several thought-provoking techniques to create problem-solving ideas, such as building metaphors, reversing goals, focusing on the people involved, remembering similar situations, and looking at the problem through someone else's eyes. In the third or evaluation step, the user ranks the ideas based on how well they meet the original objectives. The short- and long-term costs and benefits of each alternative are evaluated, in addition to the effects that each idea will have on people involved in the process. The ability to allow users to define, clarify, and focus on problems, then come up with alternative solutions, is a key feature of the Idea Generator Plus.

The Idea Screen is a very useful feature of the Idea Generator Plus. The Idea Screen tracks the user's train of thought and can be accessed via a "hot key" at any time. It incorporates a text editor to record new ideas, associations, and conclusions. Once the process has been completed, a useful summary report can be generated. This report incudes a description of the situation, a list of the people involved, and ratings of the individual's or group's goals in order of importance.

To illustrate the use of the Idea Generator Plus, two questions were asked: "What if we expand the sales force in each branch office?" and "What if we broaden the product line to include additional software solutions as well as hardware?'' To answer the first question with the Idea Generator Plus, the following steps were used. The first step was to define the problem (''What if we expand the sales force in each branch office?''). The Idea Generator Plus then prompted the user to list up to five goals. The goals of XYZ Medical Software Corporation are (1) to increase sales, (2) to gain economies of scale, (3) to lower costs, (4) to increase productivity, and (5) to broaden the product line. Next, these goals were ranked in order of importance.

The second step of the Idea Generator Plus was the idea-generation process. Here, the program offered several techniques to generate new ideas. For this analysis, other perspectives and focusing on each goal one by one were the methods chosen to address this ''what-if'' question. The program asked for suggestions that others might have. The following suggestions were given: costs will go up, revenues will increase, and product sales per employee will decrease. The program then listed all of the ideas generated up to this point and provided the option to add other ideas. Next, the program listed the goals one at a time and asked for ways to reach each. The Idea Generator Plus then gave a cumulative list of the ways to reach each goal and allowed for revision of the list if the user desired.

The third step of the Idea Generator Plus, the evaluation step, asked the user which of the ideas was to be evaluated. The user then ranked the ideas. In the report process, the final report was generated as shown in figure 8.1. This was a summary of the previous steps. Although the software did not actually generate new ideas, it did help the user to think of the advantages and disadvantages and the different ways to reach these goals, all through a step-by-step logical process.

To answer the second question (''What if we broaden the product line to include additional software solutions as well as hardware?''), the corporation evaluated the possibility of broadening the current product line. Additional products would include software packages for other industries, hardware equipment, and expansion of hardware vendors. The Idea Generator Plus was used to examine the pros and cons of expanding the product line more thoroughly. As a starting point for this analysis, the problem statement or situation was described in the first step (see figure 8.2). After the problem statement, specific goals to be achieved were listed and ranked in importance. It should be noted that goals may be ranked equal in importance. The corporation's goals in broadening the product line were (1) repeat business with current customers, (2) market penetration, (3) increase in market share, and (4) increase in sales leading to higher profitability. On a scale of 1 to 9, these goals were ranked 8, 8, 7, and 9, respectively, with 9 being most important.

The second step in the Idea Generator Plus process was idea generation (figure 8.3). Several techniques to support a more creative decision-making process were available. These included similar situations, metaphors for the situation, other perspectives, focusing on goals one by one, reversing the goals, focusing on the people involved, and making the most of the ideas. The corporation decided to use the technique of focusing on each of its goals one by one. If market penetration

Figure 8.1
Summary Report to Answer the First Question: "What If We Expand the Sales Force in Each Branch Office?" Using the Idea Generator Plus—XYZ Medical Software Corporation

```
= = = = = = = = = = = = = = = =

       S U M M A R Y    R E P O R T

= = = = = = = = = = = = = = =


- - - - - - - - - - - - - - - - - - - - - - - - - - - - - - - - - - - - - -

     YOUR SITUATION: What if we expanded our sales force

     YOUR GOALS (in order of importance) RATINGS
     - - - - - - - - - - - - - - - - - - - - - - - - -

          Increased Sales                          9
          Lower Costs                              9
          Increased Productivity per Employee      7
          Economies of Scale                       3
          Broaden the Product Line                 2

YOUR LIST OF IDEAS FROM THE IDEA SCREEN (4 altogether)
- - - - - - - - - - - - - - - - - - - - - - - - - - - - -

Increase sales territory
Broaden product line
Costs will go up
Revenues will increase

               RATINGS OF YOUR IDEAS

IDEAS (Arrows indicate those you found most promising.)  RATING
- - - - - - - - - - - - - - - - - - - - - - - - - - - - - - - - - - - -

- ->   Increase sales territory                          9
- ->   Broaden product line                              7

This report was prepared using The Idea Generator.
- - - - - - - - - - - - - - - - - - - - - - - - - - - - - - - - - - - -
```

were the only goal, the corporation came up with several ways to achieve this goal. Since it currently focuses primarily on software packages for physicians' practice management, efforts to sell any other package to this same customer base would be fruitless. However, the corporation can focus its efforts on after-sales service such as consulting, maintenance of equipment, system upgrades, and help lines. By providing such services, the corporation can become a "one-stop-shopping" facility where customers come for all their computing needs.

Figure 8.2
Problem Statement (First Step) to Answer the Second Question: "What If We Broaden the Product Line to Include Additional Software Solutions as Well as Hardware?"— XYZ Medical Software Corporation

```
                        THE IDEA GENERATOR PLUS DEMO
_____

    MAIN MENU
    ---------
    Use
          PROBLEM STATEMENT (active screens are highlighted)
    PRO   -----------------------------------------------------
    IDE --> P1   Describe the situation.
    EVA     P2   List your goals.
    PRI     P3   "People involved."

            ESC to MAIN MENU
    How
    Rea

    QUI
```

To increase market share, several alternatives are available to the corporation. By developing software packages for other industries along with medical software, it can expand the current customer base and increase market share. Along with this, consulting and programming services can be expanded to these markets as well. Furthermore, by gaining the support of large, well-known hardware vendors, the corporation can increase the potential market share available to itself.

Figure 8.3
Idea Generation (Second Step) to Answer the Second Question—XYZ Medical Software Corporation

```
                        THE IDEA GENERATOR PLUS DEMO
_____

    MAIN MENU
    ---------
    Use
          IDEA GENERATION TECHNIQUES (active sections are highlighted)
    PRO   -----------------------------------------------------------
    IDE --> I1   "Similar situations."
    EVA     I2   "Metaphors for your situation."
    PRI     I3   Other perspectives.
            I4   Focus on your goals one by one.
            I5   "Reverse your goals."
    How     I6   "Focus on the people involved."
    Rea     I7   "Make the most of your ideas."

    QUI     ESC to MAIN MENU
```

Finally, the most important goal of increasing sales was analyzed. If the corporation decides to expand its current product line, it will most likely experience increased sales due to its current solid reputation in the industry. However, the focus is on net income. Therefore, the corporation needs to make sure that such a change does not adversely affect overall profitability.

All ideas generated thus far were automatically put into the Idea Screen, which can be reached at any time throughout the program via a hot key. In the third or evaluation step, the corporation chose to look at a few good ideas (versus a single "best" idea or many ideas) (see figure 8.4). Ideas from the Idea Screen were chosen to be evaluated and were then rated on a scale from 1 to 9, with 1 being poor and 9 being excellent. The final report listed the corporation's original problem statement, each goal in order of importance, and all ideas generated from the Idea Screen, with the most promising ideas highlighted (figure 8.5).

Overall, the Idea Generator Plus that was used in evaluating the two questions helped the corporation's top-level managers organize their thoughts and facilitated the decision-making process. It did not provide them with one single "right" answer. As in most situations, these top-level managers of the XYZ Medical Software Corporation were placed at the center of the decision-making process. The results were actually generated by them and not by the machine. Hence the system provided support to them by going through a series of logical steps to arrive at a list of alternatives from which to choose.

UNIVERSAL PRODUCTS CORPORATION

The Universal Products Corporation, which specializes in the manufacture of household appliances, has current sales of $200 million per annum, projected

Figure 8.4
Evaluation (Third Step) to Answer the Second Question—XYZ Medical Software Corporation

```
                    THE IDEA GENERATOR PLUS DEMO
──────────────────────────────────────────────────────────────────
    ┌
    │  MAIN MENU
    │  ---------
    │  Use ┌
    │      │   EVALUATION    (active sections are highlighted)
    │  PRO │   ---------------------------------------------
    │  IDE │--> E1   Choose ideas to evaluate.
    │  EVA │    E2   "Rating according to goals."
    │  PRI │    E3   "Costs, benefits, and effects on people."
    │      │
    │      │   ESC to MAIN MENU
    │  How │
    │  Rea │
    │      │
    │  QUI │
    └      └
```

Figure 8.5
Summary Report to Answer the Second Question—XYZ Medical Software Corporation

```
= = = = = = = = = = = = = = =

        S U M M A R Y    R E P O R T

= = = = = = = = = = = = = = =
- - - - - - - - - - - - - - - - - - - - - - - - - - - - - - - - -

        YOUR SITUATION: What if we broaden the product line

            YOUR GOALS (in order of importance)      RATINGS
            - - - - - - - - - - - - - - - - - - - - - - - - - -

            Increased Sales (Profitability)          9
            Market Penetration                       8
            Repeat Business                          8
            Increase Market Share                    7

    YOUR LIST OF IDEAS FROM THE IDEA SCREEN (5 altogether)
    - - - - - - - - - - - - - - - - - - - - - - - - - - - - - -

    Develop software for other industries
    Expand consulting services to other industries
    Focus on "after-sale" services to all accounts
    Offer customers complete range of computer needs
    Offer more services to new and existing accounts

                RATINGS OF YOUR IDEAS

    IDEAS (Arrows indicate those you found most promising.)    RATING
    - - - - - - - - - - - - - - - - - - - - - - - - - - - - - - - - -

    Develop software for other industries                      9
    Expand consulting services to other industries             9
    Offer more services to new and existing accounts           8
    Offer customers complete range of computer needs           7

    This report was prepared using The Idea Generator.
- - - - - - - - - - - - - - - - - - - - - - - - - - - - - - - - - - -
```

to be about $275 million in five years. Its product line consists of fifty products in eight basic product categories. Variations of these basic products are for specific customers whose requirements differ owing to the markets they serve. For large orders, products are shipped directly to retailers from the company's four manufacturing plants. All other orders are shipped from its warehouses to retailers. Experience has shown that 20 percent of the corporation's dollar volume represents direct shipments from the plants and 80 percent represents shipment through the warehouses. Corporate headquarters are located in Pittsburgh; manufacturing plants are found in Cincinnati, St. Louis, Dallas, and Los Angeles. A warehouse is attached to each manufacturing plant. The present employment level for the entire corporation is approximately 4,000 employees.

Rethinking the Marketing Mix

The vice president of marketing has called in his four regional sales directors and his assistant to take a closer look at the corporation's marketing function. As a starting point, he wants them to list the typical customer's relevant demographic traits, that is, to define those factors that affect the buying of the corporation's products. In addition, he desires that they take a similar look at how to reach the typical customer more effectively using advertising. In effect, the vice president desires that his regional sales directors and assistant start rethinking the marketing mix. As noted in the first part of this chapter, rethinking the marketing mix is related to changing demographics and the marketing mix itself. That is, for the corporation to be successful in the future as presently, it is necessary that it offer the *right* goods at the *right* price in the *right* location with the *right* promotion. Hence it behooves the corporation that its marketing management get a handle on present and future considerations for its products. There are fundamental changes in demographics and consumer preferences for the next five years and beyond that will force the corporation to rethink the present marketing mix. To take an initial closer look at its customers and how to reach them via advertising, IdeaFisher 4.0 will be used by these marketing personnel.

Questions That Can Be Answered Using IdeaFisher 4.0

Because IdeaFisher 4.0 has a very strong base for the development of marketing-related strategies, one area in which it excels is market analysis. This is where IdeaFisher for the Universal Products Corporation is first considered. One of the key aspects of marketing is to understand the marketplace in which the corporation's products are marketed. IdeaFisher's QBank component allows a precise definition of the markets, all from a number of different perspectives. As seen for this first marketing example in figure 8.6a, QBank can ask many questions with regard to the demographic and sociographic makeup of the corporation's customers. By understanding more about its customers, the corporation gains a better comprehension of their requirements. This analysis can help to produce goods better suited to its customers' needs and assist in planning marketing strategies that will have the best impact on its customers.

In addition, IdeaFisher's QBank can ask product-definition-type questions, such as those seen in figure 8.6b. These questions can help to determine the market positioning of a product. They force an evaluation of competing products and how they are positioned in the marketplace. The use of QBank in this way can indicate crowded markets and resulting adjustments that may increase sales volume. By using IdeaFisher's QBank facility, the focus of the marketplace can be narrowed, and thus the corporation can produce more effective marketing strategies.

Figure 8.6a
IdeaFisher's QBank for Customer's Relevant Demographic Traits—Universal Products Corporation

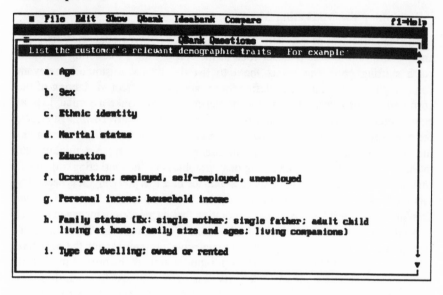

Figure 8.6b
IdeaFisher's QBank for Asking Product-Definition-Type Questions—Universal Products Corporation

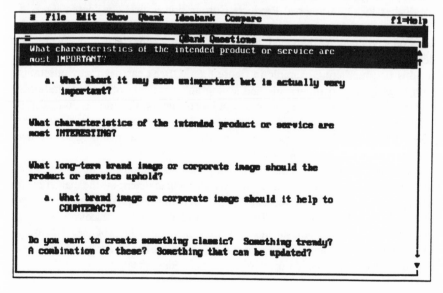

In the second IdeaFisher 4.0 marketing example, the focus is on creating a new advertising campaign for the corporation's products. The corporation is looking to modify its product image in the market place while trying to distinguish itself from competition. In IdeaFisher's IdeaBank, the topics of marketing and advertising campaigns were selected. As seen in figure 8.7a, this led to items of achievement success and "make a name for yourself." This figure displays what is being attempted in the new advertising campaign. A high level of product recognition and showing that the corporation stands for achievement are goals for this advertising campaign.

In shaping the appearance of this advertising campaign, product quality is an important trait. IdeaFisher's Idea Notepad, shown in figure 8.7b, displays the path that was taken to include quality as part of the advertising campaign. The advertising campaign will focus on products of superior quality and exceptional value. To give the products a uniqueness and to separate them from competition, they will be associated with distinctive items found in nature, such as rainbows, Saturn's rings, snowflakes, and so on. A message that the quality of some things in nature cannot be duplicated and the same is true with this product will tie the two aspects of the advertising campaign together.

As can be seen in these examples, IdeaFisher can be very helpful to the Universal Product Corporation's marketing directors, including the vice president of marketing and his assistant. Whether the corporation's marketing managers are trying to create a product, define a market, zero in on its customers, or produce

Figure 8.7a
IdeaFisher's IdeaBank to Assist in Developing a New Advertising Campaign—Universal Products Corporation

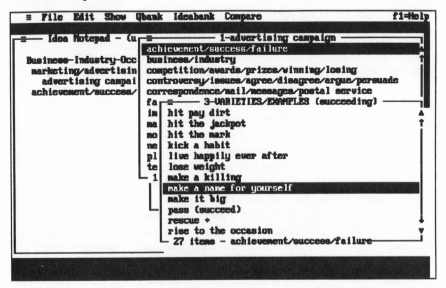

Figure 8.7b

IdeaFisher's IdeaBank to Include Quality as Part of the Advertising Campaign—Universal Products Corporation

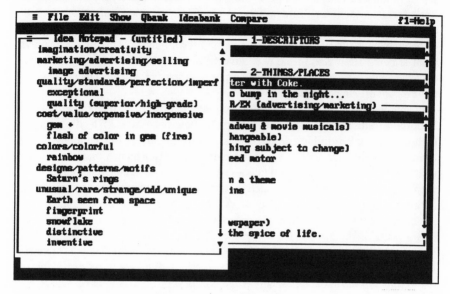

an advertising campaign, IdeaFisher can help consider items that may have been otherwise omitted. By looking at more items or looking at them from a different perspective, creativity is enhanced and a higher-quality product can be marketed.

OTHER MARKETING APPLICATIONS THAT MAKE USE OF CREATIVE COMPUTER SOFTWARE

One typical marketing application of using creative computer software can be found at the Center for Language Training (Laguna Niguel, California), which is an innovative company that develops multilingual classes to fit its clients' individual needs. When the center needed ideas for a marketing letter, the director and her administrator sat down at the computer with the Idea Generator Plus software package. They approached the task with a traditional marketing letter in mind, but they ended up with something completely different. One suggestion was that the center send flowers to the potential client instead of a letter. Another idea generated using the program—and one that the center is planning to use—is to send a series of plaques with interesting maxims on them that could be hung in an office. This unique idea fits the company's message.[14]

Another marketing application using creative computer software is that of a consumer products and information company that was in the early stages of developing its new product development plan. The purpose of this meeting was to reduce to three to five the large number of potential product ideas that could be pursued during the coming year. Prior to the meeting, various staff members of the company brainstormed a total of seventeen new or extended product ideas that they wanted to consider for the coming calendar-year development. Each of the product ideas was described in a one-page summary for review prior to the one-and-one-half-day meeting described here.

The new product evaluation and planning session was facilitated by an outside marketing consultant. The session began with a review of the company's strategic vision in order to focus the participants' attention on the context into which new products should be introduced. Present were the senior officers of the company along with appropriate business development staff, a total of eight people. Following the discussion of the vision, the facilitator used a brainstorming technique to help the participants develop a list of relevant criteria for evaluating each of the product ideas. More than thirty separate ideas for criteria were quickly developed and then, after a lively discussion, sorted into the following ten separate criteria categories:

A. - Competition.

B. - Market potential.

C. - Buyers want it.

D. - It fits our strategy.

E. - Profits and revenues.

F. - Sex appeal/pizzazz.

G. - Ramp up time.

H. - We have expertise.

I. - We tie in consumers.

H. - It builds on channel.

These ten criteria were then entered into OptionFinder. Using the software's paired-comparison procedure, the management team rank-ordered the criteria from most important to least important. This provided them with criteria weighted on a scale of 0 to 100. Once they had the weighted criteria, they used OptionFinder to evaluate each of the product ideas in terms of how well it met the criteria. A nine-point scale was used, where 1 = "Not all," 5 = "Just OK," and 9 = "Perfectly." When all of the seventeen products had been evaluated against each of the ten criteria, a separate X-Y grid was produced for each product and then reviewed by the participants. Product 17 received the highest rating and product 10 received the lowest rating from the group of eight voters. The results of each of the products were discussed to identify areas of confusion and overlap in meanings and to generate new ideas that arose in the process.

This process took a total of five and one-half hours to complete with the senior management team. After the session, the average vote for each of the criteria for each of the product ideas was analyzed using a separate software tool called Decision Pad that produced a spreadsheet. The analysis with this format helped the group to focus its attention on the four highest-ranked products. After reaching this conclusion, it immediately brainstormed a list of the possible components that might be found in each of the four final product candidates. This was accomplished in approximately two hours. The resulting lists of components provided the new product development team with information that it needed to conduct a full-due-diligence evaluation of the four most important product ideas.[15]

SUMMARY

This chapter emphasized the need to rethink the marketing function in order to make the most effective usage of creative computer software. Marketing areas that need to be rethought included the need for core competence to create new products, development of innovative products and services, influencing the direction of creating new markets, awareness that market leaders know what customers want, and a closer look at competition. Essentially, revamped marketing thinking stresses the fact that the company knows what its customers want before they know themselves and influences the direction that the market will take today and tomorrow. For many companies, profound changes in marketing policy as well as in the mind-set of their marketing managers must be undertaken. Creating a new way of thinking must come initially from top management. In addition, the chapter looked at applications that not only included the use of creative computer software, but also showed the relationship of rethinking the marketing function to this software.

NOTES

1. Richard V. Sarkissian, "Retailing Trends in the 1990s," *Journal of Accountancy*, December 1989, pp. 44–55.

2. Gary Hamel and C. K. Prahalad, "The Core Competence of the Corporation," *Harvard Business Review*, May–June 1990, p. 79.

3. Gary Hamel and C. K. Prahalad, "Corporate Imagination and Expeditionary Marketing," *Harvard Business Review*, July–August 1991, pp. 81–82.

4. Ibid., p. 83.

5. Ibid., pp. 83–84.

6. Jon Ziber, "IdeaFisher and MindLink," *MacUser*, May 1990, p. 67–69.

7. Hamel and Prahalad, "Corporate Imagination and Expeditionary Marketing," p. 85.

8. Matt DeLorenzo, "Upward Bound," *Autoweek*, April 8, 1991, pp. 22–23.

9. Hamel and Prahalad, "Corporate Imagination and Expeditionary Marketing," pp. 85–86.

10. Paula Smith, "Unique Tool for Marketers: PIMS," *Management Review*, January 1977, pp. 32–34.

11. Josh Brackett, "Strategic Computing for Corporate Climbers," *EDGE*, September/October 1988, p. 25.

12. Claudia H. Deutsch, "007 It's Not, But Intelligence Is In," *New York Times*, December 23, 1990, Business section, p. 24.

13. Hamel and Prahalad, "Corporate Imagination and Expeditionary Marketing," pp. 91–92.

14. "It's What You're Doing . . . Mediating, Selling Products, Winning Negotiations," *Thinking Software*, Fall 1990, p. 4.

15. "Evaluating New Product Ideas," *OptionFinder Application*, Option Technologies, Inc., 1990, pp. 1–2.

9

Creativity in Manufacturing

ISSUES EXPLORED

- To demonstrate the linkage of a manufacturing framework to other functional areas of a typical company
- To present a practical view of just-in-time inventories
- To show how a flexible manufacturing approach can be used to meet changing customer needs
- To focus on the need for continuing quality improvement for a typical manufacturer
- To demonstrate the usage of creative computer software in typical real-world manufacturing situations

OUTLINE

Linkage of a Manufacturing Framework to Other Functional Areas
  Elements of Computer-integrated Manufacturing
  Mobilizing a CIM Team Effort
  Steps Involved in the CIM Investigative Process That Utilize Creative Computer
    Software
Value Analysis Related to Computer-integrated Manufacturing
  Illustrative Value-Analysis Questions
A Practical View of Just-in-Time Inventories
  Avoiding High Inventory Costs of the Past
A Partnership Approach for Just-in-Time Merchandising
  Current Manufacturing Participants
Flexible Manufacturing to Meet Changing Demand
  Usefulness for a Wide Range of Manufacturers

As highlighted in the previous chapter, the marketplace is rapidly changing in new ways that are different from the past. Worldwide competition demands a renewed emphasis on product and service quality. In the United States, companies have begun to realize that quality improvement is vital. It is not just good business but is essential to a company's success. It is necessary not only to build a product faster and cheaper, but also to make the product better. This approach to quality emphasizes the cost-effectiveness of productivity in all areas of a company, from accounting to the assembly line. It is easy to forget that quality improvement in the office is as important as improvement in manufacturing or elsewhere in a company. Companies are finding that quality practices are giving them the competitive edge to survive in the world marketplace. It is from this perspective that there is need to rethink the manufacturing function so that creativity is facilitated, which is the subject matter of this chapter. In turn, the next chapter will take a new look at accounting and finance so that creativity can be applied on a day-to-day basis.

LINKAGE OF A MANUFACTURING FRAMEWORK TO OTHER FUNCTIONAL AREAS

As a starting point for relating creativity to manufacturing, it is helpful to look at the total framework that underlies all considerations for a typical manufacturing company. Such a framework today and in the future centers on *computer-integrated manufacturing* (CIM). Generally, CIM means blending manufacturing with marketing, accounting, and finance, as well as other functional areas where deemed necessary. CIM is currently crucial to the survival of manufacturers because it provides the levels of planning and control for manufacturing along with the flexibility to change with the times.

The basic objective of CIM is to change management's thinking by establishing a framework within which manufacturing operations are defined, funded, managed, and coordinated. This framework requires specific mechanisms for production planning, cost control, project selection and justification, project management, and project performance monitoring. The role of the enterprise view of CIM is to ensure that the levels and types of integration are appropriate. A most important concept in integration is the use of standards, both technical and data. Technical standards are set by and for the whole enterprise. They define what is sometimes called the computer systems architecture. Unlike technical standards, data standards cannot be obtained from a standards committee. They must be defined and maintained by the company itself.

Elements of Computer-integrated Manufacturing

Basically, computer-integrated manufacturing is a technique that enables manufacturers to be more competitive. It helps improve productivity without reliance on direct labor of the past and brings a discipline to manufacturing operations. It provides management with real-time information that allows it to be responsive to current situations. The basic components of CIM are computer-assisted design, production planning and control, computer-assisted manufacturing, manufacturing resource planning, quality control, materials inventory control, cost control, and materials handling, which includes automatic storage and retrieval. Computer-integrated manufacturing combines all of these components so that different solutions can be used for different needs. In addition, CIM currently includes going upstream, not only to product design with the assistance of the marketing function, but also to process planning—computer-aided process planning. It certainly encompasses computer-aided management and management information systems themselves, as well as distribution, which is the logistics aspect of getting products to customers. It includes all of the feedback of information, the linkages to the financial system through accounting for accounts receivable and payable. All of these areas fall within computer-integrated manufacturing from a very broad perspective. In summary, computer-integrated manufacturing is a very broad concept for more effectively managing a manufacturing enterprise. It is a way of operating a manufacturing organization using a computer-integrated business approach. In today's markets, computer-integrated manufacturing is generally necessary for a manufacturing business's survival.

In addition, CIM is increasingly critical because manufacturing itself contributes relatively less to the cost of a product. Much of the cost, quality, and time reflected in a product now lie outside the plant. In the past few years, much of CIM's emphasis has been on the "I"; greater integration has enabled CIM to impact the areas that really matter by accelerating the flow of information between manufacturing and the other functions that support it. In contrast, old CIM in the 1970s and 1980s emphasized improving a single function's productivity. New CIM is made possible by the declining cost of hardware, increased connectivity, and the widespread availability of PCs and workstations, thereby requiring that MIS contribute at the planning and delivery levels.

In planning, MIS must provide manufacturing with a vision of what is possible with information technology. MIS must stay abreast of delivery tools, such as color monitors and graphical user interfaces. It is no longer enough to merely provide a solution to manufacturing needs; the solution must be low-cost and high-quality, easy to develop, easy to use, and easy to integrate.[1]

Just getting under way is a future direction called interorganizational CIM (I-CIM) that brings vendors, suppliers, and customers into the CIM loop. This integrates factory-floor production to engineering, purchasing, accounting, upper management, and external organizations, thereby resulting in productivity gains from an enterprise-wide integration of information. Needless to say, I-CIM may take some time before it is realized.

Mobilizing a CIM Team Effort

In order to "reinvent" the organization to utilize a CIM framework, the first step is the formation of a CIM team. The team leader should be well organized and an effective communicator. This person could be drawn from any area, such as engineering, MIS, or manufacturing. A full-time commitment for the team leader will be necessary if significant progress is expected.

Next, CIM team members, drawn from all major operations within the company, should be selected for part-time participation. Within each area, a first-level manager is the ideal candidate since he or she has a working knowledge of the department, upward visibility and communication, and some measure of decision-making authority. The roster may include sales, purchasing, engineering, manufacturing (several members), production planning and control, personnel, accounting, and MIS. It is desirable for team members to attend a CIM seminar, such as those sponsored by local universities, the Society of Mechanical Engineering (SME), or the Institute of Industrial Engineering (IIE). Tours of nearby plants that have some degree of factory-floor integration are another effective way to build team enthusiasm and awareness. The team leader should assemble magazines, trade journals, and texts on the subject and then act a "CIM librarian" to circulate selected articles.

Steps Involved in the CIM Investigative Process That Utilize Creative Computer Software

In order to begin the CIM investigative process, the team needs to develop an understanding of how the business operates. A most efficient approach is to select a specific job, product, or service (depending on the type of business) and thoroughly document it as it progresses through the enterprise. This is much easier to manage and gives the team an idea of the resources available. The model selected, however, must be very representative of the product. The CIM team should arrive at a consensus in identifying this model. This will be the team's first major decision and will have lasting implications because all subsequent work will be based on this model.

The next step is to redefine the overall manufacturing cycle into a group of essential functions. Each function should represent the collective efforts of one or more departments to accomplish a major enterprise objective. For example, ensuring a steady, reliable stream of raw materials to manufacturing could be termed *procurement* and might involve coordination among sales (forecasts), purchasing (pricing), traffic (routing), receiving (unloading), and accounting (invoicing). Alternately, *production reporting* might involve interactions among manufacturing (output), quality (testing), engineering (standards), accounting (costs), and MIS (reporting). The involvement for each department in supporting a given function should be quantified in a participation matrix.

In the next step, there is need to document the flow of data and materials through each functional area. The use of a visibility technique, such as data-flow diagrams or entity diagrams, will facilitate this step if it is applied correctly and consistently. Also, each functional area must be evaluated for existing strengths and weaknesses as well as being assessed for the formal and informal systems currently in use. Concurrently, the team should identify criteria to evaluate the "as is" condition of each functional area and its opportunity for CIM.

Functional areas should now be evaluated collectively against the first CIM criterion to establish a relative ranking. The foregoing analysis of strengths and weaknesses provides direct input in deriving this ranking. This procedure is then repeated for the next CIM criterion. One of the creative computer software packages could be used at this point in the CIM investigative process.

Once all the criteria have been treated, an *opportunity score* is obtained for each functional area. It may be desirable to assign differing weights to specific criteria to account for higher priority. This is handled easily and quickly by the software package. The results of this analysis will identify those functional areas that have stronger potential for CIM. For example, accurate reporting of manufacturing efficiencies could receive the highest CIM opportunity score.

Finally, the CIM team should prepare a report summarizing its analyses, observations, and conclusions. Often this includes a recommendation to expand the group to full-time status in order to place greater emphasis on specific development and/or implementation projects. As can be seen, this CIM investigative process draws upon all the major organizational units for input and participation. Likewise, it fosters a team approach to nurture the total CIM effort.[2]

VALUE ANALYSIS RELATED TO COMPUTER-INTEGRATED MANUFACTURING

Because CIM is a very broad approach to manufacturing, it includes the final product design by engineering. To assist a manufacturer in designing products that are profitable, *value engineering* or *value analysis* is needed. This approach requires that the engineer adopt a broader point of view and consider whether the parts contained in the finished product perform their required functions both as efficiently and as inexpensively as possible. The appraisal focuses on the function that the part—or the larger assembly containing the part—performs. To illustrate, the product is dismantled and each part is mounted adjacent to its mating part on a table. The point is to demonstrate visually the functional relationships of the various parts. Each component is studied as it relates to the performance of the complete unit, rather than as an isolated element. A value-analysis checklist contains literally hundreds of questions and key ideas for reducing overall costs as well as maintaining the same level of product performance.

Illustrative Value-Analysis Questions

Illustrative general questions that can be used are as follows:

* Can the part be eliminated?
* If the part is not standard, can a standard part be used?
* If it is a standard part, does it complement the finished product, or is it a misfit?
* Can the weight be reduced with lower-priced materials?
* Are closer tolerances specified than are necessary?
* Is unnecessary machining performed on the item?
* Are unnecessary finishes required?
* Can the part be produced in the plant less expensively, or should it be bought from the outside?
* Is the product properly classified for shipping purposes to obtain the lowest transportation rates?
* Can the cost of packaging be reduced?

In addition, one of the creative software packages from chapter 6 can be used to investigate alternative creative approaches to simplify the product and reduce its costs.

When value engineering is used to appraise overall costs, possibilities for making component-part design simplifications are frequently more apparent than is possible under the conventional design conditions. This in no way reflects unfavorably on the work done by the design engineer; the discovery of such potential improvements is the result of an analysis with a substantially broader orientation than that possessed by the original designer. A value-analysis study undertaken by a typical company utilizes the background and skills of several people because it is not possible to find the multiplicity of skills and experiences of that group in the person of a single designer. Resulting design changes often permit the substitution of standardized production operations for more expensive operations requiring special setup work. In other cases, an entirely different material or production process turns out to be more efficient than the one originally specified. In the final analysis, value engineering contributes to the profitability of new products for a typical manufacturing-oriented company.

A PRACTICAL VIEW OF JUST-IN-TIME INVENTORIES

The concept of just-in-time inventories is not an entirely new one. It was originally used extensively by the Japanese and is now used by many companies in the United States and Europe, and its potential during expansionary times has been fully exploited. However, its potential during recessionary times or in declining industries is now just being realized. For example, Corning Inc., which makes kiln-baked ceramic parts for catalytic converters in cars, has lost 25 percent of its business just recently. But this time, no shutdown has been necessary. About 100 jobs have been gradually eliminated, mostly through attrition, leaving more than 800 ceramic workers employed. In effect, Corning has managed decline.

Starting in 1987, Corning installed just-in-time inventory management at Erwin, New York, a system that includes supplying its customers with products just a few days after the order is received, rather than the weeks it once took. Corning is now better able to track swings in demand and avoid getting caught with stockpiles that can take months to work down. Also, profits hold up better when operations slow.

Avoiding High Inventory Costs of the Past

Skill in managing inventories in times of slack demand as well as in declining industries is important to the U.S economy. Many manufacturers today are keeping inventories lean so that there is little risk that bulging inventories will force them to cut production abruptly and lay off large numbers of workers. These manufacturers include not just Corning but also a wide range of companies such as General Electric, Motorola, and Rubbermaid. The net effect of their efforts is that inventories throughout the economy are low not only for the onset of a recession, but also during an expansion and a subsequent contraction in the economy.

Of course, not all manufacturers have adopted just-in-time inventory management. Even those that have not, though, have learned to manage more efficiently. High interest rates in the 1980s plus other costs of carrying inventory have made running lean financially necessary. Moreover, as the Japanese have shown, efficient inventory management tends to improve product quality, efficiency, and the flexibility of work practices. In the 1990s as well as into the twenty-first century, those companies that are not getting on board with sophisticated inventory management may not remain in business. Poor inventory practices are an important contributing factor in many bankruptcies.

As an example of how not to manage inventories, reference can be made to Chrysler. In the late 1970s when automobile demand seemed set to escalate forever, Chrysler Corporation's management decided that, rather than build cars at dealer or customer request, it would stockpile vehicles to keep factories running smoothly despite swings in orders. When demand suddenly slowed in 1980, Chrysler got sandbagged. All around Detroit, thousands of its cars sat unsold on company lots. The decision to stockpile inventory was perhaps the single biggest cause of the company's near collapse. Since then, Chrysler has made significant improvements. At its Belvidere, Illinois, plant, parts inventories are used up, on the average, every two and one-half working days—a performance that matches the best Japanese standards. Even so, U.S. automobile companies still take about two weeks to make a car once they get the order, more than twice the time required in Japan. More efficient production flows—and the arrival of needed parts just before assembly—give Japanese automobile manufacturers a considerable cost advantage over U.S. rivals. Overall, if a company manages inventory properly, its suppliers carry most of a company's inventory carrying and holding costs.

That is a basic lesson Corning has learned. Before the Erwin factory adopted just-in-time practices in 1987, Corning warehoused large supplies of everything it needed, even the cardboard boxes that package the finished ceramic parts. Now, every night, its one cardboard supplier delivers what it thinks Corning will need the next day. The two eye-level stacks of cardboard near the factory's loading dock replace the pallets that once occupied the better part of a football field. Moreover, Corning pays just for what it uses and does so through one contract rather than, as before, through forty separate orders. Needless to say, savings are very large. Carrying $1.00 of inventory typically costs manufacturers $0.20 to $0.25. Corning estimates that its revised just-in-time inventory system has so far saved as much as $10 million at the Erwin plant and some $180 million throughout the company.

In the final analysis, Corning's two leased warehouses have been eliminated. Gone too are about two-thirds of the stocks formerly warehoused at the factory. Because Corning now supplies its customers only as needed, it is better able to notice a drop in demand and adjust its output gradually. In contrast, part production scheduling was less tied to current customer demand, and the company suddenly discovered a big stockpile that it needed to work off. In addition, there was very little communication with its customers back then. Now Corning can ride the economic downturns and upturns much more smoothly with a creative way to manage inventories.[3]

A PARTNERSHIP APPROACH FOR JUST-IN-TIME MERCHANDISING

In the past, the Procter & Gamble Company was known as a tough bargainer in dealing with stores that carry its products. But these days, the company is cited as a leading example of how packaged-goods and food manufacturers form partnerships with major retailers to slash costs in the pipeline that connects manufacturers to consumers. The partnerships aim to cut inventories for both parties, smooth out production schedules, and identify service and quality problems. They are looking for the same benefits that automobile manufacturers and other industrial companies have been reaping in recent years from just-in-time delivery arrangements with suppliers. To achieve such gains, some consumer goods companies and their retail customers have abandoned the traditional practice of meeting only through low-level sales representatives and buyers whose worlds revolve around the week's price margins and the size of the next order.

Today, companies like Procter & Gamble and K Mart assign teams to deal with each other. These teams mix information-processing experts, who automate and harmonize order and record-keeping systems, with sales and purchasing representatives. The companies' logistics managers share information that helps Procter & Gamble avoid sudden spikes and dips in orders for, say, Pampers, and coordinate delivery schedules with K Mart's warehouses. Marketing and finance managers share both up-to-the-minute sales data on the latest promotions and long-range plans for coordinating Procter & Gamble's new product introductions with K Mart promotional campaigns. When both companies started looking at a closer partnership arrangement, they saw a potential savings of $1 billion annually in the United States for Procter & Gamble and just as much, if not more, for its customers. Essentially, then, the underlying thrust of this partnership is the ability to obtain profits for both the company and the customer.

Current Manufacturing Participants

Among the manufacturers, Kraft General Foods (subsidiary of Philip Morris, Inc.) matches Procter & Gamble in its commitment to the team strategy and outstrips it in working with store managers on local marketing programs. Quaker Oats, Helen Curtis, General Mills, Frito-Lay (a subsidiary of Pepsico), Nabisco (a subsidiary of RJR Nabisco), Johnson & Johnson, and Pepperidge Farms (a subsidiary of Campbells) are all active proponents of extensive partnering, although not all of them rely on multifunctional teams to the extent that Procter & Gamble and Kraft do. Kraft set up almost 400 sales teams to pursue its goal of "micro-merchandising," that is, helping retailers sell more of everything, especially Kraft products, by using the growing mountain of data on consumer preferences to develop a detailed picture of each store's clientele, which products are selling best, and which displays and promotions are apt to be most effective at that site.

Sometimes Kraft sales teams even recommend that some of the company's own products be replaced with those of a competitor or with different categories of products. One reason for the drive is the increasing challenge manufacturers face in reaching consumers directly. Trends such as the declining viewership of network television make it harder to develop brand loyalty and sales through national advertising. Equally important is the fact that society has fragmented into

a number of distinctive consumer groups with different buying patterns and suscep-
tibility to brand names, discounts, and other promotions. Electronic scanning
systems give retailers the data they need to profit from such segmentation, but
few are capable of fully exploiting that information without the cooperation and
help of the large manufacturers.

In addition, the emphasis on quality in manufacturing that spread through industry in the 1980s led to a thorough reconsideration of what goes into high-quality
customer and supplier relationships in sales and purchasing departments. Total
quality concepts dictate a focus not just on today's price margins, but on cash
flow throughout a production system. Thus Procter & Gamble switched from seeking the lowest shipping price from among 250 trucking companies to ongoing
relationships with 15 major ones, many of whom were made part of teams serving the most important customers. Most of the projects seem mundane on their
own. For example, Procter & Gamble's marketing experts found that K Mart
was intent on building an image of environmental responsiveness, so they interested
K Mart marketing managers in new refillable packaging for Downy fabric
softeners. Those managers helped persuade K Mart purchasing management to
put aside its natural reluctance to place large orders for new products. The resulting
promotion sold a lot of Downy and met K Mart's strategic needs. The combination of improved information exchange and logistical adjustments has led to a
wide variety of improvement in service to Wal-Mart. As an example, the retailer's
inventories of Tide have been cut to two days from thirty.

In another case, Shaw's Supermarkets Inc. (East Bridgewater, Massachusetts)
worked with Procter & Gamble to standardize the language and structure of electronic order-processing systems. At first, Procter & Gamble was able to process
electronically only 10 percent of Shaw's computerized orders. Now that figure
is more than 90 percent, removing one of the many causes of delay and uncertainty that force retailers and suppliers to keep large inventories on hand. In addition, more error-free orders cleared the way for more electronic invoicing,
leading to prompter payments and fewer disagreements about whether orders had
been filled.

It should be noted that cooperation has allowed Procter & Gamble to automate
replenishment of supplies for twelve retailers. In one case, the automation reduced
the inventory of Procter & Gamble's products by 80 percent. For such retailers,
each order is sold out so rapidly that they have reordered and are piling up cash
from those reorders by the time the ten-day period for paying Procter & Gamble
is up. That cash cushion allows them to operate without borrowing to finance
inventories of Procter & Gamble products.[4]

FLEXIBLE MANUFACTURING TO MEET CHANGING DEMAND

Flexible manufacturing can be defined as the ability to produce quickly wide
varieties of products using the same equipment. Flexible manufacturing systems

today are far cry from the machines first installed in the 1980s. Those were highly complex, fully automated systems that people found difficult to operate and maintain. However, today's flexible manufacturing systems are usually made up of "cells" or clusters of simpler, less automated machines dedicated to a specific purpose. More important, they not only offer variation in actual manufacturing processes, but also include flexible control, which is the ability to adapt quickly in manpower levels, raw material requirements, machine availability, and customer demand.

Usefulness for a Wide Range of Manufacturers

Rather than appealing only to manufacturers with variable product lines, flexible manufacturing systems have become just as important to manufacturers with only one product line. For example, a photosensor manufacturer that produced a wide variety of products regrouped its machines, which were scattered, into flexible production cells according to product family. In addition, the company reduced the number of its suppliers, adopted just-in-time methods to cut inventory, and provided plant floor personnel with more information about the product they were assembling. With these changes, the plant cut its lead time from eight weeks to one week.

Another example is a pet-food plant with one major product that found itself facing a sudden outburst of demand. It was able to keep pace by replacing its manual procedures for controlling individual processes with an integrated supervisory control system. The control system eliminated the guesswork that occurred between each production step, thereby reducing scrap by 30 percent and boosting plant output. The new control system also made it easier to spin off variations of the plant's product line.

Not all industries have the same flexibility requirements, however. For example, a turbulent market demands that consumer product manufacturers be highly flexible. Typically, one out of every six items on supermarket shelves was introduced within the last twelve months. On the other hand, construction materials show less of a need for change. Virtually any computer-integrated manufacturing application—from manufacturing resource planning (MRP II) to computer-aided design process optimization, and statistical quality control—can play a part in making the plant more flexible.

Three Components Found in Flexible Manufacturing

There is no standard approach to flexible manufacturing, although there are three components that make up the core of a flexible manufacturing system. The linchpin is the *supervisory program*, which runs on a personal computer, workstation, or minicomputer. Such a program is known as a cell control system in the discrete manufacturing world (where parts are fabricated, built, or assembled) and a supervisory control system in the process manufacturing sector (where ingredients are blended, boiled, cooked, distilled, fermented, or subjected to chemical reaction). Depending on the plant or process type, supervisory programs may be available off-the-shelf from independent software vendors, machine tool vendors, or controller suppliers. Otherwise, they are generally custom written by systems integrators. As their names imply, supervisory and cell control programs provide overviews and coordinate the activities of the plant or a portion thereof. Their job is to collect data on work in progress, prepare trend analyses and summary reports for managers and machine operators, and transmit high-level supervisory instructions to local controllers that govern such things as machines, robots, cookers, blenders, reactor tanks, and distillation columns.

In turn, these controllers translate the instructions (the second component) into the digital or analog codes needed to operate the device or machine. Because many controllers are proprietary, then can pose integration problems. The third and final component of the flexible manufacturing system is the factory-floor network. These high-speed networks operate in real time to transmit data from the supervisory program to the machine itself. On a regular local area network (such as Ethernet), there is no guarantee that the instruction will reach its destination before the device or process fails. These networks are generally provided by the controller supplier.[5]

Finite Schedulers

There are numerous other applications that can play a supporting role in this threesome, and there are many different ways for deciding at which level of the organization or computing system each application is to be run. For instance, a relatively new type of software called a *finite scheduler* can adjust production schedules according to current demand and operating conditions. This can be valuable for companies faced with tight delivery and production schedules, many machines from which to choose, many possible ways to order their sequence, and a large number of staff deployments.

Typically, employee absences, machine downtime, and material delivery delays are usually considered outside the realm of manufacturing resource planning (MRP II) systems, which have historically been strong in long-range planning but ill equipped for the idiosyncrasies of everyday plant life. Finite scheduling programs, on the other hand, bring to the scheduling chaos not only order but optimization. Some of the newer software packages can figure how to best juggle work orders to minimize the setup procedure to readjust machines between production runs. In contrast, others can determine the most profitable job sequences to ensure that jobs are produced in order of priority.

In the last few years, several vendors have produced finite scheduling programs, some of which are stand-alone products and some of which are integrated modules to MRP II packages. Some cell and supervisory control suppliers are beginning to incorporate third-party finite scheduling products into their packages. Needless to say, there are a number of product variations. Some programs concentrate on scheduling individual production lines, while others operate at the plant level. Other distinctions are based on the method of analysis.[6]

NEED FOR CONTINUING QUALITY IMPROVEMENT

After being viewed as a manufacturing problem in the past, quality has become a service issue—not just for service-sector businesses like communications, health care, and finance but for the service side of manufacturing companies as well. The focus is on *total quality management* (TQM), that is, quality in the offering itself and in all the services that come with it. Thus, if product quality is essentially the same across the industry, service becomes the distinguishing factor.

With TQM, the postwar quality movement has moved into its third stage. When the growing popularity of Japanese automobiles, televisions, and radios forced U.S. manufacturers to take another look at themselves in the late 1970s, most companies were still in what quality experts call the first of inspection phase, relying on sampling techniques to get rid of defective items. Too often, however, they did not. In 1980—the year and NBC "White Paper" introduced audiences to W. Edwards Deming, the American statistician who had shown the Japanese how to use process controls to catch defects at the source—manufacturers who took the issue seriously started moving into the second or quality-control phase. Now, with TQM, quality is no longer solely in the quality-control department. It is sponsored by top management and diffused throughout the company.[7]

Research on Quality Improvement

In a survey conducted for the American Society for Quality Control (Milwaukee, Wisconsin) by the Gallup Organization in June 1990, the results indicated that the members of today's work force do not fully use their talents, abilities, and energies for quality improvement. Today's work force is saying to management: "Of course, we want to be paid more and we want more job security, but more than that, we want a better chance to put our ideas to work." Lack of employee involvement is a twofold problem: unwillingness or lack of motivation to participate, and lack of opportunity to participate. The most frequently cited reasons for not participating include (1) not offered/not available, (2) too busy, (3) no effect, (4) no particular reason, and (5) have not been asked.

Overall, employees see a gap between what the company says is important in regard to quality and the company's follow-through. Needless to say, this is less than a rousing vote of confidence in the quality performance of American businesses. Employees want to see better results. Substantial proportions of survey respondents said that the quality programs in their companies have had either no effect or a negative effect in specific areas (ranging from 22 percent negative on communications to 42 percent negative on their pay and benefits). Workers stated that the two most important ways the company can make it easier for them to do high-quality work are, first, to provide more training in job skills and, second, to offer job security. Beyond these two items, workers would like to see their companies do the following, in the order of importance: (1) have a more supportive attitude from top management, (2) train workers in interpersonal working skills, (3) respond faster to employee ideas, (4) offer more up-to-date tools and technology, (5) have a more supportive attitude from middle management, and (6) offer better access to available information. In each of these six points, monetary issues play a role, but they are consistently ranked by the survey respondents below other concerns. The points are a road map to quality by the people who work with the company's customers.

As an example, take Federal Express, which handles 1.5 million packages per day. The reason that customers can rely on such a complex organization is that Federal Express has made a 100 percent service level and a 100 percent customer satisfaction level as its key goals. Every employee has the right, the authority, or the backing to do whatever is necessary to satisfy the customer. Essentially, Federal Express has put much effort into mechanisms to feed information back to the people who are doing the job so that if they have a quality problem or an error, they know it and can fix it. The company has spent a lot of time training its people in quality methods. Company employees are educated on how important good quality is to the company's future viability.[8]

Accent on Total Quality Management

The concept of total quality has been around for a while. Consultant Armand Feigenbaum advocated using quality-control methods in marketing and distribution some forty years ago. But Feigenbaum's emphasis on statistical controls and quality specialists never got very far outside manufacturing. Total quality management treats quality as a strategic objective, that is, something to be built into the corporate culture.

Essentially, TQM has redefined what quality is. Quality has moved from a set of numbers on a chart to what feels right to the customer. TQM means not just delivering packages on time, but also providing a tracking system that allows customers to find out where their goods are at every point along the way. At IBM, total quality management means an electronic customer-support system that automatically diagnoses trouble and alerts service people, who have been known to show up before users know they have a problem. As another example, TQM at Ford meant getting rid of a system or regional customer-service lines so inefficient that on some days half the callers could not get through. This system was replaced with a single 800 number to provide quick satisfaction on customer complaints while giving the company an ear to the ground.

In these examples, company representatives hear things that they wish they had not. But if total quality means giving customers what they want, listening is a prerequisite. Hence there is need to see the world from the customer's point of view along with an eagerness to move quickly. Speed is critical since customers want instant gratification. Although it sounds counterintuitive, many argue that speed and quality go hand in hand. Usually, the things that take the most time are the things that go wrong. By eliminating the things that go wrong, a company can shrink the time it takes to order, produce, and deliver.

Getting the customer's viewpoint sounds easy in an age of focus groups and market research. But to see things truly from the customer's perspective is to stand at the end of a long sequence of events, all of which have to mesh smoothly. Hotel clerks, for example, may be attentive, but if the computer system is down, their courtesy is not going to help much. Within a company, total quality management is a whole chain of "internal customers" like the hotel clerk, culminating with the person at the cash register, credit card in hand. The focus is on getting everyone working together while keeping the ultimate customer in focus.[9]

UTILIZATION OF EXPERT SYSTEMS IN MANUFACTURING

In the foregoing discussion on manufacturing techniques that are related to employing creativity to improve daily operations, emphasis was placed on integrated CIM, MRP II, and JIT systems. To fit their needs in the 1990s and the twenty-first century, successful manufacturers are increasingly addressing these challenges through the development of inference-based information-processing tools. The marriage of artificial intelligence and expert-system technology with conventional information-processing techniques allows inference-based information-processing to address manufacturing application needs better. Inference-based information processing offers a number of benefits to manufacturers. First, inference-based development ensures that these systems remain malleable and flexible enough to respond to changing business requirements by decoupling complexity from change. Second, traditional MIS development cycles are reduced since the required specifications are executed directly, without the need for business rules to be translated into a language like COBOL. Third, the process of building inference-based expert systems follows a natural "protocycling" methodology where manufacturing users see results in days rather than months or years. Fourth, expert systems also change the economics of application development by making new classes of applications feasible and cost-justifiable. In effect, inference-based information processing allows manufacturers to capture and preserve the collective expertise of their most senior and knowledgeable personnel, thereby mitigating the impact of the skilled-employee shortage.

By automating its knowledge-based assets in an expert system, a company can profit by insulating these assets from human factors; that is, it can avoid loss of valuable expertise due to retirement, illness, or accident, and eliminate decision-making inconsistency. The quality and speed of business decisions also improve since junior employees can use automated expert advisors to assist them in performing their tasks at an expert level. For example, junior production engineers can consult an Engineering Design Assistant (an expert system) that embodies the design expertise of the most senior engineers and thus achieve better-quality product designs and shorter design cycles. Training and learning curves are decreased significantly, while senior personnel are also freed from dealing with routine queries and are thereby allowed to concentrate on the more difficult manufacturing and engineering problems where their years of expertise can be better leveraged.

Typical Examples of Inference-based Information Processing

Almost all facets of a manufacturing organization can benefit from applications built using inference-based information processing. For example, *Fortune* 500 manufacturers are implementing strategic and competitive applications using this technology. An Engineering Change Manager application, implemented with inference-based information processing, has helped Northern Telecom reduce the cycle time and documentation required to process product-design changes. Campbell Soup, using an inference-based application to analyze process control data, can ensure that regulatory requirements are met for its food products and has documented annual savings over $2 million as a result. Ingersol Milling is using expert systems to optimize parts purchasing, process planning, and generative numerical control to evolve from CIM toward computer-optimized systems. York International sales engineers save time and money by using a sales-support expert system that prepares supporting, quotation, explanation, and business documentation for air-conditioning proposals and ties this information into York's CAD/CAM system. These companies are using inference-based information processing to ensure that they will be formidable competitors tomorrow.[10]

APPLICATIONS SHOWING LINKAGE OF FLEXIBLE MANUFACTURING TO UTILIZING CREATIVE COMPUTER SOFTWARE

In the world of manufacturing today, winning the Malcolm Baldrige National Quality Award is a goal of many executives. Although the Baldrige Award is a marketing bonanza, it is the discipline of total quality management that brings out the very best in a manufacturer. But winning the Baldrige is no simple matter. It requires a concerted effort on the part of everyone in an organization. It requires clear focus, effective communication, and careful follow-through in a flexible manufacturing environment.

A manufacturer does not have to be a Malcolm Baldrige Award winner to utilize creative computer software. In this section of the chapter, several creative software packages will be used, namely, the Idea Generator Plus, Idea Tree, and IdeaFisher 4.0 to assist managers in a flexible manufacturing environment. Essentially, these software packages are useful in a group DSS operating mode such that a group can make paired and rating comparisons by gathering input from its members. In turn, the results can be shown in summarized form, bar charts, two-dimensional graphs, and so on. Thus the group is able to focus immediately on areas of agreement and disagreement and concentrate attention on the critical and relevant manufacturing issues. In the process, group members save time and avoid unnecessary conflict.

MERLIN TECHNOLOGIES, INC.

Running a business in today's fast-paced economy is like racing a bobsled. It seems that it is necessary to go 90 mph trying to stay ahead of the competition. The top-level executive has to think creatively and fast. No one knows this better than Walter Wilson, who runs an aerospace and automotive design company, Merlin Technologies Inc. His company has redesigned the bobsleds used by the U.S. Olympic team.

In bobsledding, the difference between winning and losing is measured in milliseconds. Wilson volunteered his services because he felt that his ingenuity could help the team improve its showing in a sport dominated by the Swiss and the Soviet bloc. One of the most important tools Wilson and his bobsled-design team used was the Idea Generator Plus. Not that Wilson's team lacked ideas. On the contrary, because it was working with seventy scientists and engineers, the problem was deciding which ideas to pursue.

Questions That Can Be Answered Using the Idea Generator Plus

As discussed in chapter 6, the first step in using the Idea Generator Plus is formulating a general problem statement—in this case, "Describe how to improve bobsled performance." The computer then guided Wilson and his group to list goals, put them in order of importance, and list people who would be involved in achieving them. Next, they were able to generate ideas using this software. The program uses seven techniques, including looking at the problem through someone else's eyes, remembering similar situations, building metaphors, and attacking the goals one at a time. One of the more interesting procedures is called "reverse goals." Instead of saying that the goal is to win the Olympics, Wilson and his group instructed the program to say, "Achieve the *slowest* bobsled time in history." Identifying all the circumstances that are guaranteed to cause certain failure underlined the factors crucial to success. They then designed ways to make impeding circumstances work in their favor. Finally, they evaluated the various ideas that had been suggested, weighed them, and chose the most promising ones.

An End Result Full of Surprises

In this groupthink situation, Wilson and his group found that personalities can get in the way of good decision making. Some strife is avoided by the subtle use of the computer software as a mediator. That is, the Idea Generator Plus allowed them the luxury of not having to address bad ideas directly and hurt anybody's feelings. Needless to say, Wilson's group came up with dozens of ideas, including experiments with wind-tunnel aerodynamics, sled vibration, and new materials.

The finished bobsled was lightning fast. In European trials before the Olympics, it had the best time in one of every four heats it entered. The bobsled demonstrated that it was as good as anything in the world. Unfortunately, the tradition-bound International Bobsled Federation got wind of what the United States was working on and got the new design disqualified. Rather than risk missing out on the event, the team bought conventional sleds and finished fourth in Calgary—a .002-second eyelash behind the Soviets. Wilson's new bobsled would almost surely have brought home a medal.[11]

UNITED GREETING CARD COMPANY

The United Greeting Card Company manufactures greeting cards and distributes them to retailers throughout the United States. It has two manufacturing plants, one located on the East Coast and one on the West Coast. Corporate headquarters are adjacent to the East Coast plant. The company's ordering policies are to "make to stock"; that is, the inventory is finished and warehoused prior to the receipt of the order to ship. There are several thousand stock-keeping units (SKUs), and each is important to the total marketing plan. While there is a definite seasonality to sales and there is a measurable long-range increasing trend, these effects are taken into account by the company's forecasting techniques. For purposes of this discussion, it is assumed that cards of different sizes that sell for differing retail amounts are of equal cost to the company and are all produced on the same equipment.

Managing the Total Inventory Effort

Managing the total inventory level and the mix among several thousand SKUs can be an arduous task. A number of questions need to be answered daily and on a periodic basis that affect the company's routine ordering policies. These ordering policies are constructed in such a way as to allow simple, low-level ordering decisions as long as the major parameters do not change.

The first major assumption is that the rate of sale has a stable and predictable trend component in the forecasting system. Stated alternatively, history is a prediction of the future. If the sales demand is increasing at an increasing rate, additional safety stock must be carried to compensate for the additive and multiplicative swings in sales. This affects the time interval over which the inventory status must be reviewed. The second major parameter is the cost of production. If the cost of materials is increasing, a decision must be made between purchasing larger quantities for price breaks and the cost of carrying inventories for a longer period of time. Factors to be weighed in this decision are the cost of money, the purchasing costs and volume breaks, and the availability of storage. The third and last major assumption is closely related to the second. Increasing costs of machinery setup must be evaluated against the costs of carrying inventory, especially in the finished-goods area.

Questions That Can Be Answered Using Idea Tree

As a way of getting started on how best to manage the total inventory effort, Idea Tree was used to organize the project into the areas that can be solved using other computer software. Because Idea Tree is not an idea generator per se but an idea organizer, it is used to group and save ideas in a form that can be shared electronically. Hence Idea Tree is looked upon as a qualitative tool rather than a quantitative one. As shown in the "tree layout" in figure 9.1, it can systematize a person's or group's thinking into developing relationships between points with which to deal.

From an overview standpoint, a number of "what-if" questions were discovered in this inventory problem to be part of a major point, "Review Ordering Policies." Idea Tree led the company's inventory group to break down the review into four work areas. The areas of review would then be handled using quantitative tools, such as electronic spreadsheets and/or SAS (Statistical Analysis System). Essentially, Idea Tree helped only in the initial layout to structure the situation. Also, it provided the necessary linkage to other computer software.

Effective production planning and inventory control for the United Greeting Card Company requires software that will support the decision-making needs of its members. One such software package is Crystal Ball (Version 2.0, Market Engineering Corporation). The goal of this software is to enable the user to find opportunities or avoid problems. Crystal Ball is a forecasting and risk-analysis program that provides "what-if" capabilities to Macintosh users. Some of its features include (1) assistance to users in understanding the relationship between variables being analyzed; (2) trend charting to forecast graphically the risk of a venture over time; (3) spreadsheet support for a variety of spreadsheet software; and (4) time and date functions useful for the analysis of project scheduling.

Another software product is available from Decisus Inc. (a company formed by Xerox). Its product, Business Wits, can help solve problems in pricing, forecasting, finance, inventory, statistics, probability, regression analysis, quality control, and more. It combines reports, graphics, and publishing capabilities into one package. It comes complete with a preprogrammed library of problem-solving tools requiring no programming skill, and also with over 300 programs based on commonly used business formulas.

NEWCOMB MANUFACTURING COMPANY

Richard Grosse, an independent manufacturing consultant, was called in by Roger Jones, the vice president in charge of manufacturing for the Newcomb

Figure 9.1
Structure of the Major Point "Review Ordering Policies" and Its Four Work Areas Using Idea Tree—United Greeting Card Company

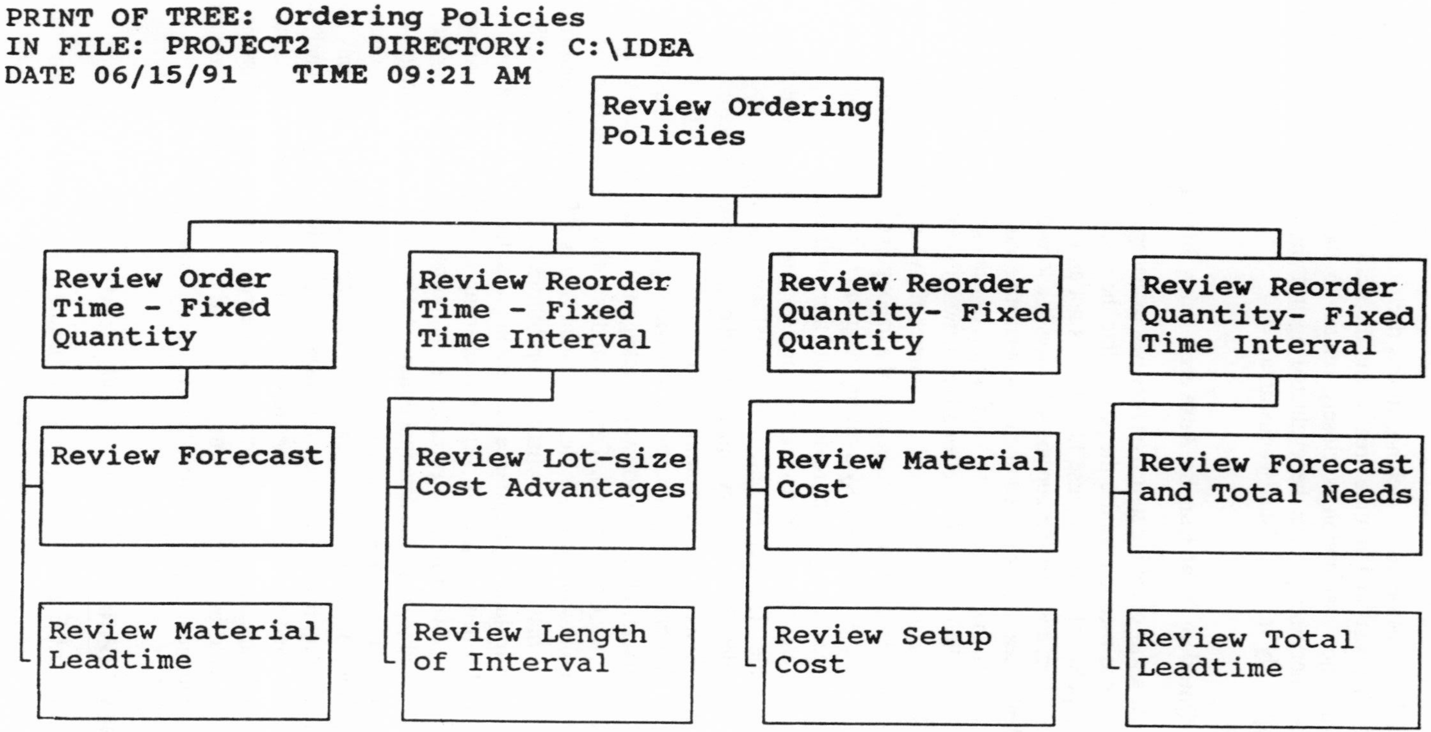

PRINT OF TREE: Ordering Policies
IN FILE: PROJECT2   DIRECTORY: C:\IDEA
DATE 06/15/91   TIME 09:21 AM

Review Ordering Policies

Review Order Time – Fixed Quantity

Review Forecast

Review Material Leadtime

Review Reorder Time – Fixed Time Interval

Review Lot-size Cost Advantages

Review Length of Interval

Review Reorder Quantity– Fixed Quantity

Review Material Cost

Review Setup Cost

Review Reorder Quantity– Fixed Time Interval

Review Forecast and Total Needs

Review Total Leadtime

Manufacturing Company, to review current manufacturing operations with the view to improve everyday manufacturing operations. The Newcomb Manufacturing Company is engaged in the manufacture of automotive parts for the Big Three car manufacturers in the United States. Additionally, the company has just started manufacturing parts for foreign manufacturers who have automobile plants in various parts of the United States. Jones was wondering whether or not the company would be able to supply automobile parts to all customers based upon changing its operations to a daily or weekly basis to meet the needs of its expanded customer base.

Inventory in a Manufacturing Environment

Flexible manufacturing, noted previously in this chapter, centers on the capability of producing quickly a number of products using the same equipment. It also includes flexible control, which is the ability to adapt quickly in manpower levels, inventory requirements, machine availability, and customer demand. Since inventory levels have a great impact on overall profitability, Grosse decided to focus initially on this important item before examining the other aspects of a flexible manufacturing environment.

From his previous consulting engagements in manufacturing companies, Grosse knew that one of the best ways to lower costs on a long-term basis is to reduce inventory levels. A reduction in inventory not only saves storage costs and space utilization, but also can increase inventory turnover. By increasing the rate of inventory turnover, the company speeds up cash flows and can better utilize scarce capital resources. IdeaFisher 4.0 was used by this consultant to assist in accomplishing inventory reduction.

Questions That Can Be Answered Using IdeaFisher 4.0

Using IdeaFisher's Ideabank, Grosse chained through a number of topics, as shown in figure 9.2a. He moved through Business-Industry-Occupations to Factories/Manufacturing to inventory turnover. From inventory turnover, he discovered topics of planning/forecasting and ways to automate that function. Computer-aided manufacturing (CAM) and computer-integrated manufacturing (CIM) have made great strides in streamlining the manufacturing process. The first way to lower inventory levels is to implement an automated solution to forecast and control inventory levels in the manufacturing process.

Once into automation, he thought that there would be additional ways to reduce inventory. Chaining through other uses of computers, such as robots and numerically controlled (NC) machines, is shown in figure 9.2b. A first way that these machines can reduce inventory is through the reduction of manufacturing lead times. If lead times can be lowered, the amount of raw materials and finished product stored during the manufacturing process is also lowered. Raw material and delivery dates can be pushed closer to the finished-product required date.

Figure 9.2a
IdeaFisher's IdeaBank to Assist in Evaluating Inventory Reduction—Newcomb Manufacturing Company

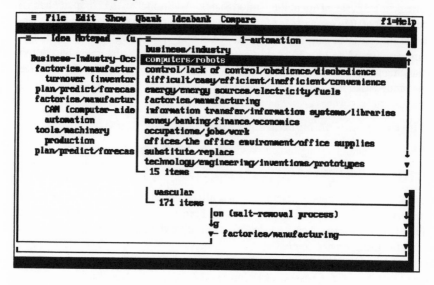

Figure 9.2b
IdeaFisher's IdeaBank to Assist in Tieing In Inventory Reduction with a Flexible Manufacturing Process—Newcomb Manufacturing Company

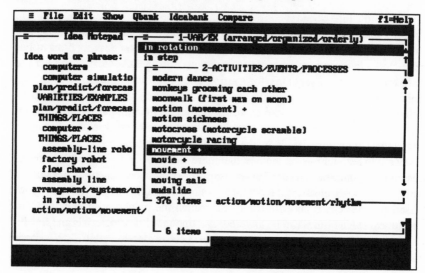

A second way that computerized equipment can assist with inventory reduction is through the use of a flexibile manufacturing process. A work-redesign program would be put into place to analyze the manufacturing flow. By using machines capable of manufacturing multiple parts and changing between them very quickly, the importance of larger "run quantities" is diminished. With short setup times, small run quantities can be manufactured almost as efficiently as larger ones. Having the ability to manufacture smaller quantities enables the company to save on storage costs and inventory levels. By using a number of flexible automated machines that are capable of producing "families of parts," the manufacturing process can be flexibile enough to produce a large variety of items in very short time spans. Hence IdeaFisher 4.0 enabled Grosse to tie in inventory reduction with a flexible manufacturing process.

OTHER MANUFACTURING APPLICATIONS THAT MAKE USE OF CREATIVE COMPUTER SOFTWARE

In applying creative computer software, Jerome Ferdinand (CEO Consultants, Inc., and the January Group, located in Chicago, Illinois) uses the Idea Generator Plus to prepare planning sessions with clients. As noted previously in chapter 6, the Idea Generator Plus can help him define the situation, consider approaches, and provide a format for the actual sessions.

As an example, a manufacturing company wanted a new approach to achieve its fourth-quarter profit goals. During a planning session with the client, Ferdinand projected the program onto an LCD screen and developed thirteen goals that would increase profits. The group then considered all possible means of reaching each goal. One of the goals was to reduce product rejects to 5 percent or less. One of the ideas they generated to reach this goal was to develop detailed inspection procedures. Another was to qualify new vendors. Still another was checking machine speeds. Next, Ferdinand exported these ideas to MaxThink, an outliner that presented the material as an action plan detailing the person responsible, short- and long-term costs and benefits, and people involved. Now each idea can be implemented easily.[12]

In another application, Motorola Semiconductor Products realizes that it is going to have to face some tough human-resource challenges five or ten years from now. It has been enlisting employees to help identify many of these challenges and a few options for dealing with them. Recently, the Phoenix-based corporation solicited input from employees using the OptionFinder software program. As noted in chapter 6, this package allows focus-group participants to enter their responses to questions confidentially into a personal computer with hand-held keypads, thereby ensuring 100 percent participation. The software immediately calculates the results and displays them anonymously to the group in the form of bar charts or multidimensional presentations.

At Motorola, OptionFinder has been used by the human-resource (HR) department to identify and rank the importance of work-force-related issues and costs of dealing with them. Several teams of HR professionals were formed to examine possible options for handling future educational, technological, and demographic issues. Part of their job was to explore ways the HR department could more effectively help the organization meet its long-term goals. The company has found that the software reduced the time for the decision-making process and allowed employees to express their thoughts in a less threatening way. Everybody was able to participate and cast his or her recommendation; employees had no choice but to buy into the process.

Brainstorming is not the only application Motorola Semiconductor found for the product. The company recently used OptionFinder to supplement its performance appraisal system. It was able to see how individuals compared to the rest of the group and determine the best career path for each person.[13]

SUMMARY

An underlying theme not only in this chapter but in the preceding ones is that fast-changing times are having a direct effect on companies. Manufacturers are finding that skilled labor is getting harder to attract and retain. Product cycles are accelerating at a breakneck pace. Applications and computer systems are becoming more complex and integral to the business. Manufacturing business processes are changing faster than the information systems upon which they depend can adapt. Hence companies need to find new and creative manufacturing approaches to make them competitive in today's and tomorrow's changing environment. Not only were newer approaches presented to assist manufacturing mangers in developing even newer ones, but also typical applications of creative computer software were presented to give them some help in directing their efforts for their own manufacturing organizations.

NOTES

1. Paul E. Schindler, Jr., "Can MIS Put Integration into CIM?" *Information Week*, December 3, 1990, p. 30.

2. James K. Kaell, "A Company-Wide Perspective to Identify, Evaluate, and Rank the Potential for CIM," *Industrial Engineering*, July 1990, pp. 23–26.

3. Thomas F. O'Boyle, "Last In, Right Out, Firms' Newfound Skill in Managing Inventory May Soften Downturn," *Wall Street Journal*, November 19, 1990, pp. A1, A6.

4. Barnabay J. Feder, "Moving the Pampers Faster Cuts Everyone's Costs," *New York Times*, July 14, 1991, Business section, p. 5.

5. Tony Baer, "Flexible Manufacturing: It's Gotten Easier to Change on Demand," *Computerworld*, February 11, 1991, pp. 59–60.

6. Tony Baer, "How to Schedule in Unexpected Events," *Computerworld*, February 11, 1991, p. 61.

7. Frank Rose, "Now Quality Means Service Too," *Fortune*, April 22, 1991, p. 100.

8. Lura K. Romei, "Quality Becomes Integral to American Business," *Modern Office Technology*, July 1991, p. 10.

9. Rose, "Now Quality Means Service Too," p. 100.

10. Andizej J. Taramina, "Expert Systems in Manufacturing," *P&IM Review with APICS News*, December 1990, pp. 42–45.

11. Dan Gutman, "The Idea Generator: This Program Makes You Brainstorm at 90 M.P.H.," *Success*, September 1988, p. 18.

12. "It's What You're Doing . . . Mediating, Selling Products, Winning Negotiations," *Thinking Software*, Fall 1990, p. 5.

13. Dave Shadovitz, "Personnel Update," *Human Resource Executive*, March 1990, p. 50.

10

Creativity in Finance and Accounting

ISSUES EXPLORED

- To show initially the linkage of financial strategic thinking to critical success factors and key performance indicators
- To examine the analysis of a company's performance versus competition from an overview standpoint
- To rethink a company's cost-accounting system such that it reflects what its true costs are
- To examine a newer cost-management system that is currently used by the Japanese
- To set forth a number of case studies that employ creativity in finance and accounting

OUTLINE

Linkage of Financial Strategic Thinking with CSFs and KPIs
Analysis of Return on Investment
  Research on ROI
  Comparison Using ROI
  Other Financial Ratios
Analysis of a Company's Performance versus Competition
  Employment of Graphics to Highlight Financial Trends
  Utilization of Creative Computer Software to Assist in Analyzing Financial Trends
Analysis of Capital Investment Decisions
  Development of Alternative Capital Investments Using Creative Computer Software
Rethinking of Cost Accounting to Reflect a Company's Real Costs
The Fundamentals of Newer Cost-accounting Methodologies
Utilization of a Different Cost-Management System
  Japan's Use of Target Cost

An important starting point for the creative process, as discussed previously in this book, is a *vision of the future*. For a typical company, top-level managers must want their companies to be the leaders in their industries, say, in five years, or their companies must do this to better service their customers. Vision is not merely corporate long-range planning intended to realize more sales but a fundamental change to corporate strategic thinking on how the company must change to become competitive or achieve a leadership role. Examples include Fred Smith's vision when he launched Federal Express. Max Hopper's vision along with that of several others created American Airlines' Sabre flight-reservation system. Emil Martini's vision helped put a terminal in every drugstore for ordering inventory directly from Bergen-Brunswig. Each of these ideas—radical changes in business operations—were answers to "what-if" questions that solved business needs and achieved phenomenal success.

In addition, visioning is linked directly to a company's critical success factors and key performance indicators. Essentially, CSFs and KPIs are tied in with a company's financial performance, which is generally captured by the accounting system. Due to the importance of finance and accounting functions in a typical company, this chapter looks at their new directions from a creative viewpoint and at important financial ratios that have been so helpful in the past to evaluate a company's total performance. Likewise, applications that show the linkage of finance and accounting approaches to utilizing creative computer software are treated.

LINKAGE OF FINANCIAL STRATEGIC THINKING WITH CSFs AND KPIs

To improve financial strategic thinking within a typical company, treasurers, financial executives, and their staffs must enlarge the scope of their thinking about the company's operations. Essentially, this means allowing them to "get the big picture'' when they review the company's total activities so that there is optimization of resources for the entire company versus one or just a few parts of it. The success that the typical company has in attaining its mission as well as its short- to long-range goals and objectives depends on the degree of integration of its operations. Enlargements of the scope of organization activities as well as the acceptance of responsibilities that lie outside the boundaries of traditional finance and accounting are illustrated in this chapter. As an example, strategic capital investment thinking is discussed below.

Because the commitment of the company's money is directed to capital projects, strategic capital investment thinking is concerned with providing the various manufacturing capacities called for in the company's corporate strategic long-range plans. It consists of the comparative evaluation of alternative projects requiring the commitment of corporate capital. While long-range plans provide the framework for strategic capital investment planning, it is at the investment stage that managers and their staffs commit portions of the company's pool of capital to specific projects. Hence individuals responsible for investing corporation resources need an understanding of financial concepts and models in order to use them effectively for decision making. In turn, they must be able to evaluate those concepts and models that indicate the expected profitability of proposed investments.

When a company is developing costs for alternative capital projects, the cost of capital needs to be included. Including these costs is essential for the meaningful appraisal of capital project proposals. To make wise decisions on the evaluation and approval of investment proposals, managers need to know how effective individual projects promise to be in using the corporation's capital to generate a satisfactory return over the long run. Projects that do not return an amount at least equal to the corporation's cost of capital should be rejected or should at least have to be justified on other than economic grounds.

An essential part of strategic capital investment thinking is determining where a company should make capital investments that are related to its most important critical success factors. For example, CSF analysis revealed that strategic control of a certain company depends on five factors: cash flow, product quality, customer services, management development, and market share. In turn, KPIs were used to measure these factors and allowed the vice president of finance and her staff to analyze and model situations affecting these five factors.

Because cash flow was an appropriate and highly visible critical success factor, the vice president used it for measuring current operations. KPIs were established to track components of cash-flow performance, namely, on-hand cash balances, accounts receivable older than sixty days, and gross profit margin. These measures were reviewed by the vice president and her staff using a group decision support system. Although cash balances and accounts receivable were lower than budgeted amounts, gross profit margin was much lower than anticipated. Isolation of the components of gross profit margin indicated that manufacturing costs were rising faster than revenues and that productivity was declining. After examining more detailed information using a group DSS operating mode, the vice president determined that an inefficient use of labor caused poor productivity, thereby resulting in increasing costs, decreasing profit margins, and lower cash flow.

The vice president then decided to access operational data in more detail to get at desired information. This strategy proved successful, and a staff assistant found that some present manufacturing equipment was obsolete, thereby causing inefficient use of labor. In turn, the vice president made recommendations to replace certain pieces of machinery in the plant that were causing poor productivity. Additionally, if the vice president of finance did not obtain needed information, she could ask for more data to answer specific questions. These specific questions could be related directly to a company's return on investment and financial ratios (which are discussed below) or to some other area of operations.

ANALYSIS OF RETURN ON INVESTMENT

Because return on investment (ROI) is a measure of good, average, or poor performance of an organization's resources, financial managers should consider various ways of improving its ROI. Divestment of business operations that have a low return, acquisitions of investments that have a high return, pruning of low-return product lines, cost reduction and profit improvement, improving asset utilization, and changes in financial structure are constructive ways of increasing an organization's return on its investments. An optimum allocation of financial resources that considers these alternatives for increasing ROI is a necessity for reaping a higher return. However, a word of caution is appropriate. If this allocation means raising ROI, it also means balancing long-term commitments and noneconomic constraints such as social responsibilities. Reduction of commitments seems preferable to taking on a whole series of marginal projects that will reduce the organization's ROI in the long run.

Research on ROI

Research findings indicate that there is an overall relationship between ROI and investment intensity. The higher the ratio of investment to sales, the lower the return on investment tends to be.[1] This conclusion was drawn from a survey of 57 corporations with 620 diverse businesses. The survey indicated that businesses with high investment intensities are not able to achieve profit margins sufficient to effect the greater amounts of investment that they require to sustain a given volume. Another important finding from this study was that market share has a major influence on profitability.[2] On the average, businesses with market shares above 36 percent earn more than three times as much relative to investment as businesses with less than 7 percent of their respective markets. Subsequent research strongly supported the proposition that market share is positively related to the rate of return.[3] Three possible explanations given are economies of scale, market power, and the quality of management.[4] These factors are quite evident in such major firms as IBM, Gillette, Eastman Kodak, and Xerox. Also, research data indicate that the advantages of a large market share are greatest for businesses selling products that are purchased infrequently by a fragmented customer group.

Comparison Using ROI

Because calculating a company's, a division's, or a product's return on investment is an excellent way to measure performance, ROI analysis can be used to judge present performance and to evaluate future investment opportunities. Managers can also use it to rate managerial effectiveness and to compare potential profitability of divisions. While the technique of ROI analysis is uncomplicated, the potential applications are varied and valuable. The basic definition of ROI is

$$\text{ROI} = \text{Profitability Rate} \times \text{Asset Turnover Rate}.$$

The meaning of this definition can be clarified by dividing it into its component parts:

$$\text{Profitability rate} = \frac{\text{earnings}}{\text{net sales}};$$

$$\text{asset turnover rate} = \frac{\text{net sales}}{\text{total assets}};$$

Thus

$$\text{ROI} = \frac{\text{earnings}}{\text{net sales}} \times \frac{\text{net sales}}{\text{total assets}}.$$

This equation can be further reduced to

$$\text{ROI} = \frac{\text{earnings}}{\text{total assets}},$$

but for managerial evaluation, it is more useful in its expanded form.

A problem in calculating ROI arises in identifying what is meant by earnings or total assets. Although there is no single, correct way to figure ROI, it is customary to use earnings from operations before taxes, sales after returns and allowances for bad debts, and net, year-end book value of assets. It is important that there be consistency and that the same measure of earnings, sales, and assets be used when figuring ROIs for different periods. Also, managers should be prepared for apparent surprises when they compare the company's ROI to another company's, because the other company may have used different measures in calculating its ROI.

To illustrate the problem with measuring a company's ROI's, reference can be made to figure 10.1 for a company with sales and assets of $1,000,000 that has two divisions. Although both divisions have equal sales and equal earnings as a percentage of sales, the return on investment for the second division is much higher. The reason is that the first division requires $250,000 more in investment than the second division to achieve equal sales and profits. The difference in ROIs for the two divisions might stem from differences in management effectiveness or from the nature of their businesses. If the former is true, it might be appropriate to reward the management of the second division and take action to improve the management of the first division. In any case, the higher ROI of the second division suggests that additional capital investment might earn a much higher return in the second division than in the first division.

Fundamentally, there are four basic methods of improving performance: (1) increasing sales faster than expenses, (2) reducing expenses proportionately more than sales, (3) increasing sales faster than investment, and (4) reducing investment more than sales. By inserting figures into the ROI formula, management can judge the effectiveness of alternative proposals. For example, reducing the first division's expenses $30,000 while holding sales steady increases its ROI from 8 percent to about 13 percent. Reducing investment $50,000 while keeping sales constant would increase the ROI to about 9 percent. Generally, reducing expenses is the fastest way to improve ROI.

ROI analysis has use in the following areas:

Figure 10.1
Comparison of the Return on Investment for Two Divisions with Equal Sales and Earnings

First Division:

Sales	$500,000		Current Assets	$125,000
Expenses	(450,000)		Fixed Assets	500,000
Earnings	$50,000		Total Assets	$625,000

$$\text{ROI} = \frac{\text{Earnings}}{\text{Net Sales}} \times \frac{\text{Net Sales}}{\text{Total Assets}} \qquad \text{ROI} = \frac{\$50,000}{\$500,000} \times \frac{\$500,000}{\$625,000} = 8\%$$

Second Division:

Sales	$500,000		Current Assets	$75,000
Expenses	(450,000)		Fixed Assets	300,000
Earnings	$50,000		Total Assets	$375,000

$$\text{ROI} = \frac{\text{Earnings}}{\text{Net Sales}} \times \frac{\text{Net Sales}}{\text{Total Assets}} \qquad \text{ROI} = \frac{\$50,000}{\$500,000} \times \frac{\$500,000}{\$375,000} = 13+\%$$

- Evaluation of capital expenditures
- Providing a basis for determining management rewards
- Providing guidelines for growth through mergers or acquisitions
- Measuring effect of reducing costs
- Measuring effect of changes in inventory levels
- Measuring effect of changing asset utilization
- Evaluation of new product development
- Providing a framework for pricing decisions

Hence ROI analysis is helpful in analyzing many areas of a company's business. A small investment of management's time can lead to important improvements in a company's total performance.

Other Financial Ratios

In addition to return on investment, there are a number of financial ratios that can be applied to a typical company. The ones illustrated in figure 10.2 focus on the overall aspects to assist in financial strategic thinking. They can be calculated as needed and thereby serve as the basis for management by exception where appropriate ranges are assigned to each ratio. For example, the ratio of current assets to current liabilities should be about 2 to 1. Typically, to calculate these financial ratios, there is need for a group DSS operating mode whereby a corporate data base is used in conjunction with a computer for determining these ratios.

Figure 10.2
Typical Financial Ratios Useful for Financial Strategic Thinking

Measurement	Financial Ratio	Calculation
Management efficiency	Capital turnover	$\dfrac{\text{Sales}}{\text{Assets employed}}$
Liquidity status	Current ratio	$\dfrac{\text{Current assets}}{\text{Current liabilities}}$
Measure of solvency	Investment status	$\dfrac{\text{Investment}}{\text{Total assets}}$
Immediate liquidation	Acid test ratio	$\dfrac{\text{Cash + securities + net receivables}}{\text{Current liabilities}}$
Operation efficiency	Return on sales	$\dfrac{\text{Net income}}{\text{Sales}}$
Inventory utilization	Inventory turnover	$\dfrac{\text{Annualized sales}}{\text{Average inventory}}$
Days of sales in backlog	Undelivered commitments	$\dfrac{\text{Backlog}}{\text{Sales per day}}$
Credit strength	Net worth debt ratio	$\dfrac{\text{Shareholders equity}}{\text{Total debt}}$

Hence, when a financial group requests a specific statistic or ratio, the calculations are automatically performed by the group DSS to obtain the desired results. Basically, these statistics and ratios provide an insight for measuring actual results against the corporate strategic plans, short range to long range. Management effectiveness can be measured by the capital turnover ratio, asset profitability, and return on investment. Also, the corporation's performance can be gauged through the return on sales, days of sales in backlog, inventory utilization, and receivable collections.

From a slightly different perspective, these financial ratios can be viewed from the standpoint of a typical manager. Managers know the problem of battling the daily, even hourly, barrage of operating data that assaults their minds. The realization that they cannot track every detail of business comes as their days get longer and their nights get shorter. Like most managers faced with this problem, they try delegating. Yet they still monitor or second-guess everything they delegate. The net result is that they do not save any time.

The most effective way for them to monitor what is transpiring in their companies is to look at the ROI and the financial ratios. Additionally, there is need for managers to have a good overview of operating information, such as that found in figure 10.3, that is available to them on a daily, weekly, and monthly basis.[5] For the most part, this operating information centers on the company's key performance indicators that are essential to its success.

If the major indicators show no warning signals, managers generally have no need to analyze further. Only by rigorously limiting themselves to the daily, weekly, and monthly checks will they find time to devote to the future of the business—to new product development, acquisitions, and to short- and long-range strategic thinking. This selective pulse-taking of the company not only gives them more time and opportunity to focus on the big picture, it also acts as a management tool by giving them clearer criteria on which to communicate goals to their subordinates and judge their performance on this basis.

ANALYSIS OF A COMPANY'S PERFORMANCE VERSUS COMPETITION

A most important factor of reviewing corporate financial performance via financial ratios is to assist in giving direction to the corporation's top-level managers and its corporate planning staff for furthering financial strategic thinking. If external environmental factors are related to internal ones for a typical company, the growth and profitability of comparable firms in its industry can be compared to it. This financial analysis gives an indication whether or not the company is increasing its market share and giving a fair return to its stockholders when the industry's current state is considered. This overview of financial ratios needs to be supplemented by a more detailed analysis of competitors' financial statements, frequently referred to as *content analysis* of periodic financial statements and annual reports.

Figure 10.3

A Summary of Operating Information Useful to a Typical Manager

	Daily	Weekly	Monthly
Total company sales	x	x	x
Sales by product groupings		x	
Sales by major product groupings, territories, and major customers			x
Average sales prices of major products or product groups			x
Gross profit margin for company, major product groupings, and major products		x	
Production costs of major products			x
Direct expenses, with particular attention to large or discretionary items			x
Other income and expenses		x	x
Net profit			x
Cash flow		x	x
Accounts receivable		x	x
Inventory		x	x

Basically, content analysis provides valuable clues to competitors' corporate strategic thinking. It is a source of both financial information and information on new directions by competition. Content analysis of competing companies can be of real usefulness for getting a handle on specific issues of corporate strategy and can serve as a primary or supplementary source of information. It can be used to analyze current changes and past correlates of performance and for more general investigations of questions of interest to top-level executives and their corporate planning staff.

As an example, content analysis may disclose that one of the company's competitors is showing improved cost performance; that is, its costs are declining. The appropriate corporate response is for a typical company to get involved in a cost-analysis technique called *benchmarking*, which focuses on what the competitor does and how much it costs him to do it. In the company's lab, analysts tear apart the competitor's products and estimate the cost of designing and procuring each part. The analysis extends beyond product costs. To pin down distribution and handling costs, top-level managers need to order some of their competitor's products, then trace where they were shipped from and examine how they were packed. Typically, cost savings on a particular product start at the earliest stage, with engineering determining the product design. The challenge is to find ways to make engineering more cost-effective without stifling its creative efforts.

Employment of Graphics to Highlight Financial Trends

In a thorough analysis of overall performance and variances that are tied in with financial ratios, there is a great need to employ graphics. Although financial ratios can be compared on a day-by-day, a week-by-week, a month-by-month, or some other time-period basis, the purpose of this analysis by finance executives is to determine whether or not the company is improving its financial stature. Of equal importance is the fact that financial ratio analysis that uses graphics discloses whether or not financial managers are really managing the company effectively over the short term and the long term.

Generally, "at-a-glance" graphic presentations of information allow managers to start their thinking processes quickly. The usual method—also the slower method—involves a lot of reading. A "picture" may tell managers immediately what they want to know. Information in this visual aid might otherwise be buried in stacks of computer-generated reports. From another viewpoint, managers may view graphs on a display screen and also employ a paper printout of graphic data to ponder later, as in problem finding. Based on either perspective, computer-prepared graphics are very effective for supporting decision making and getting managers to think about new ways of running their operations.

Research studies have shown that graphics are a valuable tool of executives and people below them. The most-often-cited study justifying the use of business graphics was performed at the Wharton School at the University of Pennsylvania. It assessed the effects of overhead transparencies in business meetings. Among the findings were the following: (1) more executives decided to act on the recommendation of a presenter who used transparencies than on the recommendation of a presenter who did not; (2) presenters who used graphics were perceived as better prepared, more professional, more persuasive, more credible, and more interesting; (3) groups in which a presenter used graphics were more likely to reach consensus on a decision than groups in which no transparencies were used; (4) individuals reported making decisions earlier when graphics were used; and (5) meeting length was shorter when overhead transparencies were used. In addition, the study found that speakers supported by visuals won approval for their projects twice as often as speakers not supported by visuals. Graphics shortened meeting times by 28 percent and generated on-the-spot decisions 33 percent more often.[6]

Utilization of Creative Computer Software to Assist in Analyzing Financial Trends

As a way of demonstrating the use of creative computer software to assist in analyzing financial trends, a starting point is the use of problem finding. Basically, problem finding is able to diagnose more types of important problems that are financially oriented facing financial executives as well as top-level executives than traditional problem-solving approaches. To illustrate the use of problem finding, consider the following example. The goal of the company is to increase the value of its investments by 50 percent in five years. Top-level executives and the corporate planning staff, working in conjunction with the company's vice president of finance, the treasurer, and the controller, can model the problem using appropriate financial software. By examining each approach to increase investment values, the bottom line for each investment approach can be evaluated thoroughly. If the investment's total return does not attain the company's goal, the important variables can be examined to determine what individual profit contributor(s) is (are) likely to fail to produce its (their) share of gains. Essentially, creative computer software can be used to assist the group in getting a handle on what changes should be made to these important variables so that the investment reaches its desired profitability. The net result of this analysis is that it is useful for identifying future potential investment problems before they happen. In turn, the financial results can be quickly recalculated based on these problems, and the effect on the aggregate returns is seen immediately. Overall, the group uses modeling analysis to perceive future investment alternatives and their relevant problems and brings them back to the present time for solution.

ANALYSIS OF CAPITAL INVESTMENT DECISIONS

Capital investment questions from finance managers can benefit from a thorough analysis of financial alternatives or other factors using appropriate financial software. As an example, a simplistic model using Lotus 1-2-3 can be employed to evaluate the purchase of a new piece of equipment costing, say, $30,000. Expected savings are estimated to be $10,000 annually, the equipment has an expected useful life of five years, and there is a discount rate of 12.5 percent, which represents what the company would have to pay on money borrowed to finance the purchase. Using the present-value method, this investment would bring future savings that have a present value of $35,606, or $5,606 more than the investment cost. Given this set of assumptions about savings, useful life, and discount rate, the equipment should be purchased. Estimates for interest rate, annual savings, and useful life, on the other hand, might deviate from these assumptions. To illustrate, assume that the interest rate has been projected accurately, but the useful life and annual savings estimates are more suspect. Lotus 1-2-3 allows the manager to perform either a one- or two-way sensitivity analysis to examine potential changes. The one-way analysis allows the present values to change in response to a variation in annual savings. In contrast, a two-way analysis allows the present values to change in response to two different variables, cash savings and useful life in years. If the financial manager prepared another two-way analysis that examined discount rate and years of useful life, the results would be much more sensitive to changes in the useful life than in the discount rate, evidenced by larger changes in results as the useful-life projections changed. Thus, specific "what-if" questions can be answered for financial managers about present values when they are related to cash savings and years of useful life or discount rate and years of useful life.

Development of Alternative Capital Investments Using Creative Computer Software

Some of the creative computer software examples presented in this book allow financial managers to compare investment alternatives. In turn, the best investment is selected. Essentially, the utilization of creative computer software is a beginning point for utilizing newer information systems technology. More specifically, a financial group DSS application that is the result of using creative computer software can be developed using the latest expert-system technology as well as traditional economic and financial modeling approaches. It can be built using a flexible knowledge-acquisition interface that requires some technical knowledge to install, parameterize, or customize. In addition, the knowledge base needs to be kept current with existing financial and production data bases. Also, the system should be tightly integrated into the mainstream transaction-processing environments in a timely manner.

It should be noted that much of the decision-making logic associated with a financial group DSS is heuristic and symbolic in nature. That is, this knowledge should be tightly integrated with more traditional financial knowledge to arrive at an overall solution to the decision-support problem. If the knowledge base is allowed to optimize problems truly, the constraints in the knowledge base should be capable of modeling the various institutional and regulatory guidelines, thereby providing decisions that are in line with current conditions. There should be great artificial intelligence opportunities in the financial area to construct an intelligent application environment that will allow the solution of financial decision-support problems requiring true multiobjective, multicriteria-based reasoning. By the use of intelligent search strategies and goal-driven programming, a flexible framework can be provided to solve these tough problems. It would be nearly impossible to achieve the same results with traditional methodologies. In addition, it would be important to construct this environment so that financial managers could easily edit the rule base as new heuristic are discovered and old ones no longer apply. Overall, new information systems technology can be used in conjunction with creative computer software to solve more difficult capital investment decisions.

RETHINKING OF COST ACCOUNTING TO REFLECT A COMPANY'S REAL COSTS

To compete in the global markets, U.S. companies must get control of their production costs. The good news is that U.S. manufacturers began meeting that challenge recently with computer-integrated manufacturing (CIM), automation, robotics, and just-in-time (JIT) methods (refer to the previous chapter). The bad news is that even with these manufacturing advances, costing systems still cannot compete in high-volume markets. If U.S. companies are doing the right things in manufacturing, then why cannot they compete? The answer is that U.S. companies have fixed just about everything except their costing systems. Generally, today's product-costing data are wrong, often by extremely large margins. Without more accurate costing methods, the bottom line is a continued competitive crisis. Hence there is need to rethink cost-accounting methods for the 1990s and beyond. More specifically, there is need to take a hard look at activity-based costing as well as other newer costing methodologies.

THE FUNDAMENTALS OF NEWER COST-ACCOUNTING METHODOLOGIES

Because today's manufacturing environment is characterized by increased automation and computerization, reduced levels of direct labor, increased attention to product and production planning, expanded global competition, and shorter life cycles, the traditional cost-accounting model can distort product cost, limit the visibility of waste, and mask the factors that actually drive the costs. As a result, companies may be emphasizing the wrong product mix in their manufacturing and marketing efforts, or worse, they could be pricing products at a loss when they think that they are making a profit.

In the prior era of manufacturing, direct labor was the most significant component of a product's total cost and was the primary method for assigning overhead and indirect costs to products. Today overhead is often the most significant component of a product's total cost. It is not unusual to find direct labor being only 10 percent of total product cost and overhead being two or three times the cost of direct labor. As a result, direct labor is no longer an accurate basis for allocating overhead, nor does it merit the priority it receives over overhead costs in monitoring and controlling costs.

The traditional cost-accounting system and techniques that prevail today are ineffective in monitoring manufacturing costs and allocating overhead. Consequently, newer cost-accounting methodologies such as activity-based costing, technology accounting, and life-cycle accounting have been developed to respond to the demands of today's manufacturing environment.

Activity-based costing (ABC) directly relates costs to the resources used to manufacture the product. A starting point is analyzing a company to determine all its production and support activities. All costs are then assigned to activities. Next, activities are measured and linked with the products that consume the activities. The total cost of the finished product is an accumulation of the activities required to produce the product. In addition to assigning the costs to the products that actually absorb the activities, the ABC method identifies cost drivers and isolates non-value-added activities. Figure 10.4 shows how product-cost reports showing non-value-added activities can reveal cost-reduction opportunities, while figure 10.5 illustrates how

Figure 10.4

Separation of Value-Added Costs from Non-Value-Added Costs for Activity-Based Costing

Product Costs	Value-Added	Non-Value-Added	Total
Direct labor	$1,600		$1,600
Rework		$250	250
Setup time		700	700
Direct materials	1,000		1,000
Scrap		100	100
Direct technology	800		800
Underutilized capacity		450	450
Material controls		400	400
Quality testing		2,400	2,400
Engineering	400		400
Productivity support	450		450
Expediting		300	300
Distribution	200	____	200
	$4,450	$4,600	$9,050

Figure 10.5

Traditional Approach versus Activity-Based Costing Approach to Engineering Department Costs

Traditional Approach to Engineering Department Costs		Activity-Based Costing Approach to Engineering Department Costs	
Engineering salaries	$510,000	Develop bill of materials	$29,500
Technology	100,000	Maintain bill of materials	118,000
Travel expenses	50,000	Develop routing	24,000
Supplies	20,000	Maintain routing	112,500
Facilities	30,000	Special orders	75,000
Total	$710,000	Capacity studies	132,500
		Process improvement	27,500
		Tooling design	41,000
		Training	41,000
		Management and administration	109,000
		Total	$710,000

activity-based cost accounting is significantly different from the traditional approach. With this information, a company can establish priorities to focus on eliminating or reducing non-value-added activities.

Technology accounting is based on the concept that technology costs, such as plant, equipment, and information systems, should be treated as direct costs, equivalent to direct labor and materials. Today's technology costs, for the most part, are accounted for by amortization (or depreciation) and included in overhead. The problem with this method of accounting is that conventional amortization methods are time based, not production based. A time-based method equates time with cost and often causes amortization of idle machinery to increase overhead costs when there is little or no production. This encourages constant and ineffective production to maintain a desired cost per unit.

Product costs are further affected by the inclusion of the time-based amortization in overhead, which must then be allocated to production. The adoption of a direct production-based amortization method such as units of production means that costs are matched more accurately with products manufactured. When one is determining the number of units over which to amortize an asset, only the planned production of the asset should be considered. Simply using the asset's total lifetime production capacity does not solve the problems associated with a time-based method. Total units used to amortize an asset should be limited by planned production, product demand, and obsolescence of the asset's technology or the manufacturing process.

As with activity-based costing, the choice of an overhead-allocation method can significantly alter product costing. As technology costs increase as a percentage of total product costs, any misallocation will improperly influence management decisions and possibly the financial results of the company.

The traditional cost-accounting model also distorts a product's true cost by expensing preproduction costs such as research and development, engineering, and start-up and marketing costs as incurred. Current expensing of costs for which a future benefit is planned makes it difficult to measure the success or failure of these costs. It also encourages companies to consider these costs as discretionary when, in fact, today's manufacturing environment requires these costs to be incurred to survive. Expensing these costs currently also encourages companies to place products into production prematurely to "improve" current period earnings. Additionally, if preproduction costs are expensed as they are incurred, the total cost of a product is unknown, and the product may, in fact, be selling at a loss while the company reports a profit.

Life-cycle accounting accumulates the costs of activities that occur over the entire life cycle of a product, from inception to abandonment by the manufacturer and the consumer. A primary objective of life-cycle accounting is a better matching of revenues and expenses. All costs are capitalized as they are incurred. These costs are charged to earnings as units are sold, based on the total planned number of units to be brought to market.

Essentially, the shortcomings in the traditional cost-accounting model are largely due to the changing manufacturing environment. To remain competitive in today's global marketplace, the time has come for U.S. manufacturers to adopt new cost-accounting methodologies so they know the true cost of their products and make informed cost-management and pricing decisions.[7]

UTILIZATION OF A DIFFERENT COST-MANAGEMENT SYSTEM

Although the foregoing cost-accounting methodologies are quite useful to assist a company in telling the true story about costs, a more pragmatic way to get a handle on costs is to follow the Japanese. That is, it is necessary to take a look at costs before the fact rather than afterwards. More specifically, a Japanese cost-management system guides and motivates planners to design products at the lowest possible cost and gives them considerable freedom in introducing new products as well as getting them to market quickly. Like its famed quality philosophy, Japan's cost-management system is ahead of that of its global counterparts.

Japan's Use of Target Cost

American companies developing a new product typically design it first and then calculate the cost. If it is too high, the product goes back to the drawing board, or the company settles for a smaller profit. On the other hand, the Japanese start with a target cost based on the price the market is most likely to accept. Then they direct designers and engineers to meet this target. The system also encourages managers to worry less about a product's cost than about the role it could play in gaining market share. This strategic thinking approach is a big reason why the Japanese so often come out with winning products.

The critical feature of the Japanese cost-management system is its focus on getting costs out of the product during the planning and design stage. That is the point at which virtually all subsequent costs are determined, from manufacturing to what customers will have to spend on maintenance. This target-cost technique, which is used by such companies as NEC, Sharp, Nissan, and Toyota, comes in countless variations. The stripped-down version has several important features. The team in charge of bringing a new product idea to market determines the price at which the product is most likely to appeal to potential buyers. From this crucial judgment all else follows. After deducting the desired profit margin from the forecasted sales price, the planners develop estimates for each of the elements that make up a product's costs: design and engineering, manufacturing, and sales and marketing. Each of these is further subdivided to identify and estimate the cost of each component that goes into the finished product.

Every part or function is treated as a component—not only windshields and engine blocks but spaces such as the trunk—and each is assigned a target cost. Essentially, this is where the bargaining process begins. It is an intense negotiating process between the company and its outside suppliers and among departments that are responsible for different aspects of the product. The sum of the initial estimates may exceed the overall target cost by 20 percent or more. By the time the process is over, compromises and trade-offs by product designers, process engineers, and marketing specialists generally produce a projected cost that is within close range of the original target.

This negotiating process is quite different from standard practice in the United States and Europe. U.S. companies design a product by going from one department to another, from engineering to purchasing, marketing, and so forth. At the end of the design phase, after about 85 percent of the product's costs have been built in, the specifications are given to the accountants, who determine what the product will cost. Costs are based on labor rates, material prices, and prevailing manufacturing standards. Slighted is the vision of what a product *should* cost, which would motivate and assist the engineers designing it.

Overall, U.S. companies tend to build a model of the product, determine what it is going to cost, and then ask whether it can be sold at a certain price based on costs. In contrast, the Japanese turn the process around; that is, they say, "It's got to sell for X dollars. Let's work backwards to make sure we can achieve it." This is not currently being done by U.S. companies with the same intensity. Western-style cost management, by basing costs on given standards, tends to maintain the status quo. The Japanese approach is dynamic and constantly pushes for improvement.[8]

A PROPER APPROACH TO REDUCING A COMPANY'S TOTAL OVERHEAD

For a typical manufacturer currently, manufacturing overhead grows until it is larger than all other costs. But as competition from lower-cost companies increases, the pressure to react mounts. Generally, companies choose one of two options. First, the company remains a broad-line manufacturer, and management fights back by dropping prices and cutting overhead, only to find costs creeping back after a few months. Second, management accepts that survival hinges on becoming a focused, low-cost company. It cuts entire product lines and pares down plant capacity, cutting overhead as it goes. Unfortunately, it compromises its long-held position of market leadership.

In both cases, companies that pursue change by focusing on cutting costs are only asking for trouble. Take the plight of a large Midwest specialty-equipment manufacturer. Facing stiff margin pressure a few years ago, the company needed to lower its overhead cost structure. At the same time, it was intent on remaining a broad-line company. It conducted make-versus-buy analyses of some major components—axles, engine shafts, and transmission shafts—and decided that it could save several millions of dollars by outsourcing a few models from each component group. In total, the company cut about 10 percent of its overhead staff. But the savings never materialized; rather, costs rose. This unexpected result came to light six months into the change program when the account department plotted overhead rates and noticed that they were rising.

When management looked at the overhead rates more closely, it discovered a number of causes for the increase. Many of the outsourced components went through the same processes as the components that remained in-house, that is, boring, milling, lathing, and drilling. But with fewer factory-floor support staff, machine maintenance and work scheduling quickly began to suffer. To solve it short-term problems, the company rehired some of the old overhead staff. Other problems became evident. As the company outsourced more components, management paid less attention to improving core-process technology. To save money, it postponed technological upgrades, including the purchase of a sophisticated, flexible multispindle tool. In addition, the logistics of outsourcing meant that the company had to keep track of a whole net set of orders, billings, and shipments. A multiple-supplier network demanded more indirect staff, so overhead increased.

Another consequence of outsourcing was excess capacity. In response, the company consolidated its operations. Over an eighteen-month period, the company reduced its fifteen plants scattered around the Midwest to just ten plants. Still, overhead costs continued to rise because little thought was given to streamlining operations. There were the obvious turf battles. Because departmental vice presidents back at headquarters fought to keep their staffs intact, few people were cut as a result of the consolidation. The final result was that the company ended up with fragmented production processes, fewer but less productive manufacturing facilities, and higher total overhead. It was less competitive than it had been, it was compromising its technology by outsourcing key component parts, and it was becoming more dependent on a much wider range of suppliers. On the bottom line it was a weaker company.

This manufacturer's predicament is not uncommon. Too often, top-level managers assume that by mechanically eliminating chunks of business or consolidating operations they will improve the company's position. In fact, only by designing flexible manufacturing processes can companies lower overhead permanently and, at the same time, remain viable broad-line manufacturers. All processes must be addressed together: product design, manufacturing, logistics, distribution, and all supplier and customer relationships. Overall, sustainable overhead reduction means a commitment to continuous improvement. This includes segmenting, mapping, and measuring existing processes and then working to improve them. As a result, overhead costs drop, and overhead employees spend time improving processes upstream instead of fixing problems downstream.[9]

APPLICATIONS SHOWING LINKAGE OF FINANCE AND ACCOUNTING APPROACHES TO UTILIZING CREATIVE COMPUTER SOFTWARE

Applications that show the linkage of finance and accounting to creative computer software vary from one company to another. Creative meetings without the use of appropriate creative software can be fun but somewhat messy, thereby leaving stacks of ideas and no conclusions in their wake. On the other hand, brainstorming software puts some order into the creative process and provides a framework to evaluate the ideas. As demonstrated previously in this book, there are a number of low-priced products for brainstorming.

Some of the newest creative meeting support products on the market are veritable "suitcases" of software tools that can take a meeting from start to finish. For example, IBM's TeamFocus includes brainstorming, idea organization, issue analysis, voting, evaluation, and policy formation, among other tools. One tool, or several, can be used in the course of a meeting to achieve the preplanned objective. The technology was developed at the University of Arizona, and the university's subsidiary, Ventana Corporation, markets a similar software. Team-Focus was originally used in-house at IBM, but customer demand prompted the company to begin marketing it.

In this section of the chapter, the focus is on PC-oriented creative applications. OptionFinder and IdeaFisher 4.0 are the creative computer software employed. As discussed in the text, the software can be used individually or within a group operating mode. Within a typical group DSS operating mode, the process begins with the development of a list of possible ideas to solve the problem under study. Participants rank ideas in order of importance, and these votes are tabulated by the computer. Special software can be used for modeling, and strategic thinking helps to analyze the strengths and weaknesses of each idea. Because comparisons are displayed graphically on the computer screen, managers determine the priorities of ideas. Finally, one or more ideas provide the means for getting the appropriate action started to solve the problem.

UNITED FUNDS AGENCY

Generally, nearly every company is faced annually with cutting the budgetary pie among competing alternatives. Companies have this problem in capital budgeting and funding new versus existing product development. Foundations and community-service funding agencies have this same problem when they review program proposals. Such is the case for the United Funds Agency.

Allocation of Budget to Competing Program Proposals

The United Funds Agency (a not-for-profit community-service agency) was faced with allocating a total of $100,000 among fourteen different program proposals totaling $814,000 in requests. The review process was conducted by a committee composed of community volunteers. Each program proposal was reviewed by committee members on their own time. They were asked to rate the proposals in terms of four equally weighted criteria on a five-point scale and enter their rating on a worksheet. The criteria used were the following:

A. Will "empower neighborhoods."

B. Focuses on agency problems.

C. Services focus on intervention/prevention.

D. Proposal is community based.

A committee meeting was scheduled over the lunch hour. Prior to the meeting, the names of each of the program proposals and the four criteria for rating them were entered into a fourteen-step OptionFinder AutoSequence. As the committee members were eating lunch, each of the four criteria for each proposal was projected on a large screen, and the committee members entered their corresponding worksheet rating via their keypads. A total of fifty-six ratings were entered in the first twenty minutes.

Questions That Can Be Answered Using OptionFinder

Prior to the meeting, a tally sheet was prepared to capture the results of the Option-Finder rating session. The tally sheet had four columns corresponding to the four criteria and fourteen rows for each of the proposals. As soon as the rating was completed, a second fourteen-step OptionFinder AutoSequence was initiated to calculate the results for each of the program proposals and then display them on a large screen. As the results were displayed, they were entered onto the tally sheet. Two results were displayed for each program proposal. First, the *average ratings* among all of the committee members for each of the four criteria were A, 3.6; B, 4.6; C, 3.8; and D, 3.6. Second, the *levels of consensus* among the committee members for each of the four criteria were A, 42; B, 75; C, 83; and D, 42.

The average ratings were added together to get an initial indication of the ranking of the different proposals. Then the consensus result was used to focus the committee's attention on ratings in which there was some or considerable disagreement. A consensus result of less than 50 (criteria A and D) triggered a rediscussion of the proposal on that criterion. Thus the committee focused quickly on the first and last criteria to identify why there were differences in perceptions of the proposal on these two criteria and whether such differences were critical to a final decision.

The tally sheets were completed forty minutes into the meeting, leaving the remainder of the time for analyzing the results and deciding which of the proposals to fund. During the analysis, it became clear that some of the criteria were more important than others. The discussion that this raised helped to focus the attention of the committee on how well the top-ranked proposals would be able to produce the outcomes in which the agency was most interested. As a result of this discussion, the rankings of the proposals were reordered and the decision was made to recommend three for funding. While there was considerable pre-meeting preparation time for both the staff and the committee members, the total time for this review meeting was less than two hours.[10]

ACE INVESTMENT CORPORATION

Richard Hope, president of the Ace Investment Corporation, decided to go a step further in analyzing the various investment opportunities presented to him throughout the year. That is, he planned to use IdeaFisher 4.0 to assist him in making better investment decisions. In this example, he was considering the purchase of a business. Since he had a good understanding of the basic background information on acquiring a business, he decided to skip the clarification process with QBank and utilize IdeaBank only. He looked at the major categories in IdeaBank and decided to start by selecting "Business-Industry-Occupations," as shown in figure 10.6a. Essentially, he chained through items of investments and business acquisitions. In turn, he decided to investigate the possibility of acquiring a chain of retail stores.

Questions That Can Be Answered Using IdeaFisher 4.0

His next step took him in a direction that he had not anticipated and that gave him surprising results. He selected the word "entrepreneur" to indicate that he had some of the personality traits associated with business owners. Some of the traits selected from the list were "imagination" and "creativity." Needless to say, these are associated with someone who is enterprising and successful. As shown in figure 10.6b, these traits are sometimes linked with venture enterprises. This gave him the idea to investigate funding of this retail chain through venture

Figure 10.6a
IdeaFisher's IdeaBank to Assist in Acquiring a Business—Ace Investment Corporation

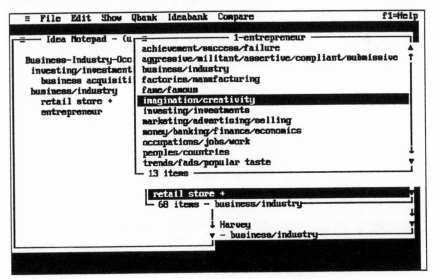

Figure 10.6b
IdeaFisher's IdeaBank to Assist in Determining Venture Enterprises—Ace Investment Corporation

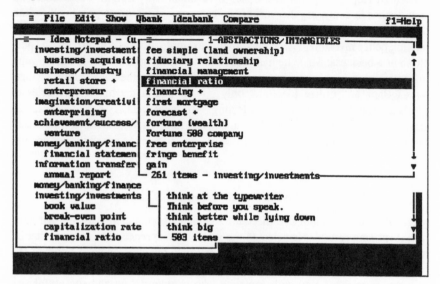

capital. Thus, while looking for a way to evaluate a business, he came up with a possible way to fund it. IdeaFisher 4.0 took Hope on a "tangent" journey, a procedure that often proves to be very useful.

Focusing once again on items that would help him to analyze a chain of retail stores financially, he selected the topic of "Money/Banking/Finance" for examination. From this point, he started to find some items that might be useful in the evaluation process. The first item was financial statements. These would most probably be available from the company being evaluated. If they are not, some published reports that are required for the government or annual reports to stockholders may contain useful information. Continuing with an investment theme, he found the last items—book value, break-even point, capitalization rate, and financial ratios—to be of help in the analysis of a company and its performance.

Overall, this example of IdeaFisher 4.0 can not only help Hope to create ideas, but also it can help him find them. In addition, he discovered that IdeaFisher can give supplemental and unexpected benefits when investigating tangent topics. This example has demonstrated that when one is trying to be creative, every attempt should be made to keep an open mind for new directions to examine the area under study.

UNIVERSAL PRODUCTS CORPORATION

The Universal Products Corporation, which was presented previously in chapter 8, will be used again. By way of review, the corporation specializes in the manufacture of household appliances. Its current sales are $200 million per annum, projected to be about $275 million in five years. Its product line consists of fifty products in eight basic product categories. Variations of these basic products are for specific customers whose requirements differ owing to the markets they serve. For large orders, products are shipped directly to retailers from the company's four manufacturing plants. All other orders are shipped from its warehouses to retailers. Experience has shown that 20 percent of the corporation's dollar volume represents direct shipments from the plants and 80 percent represents shipments through the warehouses. Corporate headquarters are located in Pittsburgh; manufacturing plants are found in Cincinnati, St. Louis, Dallas, and Los Angeles. A warehouse is attached to each manufacturing plant. The present employment level of the entire corporation is approximately 4,000 employees.

Rethinking Accounting Methods and Procedures

The vice president of finance and accounting called together the treasurer, the controller, the auditing manager, and the cost-accounting manager. The purpose of this meeting was to evaluate the corporation's financial performance, that is, to try to improve the corporation's current financial performance so that future periods would show an improvement of about 10 percent. Because there are many ways to change a corporation's financial status, the group decided to look at its current methods and procedures relating to inventory levels, cash flows, and the like with the idea of enhancing them.

One of the ways to adjust financial performance is to change the operating methods and procedures of the accounting and finance areas. Needless to say, these changes in methods and procedures must conform to federal laws as well as general business laws and accounting standards. This is done so that when the books are audited, the CPA firm will approve the business and accounting practices of the corporation. Provisions are made, within the law, to allow corporations to switch from one accounting method to another. These changes in accounting methods can have an effect on the financial performance of the corporation. For example, a change in inventory-tracking methods from FIFO (first-in first-out) to LIFO (last-in first-out) may mean that the most expensive parts are removed from inventory first. On paper, this has the effect of reducing inventory amounts when only the accounting method has actually changed.

Questions That Can Be Answered Using IdeaFisher 4.0

To assist the group in determining what approach would be best for improving the corporation's financial performance today and tomorrow, IdeaFisher 4.0 was utilized. Reference can be made to figure 10.7, where IdeaBank provides suggestions regarding accounting standards. It should be noted that ''accounting profession'' is highlighted, followed by the term ''accounting system.'' The cost-accounting manager suggested that the two could be combined, that is, the

Figure 10.7

IdeaFisher's IdeaBank to Assist in Determining New Accounting Methods and Procedures—Universal Products Corporation

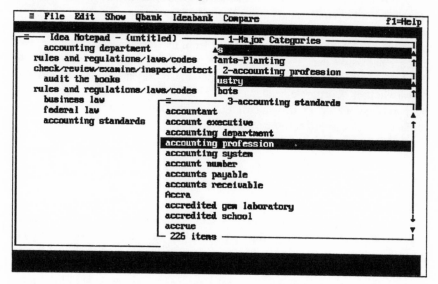

accounting profession is now advocating newer cost-accounting methods (discussed earlier in this chapter). In particular, he stressed the need to go from a standard cost-based system to an activity-based costing system, so that value-added costs could be separated from non-value-added costs. In this manner, manufacturing and marketing managers can determine what costs are logical ones for cost reduction. Hence the group felt that it had come up with a viable option for improving the corporation's financial performance today and tomorrow.

This example assisted the group in determining one method of improving financial performance. It should be noted that there are a number of other viable options available to it. It is suggested that the reader reexamine figure 10.7 for other accounting methods and procedures that might be employed by the group to improve the corporate financial performance. That is, combine some of the items in figure 10.7 or enlarge upon each of these items in new and different ways as an aid in getting a handle on new and creative ideas. It may well be that the ones you develop will be equal or superior to the one given above.

OTHER FINANCE AND ACCOUNTING APPLICATIONS THAT MAKE USE OF CREATIVE COMPUTER SOFTWARE

Creative computer software is quite helpful not only to business firms, but also to their consultants. For example, Morton Rabken, a consultant with Cincinnati-based Beechknoll Financial Group, has used the Idea Generator Plus in a number of applications. He used it to help companies that operate long-term-care facilities make the complicated "if-then" decisions that go along with restructuring, purchasing products, or developing business plans. Also, the software has many open-ended applications. As an example, he has used it to help increase earnings by a certain percentage. The ideas can be keyed in, ranked, and discussed. Because the software takes ideas in free form, the user can plug them in during the process. Although Rabken does not use the software directly in meetings, he takes notes, plugs them into the Idea Generator Plus afterward, then takes the printout to the next meeting for more discussion and refinement.[11]

SUMMARY

As seen in this chapter (and previous ones), the focus has been on applying creative computer software to typical business situations. However, this exposition was preceded by important new concepts and views on finance and accounting. The need for newer approaches is necessitated by the environment in which companies operate today. The environment in which financial decisions are made is highly dynamic, complicated, and information intense. Investment banks, commercial institutions, regulatory institutions, and brokerage houses find their staffs increasingly strained in financial times, good and bad. To help streamline operations and keep up with the times, it is necessary to provide the most intelligent, timely, and focused information. Many financial applications have been based on traditional approaches to the construction of financial decision-support systems that have centered on traditional economic modeling and proven data-base application generation. In a similar manner, the same type of comments can be made regarding accounting decisions. No matter whether reference is made to financial or accounting decisions, a creative approach is the desired one today as well as into the future. To do otherwise is to place a company at a competitive disadvantage.

NOTES

1. Sidney Schoeffler, Robert D. Buzzell, and Donald F. Heany, "Impact of Strategic Planning on Profit Performance," *Harvard Business Review*, March–April 1974, p. 143.
2. Ibid., p. 141.
3. Robert D. Buzzell, Bradley T. Gale, and Ralph G. M. Sutten, "Market Share: A Key to Profitability," *Harvard Business Review*, January–February 1975, pp. 97–106.
4. Ibid., p. 98.
5. Axel L. Grabowsky, "What to Monitor to Stay in Control," *Inc., Magazine's Guide to Small Business Success*, 1987, pp. 17–18.
6. John Desmond, "Window to MIS: Graphics Focuses Business Picture," *Software News*, April 1987, p. 54.
7. Dennis Peavey and Jim DePalma, "Do You Know the Cost of Your Products?" *Coopers & Lybrand Executive Briefing*, May 1990, pp. 7–9.

8. Ford S. Worthy, "Japan's Smart Secret Weapon," *Fortune*, August 12, 1991, pp. 72-75.

9. Mark F. Blaxill and Thomas M. Hout, "The Fallacy of the Overhead Quick Fix," *Harvard Business Review*, July-August 1991, p. 93-94.

10. Deborah Bennett-Leet, "Cutting the Budgetary Pie," *OptionFinder Application*, Option Technologies, Inc., 1989, pp. 1-2.

11. Gigi Verna, "PCs Powerful Tools for More Productive Meetings, The Record Report: Maximizing Productivity," *Greater Cincinnati Business Record, A Supplement*, April 29-May 5, 1991, p. 1B.

Bibliography: Part IV

Alexander, M. "American's Expert System Takes Off." *Computerworld*, July 8, 1991.

Ames, R. C., and J. D. Hlavacek. "Vital Truths about Managing Your Costs." *Harvard Business Review*, January–February 1990.

Anderson, H. "When Your Top Execs Want Sales Cost Data—Fast." *Computerworld*, October 3, 1988.

Argyris, C. "Teaching Smart People How to Learn." *Harvard Business Review*, May–June 1991.

Avishai, B. "A CEO's Common Sense of CIM: An Interview with J. Tracy O'Rourke." *Harvard Business Review*, January–February 1989.

Badaracco, L., Jr. *The Knowledge Link: How Firms Compete through Strategic Alliances.* Boston: Harvard Business School Press, 1991.

Badgett, T. "Accounting in the Fast Lane: Software and Procedures for Financial Professionals." *Digital News*, March 1989.

Baer, T. "Flexible Manufacturing: It's Gotten Easier to Change on Demand." *Computerworld*, February 11, 1991.

———. How to Schedule in Unexpected Events." *Computerworld*, February 11, 1991.

———. "Experts: Time to Put It Together." *Computerworld*, October 28, 1991.

Baldwin, S. R., and M. McConnell. "Strategic Planning: Process and Plan Go Hand in Hand." *Management Solutions*, June 1988.

Band, W. A. *Creating Value for Customers: Designing and Implementing a Total Corporate Strategy.* New York: John Wiley & Sons, 1991.

Barwise, P., P. R. Marsh, and R. Wensley. "Must Finance and Strategy Clash?" *Harvard Business Review*, September–October 1989.

Beischel, M. E. "Improving Production with Process Value Analysis." *Journal of Accountancy*, September 1990.

Below, P. J., G. L. Morrisey, and B. L. Acomb. *The Executive Guide to Strategic Planning.* San Francisco: Jossey-Bass, 1987.

Belton, K. "CIM—A Competitive Weapon for the '90s." *Oracle Magazine*, Fall 1987.

Bendell, A., J. Disney, and W. A. Pridmore, eds. *Taguchi Methods: Applications in World Industry*. New York: Springer-Verlag, 1989.

Bennett-Leet, D. "Cutting the Budgetary Pie." *OptionFinder Application*, Option Technologies, Inc., 1989.

Blaine, R. "The Innovator at Michigan Bell." *Learning Edge*, vol. 2, no. 1, 1989.

Blaxill, M. F., and T. M. Hout. "The Fallacy of the Overhead Quick Fix." *Harvard Business Review*, July–August 1991.

Blessing, L. J. "New Opportunities: A CPA's Primer on Performance Auditing." *Journal of Accountancy*, May 1991.

Bonoma, T. V. "Marketing Performance—What Do You Expect?" *Harvard Business Review*, September–October 1989.

Bonsack, R. A. "How to Justify Investments in Factories of the Future." *Management Review*, January 1988.

Bowles, J., and J. Hammond. *Beyond Quality: How 50 Winning Companies Use Continuous Improvement*. New York: G. P. Putnam's Sons, 1990.

Brackett, J. "Strategic Computing for Corporate Climbers." *EDGE*, September/October 1988.

Brown, C. E., and M. E. Phillips, "Expert Systems for Management Accounting." *Management Accounting*, January 1990.

Brown, J. S. "Research That Reinvents the Corporation." *Harvard Business Review*, January–February 1991.

Brunet, J. "Accounting Software: Key Considerations are Integration, Integration, Integration." *Digital News*, July 10, 1989.

Bruns, W. J., Jr., and F. W. McFarlan. "Information Technology Puts Power in Control Systems." *Harvard Business Review*, September–October 1987.

Buzzell, R. D., and B. T. Gale. *The PIMS Principles: Linking Strategy to Performance*. New York: Free Press, 1988.

Buzzell, R. D., B. T. Gale, and R. G. M. Sutten. "Market Share: A Key to Profitability." *Harvard Business Review*, January–February 1975.

Byers, C. R., and J. J. Morris. "Enhancing Sales Force Productivity with a Relational DBMS." *Journal of Systems Management*, January 1991.

Caminiti, S. "America's Fastest-growing Companies." *Fortune*, April 22, 1991.

Caroni, J. "Business Reports Get Graphic." *Datamation*, June 1, 1991.

Cheatham, C. "Measuring and Improving Throughput." *Journal of Accountancy*, March 1990.

———. "Updating Standard Cost System." *Journal of Accountancy*, December 1990.

Clark, K. B. "What Strategy Can Do for Technology." *Harvard Business Review*, November–December 1989.

Cohen, S. S., and J. Zysman. *Manufacturing Matters: The Myth of the Post-Industrial Economy*. New York: Basic Books, 1987.

Cooper, R. "You Need a New Cost System When . . . ." *Harvard Business Review*, January–February 1989.

Cooper R., and R. S. Kaplan. "Profit Priorities from Activity-based Costing." *Harvard Business Review*, May–June, 1991.

Corbin, R. H., and R. D. Gamache. *Creating Profitable New Products and Markets*. New York: AMACOM, 1980.

Cord, J. "Best Investments in Sales Software." *EDGE*, May/June 1989

———. "Making Money with Integrated Accounting." *EDGE*, July/August 1989.

Davis, L. "On-Line Applications Grow Up." *Datamation*, January 1, 1990.

Davis, L. R. "Reporting Financial Information Graphically." *Journal of Accountancy*, December 1987.

Dayton, D. "Idea Generators Spark New Solutions." *PC Week*, March 18, 1991.

Dean, J. W., Jr., and G. I. Susman. "Organizing for Manufacturable Design." *Harvard Business Review*, January–February 1989.

Dehnod, K., ed. *Quality Control, Robust Design, and the Taguchi Method*. Laguna Hills, Calif.: Wadsworth and Brooks/Cole, 1989.

DeLorenzo, M. "Upward Bound." *Autoweek*, April 8, 1991.

Dertouzos, M. L., R. K. Lester, and R. M. Solow. *Made in America: Regaining the Productive Edge*. Cambridge: MIT Press, 1989.

Desmond, J. "Windows to MIS: Graphics Focuses Business Picture." *Software News*, April 1987.

Deutsch, C. H. "007 It's Not, But Intelligence Is In." *New York Times*, December 23, 1990, Business section.

Deutschman, A. "What Me? Too Leveraged?" *Fortune*, April 22, 1991.

Drucker, P. F. "The Emerging Theory of Manufacturing." *Harvard Business Review*, May–June 1990.

Dumaine, B. "Who Needs a Boss?" *Fortune*, May 7, 1990.

Eastman, J. R. "A New Age for Marketing Analysis." *Digital Review*, September 25, 1989.

Eccles, R. G. "The Performance Measurement Manifesto." *Harvard Business Review*, January–February 1991.

Einhorn, H. J., and R. M. Hogarth. "Decision Making: Going Forward in Reverse." *Harvard Business Review*, January–February 1987.

"Evaluating New Product Ideas." *OptionFinder Application*, 1990.

Feder, B. J. "Moving the Pampers Faster Cuts Everyone's Costs." *New York Times*, July 14, 1991, Business section.

Ferranti, M. "New Criterium Elicits Praise." *PC Week*, December 11, 1989.

———. "Sygenex's Decision-Support Upgrade Takes Step toward Windows Support." *PC Week*, November 26, 1990.

Foley, M. "Post-MRP II: What Comes Next?" *Datamation*, December 1, 1988.

Forward, G. E., D. E. Beach, D. A. Gray, and J. O. Quick. "Mentofacturing: A Vision for American Industrial Excellence." *Academy of Management Executive*, August 1991.

Fucini, J. J., and S. Fucini. *Working for the Japanese*. New York: Free Press, 1990.

Garvin, D. A. "Computing on the Eight Dimensions of Quality." *Harvard Business Review*, November–December 1987.

Goldstein, D. "Modeling and Manufacturing: Preparation for CIM." *DEC Professional*, August 1991.

Gomory, R. E. "From the 'Ladder of Science' to the Product Development Cycle." *Harvard Business Review*, November–December 1989.

Goslar, M. D. "Capability Criteria for Marketing Decision Support Systems." *Journal of Management Information Systems*, Summer 1988.

Grabowsky, A. L. "What to Monitor to Stay in Control." *Inc., Magazine's Guide to Small Business Success*, Boston Mass.: Goldhirsch Group, 1987.

Gray, D. H. "Uses and Misuses of Strategic Planning." *Harvard Business Review*, January–February 1986.

Greco, A. J, and J. T. Hogue. "Developing Marketing Decision Support Systems." *The Journal of Business and Industrial Marketing*, Summer–Fall, 1988.

Grodman, L. K. "A Strategic Plan for the 1990s." *Computerworld*, December 26, 1988/January 2, 1989.

Gunn, T. G. *Manufacturing for Competitive Advantage: Becoming a World Class Manufacturer*. Cambridge, Mass.: Ballinger, 1987.

Gutman, D. "The Idea Generator." *Computer Clinic*, September 1988.

——— . "The Idea Generator: This Program Makes You Brainstorm at 90 M.P.H." *Success*, September 1988.

Hall, R. *Zero Inventories*. Homewood, Ill.: Dow Jones–Irwin, 1983.

Hamel, G., and C. K. Prahalad. "Strategic Intent." *Harvard Business Review*, May–June, 1989.

——— . "The Core Competence of the Corporation." *Harvard Business Review*, May–June 1990.

——— . "Corporate Imagination and Expeditionary Marketing." *Harvard Business Review*, July–August, 1991.

Hamilton, D. "CIM Primer." *EDGE*, September/October 1989.

Hanna, M. A. "Move Is On to Tie Vision to Information Systems." *Software Magazine*, January 1990.

Hayes, R. H. "Strategic Planning—Forward in Reverse?" *Harvard Business Review*, November–December 1985.

Hayes, R. H., and K. B. Clark. "Why Some Factories Are More Productive Than Others." *Harvard Business Review*, September–October 1986.

Hayes, R. H., and R. Jaikumar. "Manufacturing's Crisis: New Technologies, Obsolete Organizations." *Harvard Business Review*, September–October 1988.

Hayes, R. H., S. C. Wheelwright, and K. B. Clark. *Dynamic Manufacturing: Creating the Learning Organization*. New York: Free Press, 1988.

Hector, G. "Cute Tricks on the Bottom Line." *Fortune*, April 24, 1989.

Hellebust, K. G., and J. C. Krallinger. *Strategic Planning Workbook*. New York: John Wiley & Sons, 1988.

——— . "Strategic Planning Workbook." *Journal of Accountancy*, October 1989.

Henkoff, R. "Cost Cutting: How to Do It Right." *Fortune*, April 9, 1990.

——— . "How to Plan for 1995." *Fortune*, December 31, 1990.

Hertz, D. B. *The Expert Executive: Using AI and Expert Systems for Financial Management, Marketing, Production, and Strategy*. New York: John Wiley & Sons, 1987.

Hitt, M. A., R. E. Haskisson, and J. S. Harrison. "Strategic Competitiveness in the 1990s: Challenges and Opportunities for U.S. Executives." *Academy of Management Executive*, May 1991.

Ho, C. Y., and G. W. Zabrist, eds. *Progress in Robotics and Intelligent Systems*. Norwood, N.J.: Ablex Corporation, vol. 1, 1990; vol. 2, 1991; vol. 3, 1991; vol. 4, 1991.

Hodges, P. "Manufacturing: Automation's Problem." *Datamation*, November 15, 1989.

Horwitt, E. "Clearing the Obstacles to CIM." *Computerworld*, December 26, 1988/January 2, 1989.

Hosseini, J., and N. S. Ford. "A System for Analyzing Information to Manage the Quality-Control Process." *Interfaces*, March–April 1991.

Isenberg, D. J. "The Tactics of Strategic Opportunism." *Harvard Business Review*, March–April 1987.

"It's What You're Doing . . . Mediating, Selling Products, Winning Negotiations." *Thinking Software*, Fall 1990.

Jacob, R. "How to Regain the Productive Edge." *Fortune*, May 22, 1989.

Kador, J. "How Technology Can Help You Market Anything." *EDGE*, May/June 1989.

Kaell, J. K. "A Company-Wide Perspective to Identify, Evaluate, and Rank the Potential for CIM." *Industrial Engineering*, July 1990.

Kaplan, R. S. "Must CIM Be Justified by Faith Alone?" *Harvard Business Review*, March–April 1986.

Karmarkar, U. "Getting Control of Just-in-Time." *Harvard Business Review*, September–October 1989.

Kashani, K. "Beware the Pitfalls of Global Marketing." *Harvard Business Review*, September–October 1989.

Kasper, H. "One Graph Is Worth a Thousand Numbers." *Journal of Accountancy*, November 1988.

Keegan, D. P., R. G. Eiler, and J. V. Anania. "An Advanced Cost Management System for the Factory of the Future." *Management Accounting*, December 1988.

Keyes, J. "Peeling Back Layers of Quality Equation." *Software Magazine*, May 1991.

Kiechel, W., III. "Oh Where, Oh Where Has My Little Dog Gone? Or My Cash Cow? Or My Star?" *Fortune*, November 2, 1981.

——— . "Corporate Strategy for the 1990s." *Fortune*. February 29, 1988.

Knight, R. "The Black Art of CIM." *Software Magazine*, June 1988.

——— . "Focus: Banking, Now the Customer Is King." *Software Magazine*, August 1988.

Kolbasuk McGee, M. "CIM Stuck in Neutral." *Computer System News*, January 21, 1991.

Kumpe, T., and P. T. Bolwijn. "Manufacturing: The New Case for Vertical Integration." *Harvard Business Review*, March–April 1988.

Lederer, A. L., and V. Sethi. "Pitfalls in Planning." *Datamation*, June 1, 1989.

London, M. "The Promises of Cost Accounting." *EDGE*, July/August 1989.

Lotfi, V., and C. C. Pegels. *Decision Support Systems for Production and Operation Management*. Homewood, Ill.: Richard D. Irwin, 1986.

Main, J. "At Last, Software CEOs Can Use." *Fortune*, March 13, 1989.

——— . "Manufacturing the Right Way." *Fortune*, May 21, 1990.

Malone, T. W., J. A. Yates, and R. I. Benjamin. "The Logic of Electronic Markets." *Harvard Business Review*, May–June 1989.

McAdoo, M. "Building an MRP II." *Digital Review*, November 21, 1988.

McKenna, R. "Marketing in an Age of Diversity." *Harvard Business Review*, September–October 1988.

——— . "Marketing Is Everything." *Harvard Business Review*, January–February 1991.

McLaughlin, T. A. "Six Keys to Quality." *Quality Progress*, November 1985.

McLeod, R., Jr., and J. C. Rogers. "Marketing Information Systems: Their Current Status in Fortune 1000 Companies." *Journal of Management Information Systems*, Spring 1985.

Miller, R. "Accounting Software Saves Dollars and Makes Sense." *Today's Office*, July 1991.

Mintzberg, H. "Crafting Strategy." *Harvard Business Review*, July–August; 1987.

Moad, J. "Tools to Automate Quality Production." *Datamation*, April 15, 1991.

Morchove, R. "High End Accounting Software." *InfoWorld*, February 27, 1989.

——— . "Affordable Accounting." *InfoWorld*, September 11, 1989.

Morgan, G. *Creative Organization Theory*. Newbury Park, Calif.: Sage Publications, 1989.

Moriarity, R. T., and U. Moran. "Managing Hybrid Marketing Systems." *Harvard Business Review*, November–December 1990.

Moriarity, R. T., and G. S. Swartz. "Automation to Boost Sales and Marketing." *Harvard Business Review*, January–February 1989.

Norton, R. "Who Owns This Company, Anyhow?" *Fortune*, July 29, 1991.

O'Boyle, T. F. "Last In, Right Out, Firms' Newfound Skill in Managing Inventory May Soften Downturn." *Wall Street Journal*, November 19, 1990.

Ohmae, K. "Getting Back to Strategy." *Harvard Business Review*, November–December 1988.

———. "Companyism and Do More Better." *Harvard Business Review*, January–February 1989.

Ohno, T. *Toyota Production System: Beyond Large-Scale Production*. Cambridge, Mass.: Productivity Press, 1988.

Ohno, T., and S. Mito. *Just-in-Time for Today and Tomorrow*. Cambridge, Mass.: Productivity Press, 1988.

Peavey, D., and J. D. DePalma. "Do You Know the Cost of Your Products?" *Coopers & Lybrand Executive Briefing*, May 1990.

Phadke, M. S. *Quality Engineering Using Robust Design*. Englewood Cliffs, N.J.: Prentice-Hall, 1989.

Polakoff, J. C. "Computer Integrated Manufacturing: A New Look at Cost Justification." *Journal of Accountancy*, March 1990.

Polilli, S. "AA Boasts of New Systems" *Software Magazine*, May 1991.

Porter, M. E. "From Competitive Advantage to Corporate Strategy." *Harvard Business Review*, May–June 1987.

Porter, M. E., and V. E. Millar. "How Information Gives You Competitive Advantage." *Harvard Business Review*, July–August, 1985.

Putnam, A. O. "A Redesign for Engineering." *Harvard Business Review*, May–June 1985.

Quinn, J. B. "Managing Innovation: Controlled Chaos." *Harvard Business Review*, May–June 1985.

Radding, A. "PC Presentation Graphics Software." *Computerworld*, July 8, 1991.

Rapoport, C. "Why Japan Keeps on Winning." *Fortune*, July 15, 1991.

Rockart, J. F. "Chief Executives Define Their Own Data Needs." *Harvard Business Review*, March–April 1979.

Romei, L. K. "Quality Becomes Integral to American Business." *Modern Office Technology*, July 1991.

Rose, F. "Now Quality Means Service Too." *Fortune*, April 22, 1991.

Ryan, A. J. "Sales Force Automation." *Computerworld*, April 8, 1991.

Samuels, D. D. "Multi-User Accounting Systems." *EDGE*, March/April 1989.

Saporito, B. "Cutting Costs without Cutting People." *Fortune*, May 25, 1987.

———. "Companies That Compete Best." *Fortune*, May 22, 1989.

Sarkissian, R. V. "Retailing Trends in the 1990s." *Journal of Accountancy*, December 1989.

Sass, C. J., and T. A. Keefe. "MIS for Strategic Planning and a Competitive Edge." *Journal of Systems Management*, June 1988.

Schatz, W. "Making CIM Work." *Datamation*, December 1, 1988.

Schindler, P. E., Jr. "Can MIS Put Integration into CIM?" *Information Week*, December 3, 1990.

Schoeffler, S., R. D. Buzzell, and D. F. Heony. "Import of Strategic Planning on Profit Performance." *Harvard Business Review*, March–April, 1974.

Schonberger, R. *Japanese Manufacturing Techniques: Nine Hidden Lessons in Simplicity*. New York: Free Press, 1982.

———. *World Class Manufacturing: The Lessons of Simplicity Applied*. New York: Free Press; London: Collier Macmillan, 1986.

———. *Building a Chain of Customers: Linking Business Functions to Create the World Class Company*. New York: Free Press, 1990.

Scott, B. R. "Competitiveness: Self-Help for a Worsening Problem" *Harvard Business Review*, July–August 1989.

Seidman, L. W. "What Is the Future of Banking?" *Harvard Business Review*, July–August, 1991.

"Selecting the Right Accounting System." *Journal of Accountancy*, June 1989.

Sellers, P. "Winning Over the New Consumer." *Fortune*, July 29, 1991.

Shadovitz, D. "Personal Update." *Human Resource Executive*, March 1990.

Shank, J. K., and V. Govindarajan. *Strategic Cost Analysis: The Evolution from Managerial to Strategic Accounting*. Homewood, Ill.: Irwin, 1989.

Shingo, S. *A Study of the Toyota Production System from an Industrial Engineering Viewpoint*. rev. ed. Cambridge, Mass.: Productivity Press, 1989.

Skinner, W. "What Matters to Manufacturing," *Harvard Business Review*, January–February 1988.

Smith, P. "Unique Tools for Marketers: PIMS." *Management Review*, January 1977.

Snell, N. "Software to Tame the Sales Force." *Datamation*, June 1, 1991.

Sonnenberg, F. *Marketing to Win: Strategies for Building Competitive Advantage in Service Industries*. New York: Harper & Row, 1990.

Spiers, J. "A Coming Surge in Capital Spending." *Fortune*. April 22, 1991.

Squillante, J. "Computer-aided Demographic Research." *Commercial Investment Real Estate Journal*, Summer 1987.

Stancil, J. M. "When Is There Cash in Cash Flow?" *Harvard Business Review*, March–April 1987.

Stark, J. *Competitive Manufacturing through Information Technology: The Executive Challenge*. New York: Van Nostrand Reinhold, 1990.

Starr, S. H. "Marketing and Its Discontents." *Harvard Business Review*, November–December 1989.

Stern, D. E. Jr. "Tying Islands of Automation into CIM Systems." *DEC Professional*, November 1987.

Taguchi, G., and D. Clausing. "Robust Quality." *Harvard Business Review*, January–February 1990.

Taramina, A. J. "Expert Systems in Manufacturing." *P&IM Review with APICS News*. December 1990.

Taylor, A., III. "How Buick Is Bouncing Back." *Fortune*, May 6, 1991.

Thierauf, R. J. *Decision Support Systems for Effective Planning and Control: A Case Study Approach*. Englewood Cliffs, N.J.: Prentice-Hall, 1982.

———. *Effective Management Information Systems: Accent on Current Practices*. 2d ed. Columbus, Ohio: Charles E. Merrill Publishing Company, 1987.

———. *A Problem-finding Approach to Effective Corporate Planning*. Westport, Conn.: Quorum Books, 1987.

——— . *User-oriented Decision Support Systems: Accent on Problem Finding*. Englewood Cliffs, N.J.: Prentice-Hall, 1988.

——— . *Group Decision Support Systems for Effective Decision Making: A Guide for MIS Practitioners and End Users*. Westport, Conn.: Quorum Books, 1989.

——— . *Executive Information Systems: A Guide For Senior Management and MIS Professionals*. Westport, Conn.: Quorum Books, 1991.

Tucker, F. G., S. M. Zivan, and R. C. Camp. "How to Measure Yourself against the Best." *Harvard Business Review*, January–February 1987.

Verna, G. "PCs Powerful Tools for More Productive Meetings." The Record Report: Maximizing Productivity, *Greater Cincinnati Business Record*, April 29–May 5, 1991, p. 1B.

Vesey, J. T. "The New Competitor: They Think In Terms of 'Speed to Market.'" *Academy of Management Executive*, May 1991.

Viator, R. E., and C. D. Poe. "Building an Integrated Multiuser Accounting System with Micros." *Journal of Accountancy*, July 1988.

Viskovich, F. "Is Your Accounting System Right for You?" *EDGE*, July/August 1989.

Watson, R., and L. Pitt. "Remarrying Marketing and Logistics with Information Systems Technology." *Industrial Management and Data Systems*, Issue 1, 1989.

Welter, T. R. "Tools at the Top." *Industry Week*, November 24, 1988.

Wheatley, K. L., and W. A. Flexner. "Research Tool Changes the Way Marketers View Data." *Marketing News*, February 27, 1987.

Wheelwright, S. C., and R. H. Hayes. "Competing through Manufacturing." *Harvard Business Review*, January–February 1985.

Wheelwright, S. C., and W. E. Sasser, Jr. "The New Product Development Map." *Harvard Business Review*, May–June, 1989.

Whitney, D. E. "Manufacturing by Design." *Harvard Business Review*, July–August 1988.

Winkler, C. "AMR Hones Sabre to Sharpen Competitive Edge." *Computerworld*, Premier 100, October 8, 1990.

Winship, S. "Packages Stimulate Creative Process, Buyers Say." *PC Week*, March 18, 1991.

Womeldorff, T. "Distributed MRP II." *DEC Professional*, August 1991.

Worthy, F. A. "Japan's Smart Secret Weapon." *Fortune*, August 12, 1991.

Zeeck, D. "Breaking Those Mind Chains." *MacWorld*, June 1990.

Ziber, J. "IdeaFisher and MindLink." *MacUser*, May 1990.

Zipkin, P. H. "Does Manufacturing Need a JIT Revolution?" *Harvard Business Review*, January–February 1991.

Zultner, R. "The Deming Approach to Software Quality Engineering." *Quality Progress*, November 1988.

Index

About the Author

ROBERT J. THIERAUF is Professor of Information and Decision Sciences at Xavier University in Cincinnati, Ohio. He has written widely on management information systems, computers, management science, and management over the years. His books have been translated into many languages. Prior to coming to Xavier University, he worked six years for Coopers & Lybrand as a staff accountant and staff consultant on computer systems.

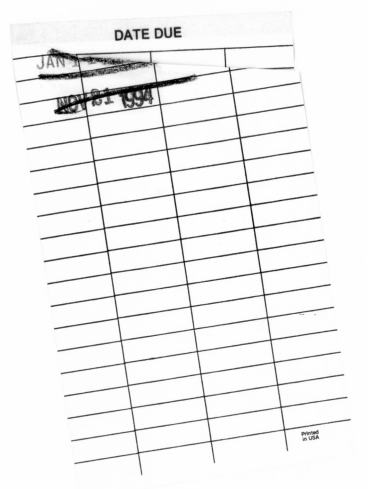